PATHS OF RESISTANCE

PATHS OF RESISTANCE

Tradition and Dignity in Industrializing Missouri

David Thelen

New York   Oxford
OXFORD UNIVERSITY PRESS
1986

Oxford University Press

Oxford   New York   Toronto
Delhi   Bombay   Calcutta   Madras   Karachi
Petaling Jaya   Singapore   Hong Kong   Tokyo
Nairobi   Dar es Salaam   Cape Town
Melbourne   Auckland

and associated companies in
Beirut   Berlin   Ibadan   Mexico City   Nicosia

Published by Oxford University Press, Inc.,
200 Madison Avenue, New York, New York 10016

Library of Congress Cataloging in Publication Data
Thelen, David P. (David Paul)
Paths of resistance.
Includes index.
1. Missouri—Economic conditions.
2. Missouri—Social conditions.
3. Missouri—Politics and government—1865–1950.
I. Title.
HC107.M8T44   1986   330.9778′03   85-7255
ISBN 0-19-503667-0

Printing (last digit): 9 8 7 6 5 4 3 2 1

Printed in the United States of America

To Esther, Jenny,
and Jerry

Acknowledgments

It would be impossible to write a book about democracy—especially in these times—without all kinds of help from many different people. Over nineteen years students and colleagues at the University of Missouri-Columbia encouraged and criticized the arguments as they evolved. Many of them steered me to cases or sources that ended up in the book. A majority of Columbia's voters demonstrated—and inspired me with—the power of democratic courage in a six-year battle with the beverage and container industries. The University of Missouri-Columbia Research Council generously provided financial assistance. The staffs of the manuscript, newspaper, and reference departments of the State Historical Society and of the University of Missouri-Columbia Ellis Library were unfailingly courteous, helpful, and patient.

Many individuals played particularly important parts. Peter Argersinger, Michael Cassity, Russell Clemens, John Hasse, Mark Hirsch, David Keyes, Susan Mernitz, and Philip Scarpino furnished information. Priscilla Evans and Curtis Synhorst assisted with the research. Exchanges with Thomas Alexander, Milton Cantor, Robert Collins, Noble Cunningham, Christopher Gibbs, Lawrence Goodwyn, Dale Grinder, Herbert Gutman, Dorothy Haecker, Darwin Hindman, Robert Hunt, Susan Mernitz, Kerby Miller, William Parrish, Pat Peritore, Steven Piott, Philip Scarpino, Arvarh Strickland, Herbert Thelen, William Williams, Dan Woods, Mary Anne Wynkoop, and an interdisciplinary "Group" of faculty members helped to shape parts of the argument. Sheldon Meyer and Tessa DeCarlo at Oxford provided encouragement and critical advice at crucial moments. I would particularly like to thank Michael Cassity, Susan Flader, Robert Griffith, Jackson Lears, and Robert Wiebe for reading and carefully criticizing the entire manuscript and then helping me through interpretive and organizational problems.

This book has been completely intertwined with the lives of three other people. They taught me about love and family and community. I could not have understood what I found in the past without what they gave in the present. Esther, Jenny, and Jerry inspired the book in every sense of that word.

Contents

PATHS OF RESISTANCE

Introduction

This book is the story of how people tried to express traditional needs for competence and security in a world that was rapidly changing the very definition of those fundamentals. It describes struggles by Missourians to maintain dignity and control over their lives even as the capacity to shape the external terms of their lives was passing increasingly out of reach. It focuses on their search to rebuild and extend a familiar sense of connectedness and community.

This struggle occurred within an all-embracing transformation of Missourians' lives that began in the early nineteenth century. In the old order, family, work, leisure, friends, community, natural surroundings, and worship had interwoven to form an integrated fabric. The new order's economic imperatives of competition and growth drove an ever-widening wedge between economic activities and social and cultural traditions. The new order replaced the authority of persons with an invisible hand that created new kinds of dependence, shame, guilt, success, and failure. Soon the relentless competitive demands pushed outward from the economic centers of change in markets, jobs, and businesses to encompass the ways people relaxed, prayed, and learned. When managers shaped the production of only-too-visible new corporations around the new market, and when those corporations assumed the power and authority that strong neighbors had wielded in the old order, Missourians discovered that the soulless new corporations felt none of the traditional communal responsibilities that had motivated powerful neighbors in the past. Few dimensions of the Missourians' lives remained untouched as the new order changed the ways they related to nature and each other.

Missourians dug in to defend their patterns of life and work against the demands of the new order, or at least to prevent the external changes from undermining innermost values. The traditions they rallied to defend had long guided their families, their crafts, their ethnic and religious groups, their communities, and their personal networks. Some people resisted by directly challenging a new doctrine or practice. Others created parallel alternatives. Still others tried to be left alone or to find temporary release and escape from the new pressures. They expressed their resistance in bars and ballot boxes and lodge halls, now and again by cheering train robbers and public prosecutors. The diverse shapes and directions of their resistance underscored the all-embracing nature of the transformation.

Since any arena is potentially a battleground on which traditional people might stand to defend their world, developers of economic growth from that day to this have concluded that control over the economic surfaces of people's lives is the easiest form of control. Over the past century developers have changed Missouri from an isolated economic backwater into part of a major empire. But the challenge has not changed. Leaders of the new empire, like their predecessors in Missouri, continue to believe that the central struggle is to control the "hearts and minds" of traditional peoples, at home and abroad. In the struggle over hearts and minds, the worker who sought escape in a St. Louis bar challenged the empire's leaders as severely as did a guerrilla movement against a client regime at the empire's extremities. As twentieth-century leaders have relied on military means to control the hearts and minds of traditional peoples, they have revealed their profound inability to secure their empire. Now, as then, traditional peoples have proved to be resourceful, resilient, and independent. They have built their own lives even when others have owned the guns or the means of production.

Scholars have disagreed strongly about the significance of popular resistance in the development of industrial capitalism, but they have generally tended to embrace languages of development that, despite differences, assume the centrality and desirability of growth and production. One group has viewed the emergence of the new order as a desirable process of "modernization" that created societies founded on greater individual freedom and economic growth that rewarded "everyone" with a higher standard of living. For modernization theorists, resistance was incidental and ignorable, since presumably only a utopian, a neurotic, or a fool would resist such an inevitable and desirable process. They simply assumed that tradition-minded peoples would jettison old habits and beliefs.

Other scholars have traced resistance to changes in the modes of production and have emphasized evolution from "feudal" to "capitalist" to "socialist" modes. In their view, each mode created social classes which developed a consciousness of their inevitable missions, and resisters must find their place in this evolution. As their opposition evolved from unorganized and "primitive" to organized and political forms, the resisters became conscious of themselves and their power as a class.

Both approaches illuminate aspects of resistance to the new order. Many Missourians came to accept the new order's values and disciplines. Many workers came to work sober and punctual, for example, because the only alternative was unemployment. Others warmly embraced some aspects of the new order while rejecting others. A majority of the state's blacks, for example, fought to replace the old order's insistence on racial inferiority, based on law and custom, with the new order's freedom, even as they struggled to preserve other traditions. Many Missourians felt profoundly ambivalent about the changes, appreciating a higher living standard while lamenting the erosion of familiar bonds and control. Some internalized their injuries and blamed themselves. Still others protected the cores of traditional values by wrapping them in coats that appeared to be new values. The yearning to excel, for example, was a part of the old order that was rooted in ancient respect for superior skill and strength. It resembled the new order's competition, except that victory in the new order, unlike in the old, required the destruction of others. Likewise, Missourians sought to acquire riches quickly both to participate in the new order and to escape its pressures. At the same time many workers came to see themselves as part of a self-conscious proletariat, but not at an accelerating rate over time. Indeed, the most dramatic example of collective working-class resistance, the St. Louis general strike, occurred in 1877—at the beginning, not the end, of this book's chronological focus.

The central mechanism for popular resistance, however, was less a law of development than a pattern of folk memories that Missourians drew upon to keep alive values and traditions that the new order threatened. They forged these memories into traditions to guide their lives and yardsticks to measure what they feared they were losing to the new order. Traditional ways were familiar ways. Missourians equated them with "natural" ways, endowing them with a special authority. The living traditions of black Baptists or of carpenters or of the people of Callaway County, for example, carried the weight of authority precisely because they incorporated both ancient and recent knowledge and experience. It did not matter that the "traditional" family or religion or craft that Missourians sought to preserve included some components rooted in the reality of the recent past, other components whose existence was so old that no one could date them, and still others that may never have existed. What gave force to the tradition was not the reality on which it had been based in the past—how a thing was made, how particular people related to each other, when the reality had existed—but the ability of people to use that memory or tradition to project resistance in the present. By providing the means to evaluate loss, folk memories energized struggles to regain control over the processes of change.

Folk memories did not follow clean lines of progression or chronology when they triggered popular resistance. For one thing, Missourians overlooked the many changes within the old order when they recreated that era in their memories as a long, unchanging epoch that contrasted warmly to their experience of constant change in the new order. There was no actual period, in fact, when the realities that shaped their living traditions remained frozen, unchanged, in time and space. For another thing, different pressures and values from the new order collided with different traditions of craft, community, and ethnicity in different ways at different places and times. Resistance, in short, grew from different traditions at different times and places. Some patterns of resistance developed their distinctive forms precisely because the transition from old to new was so long and uneven. Fraternal orders and labor unions, for example, defended values from the old order in ways unleashed by the free association of individuals which accompanied the new order. Finally, there was neither a clear evolution from one form of resistance to another nor a predictable weakening of particular folk memories over time. In fact, the very assumption of the linear development of resistance that has guided many studies of change in communities and crafts has clouded the more subtle ways that people have used folk memories to preserve dignity. Instead of progressing chronologically from traditional and defensive patterns such as religion and escape to organized and aggressive patterns such as class consciousness and political action, Missourians selected among alternative patterns as they encountered new threats. They sometimes drew on several at once to create their responses. And they came to accept some new values while struggling to retain older ones.

The challenges that stimulated folk memories emanated from the core of the new order and violated multiple traditions and ancient priorities. They reached especially explosive dimensions when they threatened several traditions simultaneously. The willingness of elected officials to vote unprecedented taxes for the building of railroads challenged the traditions that politicians should represent their constituents, that low taxes were necessary to preserve independence, and that the local community was the focus of life. Skilled British-born coal miners in Macon County revolted against a simultaneous threat to their craftsmanship, ethnicity, race, and community when the mine owners introduced machinery and unskilled blacks to operate it.

Resisters used folk memories not literally to recreate a world of the past but to create a world for themselves. They broadened the traditional meaning of family into the fraternal ethic that offered the familiar security of the family to a wider circle of people. They broadened the tradition of community into an ideal of "the public interest" behind whose banner progressives of the early twentieth century battled large corporations. In both cases they used folk memories to create alternatives to the dominant forces that had changed their lives. In both cases, too, those alternatives mobilized people across cultural barriers that had been unbridgeable in the old order.

Missourians ignored and romanticized many features of the old order, which had its dark realities of poverty, disease, hunger, ignorance, brutality, slavery, and intolerance. Many hoped to resist the new order by remembering the protection, not the constraints, of family life in the old order. They wished to overlook the grim realities of the past precisely because the promoters of the new order pointed incessantly to those shortcomings. The more they heard the new order's freedom and individualism extolled, the more traditional resisters remembered the warmth of the old order's security.

The need to reconsider connections between tradition and democracy is particularly great at this time. Conservatives have wrapped themselves in cloaks of tradition. The New Right has harnessed the traditional values of family, community, church, and flag to support a political movement whose economic policies would give greater power to business and the rich. For most of our history, however, defenders of family, community, and church have resisted the new businessmen and their values as alien invaders who threatened the most cherished traditions.

The New Right has succeeded in uniting these ancient antagonists primarily because liberals and radicals have abandoned the field, neglecting tradition as a basis for resistance and even condemning it as antithetical to resistance. The past was the province of conservatives; the future belonged to reformers and radicals. "The tradition of all the dead generations weighs like a nightmare on the brain of the living," declared Karl Marx, with characteristic impatience at the slowness of people to scuttle traditional values in favor of the radical vision of a great, bold future. Their very neglect of the traditional values of family, community, and democracy has encouraged today's liberals to defend modern bureaucratic institutions without recognizing how those institutions have grown away from the traditional quests for security that originally inspired their creation. The New Right stepped into an ideological vacuum after radicals and reformers became impatient with tradition. It has proved a fatal impatience.

I

The Integration of Life in the Old Order

1

Traditional Values and the
Old Order

Missourians remembered the old order as a time when family, work, community, church, politics, and environment intertwined to form an integrated way of life. They combined their cultural backgrounds with their natural surroundings to create a sense of permanence. Since people from each culture and region developed their own local and distinctive variations on that integrated life, each remembered somewhat different forms of the old order.

Realities from the old order continued to govern some crafts, regions, and ethnic groups longer than others. Challenges to the old order's ways of life came earlier to some parts of their lives than to others. Sometimes the threat began as pressure to change the ways things were grown or made in order to survive dramatic changes in the volume or price of goods produced by remote competitors. Other times strangers from different backgrounds suddenly disrupted the familiar sense of community by introducing different religions or languages. Sometimes children broke up traditional family unity by moving to a new place in search of greater opportunity or security or adventure. Whatever the form or timing of the initial challenge, however, Missourians drew on memories of the traditional integration of their lives to develop resistance.

1. The Land, the Rivers, and the People

Huckleberry Finn had constructed all of life around a river, and Missourians shared Mark Twain's instinctive fascination with the relation of rivers to people's lives. Rivers loomed as the most important natural feature in shaping decisions about where to locate and how to live. The Mississippi defined the state's long eastern boundary. Down from the Rockies flowed the Missouri to create the state's western boundary, until it veered sharply eastward to bisect the state and meander into the Mississippi. North of the Missouri, settlers had picked congenial homes near the Medicine and the Salt, the Grand and the Platte, the Nodaway and the Cuivre. Ozark rivers had beckoned settlers south of the Missouri to the Osage and the Gasconade, the Current, the Eleven Point, the Pomme de Terre, the St. Francis, the Niangua, and the Meramec, to Horse Creek and Dry Creek and Piney Creek and Big Creek. Near these rivers people built their homes and communities. They built their largest settlement, St. Louis, where North America's two biggest rivers met.

Rivers gave Missourians the choice of ways to live. Since God had put the rivers there and only God could change their courses, settlers were secure in the knowledge of the exact location of major links to the outside world. Those who dreamed of the wealth that accompanied concentration of people and productive capacity settled near the major navigable rivers that provided access to large markets. Other settlers came to Missouri to escape the pressures of civilization. They built homes along remote mountain or forest streams.

Rivers permitted Missourians to create self-sufficient lives. By yielding fish and attracting game, rivers supplied food. Rivers provided the energy to power mills where farmers processed agricultural products into things to eat and wear. In the 1870s the Greer Mill in Oregon County ground corn into meal, sawed timber, ginned cotton, and carded wool. While waiting for the miller to process their goods, which often took several days, settlers caught up on the latest comings and goings and in that way cemented their communities. Missouri boasted 840 mills in 1870, and 872 at their peak in 1880.[1]

Rivers reinforced dependence on nature. Sometimes nature was kind, as when fish and game were abundant, and sometimes nature was cruel, as in a flash flood, but always settlers respected nature above all forces.

Rivers strengthened local communities by serving as barriers against outsiders. During the Civil War the White River divided Union and Confederate sympathizers in the Ozarks. The largest rivers blocked Missouri's links to East and West for a long time before the Missouri was bridged at Kansas City in 1869 and at St. Joseph in 1873 and the Mississippi at Hannibal in 1871, at Louisiana in 1873, and, most dramatically, at St. Louis in 1874.

Rivers belonged to everyone. A family could control the manner and cost of transportation, build a raft or hire a steamboat. As late as 1900 the Osage River floated 83,461 tons on rafts and only 12,683 tons on steamboats and barges together.[2] Rivers encouraged Missourians to think of transporation as common property.

Providing a focus for most communities in the old order, rivers helped shape basic values. They encouraged people to evolve a local sense of community with a feeling of permanence and tradition that harmonized with nature. They encouraged a sense of self-sufficiency for families and communities. In hundreds of subtle ways dependence on the river restrained even those who dreamed of growth and wealth. "The most important factor in the evolution of St. Louis's destiny . . . is the Mississippi River, the main artery of Western commerce, the highway over which must travel the richly laden argosies on their way to other countries," declared two local enthusiasts in 1878, echoing the ways the river had long shaped promoters' visions of the city. Chicago's promoters, unrestrained by the river tradition and the "local conservatism" it bred in St. Louis,[3] based their dreams on the new railroads, and their city soon eclipsed St. Louis as the hub of the Midwest.

While some Missourians created communities within St. Louis, helping to make it the nation's fourth largest city by the end of the nineteenth century, others settled in one or another of the state's diverse rural environments. The spectacular variety of Missouri's rural landscapes attracted an equally spectacular variety of peoples. Each natural setting dictated a different way of relating to the land and attracted a different group of settlers. Nature's diversity reinforced the cultural differences that divided Missourians by the 1870s. To the forests and woodlands of northeastern Missouri came early white settlers from Kentucky and Virginia, frequently with slaves, to recreate a southern world that revolved around woodlands agriculture, slavery, and the Democratic party. These pioneers brought Missouri into the Union as a slave state in 1821. German immigrants stayed close to the broad rivers that stretched south and west from St. Louis. They led the struggle to keep Missouri in the Union. Mountain people from the Tennessee hills reestablished their familiar world in the Ozarks of southern Missouri. Closer to hunter-gatherers than to commercial farmers, Ozark mountaineers treasured the isolation they had come to Missouri to find. The prairies of northern and western Missouri attracted settlers from the flatlands of Ohio, Illinois, and Iowa. Facing fewer natural obstacles, these farmers spearheaded commercial agriculture in Missouri. The rich, swampy soil of the southeastern bootheel formed a unique ecological niche that attracted large cotton and wheat farmers who came to depend on slaves and tenants more than farmers in other parts of the state did. Natural and cultural barriers between groups and communities combined to nurture a local focus of life.

2. The Traditional Unity of Life and Work

Farmers, artisans, and merchants shared a sense of personal control over their fates in the old order because their work was governed either by the needs of their households or by personal interactions guided by custom and participants' reputations. The origins of this sense of personal control lay in the traditional capacity of each household to grow or make what its members needed to eat, wear, and use. In villages and cities many traditional features of self-sufficiency had broadened from household to community when people came to sell surplus products in order to earn money to buy their needs. Bonds of obligation and reputation between individuals who knew each other gave those individuals a wide variety of ways to meet needs and confront misfortune. The confidence that they could work out personal solutions to problems encouraged the feeling of personal control.

Farmers evolved a sense of personal control from their daily ways of meeting their needs. Many farm families constructed their own homes, barns, and furniture, sewed their own clothes and bedding, baked their own bread, butchered their own meat, and chopped their own wood for fuel; some even distilled their own liquor. Others supplemented their self-sufficient households by taking wheat, corn, wool, or trees to the local miller and returning home with flour, cornmeal, cloth, and lumber. Many farmers purchased shoes or coffee or implements from merchants or artisans who were expected to offer credit and take into account the farmers' circumstances. Farmers repaid loans at harvest time. When they needed cash, as at tax time each year, farmers could cut some trees for shingles, railroad ties, or fence rails and sell them. Others earned ready cash by selling the coal that lay exposed on many of the state's farms, for in 1879 farmers dug from their own farms 29 percent of Missouri's total coal production.[4]

The self-sufficient horizons of Missouri farmers angered promoters of the new order. The *Osceola Herald* charged that farmers in the Osage River valley were "Rip Vanwrinkles who are slumbering here content with raising sufficient hog and hominy for their own consumption."[5]

Urban Missourians developed a sense of control from their reliance on local artisans to provide goods they could not create for themselves. The familiar butcher, baker, and candlestick maker were joined by the shoemaker, carpenter, mason, tailor, furniture maker, blacksmith, cigar maker, brewer, jeweler, saddler, carriage maker, cooper, painter, and, finally, undertaker. One-fourth of all "manufacturing establishments" in Missouri in 1879 were owned by blacksmiths, carpenters, masons, saddlers, and bakers alone.[6] The face-to-face transaction between individual consumer and artisan created a sense of integration between production and consumption that led artisans in the old order to believe that neighbors and consumers, not owners or impersonal markets, should discipline the nature, quality, and price of finished products. Both artisans and consumers respected the local traditions that regulated quality and price, since they had evolved out of practices by which communities, at first through their local governments, had formally determined the quality and "just price" for many local products. To ignore consumers' expectations or to behave in ways that offended local codes was to invite social and economic ruin.

Some urban Missourians united production with consumption by joining life and work physically, just as the family farm did. Many artisans, merchants, and professionals located workplaces above, below, beside, or in front of their homes.

The real limits on personal freedom, both farmers and artisans remembered, came from nature and God. Nature largely molded what people did and when and how they did it. The disciplines of nature defined the rhythms of agriculture. Seasons dictated the activities while temperature, precipitation, daylight, and the needs of farm animals regulated the date and time of their doing.

The ability of rural Missourians to live literally self-sufficient lives depended on the preservation of land in the form that nature had created. In 1870 four-fifths of the state's land remained more or less untouched. In only four of the state's 113 counties had farmers cleared as much as half of the land for cultivation. Some areas were truly forbidding. "No clearing attests the domicile of man, the settler is as yet unheard," the Cotton Belt Railroad said of parts of southeastern Missouri in an 1893 advertisement. "The silence of the night is broken only by the solemn hooting of the owl or the blood curdling screech of the panther. Bears hide in the thicket and the graceful deer leap the fallen tree."[7]

Unimproved land was home, of course, for the fish and game on which rural residents based their self-sufficient lives. While the buffalo and elk had long since been driven from the state, rural Missourians in the 1870s could still depend on fish and game for survival. Passenger pigeons, grouse, woodcock, doves, and wild turkey joined deer, beaver, raccoon, muskrat, rabbit, and otter in the woodlands, and prairie chickens still remained on open lands. In 1870 two people landed a 315-pound blue channel catfish from the Missouri River near Morrison, and eight years later the same river yielded a 242-pound catfish. Fish and wildlife were so crucial to rural Missourians that the legislature as early as 1874 enacted both "An Act for the Preservation of Game, Animals and Birds" and an "Act To Prevent the Destruction of Fish." At subsequent sessions legislators continued to try either to restrict the commercial harvest of wildlife or to raise fish and game in captivity and release them back in the wild, in order to reinforce the basis for self-sufficient lives.[8]

For many farmers a deeply religious perspective reinforced their dependence on nature. Since only God could change what God had created, they trusted in prayer, not their own actions, to overcome nature's limits on their acts. When God invaded western Missouri in the mid-1870s with hordes of Rocky Mountain locusts that devoured everything in sight, farmers responded by praying that the scourge be removed and inventing recipes to convert nature's curse into a blessing, an edible one. Governor Charles Henry Hardin acted in the way that made greatest sense to his constituents when he proclaimed May 17, 1875, "a day of fasting and prayer that Almighty God may be invoked to remove from our midst those impending calamities and to grant instead the blessings of abundance and plenty."[9] Shortly thereafter, as the farmers expected, the grasshoppers veered sharply northward away from Missouri and into Iowa.

The seasons and weather regulated artisans almost as tightly as they did farmers. Rain, snow, and low temperatures restrained carpenters, masons, and painters. Brick makers needed sunny days for bricks to dry. In 1879 the average Missouri bricklayer lost 131 days a year to the weather, the typical painter, 111, the plasterer, 155, and the stonecutter and carpenter, 95.[10] Even major industries like meat packing and brewing could function only during cold weather and could produce goods only for local markets in the years before man-made refrigeration.

Artisans and farmers depended heavily on nature and animals for the energy to power their productive activities. Horses pulled plows and hoisted the heaviest slabs of ore from the lead mines around Joplin.[11] The amount of sunlight and warmth determined how long it took paint or bricks to dry and corn to grow, and the amount of rainfall determined how rapidly water passed through mills and thus the pace of manufacture.

Within the limits of nature, farmers shared with artisans the conviction that they could control their work because they owned the tools, knowledge, and experience which together formed what it took to create things. Shoemakers owned hammers and awls; farmers, plows and axes. The manufacture of bricks had changed little since the seventeenth century. Molders rapidly formed a mass of clay into a rough ball and then carefully dumped the clay into a wooden mold which an off-bearer carried away to dry in the open air. The best molders made up to 10,000 bricks a day. Skilled artisans hacked as many as fifty railroad ties in a single day without leaving a single axe or score mark. As late as the 1890s lead miners around Joplin required only a pick, shovel, hand jig, and half-barrel to do their jobs. The capital costs of machinery in the old order were within the reach of many. The average Missouri farmer owned implements and machines worth $84 in 1879. The entire capitalization of the state's typical blacksmith shop in 1870 was $600, of the boot and shoe "factory," $900; of the masonry establishment, $700; of the carpentry shop, $1300; and of the woman's clothing factory, $1700.[12]

From the experiences of having nature and knowledge regulate the performance of tasks, and of doing those tasks for their own households or for local consumers with whom they had face-to-face contact, traditional Missourians developed particular approaches to work. They worked to accomplish a task at a time and pace that met the needs of particular consumers within the limits of nature. They frequently relaxed for long stretches after completing particularly difficult jobs. From the task orientation of work in the old order they came to believe that they, not an employer or impersonal market, should control the priorities and timing of jobs. They frequently subordinated particular jobs to the other demands and pleasures of life.

The survival of the traditional unity of life and work depended on the survival of local markets, self-sufficiency, and personal networks as the central economic facts of life. Those realities remained powerful where the market remained local. The new wool factory that opened in St. James in 1869 manufactured cloth on a custom-order basis for consumers who provided their own wool. Fewer than a quarter of Missouri's 143 coal "mines" in 1879 marketed their products outside the county in which they operated.[13]

The length of time a rural community retained the capacity for personal control varied with the penetration of the market economy from one part of the state to the next. The cash value of a farm's products measured the extent that the market regulated its activities. In 1880 the average farm in only two counties yielded products worth more than $1,000. These two counties,

Franklin and St. Charles, surrounded St. Louis, and their farmers grew for the huge urban market. By 1900 the center of commercial agriculture had shifted along with the railroad network and its national market to the prairies of northwestern Missouri, and in that year the typical farm in sixteen counties in that region raised products valued in constant dollars at over $1,000. By 1920 the average farm in the entire northern half of the state and in sixteen southern counties reached the $1,000 mark. Even by 1920, however, farms in five of the most remote Ozark counties still did not produce goods valued as high as $500 in constant dollars.[14] While these figures only crudely measure the market's progress, they trace the long and uneven transition between old and new order, between personal and market regulation of farm life, and they underscore the survival of traditional patterns in parts of rural Missouri.

3. Family, Community, and the Variations of Culture

Missourians drew on their cultures' distinctive traditions to strengthen the family's capacity to control life. In the old order, people who had worshiped the same God, spoken the same language, worked and related to nature in the same ways had also tended to live in the same communities. Geographic isolation had encouraged each culture to develop unique ways of uniting work, life, and community. When this unity came under attack, traditional peoples concluded that the best way to preserve the familiar was to carry it with them to new places.

German immigrants came to Missouri to live more traditional lives than they could in their homeland. For centuries peasants and artisans in Germany had developed their lives around strong lords and powerful local governments, guilds, patriarchal families, traditional Catholic, Protestant, and Jewish religions, and nature. But their intensely local communities were defenseless against Napoleon's national economic and military forces. New rulers sought to create a unified Germany of unprecedented economic and military power. Peasants and artisans struggled to protect their worlds against the new ways of capitalist agriculture, factory production, and militarism. Their revolts climaxed in the great artisan revolution of 1848. The crushing defeat of this revolt convinced many Germans that the only alternative to acquiescence was to leave their homeland. Beginning with Gottfried Duden's reports in the 1820s, many German writers promoted Missouri as a place where Germans could preserve and recreate the world the new rulers were annihilating in Germany. They could fashion a self-sufficient life from Missouri's rivers, forests, fish, and wildlife. They could reestablish communal village life, and they might even be able to create an all-German state within the United States. The primitive character of manufacturing in Missouri's cities afforded artisans the chance to practice their crafts without fear of the factory competition that had eroded their position in Germany.[15]

By 1870 German-born immigrants constituted at least 5 percent of the residents of nineteen counties that sprawled from St. Louis southward along the Mississippi and westward along the Missouri. Many of these refugees from industrialization in Germany became the artisans who built Missouri. Sixteen percent of all German-born immigrants in 1870 were blacksmiths, coopers, shoemakers, carpenters, masons, or tailors at a time when only 4.5 percent of native-born Missourians practiced those crafts. Although German-born immigrants constituted only one-ninth of all Missourians listed in the occupational census of 1870, they formed 55 percent of the state's bakers and over a third of the coopers, shoemakers, butchers, cabinet makers, and tailors.[16] They had finally found a place where they could recreate the integration of traditional German life.

People from other cultures hoped likewise to reconstruct in Missouri the traditional unity of work, home, religion, and language that was disintegrating in the places they had come from. Many Tennessee mountaineers, faced with pressures from outsiders to abandon their traditional ways, escaped to the more remote Ozark valleys. The only people who could mine coal in the days when it was still a skilled craft were British immigrants who had acquired their skills earlier in England and Wales. The culture of Macon County coal miners was the culture of these immigrants. In 1870, 77 percent of Macon County coal miners had been born in England or Wales and 93 percent had parents who had been born in those two places.[17] In their remote mountain cabins or in the Italian "Hill" section of St. Louis, in the German valleys of "Missouri's Rhineland" or among Bevier's British-born coal miners, traditional peoples tried to recreate old ways of life in Missouri communities.

Missourians expected that their new communities and neighborhoods would be able to provide support as well as discipline, even when their new neighbors came from different cultures. "Everybody was everybody's friend," recalled Martha Elizabeth Smith of Pettis County. "They helped each other . . . Any misfortune to one called forth the sympathy of the neighborhood."[18] When opportunity, competition, assimilation, and intermarriage eroded the cultural isolation of many communities, traditional Missourians fell back on their families to supplement their communities' ability to assist.

The strongest folk memories were of the "traditional" family. In these memories the integration of life and work made the family, sometimes extended across several generations, the most important regulator of life in the old order. The family assigned tasks to each member. Children learned from their parents or older relatives how to milk cows, bake bread, roll cigars, sew garments, saw wood, and care for others. The household and its members' networks became the means for controlling production and consumption.

Parents in the old order had the objective ability to pass on to their children the property, skills, and knowledge their children needed to survive. This gave special authority to their attempts to guide their children's conduct and growth. The consequences of failure in everyday life were not overwhelming because parents could rescue their children in the same way that personal networks mediated the consequences of misfortunes for the parents. Parents controlled their childrens' values and how they acquired them.

Bonds between husband and wife, brother and sister, and parent and child shaped the ways people were expected to relate to each other in the larger community outside the family. These bonds both linked individuals and restrained individual activities. They were two-way connections that promised mutual aid on the one hand, and deference and obligation on the other. Communities joined the authority of law with that of custom to require people to honor these mutual responsibilities. Within a year after they acquired the right, 600 former slaves in Boone County alone adopted the legal sanction of marriage to bind their relationships formally. The laws of marriage bound husband and wife. More than a decade before Missouri became a state its legislators formally defined the mutual responsibilities of employer and new employee by enacting a law governing apprenticeship that was patterned after the idealized relationship of parents to children. Slave codes defined the obligations of master and slave.[19]

From their experience inside the family, traditional Missourians grew up with the security of having fixed "places" in the social order and knowing their specific obligations toward people in other places. From the paternal bond between father and children came the traditional belief that the strong should care for the weak. From the fraternal bond between brothers came the traditional belief that people should come to the aid of others in distress.

Out of mutual bonds and face-to-face transactions Missourians constructed personal networks and even institutions to strengthen the family's ability to control life. Through these networks and institutions families broadened their social authority to incorporate community. They turned naturally to people who shared their race, language, and religion as they tried to maintain their autonomy. When large numbers of former slaves flocked to Columbia during the emancipation winter of 1864–65, the city's blacks organized their own "African Court," with three judges and a sheriff, so that only blacks would discipline the behavior of blacks.[20]

Parents reached out to others who shared their backgrounds to help control their children's values and how they were learned. By 1870 St. Joseph's German parents, for example, had created separate schools for their children under the sponsorships of the secular Schul-Verein, the Zion Evangelical Lutheran congregation, the Adath Joseph Jewish congregation, and the Catholic Church of the Immaculate Conception.[21] Among St. Louis Catholics, Greeks, Italians, and Croats maintained separate parochial schools.

Native-born Protestants, both black and white, concluded that denominational schools were necessary for the survival of their religions because a common language and similar doctrines allowed Missourians to shift denominations. Missouri's white Baptists formed the Missouri Sunday School Convention in 1868 for the purpose of establishing sectarian Sunday schools for Baptist families. Within five years two-thirds of the state's congregations had Sunday schools for children, and by 1906 Missouri's 1,300 Baptist Sunday schools enrolled more than 100,000 children. The Disciples of Christ established their first Sunday schools in 1876 and by 1906 three-quarters of their congregations had them.[22]

The Sunday schools, like other parochial schools, simply helped introduce children to a whole system of beliefs and disciplines which traditional Missourians expected would guide their conduct throughout life. Immigrants brought their religious traditions. Italians created their own church in St. Louis by purchasing and refurbishing an old Episcopal church, modeling it after the church of St. Lawrence Outside the Walls of Rome. In 1872 it was reopened, with an Italian priest, as the Italian parish of St. Bonaventure. St. Louis Bohemians built St. John Nepomuk Church in 1854 as the first Bohemian Catholic church in the United States. In 1879 Latvian Jews established Beth Hamedrosh Hagodol congregation in St. Louis, and in 1890 acquired their own building. By 1916, two generations after the peak German immigration, the German Evangelical Synod was the largest Protestant denomination in rural Franklin, Gasconade, St. Charles, and Warren counties as well as in the city of St. Louis.[23]

The decision to join a particular English-speaking Protestant church signified commitment to particular beliefs, rituals, and people. Individual Baptists forged a powerful bond when they pledged to "solemnly and joyfully covenant with each other, to walk together in Him, with brotherly love, to His glory, as our common Lord." Members of the Church of Christ covenanted "to live together as a Church of Christ; to take the Word of the Lord as the rule of our faith and practice." "In all our struggles with the forces of evil within us and without," wrote the chronicler of Missouri's Baptist heritage in 1906, "each one who tries to serve the Lord feels the need of companionship with others of life's precious faith," for "union intensifies and enlarges individuality and greatly increases its potentiality." Methodists likewise emphasized the obligation of each member to subordinate individual desires to the welfare of the sect. "If we are united, what can stand before us? If we divide, we shall destroy ourselves, the work of God, and the souls of our people," proclaimed the Methodist book of discipline.[24]

Traditional Missourians turned their local congregations into an extension of the family that they used to establish and enforce rules of conduct. Baptist congregations at first had formal tribunals to discipline members. In 1822, for example, Ezekiel Hill formally charged himself before the Bethel Baptist Church tribunal in southeastern Missouri with the sin of killing a deer on Sunday. Writing in the early twentieth century, the chronicler of the Salt River Baptist Association recalled fondly that his association in earlier days had "maintained a healthy, consistent, corrective church discipline, in which horse-racing, gambling, swearing, dancing, adultery, Sabbath-breaking, lying, drunkenness and such like sins were forbidden to be practiced by church members." Lexington's Methodist church in the 1870s held regular meetings where members asked, "Are there any who walk disorderly and will not be reproved?" Members then tried to persuade the erring individuals of the obligation to follow the congregation's wishes. Lexington's Christian Church expelled one member in 1874 and disciplined another in 1878 for "unchristian conduct," an offense far more serious than any in secular statute books. Fourteen members of the same church wrote to the congregation in 1872 that they "promise the brothers and our Heavenly Father that in the future we will by the help of God, live better lives."[25]

Church discipline strengthened the bonds that had originated in the family and reinforced the family's ability to withstand new threats. Religion, commented the Sedalia *Harmony Baptist* in 1899, kept the family together as it worked to "ennoble" family relationships, while the strong family provided "the best atmosphere for the practice of religion and the development of godly character," according to the Methodist's *Central Christian Advocate* in 1886.[26]

Local congregations formed crucial personal networks in the old order. Emancipation permitted blacks to bring their invisible—and illegal—congregations out of the shadows so that they could erect churches where they could worship and control members' conduct. Methodist businessmen, for example, were formally required to help other Methodist businessmen and to give first preference in employment to Methodist workers. As late as the turn of the century, Sedalia's *Harmony Baptist* and *The Christian* and Boonville's *Western Christian Union* urged their readers to patronize only business and professional men who were members of their denomination.[27] The ability to buy, sell, hire, lend, and borrow within the congregation's ranks provided an important measure of security.

4. Politics and Government

Politics and government had evolved by the 1870s to resolve conflicts between traditional cultures by rules that grew out of the old order. Missourians expected to control government by keeping its size small, its focus local, its policies obedient to majority local sentiment, and its officeholders responsive to family, friends, and neighbors.

In this world of personal networks the holding of office was the highest goal of politics, and officeholders were expected, above all else, to be loyal to family and friends. In the most ancient chambers of folk memory the eternal criterion for political advancement was loyalty to the chieftain, who had acquired his office by birth or by bullets and was expected to defend his subjects against hostile tribes, cultures, and communities. Although the addition of popular elections to older ways of governing shifted the weapons from swords to ballots (in most cases), shifted the rewards for the loyal from fiefdoms to post offices, and ultimately shifted the mobilizing agency from clan, sect, or community to political party, what attracted people to politics and government changed very little.

Irish-born blacksmith Edward Butler mastered traditional political practices as he rose from poverty to dominate St. Louis Democratic politics in the

1880s and 1890s. Butler was popular among Irish Catholics of the Fifth Ward. They chose him to represent them in the political extension of their culture, the Democratic party, and by the 1870s in the city council. Since the point was, as it had always been, to get and keep office, rather than to worry about the niceties of elections, which were only a recent addition to the selection process, Butler organized his followers into bands of rowdies who came to be called "Indians" as they intimidated and assaulted supporters of other candidates, moved the "polls" all over the ward, physically over-powered unsympathetic election judges, and voted early and often for their leader. In one election, judges threw out half the Fifth Ward's ballots because they had been fraudulently cast. Butler rewarded his friends and family with jobs and privileges, and he seized the perquisites of power. He persuaded the Board of Police Commissioners in 1873 to award him the department's horse-shoeing contract, and by taking advantage of similar opportunities he amassed five million dollars by his death in 1911. But he used the money and power of office for the traditional goals of rewarding loyal friends and helping the weak. He donated food and medical assistance, for example, to his poor constituents.[28]

Across the state saloon keeper Jim Pendergast rose to power in Kansas City by the same means as Butler had used in St. Louis. Pendergast represented the First Ward in the city council from 1892 to 1910. Recognizing the essentially military nature of the conflict, Pendergast based his organization in the police department. Between 1900 and 1902, for example, he selected 123 of the city's 173 patrolmen. Not surprisingly, they did not raid Pendergast's gambling rooms. Pendergast paid the grocery and fuel bills of poor voters, and provided city jobs for many others. "I've got lots of friends," he explained. "You can't coerce people into doing things for you—you can't make them vote for you. . . . All there is to it is having friends, doing things for people, and then later on they'll do things for you."[29]

The patronage system of appointments not only provided rewards for the loyal, but also meant that someone's loyal friend would be interpreting and enforcing the law. Traditional Missourians preferred to trust someone's loyal lieutenants to decide whether an action should be punished rather than to enact laws that impartially proscribed many actions. Diversity and conflict among Missouri's cultures reinforced patronage and loyalty as values that alone could unite the Ozarks and the cities, blacks and whites, Unionists and secessionists, immigrants and the native-born. There were plenty of offices for friends to hold. By 1891 the mayor of St. Louis directly and indirectly appointed 1,717 patronage employees. By 1909 the governor appointed be-tween 6,000 and 7,000 employees. Traditional cultures dug in to protect the world of personal networks against businessmen who tried to make compe-tence, not loyalty, the basis of these appointments. When the Republican mayor of St. Louis, William L. Ewing, decided in 1883 to retain competent Democratic officeholders from the previous administration, outraged fellow Republicans on the city council came within a few votes of impeaching him. Governor Lon Stephens explained in 1898 how loyalty and patronage bound diverse groups around a common principle: "No organization could long stand if those placed in the forefront would be ungrateful to its benefactors and to those to whom it is indebted for success and power.[30]

The agency that traditional cultures devised in the nineteenth century to mobilize for the winning of offices was the political party. Parties became the political arm of ethnic, religious, and sectional cultures. Each new group from Europe joined the party opposite to the one that had attracted its most bitter enemy from the homeland. Irish Catholics became Democrats when they spotted their ancient enemies, English Protestants, in the Republican party and its forerunners. The Fourth Ward of St. Louis was the most heavily Irish and the most heavily Democratic of the city's twenty-eight wards in 1880. German immigrants subordinated their religious differences to their desire to protect things German, particularly their language, and this led them to become the most important voting base for the Republican party in urban and rural Missouri alike. Six of the seven St. Louis wards with the highest concentration of first- and second-generation Germans in 1880 were also six of the seven wards with the highest proportion of Republican voters in that year's presidential election. Republican Henry Ziegenhein won the mayor's office in St. Louis in 1897 with the boast that he knew German better than English.[31]

In the decades after the Civil War other Missourians voted for the political arm of the army in which their fathers had fought. Blacks repaid the Republicans with their votes for the next half-century. Confederate support for the Democratic party was so obvious that Republicans could overlook the Unionist Democrats and plausibly charge in 1886 that naming the Democrats' state officeholders was "like calling the roll of the Confederate army." Among circuit court judges and state legislators elected in 1890, all twenty-three Republicans who had fought in the Civil War had fought on the Union side, and all twenty-seven Confederate veterans were Democrats. Only sixteen Union veterans became Democratic officeholders. At the Democratic state convention as late as 1904 the band's performance of "'Dixie' sent the audience wild."[32]

Missourians mobilized the quest for offices around ethnic and sectional loyalties, not wealth or occupation. In the St. Louis election of 1880 unskilled laborers, factory workers, managers, and merchants were equally likely to vote Democratic or Republican. The state's most prosperous farms in 1890 were in northwestern Atchison County, averaging an income of $1,160 per farm, while Douglas County in the Ozarks had the least prosperous farms, with an average income of $176. Both counties ranked among the top third of Republican counties in the 1888 presidential election.[33]

Voters subordinated candidates' claims to the all-important mission of aiding the party as the agency to protect their cultures. Over 680,000 Missourians voted in the election of 1900, and the Democratic candidate received 51.65 percent of the vote for state supreme court judge, 51.64 percent of the vote for attorney general, 51.62 percent for railroad and warehouse commissioner, 51.58 percent for both secretary of state and auditor, 51.57 percent for treasurer, 51.52 percent for lieutenant governor, 51.48 percent for president, and 51.15 percent for governor. Nor did most voters change their affiliations between elections. The Democratic percentage in presidential elections was 58 in 1876, 53 in 1880, 54 in 1884, 50 in 1888, 50 in 1892, 54 in 1896, 51 in 1900, 46 in 1904, 49 in 1908, 47 in 1912, and 51 in 1916.[34]

"The only government that we know in this country is party government," concluded Governor Herbert Hadley in 1912. The good of the party came first with both voters and officeholders. "The Ethiopian may change his skin and the leopard his spots," wrote the Jefferson City *Tribune* in 1892, "but the southeast Missouri Democrat never changes his politics." Officeholders, in turn, promised that they would keep the faith. Recalling the close links of section and party, State Representative Clement W. Bank of Saline County proclaimed in the official state manual for 1894 that he was "sired by a Kentucky democratic father and nursed by a Virginia mother, and have ever been classed as a strict partisan Democrat." The party's newspaper editors created a common vocabulary for viewing politics and government through partisan lenses, for relating office seeking to the day's events. They served between elections to preserve partisanship and often depended for survival on government printing contracts when their party was in power. Of Missouri's 584 daily and weekly newspapers in 1894, 49 percent were officially Democratic, 29 percent were Republican, 5 percent were Populist, and only 16 percent were officially "neutral" or "independent."[35]

If traditional Missourians believed the ends of politics to be the preservation of ethnic and sectional cultures within a world held together by personal networks and patronage, they had considerably more modest expectations of government. They treasured the independence that they associated with low taxes and freedom from debt, and they were suspicious of anything that swelled the size of government and taxes. They further assumed that government was most reponsive at the levels closest to each community. Believing that the greatness of the American experiment was the ability of citizens to make policy at the polls without regard to wealth or rank, they concluded that elected representatives were obligated to follow majority sentiment among their constituents.

II

Creation of the New Order

Some impatient Missiourians, inspired by a combination of vision, greed, and restlessness, sought to break the restraints by which local markets and traditions bound individual ambitions in the old order. They believed that the creation of a new order based on economic growth would require dramatically new and interrelated policies for transportation, education, labor, and public life both to shatter traditional limits and to unleash entrepreneurship. Victorious on the battlefield and at the ballot box in the 1860s, the new leaders created the railroad network that brought Missourians into ever-increasing contact and competition with the rest of the world. Soon no traditional ways of making or growing products were safe from the relentless imperatives of growth, competition, and "progress."

2

The Engine of Growth

From all over the world visitors thronged to Forest Park, St. Louis, in the summer and fall of 1904. "Meet Me in St. Louie, Louie" was the hit song of the season. Streetcars and special trains arrived at the gates of the Louisiana Purchase Exposition that season loaded with sightseers who had come to marvel at exhibits showing the profound changes that had overtaken the ways people worked and lived over the past generation. More than 100,000 people entered the fairgrounds on a busy day. Staged to commemorate the Louisiana Purchase and territorial expansion, the fair itself cost more than three times the amount the United States had paid France in 1803 for the entire Louisiana Territory from the Gulf to Canada, the Mississippi to the Rockies. The fair's 70,000 exhibitors covered 1,240 acres, nearly twice the area of Chicago's Columbian Exposition of 1893.[1]

The Louisiana Purchase Exposition differed from earlier world's fairs by trying to portray how changes in business and science dictated changes in social life and culture. This fair went beyond exhibits of railroad locomotives and electricity, beyond the diversions of fireworks and the Ferris Wheel, to display how people were adapting education, statecraft, the arts, and social institutions to the new economic world. "The development of man from his primitive condition to the present height of achievement was illustrated in the Louisiana Purchase Exposition by object lessons . . . in such sequence as would show the evolution of industrial art, and the expansion of those mental and moral forces which obtain in modern civilization," concluded one souvenir history of the fair. Many older visitors left the fair feeling that change had sped up so dramatically within their lifetimes that they seemed to have entered a whole new order of things. In fact, this rapid acceleration of all change, rather than any single qualitative aspect, seemed to characterize the new order. "Civilization is advancing by bounds so tremendous that the average human being can scarcely measure them," concluded *Cosmopolitan* editor John Brisben Walker in his magazine's special review issue on the exposition.[2]

The exhibits at St. Louis displayed the economic transformation of Missouri that had exploded since the Civil War and would continue in the years ahead. Champions of progress pointed proudly to the statistical dimensions of the transformation. The value of Missouri's manufactured goods jumped almost ten times between 1879 and 1919, from $165 million to more than $1.5 billion. Over the same period the value of the state's farm products also rose almost ten times, from $96 million to $953 million. The cause of these stunning increases lay not so much with population growth, for the number of Missourians rose only from 2.2 million to 3.4 million, as with the development of a new economic system in which impersonal, ever-expanding markets dictated rapid changes in production.[3] In this new economic system "man's competitive instinct" was indeed "the spontaneous lever that arouses human activity and exalts human effort," as President David R. Francis of the Louisiana Purchase Exposition Company proclaimed in the fair's *Official Guide*.[4]

A few pioneers created the new system that stimulated this competitive "instinct," explained the state's most perceptive observer, Mark Twain, in *A Connecticut Yankee in King Arthur's Court* (1889). Like Mark Twain's Yankee, who tries singlehandedly to convert feudal Britain into an industrial society, Missouri's pioneers felt that they were the torchbearers of civilization. Like the Yankee, they offered a new social vision as they battled popular resistance. Their new world would encourage those who chafed at the old order's constraints to break loose from the bonds of family, church, and community. These new leaders in business and agriculture, journalism and education created an official culture that defined their mission.

They dreamed of a new civilization founded on economic growth. Missourians would enjoy more of everything when farms and factories were freed from the constraints of local markets and traditions: more money, more time, more possessions, more education, more freedom, more opportunities. "We are at a parting of the two systems," declared J. W. Sanborn, secretary of the state board of agriculture in 1887. To resist modern methods would only mean "deliberately farming toward poverty, and inability to educate children, adorn homes, build roads and enlarge the comforts of life." "Every new invention opens the way for further advance," announced M. W. Serl in 1891. "Our expensive schools and churches, our asylums, and all the superior facilities for travel and communication, are only made possible by increased production." All these blessings depended on competition between the largest possible number of producers. Large-scale competition, in turn, required the expansion of markets so that the price and quality of goods would no longer be restrained by local consumers. "We cannot succeed with a Chinese wall around each community," explained state highway engineer Curtis Hill in 1910.[5]

1. Expanding the Market

Before the Civil War some businessmen and farmers had campaigned for new roads, river improvements, and railroads to link their communities to wider markets, but they had had only a slight impact. In the thirty-three years since the first steamboat had churned up the Osage River in 1837, promoters of improvements on the Osage had received a grand total of $50,000 in combined federal and state aid. Their meager improvements lay in ruins in 1870 when the Army Corps of Engineers began to take surveys that would be the basis for plans to develop the river into an avenue for expanding commerce. From the beginning of public aid to railroads in 1851 until the end of the Civil War, Missouri's railroads had laid only 925 miles of track, and all but one of them had gone bankrupt.[6]

The commitment to freedom and growth by the victorious Union armies and Radical-Unionist party in the 1860s encouraged potential investors to dream that they might finally win public support for their hopes of expanding markets. Radical governor Thomas Fletcher reflected the new leaders' vision in 1866: "The Atlantic & Pacific railroad, or the southern road to California, has been my dream and occupied my waking thoughts for ten years past. . . . It is the greatest enterprise of the age." Stimulated by the war's victories, developers emerged across the state to promote railroads that would draw communities out of isolation and unleash a spirit of improvement, enterprise, and civilization. "The trifling amount of taxes to be paid" to build the railroads "bears about the same relation which seed does to the crop in value," promised the champions of the Osage Valley and Southern Kansas Railroad. The Jefferson City *Tribune* could hardly contain its enthusiasm as a new railroad approached the capital city in 1879: "We increase the trade of this city double, we add thousands to our population, double the value of our property and hold the capital of the state. . . . The future of our city brightens daily, and the confidence of all our citizens takes an upward bound. . . . Property owners are planning . . . improvements such as they would not have thought of undertaking, had the railroad movement failed." By linking Springfield and the Ozarks to remote markets, promised the *Missouri Weekly Patriot*, railroads would finally encourage people to convert nature from a barrier into a stimulus for growth. "Our forests are waiting for the saw mill; our prairies lying waste when they should be covered by herds of cattle and sheep; our splendid water power is running to waste as it did a thousand years ago," the *Patriot* declared. "What is now wanted to develop these latent sources of wealth is the completion of the Southwest Pacific Railroad, so as to give us an outlet to market, and place us in communication with the rest of mankind."[7]

The promotion of railroads against the obstacles of popular prejudice and conservative fiscal traditions became the mission around which new local elites formed after the Civil War. Most leading promoters owned large investments whose value would skyrocket when the railroad arrived. Large farmers served as officers for the Pike County Short Line. At Kansas City, realtors and speculators who owned huge tracts in the newer parts of town designed and executed the railroad promotions of the 1860s that lifted their city from a sleepy village into the major metropolitan center of the region. Large landowners and lumber companies provided the support for Louis Houck to build his railroads in the bootheel after 1880. Newspaper editors joined professional men like Nevada City physician J. H. B. Dodson as cheerleaders in campaigns by the new elites for railroads and growth.[8]

At the peak of railroad promotions, in 1873, Mark Twain and Charles Dudley Warner created in *The Gilded Age* a fictional railroad promoter, Colonel Beriah Sellers, whose hometown of Hawkeye, Missouri, could have been any real city in the state. Sellers dreams of schemes for instant wealth. He plans to sell a patent medicine to cure sore eyes, whose market would extend from his Missouri headquarters all around the world. The key to success was to serve the largest number of consumers and their needs. "I'm engaged in the invention of a process for lighting such a city as St. Louis by means of water; just attach my machine to the water-pipes anywhere and the decomposition of the fluid begins, and you will have floods of light for the mere cost of the machine," Sellers announces at one point. "I've nearly got the lighting part, but I want to attach it to a heating, cooking, washing and ironing apparatus."

The problem was to convince people to buy things they had never bought before. After all, people had survived for centuries without patent medicines for sore eyes. The basic solution was to replace the old order's self-sufficiency, and its ranking of people by station and skill, with a new ethic which conferred status on the ability to consume lavishly and conspicuously. Sellers appalls the people of Hawkeye when he uses his possessions to try to impress people rather than to meet traditional needs. Through an isinglass window on Sellers's stove a young relative sees a brightly glowing fire, but he feels as cold as if the stove were unlit. As he edges closer, he accidentally knocks the door open and discovers that the only thing inside the stove is a lighted candle. Sellers explains to the embarrassed young man that in the new order "what you want is the appearance of heat, not the heat itself."

Sellers's missionary zeal is only spurred by the popular hostility and indifference that surround him. Missouri cabin dwellers are baffled and angry when he builds a railroad through their midst. His railroad workers are furious that he bribes politicians with the funds that were to have been their wages. Traditional people resist him because he "expected to get on in the world by the omission of some of the regular processes which have been appointed from of old." Driven by dreams and greed, Sellers and other speculators in *The Gilded Age* hope to "come into sudden opulence by some means which they could not have classified among any of the regular occupations of life." In real life as in fiction, the passion to prevail over popular ignorance and opposition provided the permeating sense of mission for the new speculators.

Promoters, inspired by the same vision as was Beriah Sellers, succeeded in constructing railroads with the aid of public funds. Railroads began to crisscross the state, linking Missouri communities to the national market. The number of railroad miles, which had risen only from 817 in 1860 to 925 in 1866, reached 2,000 in 1870, 4,000 in 1880, 6,000 in 1890, and 8,000 by 1909.[9]

A railroad's impending arrival signaled feverish speculation in land, whose value could soar overnight. The Atlantic and Pacific stopped its southwestward push from St. Louis at Jerome, where 700 people sold town lots in 1867. After making a quick profit of $100,000 in land sales in Lebanon, the South Pacific hastily established thirteen new railroad towns before halting again for another major speculative project at Springfield. Springfield's local speculators persuaded the railroad's owners to establish the depot a mile north of the existing city in exchange for a share of town lot sales in the new community that would spring up around the depot.[10]

The new railroads brought communities into competition, and local leaders feared that failure to attract railroads would turn their communities into backwaters. Leaders of older river towns who permitted their worlds to be bounded by the river's rhythms instead of the locomotive's found their communities eclipsed by nearby railroad towns. The arrival of railroads in the Osage Valley soon drew population and influence from Osceola, the river's old "Queen City," to the valley's new railroad towns. Osceola's township declined from 2,077 residents in 1860, to 1,162 in 1880, while the railroad city of Clinton jumped from 640 in 1870 to 2,868 in 1880. The promoters' greatest triumph came at Kansas City, where the new railroads spurred an explosion of population, from 4,418 in 1860 to 32,250 in 1870, 55,785 in 1880, and 132,716 by 1890.[11]

The railroads concentrated manufacturing in the cities that grew at the points where rail lines converged to create the greatest competition. From rural Europe and America came the people to work in and buy from the new urban factories. Between 1860 and 1900 the number of Missourians who lived in cities over 2,000 rose 466 percent, while the rise in the number of people living in smaller and rural communities was five times slower. The proportion of Missourians living in communities over 2,000 rose from 17.4 percent in 1860 to 37.5 percent by 1900 as manufacturing followed the new railroads from rural to urban Missouri.[12]

The railroads brought such immediate profits from land sales and such dramatic growth in population that they unleashed among businessmen a spirit of optimistic confidence, stimulating them to invest in projects based on the community's new links to remote markets. Freed from dependence on neighboring consumers, businesses could now produce for the huge markets that the railroads brought to their doorsteps. At the same time, however, they lost the security of local markets to faceless producers from distant places who now sold in their communities. One statistic traces the spectacularly new dimensions of the resulting competition. It cost as much to ship wheat the thirty-five miles from Huntsville, Missouri, to Glasgow, Missouri, before the railroad's arrival as it cost after the railroad, in 1880, to ship it from Huntsville, Missouri, to Glasgow, Scotland.[13] Cheaper transportation forced businesses to produce more goods at lower prices. Failure to cut costs and increase production meant that a distant competitor would drive them out of business.

The railroads stimulated dramatic changes in extractive industries. The Missouri, Kansas, and Texas Railroad radically transformed coal production when it entered southeastern Bates County in 1880. Originally a small operation in which farmers gathered coal in bushels and sold it to teamsters for local delivery, coal production now became a large-scale enterprise. In 1879, before the railroad's arrival, 95 percent of the county's coal was sold within its borders; a decade later only 6 percent was sold locally, and the rest was shipped on the new railroad. Farmers dug 94 percent of all the coal produced in Bates County in 1879, while actual mines produced only 19,385 tons, or 6 percent of the county's total. By 1889 mine production jumped forty times, to 755,989 tons. Over that same decade the average local mine's capitalization rose from $2,023 to $30,051, the number of workers rose from six to seventy-one, and steam engines replaced people and animals as its energy source.[14]

Large-scale lumbering in the Ozarks likewise arrived with the railroad. The Missouri Lumber and Mining Company began to log its huge Ozark forests in 1880, but the company quit in 1884 because the ten-mile oxen-drawn trip to the railroad was too slow and costly to permit large oeprations. In 1889 the company attracted a rail spur to link a new mill in Carter County at Lakewood, soon renamed Grandin, to markets in Kansas City and the West through the Kansas City, Fort Scott and Memphis Railroad and to St. Louis and the East on the Cape Girardeau and Southwestern. The old mill had possessed an annual capacity for six million board feet in 1880, but the new mill, with its two huge band saws and one circular saw, could produce seventy-five million board feet by 1899. Devouring Ozark forests at the rate of sixty or seventy acres a day, the mill was Missouri's largest. The company's work force rose from 125 before the railroad to 1,500 in 1905. By 1902 the company had denuded 213,017 acres in southern Missouri. The Grandin mill was the largest seller of lumber in the markets of Illinois, Indiana, and Ohio.[15]

The railroads created large-scale competition by expanding markets beyond even the speculators' dreams. The number of railroad carloads of general merchandise loaded or unloaded at St. Louis, a good quantitative index of the market's size, soared from 20,542 in 1870 to 125,939 in 1880, 323,506 in 1890, 382,518 in 1900, and 710,306 in 1910. Over these forty years the population of St. Louis barely doubled, but shipments of freight increased almost thirty-five times. The number of tons of freight carried on Missouri's railroads rose from 20,042,671 in 1881 to 129,518,033 in 1904.[16] Railroads transformed the size and shape of the market economy, forcing businessmen and farmers to produce at unprecedented rates to survive the new competition.

The evolution of the Granite Iron Rolling Mills in St. Louis typified the ways that manufacturers developed new methods to reach the new large-scale markets. In the 1850s Frederick G. and William F. Niedringhaus emigrated from Germany to St. Louis as apprentice tinners. They opened their own shop in 1857, where they made pots and pans from pieces of tin that they cut by hand and soldered together. Importing a machine that stamped pots and pans from a single sheet of tin, they launched the St. Louis Stamping Company in 1866. By the 1870s they found still larger markets by converting ground granite into enamel that they applied to sheet iron to produce more popular utensils. To grow still further they needed a large, cheap supply of the ground graniteware ingredients, and so they erected the Granite Iron Rolling Mills in 1878. The new factory contained two heating furnaces, one bar mill, three sheet mills, three pan furnaces, three sheet furnaces, three hammers, nine charcoal fires, two puddling furnaces, and a coal mill. In 1895 the brothers completed the Granite City Steel Works, with its open-hearth furnaces and its blooming, plate, jobbing, and bar mills. In four decades the apprentice tinners had demonstrated how machine production reached wider markets.[17]

Driven by the new railroad markets, businessmen defied the traditional restraints imposed by nature. Trees and coal, once harvested by local users with axes and shovels, now were stripped by huge mills and mines to be sold to faceless consumers.

For centuries people had made refined foods from raw agricultural products, but nature had severely limited these processes. People produced meats, poultry, eggs, milk, beer, and butter for their familes or communities, usually in cold weather, because these things spoiled or perished in the Missouri summer. To take advantage of the new markets, businessmen invented ever more complex forms of artificial refrigeration so that they could manufacture and ship goods across the ancient barrier of perishability. The Anheuser-Busch brewery in St. Louis grew to preeminence by developing refrigerator cars and pasteurization, which allowed it to brew lager beer throughout the year and ship it across the country. Inaugurating its man-made refrigeration in the 1870s, the brewery boasted 1,250 refrigerator cars and thirty ice plants by 1895. With these developments Anheuser-Busch expanded its production of beer from 38,412 barrels in 1873 to 200,053 in 1881 and 825,548 in 1898.[18]

Artificial refrigeration converted meat packing from a local, part-time operation into one of the nation's largest and most concentrated industries. The Plankinton and Armour company in Kansas City developed a chill room in 1877 that permitted it to pack hogs throughout the year, but it still could not ship meat in warm weather. The Kansas City firm of Nofsinger and Company had solved that problem in 1875 by shipping beef in primitive refrigerator cars which expanded the beef-packing season by a few months. The railroads killed Nofsinger's experiment in 1879, because the packer's refrigerator cars competed with the railroads' cattle cars. Not until the late 1880s and early 1890s did Missouri's meat packers overcome railroad opposition so that they could finally reach the distant urban markets throughout the year. And reach they did. At St. Louis the amount of pork carried by railroads jumped from 63 million pounds in 1875 to 500 million pounds in 1890. Packers built huge plants to produce for these markets. In 1887 Swift and Company erected a half-million-dollar factory at Kansas City, and five years later P. D. Armour constructed a million-dollar plant there. By 1901 the Armour factory was the largest business in Kansas City, employing 4,000 people and producing more than $50 million worth of meat products. The new factories consumed animals as voraciously as the mills consumed trees. The city's total slaughter of hogs, sheep, and cattle rose from 588,177 in 1880 to 4,555,950 in 1900.[19]

Businessmen further conquered perishability by sealing products in tins and cans which retained some of the product's original qualities. In their zeal to reach new markets, meat packers also pioneered large-scale canning. Kansas City's Slavens and Oburn began to can beef in 1878, and within two years half of Kansas City's beef was marketed in cans. The number of tins of beef canned in Kansas City rose still further, from 778,720 in 1880 to 4,095,410 in 1885. Processors of other agricultural products soon copied the packers, and the value of Missouri's canned goods skyrocketed from $155,000 in 1880 to $1,480,000 in 1890.[20]

The rapid explosion of markets and the accompanying shift of manufacturing from its rural origins to the new cities convinced many businessmen that nature shackled them in other ways. The mills that ground wheat into flour, sawed trees into lumber, and converted raw wool and cotton into cloth depended for power on either the leisurely pace of harnessed oxen or the flow of water from rain, rivers, and springs. Although millers since colonial times had found waterpower flexible enough to allow expansion of production, they turned increasingly to steam and finally to electricity in the new order because they could regulate output far better and thus take advantage of the new markets. The mill on Big Cedar Creek in Callaway County had been powered by the stream's water for three generations before its owners turned to a steam engine around 1900. The oxen that drove the Locke Milling Company's mill on Loose Creek in Osage County by plodding around a capstan were replaced with steam power in 1886. The new millers of the 1870s built their plants at major railroad junctions. The huge new City, Diamond, Gate City, and Central mills opened during the 1870s in Kansas City to take advantage of the city's railroad connections. The new mills increased their productive capacity by harnessing the seemingly unlimited power of steam to expand processes like roller milling in the 1870s and 1880s. Kansas City's new mills raised that community's flour production from 52,708 barrels in 1878 to 1,820,250 in 1907.[21]

Nature had further limited production by confining it to daylight hours. Now entrepreneurs introduced artificial lighting by kerosene, gas, and finally electricity and manufactured around the clock. The new pottery at Clinton, for example, was noteworthy to a local editor in 1892 because "You can pass the pottery day or night and can hear the engines puffing, the rattling of the clay mills. They run day and night in order to keep the shop in clay."[22]

In the new market society the age-old restraints of nature could no longer be tolerated. Nature, like other traditional barriers in the way of producing more goods at lower prices, would have to be conquered.

2. The Developers of Agriculture

Great obstacles faced promoters who tried to convert farming from a traditional way of life into a profitable business. Farmers, unlike workers who had to accept available jobs, would only use their property in new ways if they possessed enough capital and shared the promoters' vision. Farmers could refuse to change. The result was that the movement to transform agriculture lasted much longer and required far greater organization and pressure than the movement to change industry. Inspired by visions of more profitable tomorrows, the developers constructed a network of economic, educational, and political agencies to persuade and pressure the state's farmers to adopt the new ways. Like the railroad promoters, they felt hampered by popular opposition and conservative fiscal traditions as they pursued the large public subsidies that they counted on to fulfill their dreams.

The promoters felt isolated from most of the state's farmers because they came from different worlds. The railroads wanted large-scale farm production because that meant more rail freight and higher prices for their land holdings. To sell the idea of increased agricultural production the Missouri Pacific railroad published *Missouri Lands* and *Money in Sheep*, while the Iron Mountain Railroad printed *Practical Suggestions for the Fruit Grower* by J. C. Whitten of the state agriculture college. Processors of farm goods and land speculators operated model farms to encourage increased farm production and land sales. Edwin Douglass ran a model dairy farm in Jefferson County both to promote new dairying methods and to stock his wholesale butter and cheese business in St. Louis. The Scottish-owned Missouri Land and Live Stock Company stimulated sales of its 369,427 acres in southwest Missouri in the 1880s by operating the model 3,150-acre Sandyford Ranche near Neosho. Most of the state's earliest promoters, the fruit growers, did not even live in rural areas. More than half the members of the State Horticultural Society in 1872 lived in St. Louis, Kansas City, or St. Joseph.[23]

Despite their diverse and tenuous ties to farming, the agricultural promoters shared a common perspective. They based their dreams and programs on new imperatives created by railroads. "As by the wand of a fairy," reported the secretary to the State Horticultural Society in 1876, "the railroad era changed" farming by suddenly depriving the state's farmers of their secure local markets. "Distance and time, if not annihilated, became as dust in the balance . . . and the market was no longer St. Louis or Kansas City, . . . but the world. Competition was the ruler," observed a fruit grower to the State Horticultural Society in 1878. "Henceforward Missouri has no market of her own. She sells to the nation; her mart is taken from her" by the railroad. But the new markets created opportunities, too, for "proximity to markets makes farming profitable," according to the Warren County correspondent to the state agriculture board in 1880.[24]

Farmers, the developers believed, needed to copy industry. Appealing "to the farmers to get out of the worn-out rut that has but little of system, no economy, and is generally short in profits," the president of the state board of agriculture in 1885 called for "a higher type of farmer" who understood that the central problem was to produce "larger yields with an equal amount of labor, thus giving us a larger net profit." Farm educators shared the vision. George C. Swallow, dean of the Missouri Agricultural College, promised in 1872 that the new college "will teach the science of high production."[25]

The political and military victories of the Radical-Unionist forces in the 1860s gave public support to the agricultural promoters. Prior to those victories the State Agricultural Society, formed in 1853, and the State Horticultural Society, formed in 1859, had unsuccessfully agitated for state aid for agricultural education and development. Although many of the largest agricultural operations in the old order had been operated by slaves, the new promoters shared a common outlook with the victorious Radicals. Believing that individual initiative sparked economic growth, Radicals hoped to create a new society based on free labor to replace indolence-breeding slavery. They sought government support to impose new institutions that would encourage individualism, competition, and growth. The 1863 legislature accepted the federal offer, under the 1862 Morrill Act, of 330,000 acres to establish an agricultural college. This became the developers' educational arm. In 1865 the Radicals created an official state agency, the State Board of Agriculture, to promote and supervise the development of large-scale agriculture.

The horticultural society, board of agriculture, and agricultural college cooperated in trying to convert the state's farmers to their dreams. The three organizations had so many members in common that they were virtually indistinguishable. By 1876 six members of the board of agriculture had previously served as curators of the University of Missouri and its agricultural college. The developers agreed with university curator James Rollins that "the great difficulty . . . is that the farmers themselves do not take sufficient interest" in their own educational agency, the agricultural college. "The great point now," declared Rollins to the agriculture board in 1875, "is to engraft the idea of this institution, and similar institutions, on the people of this State."[26]

Since colleges and railroads reached farmers slowly, Radicals and agricultural promoters developed a more direct program to engraft the new values of competition, profit, and production onto farmers. In 1867 they secured a law that encouraged each county to establish an association to stage local fairs and exhibitions where farmers could compete for prizes for the best livestock, crops, and implements. When counties resisted appropriating prize money for the fairs, the State Board of Agriculture formally lectured them in 1876:

We believe that a general exhibition, once a year, of the products of a county where one person's "best" is brought into competition with another person's "best," and the community have an opportunity of seeing the finest and the best the county can produce, does more than anything else can do to encourage and promote these general interests, and that those counties sustaining such organizations, will surpass those that do not, in all of their improvements, and lead them in growth and prosperity.[27]

While trying to graft competitive roots onto farming at the county level, agricultural promoters encouraged competition in other ways. The State Horticultural Society offered cash prizes in the 1870s for the best fruits. Distressed by the state's low yield of corn per acre, the State Board of Agriculture in 1887 sponsored a $100 contest for the farmer who could produce the highest yield from a five-acre plot. And in 1899 the state board established a state fair whose prizes, its members hoped, would stimulate farmers to reach new competitive heights.[28]

George Husmann typified the tangled motives of these developers of the 1860s and 1870s, and contributed mightily to the world's agriculture. Emigrating with his parents from Prussia to the German community of Hermann in 1838–39, young Husmann grew up fascinated with nature and eager to get rich quick. He joined the gold rush in 1850 but failed to make his fortune in California, and returned to Hermann two years later to manage a farm. Sharing the dream of many Germans that the soil around Hermann might nurture wine grapes, he spent the next seventeen years cultivating grapes and other fruits. Soon his orchards and vineyards became models, and the hilltop winery at Hermann became the world's third largest. Believing that his model farm required ever-expanding markets for its products, Husmann became a leading promoter. He helped to found the State Horticultural Society in 1859 to promote Missouri fruits and wines in distant markets, and helped form the State Board of Agriculture in 1865, serving as a board member for sixteen years.

Like other agricultural developers, Husmann deeply believed that competition would create incentives for farmers to adopt new methods. "The grape can only flourish on *free* soil, and by *free* intelligent labor," he wrote in 1866. "The demon of slavery" had retarded agricultural development, because the obligation of the master to care for the slave, however incompetent the slave might be, destroyed individual incentive in both. The promotion of agriculture required victory for the Union and the Radicals. Husmann served in the Union Army, was elected a delegate to the Radicals' state constitutional convention of 1865, and acted as a presidential elector for Ulysses S. Grant.

After the Civil War, Husmann moved comfortably between patient study of grapes and wines, zealous promotion of competitive agriculture, and personal schemes to make money. As a scientist and publicist, he wrote his classic *The Cultivation of the Native Grape, and Manufacture of American Wines* in 1866, and he published *Grape Culturist* from 1869 to 1873. As a promoter, he served on the governing board of the horticultural society, agriculture board, and state university. Aware that wealth came from selling, not growing, products, Husmann organized several enterprises. He launched Hermann's first bank in 1867. He served as president of the 1,500-acre Bluffton Wine Company from 1869 to 1872. When that company failed, he moved to Sedalia to organize Husmann Nurseries, which sold fruit and shrubberies in that booming railroad city.

Husmann's most significant contribution combined the missions of scientist, developer, and entrepreneur. Soon after the Civil War phylloxera insects increasingly destroyed the vineyards first of France and then of California. Scientists, including Charles V. Riley, Missouri's state entomologist, discovered that these root lice had originated in America and that some American grape plants had evolved a natural resistance to them. Desperate French vintners began to import grape cuttings from Missouri to graft onto their vines so as to preserve their grapes from the insects. From 1870 to 1875 Husmann exported millions of phylloxera-resistant cuttings, and in so doing helped save the French wine industry. He was joined by two other Missourians, Isidor Bush of St. Louis and Herman Jaeger of Neosho, in rescuing the world's major vineyards. "Our state is destined to furnish the stock by which the grape-growing interest of Europe and California will again be established," he wrote in 1876. The French ultimately rewarded Husmann with a gold medal and conferred on Jaeger the Legion of Honor.

Husmann, like other promoters of the 1860s and 1870s, hoped that the Agricultural College at the University of Missouri would inspire the state's farmers with grander visions. In 1878 he moved to Columbia to become its first professor of horticulture. He organized displays of Missouri fruits that won major prizes and national markets for large fruit growers. He published *American Grape Growing and Wine Making* (1880), in which he described the experiments that had led to control of the hated phylloxera. Sharing with many other German immigrants a dislike for both slavery and blacks, and convinced that slavery had bred ambition out of blacks, he replaced the university's black farm workers with white students. But college responsibilities deprived him of the excitement of making money, and in 1881 Husmann left Missouri to manage the Talcoa Vineyards in California. There, at last, he could produce wines from the vinifera grapes that had never flourished in Missouri.[29]

The College of Agriculture that Husmann left behind in 1881 was evolving into the central agency for a new generation of agricultural developers in the 1880s. The first step was to redirect the college to fulfill their vision. Geologist George C. Swallow, dean of the college since its founding in 1870, had agreed with university officials that agriculture was simply another of the liberal arts and that, as a result, the college's federal endowment could pay for programs in mathematics, philosophy, and literature. Led by large farmers and the State Board of Agriculture, promoters fought to convert the college into an agency whose teaching and research would be confined only to practical matters that directly benefited farmers. "In these days of specialization when men succeed only by division of labor and division of study," declared state entomologist Charles V. Riley in 1876, "the agricultural student needs a special education," because "those who spread themselves out too widely . . . are the most impractical and least successful." The college answered developers' demands that it test the value of particular breeds and methods. Beginning in 1878 the college published reports of its experiments on the yields of different varieties of corn, wheat, and oats. To appease the powerful fruit growers the college created a chair of horticulture in 1878. Many promoters were relieved when university president Samuel Laws fired Swallow in 1882.[30]

The new dean, J. W. Sanborn, worked closely with large farmers and promoters to make farming into a business and to convert farmers to their vision. Serving both as dean and secretary of the State Board of Agriculture, Sanborn directed the college to issue bulletins on such topics as the feeding of stock, the growing of strawberries, and the harvesting of corn. Over the course of the 1880s, as these bulletins came to dominate reports by the State Board of Agriculture and to replace papers by individual farmers, the new thrust of agricultural development became clear: the college itself was the senior partner with large farmers in directing the future course.

The federal government further encouraged agricultural development along industrial lines dictated by markets, science, and specialization. In 1887 Congress offered annual appropriations of $15,000 to each state to operate agricultural experiment stations that would stimulate specialized production. Missouri quickly attached its experiment station to the College of Agriculture, with the dean of the college to serve simultaneously as director of the station. In setting the station's research priorities in 1888, the Board of Curators resolved that "unscientific and, therefore unprofitable methods" formed the "chief hindrances" to agricultural development and, ignoring the majority of unspecialized farmers, that "the chief agricultural interests in Missouri are grain and stock growing, fruit and dairy products." The station was proudest of its experiments in the 1890s to discover an inoculation against Texas fever, which would remove the main obstacle that kept Missouri's cattle industry from shipping purebred animals to southern buyers. This discovery clearly benefited only farmers who both owned purebred cattle and produced enough to worry about the southern market. The station received its first state appropriation, $3,500, in 1901, and by 1914 its total budget exceeded $100,000.[31]

The basic problem was to conquer nature's barriers to profitable production. Disease and death, the traditional fate of livestock that farmers kept to sustain their families, became intolerable costs of production with the development of expensive purebred animals. In 1891 the State Board of Agriculture assumed direction of the fledgling State Veterinary Service in order to conduct research on curing farmers' sick animals. By 1905 the state veterinarian employed twenty deputies.[32]

The promoters believed that the study of nature would lead to its prediction and control. Unwilling to accept the cycles of rain and drought, cold and heat, as acts of God to which farmers must accommodate themselves, specialized farmers wanted to know the amount of rainfall and dates of frosts. The new United States Department of Agriculture encouraged weather reporting as a crucial part of the new market agriculture by offering to pay each state for a director of a weather service. In 1889 the Missouri legislature created the State Weather Service under these terms.[33]

Animals, trees, and plants became sources for specialized products. "We call a cow a machine for converting hay, grain and grass into milk and butter," explained an expert to a Linn County farmers' institute in 1890. "We must follow the lead of the manufacturer in this, and develop more efficient types of animal machines," Dean F. B. Mumford of the College of Agriculture told a 1912 Farmers' Week audience. I. T. Van Note, a dairy employee at the college, observed in 1909 that "the dairy cow is . . . an invention of man, as much so as is the dynamo, circular saw or steam engine. Her value is measured by her ability to produce a paying quantity of milk in one year." Pointing to the manufacturers' example of conquering nature's limits to cheapened production, for expanding markets, developers repeatedly echoed John Hosmer's 1913 warning that "If as a dairyman you have not the sense to appreciate the significance of this better machine matter, you had better shut up shop and quit, for that will be the final result when you compete with the fellow who does."[34]

Developers promoted the acceptance of more profitable breeds and varieties. Alarmed that Nodaway County lacked pedigreed animals in 1870, local businessmen took the lead in organizing a county fair in 1871 at which they displayed the new breeds to farmers. Developers created organizations to stimulate farmers to adopt the new breeds. Producers created organizations of dairymen (1890), poultry growers (1892), swine breeders (1893), horse breeders (1896), improved livestock breeders (1897), sheep breeders (1898), corn growers (1903), draft horse breeders (1909) and cattle feeders (1911). The state board encouraged these "industrial associations" in the 1890s by staging a week-long meeting for all such groups at one place. Soon the College of Agriculture hosted the annual meeting, and in 1906 it became formalized as Farmers' Week.[35]

The new animals were expensive investments that required farmers to make further investments to improve on nature. By most traditional standards it was absurd to board animals in buildings. But the new specialized breeds were so expensive that their owners had to protect their investments against nature's uncertainties. "When you show me a man who has a large barn," declared William R. Williams of Cedar County in 1887, "I will show you a man that is prosperous," and—what was most significant of all in the new order—"always has something to sell." Missouri's "Cattle King," David Rankin, built the state's largest barn in 1892 on his 23,000-acre spread in Atchison County, and by 1909 his 250 workers cared for 13,000 head of cattle, 25,000 hogs, and 640 horses and mules.[36]

In their application of industrialists' methods to rural life, the agricultural developers created in home economics a field whose very existence measured the extent of their enthusiasm. Of all the activities on the farm, developers believed, homemaking was one of the most unspecialized, inefficient, and, finally, unprofitable, of farm industries. In 1900 the college established a Department of Household Economics so that farmers' wives could be taught the new principles. "Housekeeping should be considered a business or profession," explained a speaker to the state's home economists in 1912, because "the woman who keeps her husband and other bread winners of her family healthy and strong in body and cheerful in spirit certainly adds to the family exchequer." The hallmarks of the successful homemaker, Mrs. Rosa Russell Ingels told the same conference, were "system, conservation of time and energy and the use of labor saving devices."[37]

The developers continued to be haunted by the problem of how to convert farmers to their vision for agriculture. Sanborn persuaded the State Board of Agriculture to create farmers' institutes at which representatives from the board and college traveled to farm communities to join successful local farmers in demonstrating the latest methods. The board held the first farmers' institute at Higginsville in December 1882. Convinced that institutes were the best method but faced with unenthusiastic local farmers, the promoters provided most of the funding and organization from the state level. The board authorized $700 for the institutes in 1885, and in 1891 the legislature began to make annual appropriations. The board organized three institutes in the winter of 1883–84, and the number grew to reach eighty-one in 1891–92. The board promoted institutes even more zealously in the twentieth century. The number reached 147 in 1903–4 and 260 in 1908.[38]

The board, experiment station, and college tried other methods to reach farmers. In the early 1890s the board distributed 80,000 copies of its monthly crop bulletins. The college and station developed a news service that publicized farming methods, for use by rural editors. In 1908 this news service in Columbia distributed weekly articles. The most dramatic scheme was the Seed and Soil Special Train that stopped in 1907 at all seventy-four stations on the Alton and Wabash railroads so that speakers from the college and state board could demonstrate methods of crop and soil improvement. By the 1910s these trains were a major feature of the developers' plans.[39]

These sporadic efforts failed to establish the permanent local bases of year-round support that developers increasingly believed were the best hope for reaching local farmers. Continuing its quest for local bases for "improved agricultural practices and more profitable systems of farming" in each community, the College of Agriculture in 1912 launched a program to create resident "farm advisers" who would be sponsored by county "farm bureaus" but hired and directed by the college. Their salaries would be paid one-quarter by the college, one-quarter by the U.S. Department of Agriculture, and one-half by the participating county. The college persuaded the 1913 legislature to appropriate $25,000 over two years to entice supporters of agricultural development to organize farm bureaus in their counties. The problem, as in the past, was to locate local supporters for agricultural development.[40]

The local supporters for the farm bureaus came from a consensus emerging in the 1910s among businessmen and large farmers that their businesses were becoming increasingly intertwined in a market economy in which survival depended on growth and profit. In 1912 the faltering Commercial Club of Trenton raised its membership tenfold, to over 500 members, by inviting farmers to join merchants in a common campaign to promote growth that became known as "The Trenton Idea." A clergyman explained at the 1913 Farmers' Week that "'The Trenton Idea' means that in Grundy County, Missouri, at least, agriculture and commerce are married."[41]

"Commercial clubs and business concerns of every kind are taking every step within their power to encourage better work upon the farms because the town is directly interested in only the surplus produced upon them," farmers' institute lecturer S. M. Jordan explained in 1912. Jordan warned that "if the business men do not solve this question" of development, "the farmer must be driven to do it himself, and his solution does not suit the town." Two months later the Sedalia Boosters' Club hired Jordan as county farm adviser to manage its new creation, the Pettis County Bureau of Agriculture. A mutual desire for farm surpluses meant "there is no reason why our Pettis county farmers and the Sedalia business men should not be closely aligned, and the commercial club is an instrument to enable them to gather very successfully for the benefit of both," declared the Boosters' M. V. Carroll in 1913.[42]

Businessmen hoped that by turning agriculture from a way of life into an industry the new experts would also help transcend the barriers that had grown up in the new order between farmers and the bankers and middlemen who lived in town and upon whom they depended. S. M. Jordan, first county agent in Missouri and perhaps the nation, explained how local championship of growth could overcome the traditional conflict between farmer and banker. Bankers agreed to make unprecedented loans to large farmers for feeding and breeding livestock, and Jordan agreed to assess the farmers' chances for success: "When a man makes an application for a loan it will be my business as a county man of Pettis county to investigate that fellow, see what he is doing, how he farms. . . . If he farms mostly in town he is counted out at once; if he is not industrious he is counted out, and if he 'boozes' just a little he is counted out."[43]

Local businessmen and large farmers looked to the College of Agriculture and its new program to provide both the form and content of the knowledge that they hoped farmers would turn into the surpluses whose sale would stimulate local growth. They welcomed the offer of farm advisers. During the program's first year, 1912, Pettis and Cape Girardeau counties funded local advisers. As merchant groups increasingly paid the local half of the advisers' salaries, the sponsoring groups became known as farm bureaus. Eight more counties joined in 1913. The federal Smith-Lever Act of 1914 provided further financial support for the creation of an Agricultural and Home Economics Extension Service, with the federal government agreeing to split evenly with states the costs of local extension agents and removing some of the initial financial burden from local communities. By early 1915 the College of Agriculture had staffed extension advisers, increasingly called agents, in fourteen counties. These county agents and their sponsoring bureaus met together at Slater in 1915 to found the Missouri Farm Bureau Federation.[44]

The county farm bureaus and their agents from the College of Agriculture provided, at last, permanent local roots for the state's agricultural developers. They encouraged local farmers to acquire the skills and invest the capital to produce for large markets. But the developers' real allies, in the end, were market-oriented businessmen, not the state's traditional farmers, who continued to cling tightly to their dreams of independence.

3

The New Insecurities

H. W. Roe brooded as he surveyed his Henry County farm in 1904. First the crops had failed, and then his hogs mysteriously started to die. Panic gripped him as he foresaw that he would have no surpluses to sell that autumn. He concluded that he was a personal failure: he could not produce enough to sell in a new market over which he had no control. There was only one escape. In October H. W. Roe killed himself.[1]

The new order seemed constantly to invent new ways of stripping Missourians of their familiar forms of social, economic, and psychological security as increasingly it forced them to compete with others in order simply to survive. As everything seemed to become a commodity to be bought or sold, people could no longer rely on families, friends, churches, political representatives, or communities to provide the support they had depended on in the past. The huge, new, impersonal markets reduced production and consumption to the single imperative of constant growth. Survival depended on producing more goods at lower prices than competitors.

The sheer size, interdependence, and specialization of the new markets created a vast increase in the number and kind of middlemen who intervened betweeen what Missourians grew or made and what they ate or wore. Between producer and consumer there now stood railroads and express companies to transport products, banks and insurance companies to lend and protect investments in expensive production methods, processors such as packing houses, implement manufacturers, bakeries, shoe factories, and hordes of salesmen and mail-order houses to peddle the new products.

As the world narrowed to impersonal competition and middlemen, the exchanges between producer and consumer were no longer personal relationships governed by reputation and custom. Both the common bonds of mutual obligation and the personal networks of the old order lacked the power to control life. What took their place were staggering new kinds of insecurity.

1. The Invisible Hand

When the new railroads brought their goods into competition with those from the rest of the nation and the world, Missourians lost an important measure of control over what they produced and how they produced it. Failure to expand, cheapen, and specialize meant economic ruin. "Crops once profitably cultivated in various localities must be abandoned, for the reason that rapidly increased facilities for cheap transportation bring ruinous competition from more favored regions," observed Lebanon's M. W. Serl in 1891. Missouri's many small hand potteries, for example, were driven out of business by 1890 when they lost their local markets to cheaper products from steam-powered potteries in Ohio, Indiana, and Illinois.[2]

As the price in remote markets came increasingly to dictate how Missourians worked, each group encountered special crises. Farmers created and then faced an excruciating dilemma. Those who chose to expand their production by clearing their land destroyed the habitat for the game that had allowed them to remain self-sufficient. The original landscape vanished as the proportion of property that farmers cleared for agriculture rose from 14 percent in 1860 to 38 percent by 1880 and 52 percent by 1900. The number of counties where at least half the area was improved farmland rose from four in 1870 to sixty-one by 1890. The rapid spread of aricultural cultivation and the resulting destruction of wildlife habitats forced farmers to produce for markets instead of relying for their survival on the familiar gun and dog, N. W. Clothier told a Gasconade County farmers' institute in 1891. Once farmers had cleared their good timber, as in the Osage Valley in the 1880s, they lost another basis for self-sufficiency, because they could no longer sell shingles, ties, and fence rails in local markets when they needed cash.[3]

The only way to compensate for the loss of self-sufficiency was to grow more for market. Farmers then bought new implements or animals in order to increase their surpluses. Soon one investment dictated another. Expensive pure blooded animals required barns, feed, and veterinarians. The more they invested, the more dependent farmers visibly became on the invisible hand. And there was nothing they could do about the selling price. The fundamental fact, as James A. Fulbright of Laclede County explained in 1886, was that "Some one else . . . decide[s] just how much the farmer is to get for every bushel of wheat, every pound of pork and every other product of the farm." When Missouri's farmers planted in the spring, they had no idea what their labor would be worth in the fall. The price for a bushel of corn in Missouri rose from $.36 in 1880 to $.65 in 1881 before skidding to $.39 in 1882. It rose from $.32 in 1900 to $.67 in 1901 and fell to $.33 in 1902. They had little better luck with wheat: the price for a bushel in Missouri fluctuated between $1.19 in 1881 and $.85 in 1882, $.85, in 1897 and $.59 in 1898.[4]

Growing dependence on the market left farmers even more vulnerable to the inevitable rhythms of nature. The failure of a crop, the illness of a family member, or the death of a cow became devastating events because survival depended first on producing surpluses and then on the price those surpluses commanded.

The competitive pressure to produce more goods at lower prices gripped businessmen as tightly as it did farmers. For most, the invisible hand reached out a death grip. From 1870 to 1920 the number of boot and shoe factories in Missouri fell from 1,144 to 73, of cooperages from 291 to 30, of furniture manufacturers from 271 to 93, of iron and steel factories from 61 to 5, of breweries from 87 to 20. Losing their local markets to cheaper goods manufactured elsewhere, many small businessmen were forced to close their doors and work for someone else. At St. Joseph independent proprietors declined from 21.1 percent of the city's white males in 1868 to 7.6 percent in 1908, and at Springfield they declined from 13.2 percent in 1873–74 to 8.2 percent in 1911–12.[5]

The harshest insecurities fell to workers, who were generally incapable of influencing the demand for what they sold, their labor. As their jobs and wages increasingly depended on the price for their employers' products in remote markets, they lived in growing fear of the periodic wage cuts and depressions that seemed to become more and more frequent and severe as the market economy spread. "Unreasonable and suicidal competition . . . necessitated severe" cuts in wages paid railroad workers, observed the *St. Louis Republican* in 1877. During the depression of the 1870s the *St. Louis Globe-Democrat* saw the consequences of competition in the "thousands of hungry and hopeless workmen, their once strong frames reduced by privation, their decent clothing replaced by tatters, and their wives and children reflecting at home the squalid misery of the father who haunts the streets in the vain search for work." During the depression of the 1890s at least a fifth of the workers were laid off in Missouri's boiler, railroad car, agricultural implement, bagging, clothing, machine and foundry, stave, and smelting industries. In the Panic of 1907 (as employers designated the next downturn), sixty-one St. Louis local unions, representing 15,228 workers, reported that at least half of their members could not find work for at least one-quarter of 1907.[6]

Competitive pressures deprived workers of the security of regular work in the new order. Even during prosperous times nothing cushioned their families from loss of even a single day's pay or the uncertainty of not knowing when they would work again. At the Doe Run Lead Mine in St. Francois County in 1893, for example, nearly half the employees were laid off more than half the year. A majority of Kansas City's black heads of families were unemployed for at least one-third of 1911. Appalled by the irregularity of employment for those workers who remained on payrolls in 1895 despite the depression around them, the state labor commissioner reported that 26 percent of employees of Butler County's stave factories and 46 percent of workers in St. Louis stamping plants were actually employed fewer than three out of every five workdays.[7]

Gripped by the invisible hand when they tried to sell their labor, many workers were denied the advantages of a market economy when they purchased their needs. Instead of being able to use their paychecks to buy their own groceries, provisions, medical care, and housing in a competitive market, 22 percent of the state's workers in 1880 were paid in some kind of scrip that obligated them to buy goods and services from their employers on the employers' terms, according to a survey by the state labor commissioner. Many bricklayers, blacksmiths, coopers, iron workers, coal miners, and mill hands were paid in scrip. Kansas City cigar makers and bakers, along with coal miners, were required to rent housing from their employers. Although the legislature in 1881 required employers to pay their workers in cash, employees soon encountered subterfuges that kept them dependent on the company stores. By withholding the first paycheck for twenty-five to ninety days and advancing credit at the company store, iron and coal mine owners compelled employees to shop there and pay the store's inflated prices. Employers and courts successfully thwarted coal miners' struggles to free themselves from company stores until well into the twentieth century.[8] In the meantime many workers and their families felt trapped between the invisible hand that controlled whether they would work and how much they would earn and the very visible hand that dictated how they would meet their needs.

2. The New Tools

Profit's command to produce more goods at lower prices drove employers to revolutionize the character of work in ways that stripped workers of their traditional control over what they did, separated work from life, and ignited social conflicts. Artisans fought tenaciously to defend traditional patterns of work. The creation of a product, artisans believed, was a craft that depended on their own skill, knowledge, and tools. They controlled access to the craft by selecting apprentices. They accepted guidance more readily from local consumers than from new employers.

Artisan traditions were both expensive and obstructive to employers who felt constant pressures to cut costs and control production. "The struggle for existence among the railroads leading to keen competition and low rates," observed the *St. Louis Globe-Democrat* in 1877, "has compelled the companies to be economical in the pay and employment of labor." The simplest way to cut labor costs and assume control over production was to replace the skilled artisan with specialized machines and unskilled machine tenders to operate them. Machines produced more goods at more controllable speeds, at lower prices, and without resisting their owners' commands. For centuries printers had set type by hand, and by the 1890s a skilled printer could set 1,500 ems an hour. In that decade newspaper publishers in St. Joseph, St. Louis, and other cities invested $3,000 for a new machine that could set 4,800 ems an hour, allowing one low-paid machine operator to replace three skilled printers. Mixing, molding, pressing, and conveying machines supplanted the skilled brick maker. By 1889 the new six-mold dry-press machine of the American Pressed Brick Company in St. Louis could produce six bricks with each stroke of the plunger and a million bricks a month.[9]

Boot and shoe workers soon learned how cost had replaced skill as the guiding principle of labor in the new order. On the eve of the Civil War one artisan performed sixty-seven different steps to make a shoe, and it took 1,025 hours at a labor cost of $256.33 to make a hundred pairs of cheap women's shoes. By 1895 the new factories made the same number of shoes by hiring eighty-five unskilled workers to do ninety-five operations with each worker tending the same machine all day. The new process took less than eighty-one hours at a labor cost of $18.59. As manufacturers replaced artisans with welt, turn, and lasting machines to cut costs in the huge new shoe markets, the number of boot- and shoemaking establishments in Missouri shrank from 1,144 in 1869 to 73 in 1919, while the capitalization of the average plant rose from $1,000 in 1869 to $997,000 and the number of its workers soared from 2 to 324.[10]

Employers rapidly transformed work. The exhibition of new machines at the Louisiana Purchase Exposition in 1904 was "the most startling showing ever made of the displacement of man's labor and hand-work skill by automatic devices," and "seemed to proclaim that the time is near when all the work formerly done by deft human hands is to be done by power-driven machinery," according to a souvenir history of the fair. But this bright prospect for employers meant horrifying new insecurities for workers. *Amerika*, a German Catholic paper in St. Louis, explained that "the use of steam power for thousands and thousands of practical tasks . . . put hundreds of thousands of diligent hands out of work, and reduced to the proletariat other hundreds of thousands, who as master craftsmen had enjoyed a certain independence. And for all it obstructed the once so easy step from laborer to employer by the erection of an almost unscalable cliff." Numbers supported *Amerika*'s conclusions. In St. Joseph artisans had outnumbered unskilled workers by more than two to one in 1868, but forty years later unskilled workers outnumbered artisans. Unskilled workers rose from 17 to 28 percent of the city's white males, while artisans dropped from 37 to 25 percent. At Springfield the proportion of unskilled workers among the city's males nearly doubled from 1873 to 1912, from 15 to 28 percent, while the percentage of artisans fell from 47 to 36 percent.[11]

The new machines created unprecedented alienation between workers and their tools. The new tools, owned by employers instead of workers, became the enemy of the men and women who used them. They threatened workers not only with the loss of traditional independence, but with injury and death.

Workers lived in growing fear of the accidents that might injure or kill them and deprive their families of the income necessary for survival. The new Eads Bridge at St. Louis, completed in 1874, was an engineering marvel that symbolized the coming of the new order by linking Missouri by rail to eastern markets. But one-fifth of the 600 workers who sank the bridge's foundations got the dreaded bends, and 14 died from this occupational hazard.[12]

"By the introduction of machinery into all departments of labor," con-cluded state labor commissioner W. H. Hilkene in 1880, "numerous accidents to life and limb occur from various causes. Not a day passes but that some one, is reported through the medium of the daily press, having been maimed or disabled by machinery." The accidents were as varied as the new machines. On May 11, 1897, a fifty-year-old worker sliced off his arm at the elbow on a planing machine at the St. Louis Manufacturing Company. Six days later in the same city thirty-four-year-old Richard Hayes died at the Charter Oak Stove Company when his leg caught on a set screw on a shaft. Four days after that, nineteen-year-old Edward Scherer died a hideous death at Kansas City's Beham Manufacturing Company when he stumbled and was caught by a loose drive belt and bound to a revolving shaft. Four employees died when the boiler exploded at the Churchill and Owsley flour mill at Windsor in February 1891.[13]

Although statistics on manufacturing accidents remain shadowy until the twentieth century, it is clear that the number and severity of accidents mounted as the years went by and the machinery became more complex and dangerous. Missouri's accident rate rose from 4.0 percent of manufacturing workers in 1905 to 14.1 percent in 1913, according to state labor commis-sioners. By 1913 the injury rate reached 53 percent for electrical workers, 38 percent for smelting and refinery workers, 34 percent for railway car shop-men, and 30 percent for meat packers and toolmakers.[14]

Miners and railway workers dreaded accidents as much as factory workers did. Instead of patiently angling into the coal face and shoring it up, the Keith and Perry Mine near Rich Hill in 1888 tried to cut costs by blasting with new explosives. Throughout March they blasted the coal face 247 feet below ground. Coal dust accumulated. Finally, on March 29, two massive explo-sions ignited the loose dust and a fire roared through Shaft Number 6. Twenty-four miners died and many more were critically injured. The rail-roads that created the new order provided some of its most dangerous jobs. A brakeman became the first fatality of railroading at Marshall within a month after the arrival of the first train in that city in 1879. In 1914 alone railways reported 398 killed and 6,768 injured in Missouri.[15]

But the cheapened production of the new order undermined workers' health in less obvious ways as well. The new workplaces, engulfed by dusts, fumes, chemicals, and exhausts were poorly ventilated environments where extremes of heat and cold were common. Sweating in overheated factories, molders fell frequent prey to rheumatism and lung diseases. Only young workers could stand the constant headaches that came from working in the new breweries' freezing lager cellars, filled with carbon dioxide that escaped from the beer tanks. "Painter's colic" was a disease caused by handling lead and turpentine. Victims first stiffened in the joints, then their limbs became paralyzed, and finally their kidneys became infected. Poisonous dusts took their toll on cigar makers, printers, tailors, flour mill workers, smelter workers, and others. Doctors called the resulting ailments consumption, catarrh, lung disease, liver disease. Springfield's printing pressmen claimed in

1910 that 58 percent of their members died from inhaling dusts. Touring coal mines in 1880, the state labor commissioner found one where ventilation was so poor that the lamps would not stay lit, another where he felt dizzy and unable to breathe, another where miners complained of constant headaches. Twenty years later, in 1912, coal miners at Neck, Missouri, still complained that "bad air is killing more men than anything else." After ministering to lead miners in the Joplin area for nine years, Dr. S. C. Price reported in 1880 that lead mining caused constipation, neuralgias, and intestinal spasms that were so severe that the only cure was for the patient to leave the lead-mining district.[16]

Workers' fears about their increasingly unsafe workplaces were also fears that their families could not survive any loss of income. Most employers gave little help to their disabled workers and quickly replaced them with stronger and healthier employees. When a band saw cut off the arms of two men in a planing mill in 1880, the employer fired them on the spot. That same year another employer stopped paying a carpenter who broke three ribs when he fell off a scaffold. An iron worker lost his wages when he lost three fingers in 1880.[17] The fear of disabling accidents and diseases was the fear of the isolation of each family in a new order that pitted each against all.

The new machines created further insecurities by eroding familiar avenues of recruitment and mobility and thereby undermining the bonds of deference and obligation between older and younger workers. Since the knowledge and skills of the worker were the basic ingredients of production, artisans controlled work by controlling the apprenticeship process through which young workers learned those skills. Missouri's official policy that older workers could best teach young men and women the things that would equip them for life dated formally back to a law passed in 1807, fourteen years before Missouri became a state, that required orphans to serve bound apprenticeships to craftsmen who would teach them occupational and literacy skills in return.[18] After serving the apprenticeship the young worker would know how to build a house, make a shoe, construct a saddle, or print a newspaper, and soon he could buy his own tools and ultimately hire apprentices. Control over apprenticeship was thus control over mobility.

When employers replaced artisans with machines, they also ensured that new workers would never have the skills to make the whole product and thus to rise from worker to employer in the time-honored manner. State labor commissioner Lee Meriwether observed how the new shoemaking machines had changed that craft by 1895: "Thirty years ago a shoemaker could make a shoe; put him on any spot on earth, and with the proper tools and materials he could have fashioned you a shoe. The shoemaker of today can no more make a shoe than he can make a wagon." Harness makers struck the J. B. Sickles Saddlery Company in St. Louis on February 3, 1893, because their employer had ordered them to teach young boys only enough of the trade to make a small part of a harness and saddle. By not teaching young workers the full knowledge of the craft, employers not only cut off the traditional route to mobility but also ensured that skilled artisans could be replaced by cheaper workers. Asked which workers he would fire when he installed a typesetting machine in 1895, the publisher of the *St. Joseph Gazette* replied: "The old ones, because old men cannot work the machines or adapt themselves to new conditions. A young man can learn to operate the machine in a week."[19] In the new order one could learn everything necessary to survive in the printing trade in a single week!

The new machines gave employers the victory in the battle over whether young workers would be introduced to work by employers who wanted to teach them the minimal skills to tend machines or by craftsmen who wanted to teach them the entire craft and thus the route to mobility. The employers' victory spelled the death of the apprenticeship system. In 1884 the state labor commissioner surveyed sixty-seven occupations and found that 79 percent of the workers had themselves served some kind of apprenticeship for their work but that only 35 percent of them were working in establishments that used apprentices in 1884. Twenty years later, in 1904, only 3.5 percent of the state's 663 local unions had any kind of apprenticeship agreement. By 1915 apprentices were only 1 percent of the state's manufacturing workers. In 1917 the legislature formally acknowledged the artisans' loss to the new machines by repealing all apprenticeship laws and thus terminating Missouri's 110-year-old legal tradition of apprenticeship.[20]

The new machines eroded security for farmers, too, as some turned to the new implements to produce more for the new markets. Farmers worried about how they would pay off debts for the machines as well as how family members would escape injuries when they operated them. But they worried most about the particular people the machines threw out of work in rural Missouri. "The very same power of invention and machinery [at work in cities] is fast throwing idle the hand laborers employed on farms," noted Commissioner Hilkene in 1880. By the 1890s new farm machines had supplanted the work of agricultural laborers by cutting the amount of labor it took to farm an acre of wheat from 61 hours to 3, of corn from 39 hours to 15, and of oats from 66 hours to seven. Each new thresher and twine binder in the 1880s displaced five farm workers. The basic problem was that the workers who lost jobs to the machines were generally the children of farmers. The new farm machines eroded families by forcing younger members to migrate to cities, where they competed with other unskilled workers for the new factory jobs. [21]

3. The New Competitors

The loss of control over access to the workplace led established workers to view new arrivals to their workplaces as competitors, not comrades. When employers hired unskilled employees who would work for low wages to tend the machines, they fueled new social tensions and insecurities as they widened the gulf between workers and their tools. "When a citizen has devoted the most important years of his life in acquiring a practical knowledge of some useful and wealth-producing occupation, and finds himself, before he has reached his prime, supplanted by his own or another's child, through the introduction of some new device or improvement in machinery, it is no wonder that hundreds . . . should look upon the introduction of machinery as a curse," wrote Commissioner Hilkene in 1880. With anger, fear, and contempt, the coopers' local at Alexandria as late as 1901 condemned a local employer who "would rather hire boys that ought to be in school than experienced men.[22]

The new competition from children and women posed a double-edged threat to traditional family relationships. It threatened the status, dignity, and authority of the father by challenging his ability to provide the income and skills the household, and particularly his children, needed to survive. "The child drives the father out of the factory because it works cheaper," cried John Nolde to a St. Louis rally at the peak of the 1877 general strike. And the new competition threatened "tender" children and women, who were forced into dangerous and sometimes "immoral" activities to support the family instead of following their traditional patterns of development. Small wonder that abolition of child labor became one of workers' two demands in the St. Louis general strike in 1877. Other Missourians agreed. "That certain classes of goods may be made a little cheaper than they otherwise might be, the State permits her children by hundreds and thousands to be taken into industrial establishments at tender years and put to hard labor. There they remain and grow up to be men and women, in almost every instance deteriorated physically, and mentally and morally blunted, if not vitiated and ruined," summarized labor commissioner Henry A. Newman in 1884.[23]

But child labor persisted because many households depended on their children's earnings to survive. Feelings of anger, guilt, and helpless dependence merged as parents sent their children to work. From the Civil War to World War I, Missouri's manufacturers relied on the labor of children under sixteen to a larger extent than was true in the nation as a whole. In 1869 children were 8.5 percent of Missouri's manufacturing workers and 5.6 percent of the nation's. Child labor remained greater in Missouri even when employers found other cheap workers. In 1919 children were 2.1 percent of Misouri's manufacturing workers and 1.3 percent of the nation's. Even so, the proportion of Missouri's boys and girls between ten and fifteen who were forced to work for a living fell only from 14.9 percent in 1900 to 11.3 percent in 1910, despite passage of tough child labor and school attendance laws. A majority of Kansas City's black households in the early twentieth century depended on income from children and wives to supplement income from irregular work by husbands and fathers.[24]

Skilled workers did not escape competition from cheaper workers when child labor declined, because Missouri's employers increasingly turned to young women as their source of cheap labor. In the state's box industry, for example, the proportion of women workers rose from 18 to 33 percent between 1870 and 1890 as the proportion of children declined from 24 to 5 percent. Women rose from 5.9 percent of the state's manufacturing workers in 1869 to 29.1 percent in 1919. Employers believed that women were particularly suited for the new machines that displaced male artisans in the clothing, shoe, and tobacco industries. In 1880, for example, seven tobacco factories in St. Louis fired 800 skilled tobacco rollers and replaced them with rolling machines and young women.[25]

Most of Missouri's female workers were young, unmarried women who still contributed to their parents' income. At St. Louis in 1891, 92 percent of working women were single, 93 percent lived at home, and "most of the women give their wages to their parents," according to the labor commission's survey. The average working woman in St. Louis in 1891 was slightly less than twenty years old. Most married women remained at home, for they formed only 8 percent of St. Louis's women workers and 16 percent of Kansas City's. Only 3.1 percent of Missouri's married women were "gainfully" employed in 1900, and that proportion reached only 7 percent in 1920.[26]

Missouri's adult male workers and their families lived in growing fear of cheap competition from the young people who increasingly tended the new machines. Missouri's manufacturing employers in 1889 paid the average adult male $532 a year, the average adult female $252, and the average child $147. The availability of cheaper workers led employers to lay off some adult male employees and cut the wages of others.[27]

Skilled workers soon encountered a new form of competition that threatened their traditional cultures at least as deeply as competition from children and women did. Since skills were usually passed among people who knew each other, they tended to be the province of particular ethnic and racial cultures in each community. Blacks predominated in personal service, Germans in many skilled crafts, British immigrants in many coal-mining communities. With their work bordered by their ethnicity, traditional Missourians frequently escaped contact with and competition from people with different backgrounds. When employers chose workers for their cheapness instead of their skill, they threw people from different cultures into competition and undermined the security that had come with ethnicity.

The new competitors came from different ethnic and racial groups. British-born coal miners in Macon County fought tenaciously to prevent competition from cheaper workers, but their defeat in that battle could be measured by the decline in the percentage of coal miners' parents born in England and Wales, from 93 percent in 1870 to 23 percent in 1900. When owners of St. Francois County lead mines sought cheaper workers to operate the new machines, they fired the established Ozark miners and replaced them with Italian and Hungarian immigrants. Cheapened production stripped members of traditional ethnic cultures of their control over their work. Germans lost control over shoemaking to the new shoe factories. Almost half as many first- and second-generation Germans worked in the boot and shoe industry in 1900 as had first-generation Germans in 1870. Irish immigrants lost their supremacy in railroading. In 1870 one out of every twelve Irish immigrants in

Missouri had worked for railroads, but by 1900 only one of every twenty-seven first- or second-generation Irish did.[28]

The most dramatic job competition between traditional cultures in the new order was between races. This competition stripped each race of the security that had accompanied control over particular jobs. At stake in this competition were the badges of pride, dignity, and independence that each race had developed separately under slavery and segregation. For at least a generation after the Civil War, blacks continued to be confined by racial prejudice to jobs in personal service and agriculture that grew from skills and experiences they had acquired as slaves. When employers finally challenged racial traditions in their quest for cheaper workers, they kindled racial conflicts in rural and urban Missouri alike as both races lost their control over their traditional jobs. Macon County's coal mine owners hired their first black workers in the 1880s, and by 1900 blacks constituted one-fifth of that county's coal miners. By the early twentieth century steel mill owners in St. Louis and meat packers in Kansas City concluded that they could best break unions and keep wages down by exploiting the racial tensions that had kept blacks out of the new unions. "The Negro was introduced" to the iron and steel industry, concluded William A. Crossland in his study of St. Louis blacks in 1914, because "he was a willing worker; he worked at low wages; and could be depended upon to break a strike." From 1890 to 1920 the percentage of blacks among iron and steel workers rose from zero to 10 percent at Kansas City and from 4 to 18 percent at St. Louis. Blacks increasingly competed with whites as unskilled workers in all industries. Between 1890 and 1920, they rose from 14 to 31 percent of laborers in St. Louis and from 25 to 39 percent in Kansas City.[29]

As blacks increasingly competed with whites for factory jobs, they lost their dominance over personal service trades to white competitors. "St. Louis has . . . become more of a northern metropolitan city, and so a less favorable location for colored personal service workers," noted Crossland in 1914. Racial prejudice combined with the arrival of unskilled immigrants and strong white labor unions to drive blacks from their traditional and desirable jobs as barbers and waiters in prestigious downtown establishments. From 1890 to 1920 the percentage of male servants who were black declined from 59 to 32 in Kansas City and from 39 to 28 in St. Louis, while the proportion of blacks among barbers fell from 31 to 14 percent in Kansas City.[30]

Established workers came to view newcomers from different backgrounds as enemies instead of allies. Sometimes they expressed their anger by resisting the employers and their machines, and sometimes they attacked the new competitors. But the basic cause remained the same. The German Catholic editor of *Amerika* reacted characteristically in 1877:

> But since the Negro emancipation has thrown an enormous mass of new workers into the East and North and West, and since the importation of the horrible coolies has added a second innumerable quantity, the bloodsuckers can take a much greater freedom over against the white worker. . . . And if . . .

the deluded money-grubbers continue to tread these hundreds of thousands of white workers underfoot, then these bloodsuckers will soon have the most unwelcome experience that the great strike of 1877 was not the last or the worst.

Skilled English and Welsh miners at Bevier struck their employer in 1878 to prevent the hiring of Chinese miners. In the 1880s they used both strikes and terrorism to block employers from introducing cheaper Scandinavian and black miners. They boycotted mines that employed competitors from different backgrounds, set fire to a pit where black miners worked, and murdered mine owner Thomas Wardell in 1888 for his prominent part in undermining their job security. St. Louis railway car builders struck against importation of immigrants. Tension between Italian and native-born workers became so explosive during a 1910 strike at a cement factory in Italasco that Governor Herbert Hadley had to call out troops to keep peace between the rival ethnic groups.[31]

Traditional ethnic and racial conflicts flared into violent confrontations when employers subordinated skills and cultural values to cheap wages and unskilled work. The new workplace competition was the torch that set ancient feelings of craft, ethnic, and community pride aflame. Resenting newcomers who threatened their skills, jobs, and wages, established workers frequently expressed their new insecurity by condemning the newcomers' culture. Newcomers felt insecure in their relationships with established workers and resented the ways they were treated. Employers thus created a dramatic new process by which workers in the same workplace came to view each other as enemies and the workplace as a constant assault on their traditional ways of living and working.

4. The New Authorities and Secularism

The new invisible hand seemed to replace traditional values and authorities as the regulator of life. By forcing Missourians to compete against growing numbers of faceless people in a world in which money alone seemed to ensure survival and success, the new order cut individuals adrift as it rapidly undercut familiar economic and moral bases of security. "That fierce spirit of competition . . . seems to dominate our life in all its avenues," lamented President Clara Hoffman of the Missouri Women's Christian Temperance Union in 1896. The most frightening impact of this new competition for many Missourians was its secularizing erosion of religious authority and its creation of a mass market for immoral new authorities. Conferences of southern Methodists declared in 1897 that "one of the greatest perils of the church today is the cheap, secular newspapers" and "books of a like, trashy kind," which, it charged, were "almost entirely godless." "The young mind is being inundated with theories and inculcations which create doubt and uncertainty on almost all high moral questions. Already the absence of moral conviction is simply appalling."[32]

The new order further eroded the security provided by traditional authorities by reducing Missourians to strange new dependence on people whose only claim to authority was their wealth or ownership of tools. In their daily lives farmers and workers felt their independence ebbing as they encountered employers or middlemen who had grown wealthy—and hence, in the new order, powerful—without ever making or growing anything. These daily experiences of subservience, of deference expected toward those with no traditional claim, intensified their feelings of isolation. E. T. Behrens, who rose from his position as a railway clerk in Sedalia to become a national union leader, never forgot an early experience that epitomized the new feelings of powerlessness that gripped workers as they faced the new leaders. One day in 1878 Behrens and other clerks in the Sedalia office of the Missouri, Kansas, and Texas Railway glanced up as their supervisor and a portly man entered the room. Behrens recalled:

> The supervisor clapped his hands, and, as one man, every clerk in that room rose to his feet. They stood thus for a brief moment and at another signal resumed their seats. The portly gentleman was the president of the road. I couldn't figure out just what it all was about. I had witnessed similar performances at church when members of the congregation rose to their feet while prayers were being offered. But why this display of servility toward this bald-headed guy?[33]

Many employers acted as though their wealth and power alone entitled them to command servile behavior. The superintendent and chief operator of the Home Telephone Company at Joplin attempted to use their positions to force unwanted familiarity and other indignities on the thirty young women who operated the telephones. Although the operators forced the supervisors to quit these particular demands for subservience by striking the company in January 1903,[34] many other workers silently suffered daily loss of independence to men with no traditional claims of prestige who commanded them to behave in ways that eroded traditional values.

The new order seemed to be erecting an insurmountable barrier that doomed those without wealth to a life that would be increasingly controlled by those who had it. "Steadily but surely," wrote the Hannibal *Daily Clipper* in 1877, "the mechanic and workingman have been ground down by the exacting demands of a bondholding aristocracy, until it has reached the point where a man can scarcely in any instance derive an honest and respectable living for himself and family by the sweat of his brow." Farmers were "the real wealth producers," observed Missouri agriculture leader Norman J. Colman in 1890, but in the new order the farmer was destined to become merely "a hewer of wood and drawer of water for the privileged classes."[35] There seemed no limit to the insecurities the future might hold.

III

Primitive Resistance to the New Order

Out of the traditions that had guided their lives Missourians dug in to resist the new world that the promoters of change were trying to impose on them. They resisted on many levels and in many ways. It was war on many fronts. Some patterns of resistance were offensive, others defensive. Some were the resistance of armies, others of guerrillas. Sometimes the resistance was stony silence when promoters wanted cheers of support. These diverse patterns of resistance reflected the dimensions of the struggle for the hearts and minds of Missourians as they grappled with economic and cultural changes they had not sought. Traditions gave Missourians the strength and vision to make worlds of their own whose cores the promoters could never reach.

Civilizations collided with elemental force in Missouri. So powerful was the clash that the first struggle was over the very legitimacy of the new competitive order. The basic issue was whether the agents of the new order could secure their new forms of property against growing—and increasingly violent—attacks by defenders of old ways. Accustomed to personal control and direct action, traditional Missourians at first struck directly at the new sources of injury. They destroyed the new machines that threatened their lives and livelihoods. Machine wrecking and arson left the battle's outcome uncertain. "The man who set fire to the self-binding reaper was of course a vandal and a criminal," warned an Adair County resident in 1879, "but behind all that lay an ideal, small now . . . but in the future destined to break into a storm of fury, perhaps over all this fair land."[1] And behind that issue was the battle over whether law could be restored as a means by which traditional cultures could restrain individuals and institutions that threatened cherished social patterns, or whether it would become the instrument of the champions of progress.

Missouri had acquired a national reputation by the 1870s as a state where armed conflict between groups and individuals would determine whether the new economic leaders would be able to translate their economic power into social and political legitimacy. Train robbers and railroad detectives in the woodlands of western Missouri, armed businessmen and striking workers on the streets of St. Louis, mountain folk and hooded vigilantes in the steep Ozark valleys shaped Missouri's initial response to the market economy. The people charged with making, interpreting, and enforcing the law recognized that the conflicts were too large to be confined to courtrooms or legislatures. They simply abdicated when faced with a choice between upholding formal law and pursuing popular lawbreakers who defended traditional values. Missourians placed their faith in robbers, vigilantes, and mobs, not public officials, to help them defend their traditions. Not far beneath even formal political disagreements was the threat of renewed violence, even warfare, where the new order challenged cherished values. Order, if not justice, truly came out of the barrel of a rifle in post–Civil War Missouri.

As they developed direct, frequently violent and illegal ways of defending their familiar understandings of law against its menacing uses by new economic leaders, Missourians joined traditional peoples around the globe whose initial resistance to a market economy was primitive. But there was an important difference. In most parts of the world traditional resisters lacked the right to vote or familiar access to the state. Their primitive resistance was "pre-political," and over time it evolved into organized and self-consciously political movements to capture the state. For Missourians, on the other hand, the relationship of primitive to political resistance was more subtle, because organized and political action was always possible. Missourians adopted primitive patterns as alternatives to, not evolutionary steps toward, organized and political action.

4

The Law, Outlaws, and Railroads

To traditional Missourians law was the means by which the community restrained behavior that challenged accepted ways. To the new railroad promoters law was a means of creating a market economy. As they fought to shape society's rules, each side believed the other to be "robbers" and "traitors." The collision of values was too fundamental to be resolved by political institutions, whose legitimacy in any case had collapsed during the Civil War. In the end the central issue was whether the railroads had enough military, economic, and political power to secure their property from taxpayers, workers, and bandits who had concluded, with the public's agreement, that collective, direct, illegal action was the only alternative to submission to the railroads' world.

1. The Civil War and the Crisis of Law and Authority

The Civil War shaped the primal character of postwar struggles by deeply eroding Missourians' confidence that government was capable of performing its most important function: protecting the security of families, homes, and communities. The wedge that the war drove between government and the people made formal law into something alien and oppressive, and convinced many Missourians to act on their own. Moreover, the governments of both the United States and the Confederate States legitimated violence as the most effective means to resolve conflicts.

From the start Missourians had been more interested in security for their families than in either the issues or political parties that beckoned voters in 1860. More than seven-tenths of the state's voters cast ballots for the two moderate presidential candidates. When war broke out, most Missourians

59

hoped that the state could somehow remain aloof, neutral. When military events by the summer of 1861 ensured that the state would remain part of the Union, not neutral, many Missourians chose sides based on which government would best protect them.

During the Civil War Missourians lived in constant fear of the next attack by regular or irregular forces from either side. Outside St. Louis, the military reality of war was one of constant raids, skirmishes, and guerrilla attacks. Unionist and Confederate leaders and guerrillas used terror, conscription, and confiscation to try to compel allegiance from citizens who merely wanted to be left in peace. No family or home was safe from a sudden visit by guerrillas or militiamen who demanded food, property, sex, lodging, and even lives. The chaotic military situation encouraged individuals to rob, burn, loot, torture, and murder more for private motives of greed, anger, and jealousy than out of patriotic devotion to their cause. Many shifted loyalties with each new atrocity. One Saline County Confederate supporter converted to the Union in 1862 because security was all-important to him: "I have no use for any government except to protect my property, and I intend to support the federal government hereafter because it affords some prospect of protection to property." Missourians discovered the bitter truth that neither government was capable of protecting their homes and families, but men waving flags of both governments were very capable of threatening them.[1]

The military end of the war merely confirmed the inability of governments to restore order and security. Missourians continued to fear for their homes. The war had taught many that robbery was the quickest way to get money or property. Others wanted to settle debts. The state drove many guerrillas to outlawry by excluding them from the general amnesty. Lawlessness soon became so common in St. Clair County, for example, that an editor figured in 1866 that "rogues, thieves, vagabonds, and highwaymen" dominated the county's population. The epidemic spread even to St. Louis, where the *Missouri Democrat* reported in November 1865, "Never in the memory of the most ancient citizen . . . has rascality stalked so boldly about our streets as at the present time. . . . The police seem to be unable to meet the exigency of the times."[2]

Lawmen, prosecutors, and courts failed after the Civil War to restore the traditional workings of criminal law. In northeastern Missouri prosecutors were afraid to arrest lawbreakers. After declaring most of the state's judgeships vacant, victorious Radicals imposed unwanted judges on some communities. Bootheel voters trounced unpopular James H. Vail for circuit court judge in the 1868 election, but Governor Thomas C. Fletcher overturned the election and made Vail the judge nevertheless.[3]

Since the law was ineffective and sometimes illegitimate, Missourians asserted raw popular authority on their own. They banded together to protect their communities. They formed vigilante groups, sometimes together with wartime enemies, to curb the epidemic of murder, robbery, arson, and horse stealing. They formed formal organizations such as the Honest Men's League of Greene County or the Ku Klux Klan in central and southeastern Missouri.

Experienced in California's vigilante methods, David McKee revived a secret Anti-Horse Thief Association to capture and prosecute criminals after the breakdown of the local courts in northeastern Missouri. "Vigilance committees" finally ended the crime wave around Aullville in the 1870s.[4]

Formal legal machinery lacked the popular authority to restore order in many counties. "Everyone . . . knows that the law has been violated with impunity, and that the red hand of murder . . . has swayed the gory scepter of terror over our community ever since the war of the Rebellion," wrote the Osceola *Voice of the People* on May 12, 1880. "Murder after murder has been committed and yet not a single transgressor has been made to feel the force of the penalty of outraged justice. . . . We say emphatically that it furnishes more than the shadow of justification for the people taking the law into their own hands. . . ." That night two hundred people stormed the Osceola jail, seized three accused murderers, took them to Happy Hollow south of town, and lynched them. Two weeks later Osceolans read in the paper a letter that proclaimed the new way to restore security:

> We, the Moderators of St. Clair, have hung Smith, Park, and Pierce. We have done the work . . . for the benefit of the honest people of St. Clair county, that try to make an honest living for their families. . . . We don't want to hurt or damage anybody, only the ones that we think is guilty. . . . This country has been imposed upon by a certain class of men and they are mostly lawyers, and we are getting tired of it. The law is not any account and we propose trying Mob Law.
>
> *Moderators*[5]

The Civil War further contributed to the popular crisis of law and authority by bringing to power in Washington and in Jefferson City new leaders who were determined to use law to create a large-scale market economy. Amid lurid charges of corruption, the state's new political leaders in the 1860s surrendered the state's interest in railroads, which had cost the taxpayers nearly $32 million, to private promoters for a mere $6,131,496. The lawmakers argued that private developers would be whipped by economic incentive to complete the railroads more quickly than the state would. To the public, however, the new leaders seemed more loyal to the railroads than to the taxpayers. They sat in distant places and created law for alien purposes. The *Boonville Weekly Eagle* reflected the popular feeling of remoteness from the new leaders when it derided Governor Charles Hardin's claim to be "a safe man and a man with an iron will." Hardin, explained the *Eagle*, was " 'Safe,' because there is no danger of extricating himself when once the robbers encircle him. 'With an iron will,' because it seems to be his will to support the roads of iron rail."[6]

In their zeal to promote a competitive society, the new leaders seemed to ignore the tradition that law existed to represent local majority sentiment and community control. Governor Thomas T. Crittenden urged Missourians in 1885 to abandon this tradition: "The trouble is, each community and individual wants the railroad operated for his or its special convenience. Of course, it is impossible to do this." Railroads were not only beyond the reach of community control, but they soon sapped the community's ability to control other things. "We have seen this Company a thing, nebulous and intangible, quietly but persistently asking life of us," sadly noted a Springfield resident in 1870. "We see it to-day, bland, insatiable, and immense, taking in our towns as nutriment, before starting on its march to the Pacific." Both the new leaders and their creation were beyond the ability of communities to control them in traditional ways.[7]

Law and authority in postwar Missouri were squeezed between these two consequences of the Civil War. The military victory of the Union armies and the political victories of the Unionist-Radicals promised that law would be used to encourage remote markets, eroding both the community's isolation and its ability to regulate behavior. Those victories required Missourians to obey laws from the newly powerful capitals of Jefferson City and Washington. But the social consequences of the war contrasted sharply with the implications of these victories. After the war only local communities had the legitimacy to define what behavior was acceptable and what was not. And only local communities had the effective means—collective direct action—to punish aberrant individuals. The desire to protect homes and families from outside attack and the traditionally local focus of farming and manufacturing came together. The war thus created a desperate paradox: victorious leaders in remote places hoped to create a new order that would destroy the autonomy of local communities at the very time that most Missourians believed that only local communities were capable of providing order, security, and justice. This profound split between remote formal law and immediate social authority shaped the collisions between the old and new orders.

Since railroads were beyond the reach of traditional disciplines and certainly of formal law, many Missourians concluded that they had only two choices. They could submit, or they could follow their recent experiences in restoring order after other criminals threatened their community and take possession of the law themselves.

2. The Battle over Railroad Bonds

The primitive and frequently violent struggles between local taxpayers and railroad promoters over the construction of Missouri's railroads attracted national attention. Taxpayers fought to defend the traditions of independence—low taxes, majority rule, and community control—against the railroad promoters' dreams and schemes.

The developers believed that taxpayer subsidies were the necessary source of capital to build their railroads. Leaders of state government in the 1860s assisted developers mightily by surrendering the state's interest in railroads, acquired over the 1850s, to private owners, but they also created a problem for postwar speculators. Hoping to encourage businessmen to replace the state government as the owners and directors of railroads, drafters of the 1865 state constitution prohibited any further state aid to railroads. As a result, promoters had to ask counties, townships, and cities to subsidize their plans with local taxes. In this quest the developers' basic problem was to overcome the resistance of local taxpayers. Fortunately for them, between 1865 and 1875 the legal requirements for local bond issues were ambiguous. Local legislatures, known in Missouri as county courts, could issue a bond with or without a popular vote and could determine whether they wanted to exclude Confederate supporters, for example, from voting on bonds. The pattern was the same everywhere. Prominent local businessmen, farmers, and editors convened public meetings to resolve in favor of local aid to the proposed railroad. County courts then decided whether to hold a popular election, whether to abide by the election's results, and finally whether and in what amounts to issue bond subscriptions.

The outcome was frequently the same in northern and western parts of the state. Between 1865 and 1875 promoters persuaded county and local governments in 55 of the state's 114 counties to subscribe a total of $18,319,850 in public aid to a total of forty-three proposed railroads. By 1880 Missouri ranked third in the bonded debt of counties and townships for railroad aid. Between 1866 and 1875 the average Missourian accumulated three times more in local public indebtedness than the average taxpayer in the seven states that bordered Missouri.[8]

To people who had always measured their independence by freedom from debt and taxes the magnitude of the railroad debts was overwhelming. In nine counties the principal alone on the railroad bonds issued between 1866 and 1875 came to more than one-tenth of all the real and personal property in the county. Over time the interest frequently amounted to even more than the principal. Between 1869 and 1900 Pilot Grove's taxpayers paid in principal and interest for a single bond an amount that equaled more than half the township's total assessed wealth in 1900. Over forty years Callaway's taxpayers paid nearly a million dollars in interest on a $550,550 subscription in 1867 to the Louisiana and Missouri River Rail Road. In counties such as Henry and Dallas, taxpayers suddenly owed more for a single railroad subscription than they had paid in taxes for all county and local services over an entire decade. The burden was greatest in eleven central and western counties. (See chart on page 64.)

The worst feature of these huge debts for many Missourians was that the local legislatures, the county courts, frequently issued these bonds regardless of their constituents' wishes. Often in defiance of the voters' will, and even more often without consulting voters at all, the county courts subsidized the railroads, and seemed eager to please only the railroad promoters. In thirty-five popular votes on postwar railroad bonds, voters approved twelve subscriptions in ten counties while rejecting twenty-three subscriptions in thirteen counties. Between 1866 and 1871 voters rejected proposals for railroad aid in Bates, Clark, Greene, Grundy, Lafayette, Lewis, Livingston, McDonald, Pike, Polk, Putnam, Schuyler, and Sullivan counties. In Bates and

County and Local Railroad Bond Subscriptions, 1866–75[9]

	Railroad debt per capita, 1866–75	*Tax per capita for all county and local purposes, 1870*	*Railroad debt as percent of property, 1870*
Howard	$49.35	$5.25	15.7%
Lafayette	47.28	10.48	12.8
Cass	39.39	8.50	10.8
St. Clair	37.08	7.50	9.4
Buchanan	35.60	32.98	10.3
Henry	34.48	3.21	9.7
Pettis	32.08	10.34	9.6
Dallas	29.23	2.63	17.2
Cooper	28.74	8.50	10.2
Callaway	28.67	7.27	10.4
Vernon	28.19	4.45	10.5

Grundy alone taxpayers voted down nine separate subscriptions at six different elections. The courts simply defied the popular verdict and issued the bonds anyway. In 1869 Greene County voters rejected two subscriptions for $400,000, but the county court approved both in 1870. Clark County taxpayers voted down railroad aid in 1870, but the court granted it the next year and, shelving a protest from 1,760 taxpayers, raised the amount later that year. In the northern counties of Putnam, Schuyler, Livingston, Grundy, and Lewis, courts authorized railroad subscriptions within a year of popular votes against them. Even when the bonds received popular support courts defied local opinion by adding generously to the amount approved by voters. The Knox County court defied angry protests and piled $185,000 on top of the $100,000 approved by voters in 1867, and the Howard County court added generously to two voter-authorized subscriptions.[10]

At first stunned, Missourians soon embraced increasingly desperate and direct methods to reclaim popular control over taxation and representation. In 1869 a surly mob in Knox County threatened to lynch the county court's judges if they voted any more railroad aid. Taxpayers packed the streets of Macon on June 6, 1870, former Confederates joining former Unionists to attack the county court for issuing railroad bonds in defiance of a public vote. The crowd roared its approval of a resolution. Noting "the great anxiety" of the judges and railroad attorneys "to get possession of the bonds before this mass meeting assembled" and the haste with which "the judges have abandoned their posts this day, instead of holding court as honest men would have done," the resolution accused the judges of taking bribes, demanded their immediate resignations, and resolved never to pay "one cent of this last subscription as long as we have men and money to oppose it."[11]

In Pettis County popular anger exploded in 1869 into a movement to abolish representative government itself, if that was what was necessary to reassert political control by the majority, not the railroads. It began as a petition campaign to recall the unresponsive officials. Taxpayers charged that the court defied the people's will when it had approved railroad aid. A local poet explained:

> A reckless spirit's been unearthed,
> And all the records show it.
> The people's will has been defied,
> 'Tis well the public know it.
>
> A petition has been sent forth,
> The people, willing, sign,
> Asking the Court, also the Clerk,
> Their offices to resign.

The petitioners further demanded that taxes earmarked to pay off the railroad bonds be used instead to contest the bonds in a lawsuit. Some Pettis taxpayers were so angry at the court's betrayal that they proposed the revolutionary alternative of a provisional government that would be accountable only and directly to the public.[12]

Primitive rebels, sanctioned by local opinion, developed more direct methods to halt the erosion of popular sovereignty and the loss of local control to the railroads. In Cass County, where Confederate supporters had been banished from their homes during the last two years of the Civil War and stripped of the right to vote after the war, taxpayers grew increasingly desperate as Unionist politicians and railroad promoters saddled Cass with the third highest per capita railroad debt in the state. The explosion began in 1871 when the county court issued $300,000 in bonds to the Kansas City and Clinton Railroad. Outraged taxpayers formed a Protective Union Association of Cass County to resist taxes that were "illegally and oppressively imposed" on the people. Calling its officers "commanders" and pledging to uphold "the law of self-defense" if necessary, the association soon developed into a huge mass movement when the county court, circuit attorney, and St. Louis and Santa Fe Railroad concluded a corrupt deal by which the court issued $229,000 in bonds to the railroad. The malefactors were exposed and indicted. As they awaited their trial, scheduled for May 6, 1872, they became frightened by local residents' growing anger at their corruption. Three of the conspirators—a county court judge, the circuit attorney, and a Harrisonville city councilman—decided to escape by train to Kansas City on the evening of April 24, 1872. Twelve miles outside Harrisonville, near Gunn City, the train ground to a halt before a crude barricade. At least fifty Case County men, clad in white cloths, began firing at the train. "Turn out the bond thieves," raged the crowd. They dragged the conspirators from the train and murdered them. They fired more than forty bullets into one victim and "vented their fiendish fury" on another, according to the *Kansas City Times*. The mob swelled to two hundred as its members continued to batter the corpses with bullets in "one of the most terrible and atrocious massacres of the nineteenth century." Passengers recognized twenty of the mob before they rode off.

Panic gripped railroad promoters. At Sedalia an official of the Missouri-Kansas-Texas Railroad hired bodyguards. Others demanded that President Grant invoke the Ku Klux Klan Act to punish the mob. They appealed to Governor B. Gratz Brown to send the militia. Brown called out the militia from Kansas City, but Adjutant General Albert Siegel halted the troops at the Cass County border when local lawmen warned that the troops' arrival would set off another civil war. "The whole county" would resist the troops because practically everyone sympathized with the murderers. "The sheriff dares not summon a posse, lest he only organize a posse to hang himself," reported the *Kansas City Times.* "Our people have been imposed upon, insulted, brow-beaten as it were, cursed and defamed until forbearance has almost ceased to be a virtue. . . . There is no doubt . . . that the people may have had some cause to take the law into their own hands," declared the local *Pleasant Hill Leader.* The mob achieved its purpose: its members had recovered $174,000 of the bonds that the ring had not yet sold, thus saving taxpayers from having to pay for that portion. Special investigators John F. Philips and F. M. Cockrell reported to Governor Brown that the best way to prevent the vigilantes from unleashing "a forward military movement and a new carnival of blood" was not to prosecute them, but instead to "open to them the ways of peace, and return to their homes the fugitives. . . ."

The Gunn City murders attracted national attention and revealed the law's inability to contain the conflict over railroad bonds. For Missouri public officials who had violated local opinion the message from Gunn City was more urgent. Framed, along with one of the "bloody bonds," in the Cass County clerk's office was a reminder to local officials "that the public servants of old Cass may remember when they trample upon the rights of the people and refuse to hear their prayers, that they will appeal to a higher power and serve an injunction that will stick—which means death to tyrants."[13]

Local anger soon hardened into a concerted taxpayers' revolt that left politicians with the choice of obeying popular demands or facing lynch mobs. County courts began to listen. Beginning in Callaway and Ray counties in the summer of 1871, courts began stopping payment on the bonds, or at least on the interest. Within eight months the taxpayers' rebellion spread to Henry, Cass, Johnson, Lawrence, Jasper, Vernon, and Bates counties. Taxpayers soon learned, alas, that in a market economy these things were no longer local matters. The actual bonds had passed out of the state and into the hands of "innocent investors" who cared little about the social traumas in the Missouri counties whose bonds they now held for profit. In 1873 the "innocent investors" hired lawyers to sue sixteen Missouri counties and five local governments to compel them to resume payment on the bonds. From 1873 to 1880 the state courts and the U.S. Supreme Court ruled that local residents would have to pay. The main thing in a market economy was to protect the security of investments so that people would invest again, even if those subscriptions violated public opinion or were corruptly obtained.[14] The courts had spoken. The law was clear.

The county courts were now squeezed between formal law and local authority. Taxpayers threatened them with murder, and the courts threatened them with jail for contempt. The Vernon County court resolved the dilemma in 1874. A mass meeting threatened the judges that payment of any interest on the bonds "would be at their peril." The judges replied:

> Being . . . the servants of the people, we have felt our duty to obey their instructions. In obeying these instructions we have been compelled, though against our own convictions of right, to refuse to levy a tax for the purpose of meeting the rapidly accumulating interest of our railroad bonds. In thus refusing we have placed ourselves before the higher courts in such a position that we are not only liable, but certain to be arrested, imprisoned and fined for contempt of their authority. From which, resignation is our only means of escape.

County courts in Lafayette and St. Clair counties soon copied the judges' solution in Vernon. But Governor Charles Hardin refused in 1875 to accept these resignations, thereby compelling local governments to levy the taxes.[15]

Undaunted by the governor, local taxpayers tightened the vise that gripped the local legislators. Under renewed popular threats of physical harm, county courts in Knox and Macon devised schemes in 1879 that prevented the county treasuries from ever having enough funds to pay railroad debts. The higher courts rejected this dodge and ordered an end to civil disobedience by local taxpayers and county courts. Fearing endless popular resistance in Missouri, investors offered to compromise on the amounts to be repaid. While some counties responded to inducements from investors and threats from higher courts, others rejected any compromise with the investors and their alien law. In Macon County voters turned down proposed compromises by votes of 1,278 to 128 in 1879, 5,020 to 67 in 1894, and 2,729 to 2,397 in 1904 before finally accepting a compromise in 1911. Knox County rejected a compromise by 1,047 to 314 in 1891, and only agreed to settle in 1894 when it became clear that the secrecy that necessarily shrouded public business in order to evade the investors also led to corruption. Voting down an 1878 compromise by 791 to 131, Dallas County taxpayers did not finally repay the local bonds until 1940.[16]

The ensuing struggle between local taxpayers and federal marshals created new forms of representative government. Federal marshals began in 1878 to arrest local officials for disobeying judicial orders to levy taxes for railroad bonds. Candidates for county courts pledged they would go to prison before they would levy railroad taxes. Federal judges imprisoned all three judges of the Scotland County court in 1881 and the Cass County court in 1882. Judges from St. Clair, Lafayette, and Dallas counties also spent time in prison for refusing to levy the railroad taxes. Since local taxpayers believed that the judges were, finally, obeying public opinion, they helped the judges evade the marshals and the law. Homeowners welcomed and hid any judge trying to escape the marshals. In Dallas County the court met in the woods, under culverts, in barns, and other places where marshals were not likely to look. At the county seat of Buffalo, residents developed an elaborate network to warn the judges whenever a stranger appeared who might be a marshal.[17] These new forms of representative government, featuring imprisoned local officials and court meetings in the woods, restored to taxpayers the traditional control that citizens had exercised over elected officials. The plain truth was that those officials had abdicated their governing function, leaving the field of battle to local taxpayers and remote investors.

Primitive resistance in St. Clair County's bond war measured the distance between formal law and local authority. St. Clair's taxpayers joined the movement in the 1870s to repudiate the debts, but the county's new leaders wanted to repay the investors. Afraid to try taxing the residents, they decided to raise the interest by staging a huge livestock auction in 1876, the proceeds to pay off the railroad bond interest. On auction day, however, "no one seemed to want to buy" any animals. To bondholders the "great shock" of the auction's failure proved the depth of local resistance to railroad taxes.[18]

By the 1877 tax season rumors began to circulate that the county court was planing to tax residents for the bonds. On the night of December 15, 1877, a gang of armed men rode into the county seat of Osceola and held tax officials at gunpoint while its members stole all the official tax records. The gang warned the county court judges that they would be lynched unless they resigned immediately. Lawmen recognized individuals in the gang but took no action because they knew residents admired the gang more than they did the court. The gang destroyed the tax records, and that meant that the county had no way of taxing anyone. All three judges resigned and, at a special election, voters selected three dedicated Greenbackers, one of them a relative of train robber Cole Younger who could presumably be trusted not to ally with railroads. From Putnam County came the opinion that St. Clair residents had the right to "try to undo by violence what courts and legislatures have done by trampling down the constitutional rights of the whole people." A Clinton editor maintained, "Many of the St. Clair people may be rude, and to an extent, unlettered, but their idea of justice is not far wrong."

Early in 1879 rumors of new taxes began to circulate again. Around midnight on May 20, 1879, an armed gang forced Deputy Treasurer K. B. Wooncott to take its members to the county offices. The gang seized the railroad tax book and escaped into the night. Once again the county was incapable of collecting taxes. After an "investigation," the prosecuting attorney, J. B. Jennings, announced that he could only discover "the charred remains" of the tax book. No one was prosecuted. No one paid railroad taxes.

The people of St. Clair shielded the guerrillas from champions of the new order. One such champion, Joseph Pulitzer of the *St. Louis Post-Dispatch*, upbraided local residents for damaging Missouri's reputation with investors. After all, wrote Pulitzer, the robbery of a single tax book retarded investment in Missouri by more than all of St. Clair County was worth. The Osceola *Sun* preferred the robbers' values to Pulitzer's: "Our people take a tax book on which there is due some $20,000, and in the same issue of the *Post and*

Dispatch referred to we read of over Three Hundred Thousand Dollars being stolen from the poor, trusting depositors by St. Louis bankers. Bring your moral optics to bear, now, Joseph, and say which is the greater crime."

During the 1880s and 1890s local residents shifted their resistance from destroying tax records to hiding judges from federal marshals. Even Jo O. Shelby, once a popular Confederate general, could not penetrate the hiding places of St. Clair's county court. His bill told the story: "116 days searching for Judge George H. Lyons of St. Clair county at $2 per day, $232." For twenty years successful candidates for the county courts pledged to go to jail rather than levy railroad taxes. Sometimes the marshals found the judges, but the judges still refused to levy the taxes. Indeed, in 1893, Judges Copenhaver, Lyons, and Nevitt spent the fall and winter in the Jackson County jail. Not until 1910 did the county's taxpayers finally agree to a compromise.

Local taxpayers built outward from the traditions of majority rule, local control, and low taxes to encourage primitive resistance to such agents of the new order as railroad promoters, bondholders, supreme courts, and finally the law itself. By the late 1870s outlaws, including armed gangs and disobedient county court judges, seemed to uphold traditions better than did the law. The outlaws saved taxpayers from railroad debts and restored local governments to control by the community, not bondholders.

Local taxpayers strengthened their support for the lawbreakers by creating an organized movement to protect future Missourians from any similar experiences. They campaigned for a new state constitution to prohibit public officials from straying so far from accepted ways. The taxpayers' revolt against public subsidies to railroads and public schools that taught the developers' new values shaped the background for the new constitution in 1875. The constitution increased the number of areas in which the legislature was prohibited from intervening in people's lives from thirteen in the 1865 constitution to thirty-two in 1875. It asserted the public right to regulate and tax the new railroads. It prohibited county and local governments from lending credit to corporations. The new constitution mandated a popular vote for all county and local debts and required approval by two-thirds of the voters. It prohibited local governments from acquiring debt that exceeded 5 percent of their taxable property at a time when thirty-five counties had bonded over 5 percent of their wealth for railroad bonds issued between 1866 and 1875. For the first time in the state's history a constitutional convention specifically spelled out the tax rates that state and local governments could charge taxpayers. State taxation was limited to twenty cents on every hundred dollars of assessed valuation until the total taxable property reached $900 million, at which time the maximum rate would fall to fifteen cents. (The $900 million mark was reached in 1894 and created a major fiscal crisis that racked the state government for the rest of the decade.) The new constitution created a formal structure within which Missourians could recapture traditional independence. Although relatively few Missourians demonstrated much faith in constitutional resolution to the crisis of law and authority by voting in the 1875 ratification election, the new constitution was overwhelmingly approved—91,205 to 14,517—among those who did vote. "The people of this State have sensibly felt the inconvenience and misfortune of a public debt" and had acted "to prevent its increase, or a recurrence of that evil," explained Governor John Phelps in 1877.[19]

"This bond business has made the people conservative," concluded Carroll Hawkins, a Dallas County banker.[20] Local, state, and national governments had sided with the champions of the new order, had deprived taxpayers of the popular control over their lives that had come from representative government and of the freedom from debt that had come from low taxes. As a result, Missourians developed a profound suspicion that government action generally eroded their personal independence. Law itself became alien. Encouraging outlaws, and restraining local and state governments in the strait-jacket of the 1875 constitution, desciplining them by informal direct action, local taxpayers were indeed conservative. But that conservatism fed resistance to the new order.

3. Jesse James, America's Classic Social Bandit

There are times and places where defenders of traditional values have felt so desperate in the face of onrushing change that they have placed their hope for deliverance not in traditional leaders, such as priests and politicians, but in men who fearlessly attacked the symbols of the new order while upholding the old. Regarded as criminals by the promoters of change and their law, these social bandits were nurtured and shielded by people who shared their values. Since the bandits seemed capable of striking at will and made their victims look ridiculous and ineffectual, their supporters made them into the object of heroic legends that confirmed the power of tradition.

Out of the ferocious railroad wars Missouri spawned the nation's most famous social bandit, a man whose fame would outlive that of governors and presidents. He became a legend of defiance. Railroads and their allies might triumph in legislatures or courts, but they could never secure their property or their world until they captured Jesse James. At a time when Missourians imposed on their officials the choice of prison or lynching, elected representatives abdicated in the war between railroads and bandits. When Senator Carl Schurz complained that he was often taunted in Washington as the representative of "the Robber State," Missouri voters added his complaint to their other grievances and firmly turned against him. They wanted politicians who were not embarrassed by "robbers."[21]

Robbers were the leaders who seemed most capable of stopping the promoters. Many Missourians wanted leaders who could take away the very root of the railroads' power, their money. Both sides agreed that the railroads would never fully triumph so long as train robbers, shielded by the public, could steal the railroads' money, publicly humiliate them, and escape. In order to cast Jesse James as a heroic deliverer his supporters interpreted his activities to meet their own needs rather than those of accuracy. And James, for his part, gloried in the role Missourians created for him and did his part to expand the nobility of that role.

Jesse James rose to fame following the classical pattern of the world's great social bandits. He did not choose a life of crime out of a depraved nature. Rather, as the friendly Sedalia *Daily Democrat* observed, "Fate made him so." Jesse and Frank James first fought to preserve the homes and communities of their people from outside attack when they rode with Quantrill's Raiders during the Civil War. As Confederate guerrillas they became skillful at raiding Unionists and railroads. And they developed local networks of support to escape capture. The mystique that grew up around Quantrill's Raiders and other western Missouri guerrillas came to overshadow their murderous terrorism. Loyalty to comrades was the sacred obligation that united guerrillas and transcended not only the temptations of money or the flesh but even the instinct for self-preservation. "In the name of God and the Devil" Quantrill's Raiders had sworn "never to betray a comrade" and to "suffer the most horrible death, rather than reveal a single secret of this organization, or a single word of this, my oath." Bonded in a kind of expanded kinship of mutual protection, the guerrillas had great difficulty resuming civilian life after the war. They were excluded from the general amnesty. Made outlaws by the state, and experienced in the art of robbery, many of Quantrill's Raiders resumed their familiar activities once the war ended.[22] It was only after Missourians experienced the new processes of railroad promotion and isolating competition that the guerrillas' strong sense of brotherhood and mutual aid became attractive alternative visions to people who had fought on both sides of the Civil War.

No one knows precisely when the James Brothers, Frank and Jesse, leagued with the Younger Brothers, Cole, James, Robert, and John, to begin their careers as bandits. They were accused of bank robberies as early as 1866. But there is no doubt when their legendary reputation began. In 1872 promoters of economic development staged a huge fair in Kansas City to advertise their city. On the evening of September 26, 10,000 spectators were moving slowly toward the exits when three bandits—two of them soon identified as Jesse James and Cole Younger—rode through the throng, held the spectators at gunpoint, robbed the ticket booth of $978, and vanished toward the east. "Whence they came or whither they went no one knows," reported the *Kansas City Times*, "but they came and went, and while they stayed they made a page in the criminal history of the country that will probably stand for many years single and singular for wild audacity, reckless courage, invincible nerve and utterly indescribable daring." They struck directly at a spectacular exhibition of the new order, in the middle of a city, in broad daylight, and at a place where any one of thousands of people might have killed them. The *Times* confessed, "It was a deed so high-handed, so diabolically daring and so utterly in contempt of fear that we are bound to admire it and revere its perpetrators for the very enormity of their outlawry."[23]

The idea of robbing a train was even more spectacular. It took both courage and imagination to conceive of ways to stop a speeding locomotive, since, unlike a stagecoach, a train could shield its passengers from the robbers' guns and outdistance the robbers' horses. The James Gang's first solution, tried in Iowa in July 1873, was to remove rails on a blind curve, thereby wrecking the train. This tactic yielded loot but cost the gang public support, because the engineer was scalded to death beneath his locomotive. Their second train robbery, at the Gads Hill flag station a hundred miles south of St. Louis on January 31, 1874, ranked with the Kansas City fair robbery in building their fame. They used the railroad's own signals, switches, and employees to halt the St. Louis–Little Rock Express. Taking station employees hostage, they ran up a signal that halted the train. When the train stopped and its crew searched the platform for the expected passengers, the Jameses and Youngers walked out the station door and robbed the train's express company safe and its wealthy passengers. They continued to rob banks and trains without getting caught until September 1876, when they made the mistake of venturing into the commercial wheat-growing area around Northfield, Minnesota, a place where the people supported the market economy. Eight men robbed the First National Bank of Northfield, but local residents responded differently than in Missouri. Two of the gang were killed before they could escape from town. Local residents organized the largest manhunt in Minnesota history and captured most of the other robbers, including Cole, Robert, and Jim Younger. But two robbers escaped their pursuers and fled back to Missouri. Jesse and Frank James now seemed invincible. They recruited new members for their gang and continued to rob trains in Missouri until 1881.[24]

The railroads, the banks, and their allies believed that the James Gang formed a major barrier to Missouri's economic development, and they demanded that officials use the law to protect their property and capture the bandits. The state Republican platform of 1874 had charged that the Democrats' failure to capture the train robbers had led to "insecurity of person and property; the prevention of immigration; the utter prostration of business, and the most ruinous depreciation of all values of property." Six years later the Republicans again charged that the Democrats' failure to catch the Jameses had "prevented immigration into the State and the introduction of capital and the growth and development of industries." Most Missouri politicians believed that the bandits were popular precisely because they exposed the weakness and fragility of the new order, and they offered little encouragement to the railroads and express companies in the 1870s. The 1874 legislature did authorize a special police force to suppress banditry, but it defeated proposals to single out the Jameses and Youngers and to reactivate the militia. In 1875 the Missouri House of Representatives passed a measure granting amnesty to the Jameses and Youngers, but it failed to get the needed two-thirds vote.[25] Aside from these actions, the state's politicians abdicated just as local politicians had abdicated in the bond crisis. They stood back to see whether the railroads had enough money to hire enough detectives to crush these challengers to the developers' power.

After watching railroad promoters force unwilling taxpayers to subsidize railroads, many local taxpayers concluded that the railroads were the real robbers, while the Jameses were the only Missourians who seemed capable of stopping, or at least humiliating, the railroads. The bandits themselves had sharpened the issue of who the real robbers were when they wrote the *Kansas City Times* in 1872 to condemn the new morality that condemned them while the Grant administration "can steal millions and it is all right." The Lexington *Caucasian* argued in 1874 that the train robbers' loot was "just as honestly earned as the riches of many a highly distinguished political leader and railroad job manipulator." Many taxpayers agreed with the *Carrollton Journal*'s 1874 assessment: "The people in this part of the state, who have been so handsomely plundered by the highwaymen who have absorbed their means under the name of the B[urlington] and S[outh] W[estern] R[ail] R[oad], will ask themselves, . . . What other fresh class of tax-payers . . . have been captured, and will now be ordered to stand and deliver? What new set of victims are to be fleeced?" The *Journal* concluded that the "humbler transactions" of the Jameses "only have the effect of drawing off attention from these more gigantic scoundrels" who promoted the railroads. "Many look upon a railroad with distrust and aversion, almost placing it in the catalogue of public robbers," observed Governor Thomas Crittenden. Even Union veterans agreed with the St. Louis *Dispatch* that the real result of the Civil War was "such a destruction of the old order of things as taught to the rising generation only the lessons that have borne fruit . . . at Gads Hill." "Everything that was venerable and sacred in the country," maintained the *Dispatch*, the Radical victory "has taught the people to despise." In the new order based on greed and competition, "the courts were marketable things and . . . the higher the judge the greater his capacity for bribes. . . . It is no longer disgraceful to steal."[26]

The conflict between the social forces behind the two approaches to law and authority focused on the railroads' hiring of private detectives to hunt the bandits. Communities expected elected sheriffs to enforce laws in locally popular ways. But the railroads, fearing local support for the bandits, hired outsiders, "those dastardly dogs who were hunting human flesh for hire," as the St. Louis *Dispatch* put it. Local residents repeatedly warned the Jameses and Youngers whenever the "dastardly dogs" were seen approaching the gang's hideouts. They applauded when the bandits, so warned, surprised and killed the detectives.[27]

The detectives retaliated on the night of January 26, 1875, in a manner that solidified popular support for the Jameses while confirming fears that in the railroads' new world ancient restraints could no longer leash individual greed. That night the detectives sneaked up on the Clay County home where the Jameses's mother, stepfather, and stepbrother lived. They hurled a fire-bomb into the house and ran away. The explosion killed the brothers' nine-year-old stepbrother, Archie, and mangled their mother's right hand so badly that it had to be amputated. So great was the anger at the railroad's hired assassins and their attack on defenseless victims that Clay County residents turned out in huge numbers for Archie's funeral, and the state legislature demanded, nearly unanimously, an official investigation to identify the midnight culprits. The Clay County grand jury indicted eight detectives for Archie's murder, including the boss of the agency, Allan K. Pinkerton of Chicago.

The murderous raid on the James home exposed the two sides' contending values. For most Missourians preservation of home and family was the highest obligation. "The monstrous crime of attempting to destroy a whole family . . . calls for instant redress," editorialized the St. Louis *Dispatch*. The detectives' willingness to attack a defenseless family contrasted starkly with the guerrillas' and bandits' code of brotherhood, which exalted loyalty between comrades as the highest obligation. The guerrillas had raided so that Confederate homes would be secure; the detectives had raided for money. In the 1870s Missourians bitterly rejected the railroads' vision that money was the tie that bound people. Frank James would observe in 1897 that "Love is something [corporate] syndicates can't control. And it's about the only thing."[28]

The James brothers, at least as portrayed in popular legend, felt deep obligations to family and community. Their mother told reporters that "no mother ever had better sons; more affectionate, obedient, and dutiful." Jesse James reportedly spared the life of a Union soldier when the soldier told his captor that he was deserting to join his mother. The Jameses' father, a popular Baptist preacher, had taught them to shun all temptations to sully their souls or their family's sanctity. Jesse James reportedly carried a Bible with him at all times. Friends told reporters that Jesse James was a loving and devoted husband and father.[29] From such tidbits Missourians created the legend that the Jameses upheld in their own lives the traditional world in which loyalty to family and friends took precedence over the greed and secularism the railroads had unleashed.

The railroad detectives' willingness to kill for cash frightened traditionminded Missourians by revealing unspeakable horrors in the emerging competitive society. In Clay and neighboring counties local residents reacted by shielding the bandits. Local residents could only hope for deliverance from the railroad and its allies if the James brothers escaped to attack again. They imposed on the Jameses the obligation never to get caught. Everyone believed that the succor of their neighbors was all that saved the Jameses and that the only force capable of subduing them would be betrayal from within the rebel band or the supporting community. The *St. Louis Globe-Democrat*, a friend of progress, angrily reported that the James brothers "were supported to a considerable extent by a depraved public sentiment in their own localities, and this fact added greatly to the difficulty of apprehending them.[30] In return for this support, the rebels understood that they must attack only popular villains and defend the defenseless.

Frank and Jesse James carefully appealed to other popular traditions. Owning the finest tools of their trade, guns and horses, they expected the respect traditionally given to gifted artisans. The *St. Louis Republic* insisted that the Jameses had made robbery into an art form. "Highway robbery as a fine art has been cultivated only in a way that has tended to bring it into disrespect," maintained the *Republic* in 1874, until the James Gang "burst upon us, and revealed a new field of worthy labor." Frank James once traced the lineage of their craft back to the great social bandits of Europe, Robin Hood, Dick Turpin, and Claude Duval. Jesse James proclaimed Robin Hood his hero, and signed an 1872 letter to the *Kansas City Times* with the names Jack Shepherd, Dick Turpin, and Claude Duval. Boldness of plan and execution marked a great robbery, and ever since the Kansas City fair robbery Missourians looked for these hallmarks from the Jameses.[31]

Frank and Jesse James, fully understanding the popular desire to discipline remote railroad owners, graded their victims by the extent to which they internalized and expressed the institutionalized greed of their employers. The greediest and most vile were the railroad detectives, who would kill for their employers. They deserved to be killed. In the middle were most railways employees, who rarely defended their employers' property; the James brothers usually left them alone. Finally, there were a few like conductor Lew Eveland, who ignored the railroad's orders to collect fares from all and "passed" hundreds of penniless war veterans, and Jack Foote, engineer on a train they robbed in 1881. During the robbery Foote and his crew tried to keep passengers from being killed by a train he knew to be approaching from the rear. A crew member broke loose from the gang and ran to halt the approaching train before it rammed into them. Jesse James was so impressed by Foote's courageous concern for his passengers that he offered to help remove the boulders with which the gang had blocked the locomotive's progress. When Foote said that he would remove the rocks himself, the bandit reportedly gave him two silver dollars, exclaiming, "You are a brave man and I am stuck on you, here is $2 for you to drink the health of Jesse James."[32]

At the center of popular support for the bandits was the belief that they sought to reunite the community and reassert tradition by making the reluctant rich and powerful support the weak and defenseless. Jesse James, emulating his hero, Robin Hood, told the *Kansas City Times* in 1872, "We rob the rich and give to the poor." In the most famous James Gang story the bandits gave some of their loot to a poor widow so that she could pay off her mortgage just before a banker was to foreclose on her. During the 1874 Gads Hill robbery the gang examined the hands of all male passengers. They explained that they did not want to rob "workingmen or ladies," only the "plug-hat gentlemen."[33]

The end came in a dramatic way that escalated and recapitulated the legend. Everyone, including the Jameses, expected that no posse or army of detectives would ever take Jesse James alive. The end, like that of all classic social bandits, would have to come through betrayal by a new recruit to the gang, who would see it as a way to collect reward money and receive amnesty.

The final chapter began when Thomas T. Crittenden became governor in 1881. On July 15, 1881, the James Gang robbed a Rock Island train in

Daviess County and escaped. Using money donated by the railroads and express companies, Crittenden surprised voters but not his friends among railroad officials by offering a reward of $10,000 for the capture and conviction of Jesse or Frank James. Mocking the authorities as their supporters expected heroic bandits to do, the James Gang a few weeks later robbed another train just outside Kansas City. Jesse James told the railroad employees that the purpose of this robbery was to take revenge on the railroad and the governor for offering the reward. Crittenden, Kansas City police commissioner Henry H. Craig, and Clay County sheriff James R. Timberlake now coordinated a campaign to let gang members know that riches and amnesty awaited the first to betray the James brother. On April 3, 1882, Jesse James unstrapped his guns to dust a picture in his St. Joseph home, where his family had been living for several months, appearing to the neighbors to be a respectable, close family. A new gang member, Robert Ford, shot him dead through the back. Ford wired for the reward. The grand jury immediately indicted Ford for murder, he pleaded guilty, Crittenden pardoned him, and Ford collected the reward. Six months later Frank James marched into the governor's office in Jefferson City and surrendered, preferring to trust his fate to a jury of his peers.[34]

The murder of Jesse James in 1882 was a victory for the new order, in which money commanded a higher allegiance than brotherhood. Governor Crittenden boasted, at least in legend, that he had triumphed because "the cupidity of man is only equaled by the force of the 'root of all evil'—money." He solemnly told the legislature a few months later that the state of Missouri "is fully redeemed and acquitted of that unwarranted appellation of 'robber State.'"[35] With the murder of Jesse James, Crittenden had finally made Missouri attractive for investors.

Most Missourians angrily denounced their governor's act. Jesse James's murder confirmed their worst fears about the future. They agreed with the Sedalia *Daily Democrat*: "There never was a more cowardly and unnecessary murder committed in all America than this murder of Jesse James. It was done for money. . . . It was his blood the bloody wretches were after—blood that would bring money in the official market of Missouri." Bob Ford was a villain, the St. Louis *Chronicle* cried, for "there is no precept which can make anything but hideous the act of a man who assassinates his friend for dollars." But most of the outrage was directed at Crittenden, who had defied his constituents and supported the railroads. "The great parallel that will go down in history will be Crittenden and James," observed the *Howell County Journal*, "and the very ashes of Jesse James will cry out in disgust at the comparison." The *Journal* demanded that the governor stand trial as an accessory before the fact of Jesse James's murder. Under the new order, the *Daily Democrat* warned, "the law itself becomes a murderer."[36]

Missourians rallied behind their fallen deliverer and punished everyone who had anything to do with his murder. The Democrats refused at their 1882 convention to give the customary endorsement to their party's incumbent governor. In 1884 they turned to the Confederate wing of their party for the first time because it had John Marmaduke, who, as railroad commissioner between 1875 and 1880, had led the campaigns to regulate railroads. By choosing Marmaduke in 1884, Missouri Democrats nominated and elected the most antirailroad governor the state had yet seen. Defended by prominent politicians and military leaders from both sides of the Civil War, Frank James was acquitted in his 1883 trial for a train robbery in Daviess County. In 1889 most members of the Missouri legislature petitioned the governor of Minnesota to pardon the Youngers so they could return to Missouri.[37]

In the end the railroads may have had enough money to buy the allegiance of Bob Ford. But the fame of Jesse James far outlived that of Governor Crittenden or other politicians. Many Missourians, and many other Americans, refused to believe that money should become the cement of society. Fearing that representative institutions were inadequate to protect older values, they took solace in the memory of a bandit who had stolen from the railroads and mocked the authorities. In the twenty years after his murder publishers turned out at least 450 books, weeklies, and dime novels about Jesse James. Twenty-six different people came forward to claim that Bob Ford had missed his target, that they were the real Jesse James. People believed them for a time because they wanted Jesse James to return. And a folk song with the theme "He stole from the rich/ And he gave to the poor" was first heard from a black farmer in the 1880s, accompanying himself on a banjo. Half a century later Ozark farmers sang at least six different versions of that song.[38] Like the spirituals of the slaves, songs about Jesse James showed that a great many Missourians prayed for deliverance from the social setting in which they found themselves.

4. The Great Strike of 1877 and Ownership of Law

Followers of Karl Marx seemed to seize control of St. Louis for a few days in the summer of 1877 when Missouri's metropolis became the scene of the nation's first general strike. "Three more days like the past three," gasped the *Globe-Democrat* on July 27, 1877, "and the City of St. Louis will be hopelessly in the hands of the worst set of marauders that ever disgraced the earth." In England, Marx himself, inspired by news from America, wrote his friend Friedrich Engels that "a nice sauce is being stirred over there." Marx and Engels must indeed have enjoyed the sauce that workers were cooking during those hot July days, for workers from diverse backgrounds seemed to be forming a self-conscious proletariat that could take power.[39] Public officials nervously tried to measure the strength of both sides as the nation's first direct confrontation between the new railroads and their employees exploded into a general strike at St. Louis and spread quickly across the state.

To most Missourians the central underlying issue in the Great Strike of 1877 was the same as in the battles over railroad bonds and social outlaws: ownership of law, not ownership of the means of production. In folk memory, law was the codification of popular values, not the means by which those with economic power obliterated popular traditions. By this yardstick, "the largest and most lawless money interest in this country is the railroad interest," cried the St. Joseph *Herald* in 1877. "It has walked over the people like a remorseless and tyrannical giant defying the general government, the State governments and the people; it has bribed, bullied, brow beaten and bombarded every popular interest until men despaired of any remedy or relief."[40]

The strike and the struggle over ownership of law focused on the ways employers discharged their traditional obligations to their employees. According to familiar standards, workers were entitled to what the *St. Louis Journal* called a "living wage" to support their families. Each worker was "worthy of his hire," as the Sedalia *Democrat* put it, because of unique qualities of craftsmanship and character. The typical new railroad boss, by contrast, was simply a "money-grubber," according to the German Catholic *Amerika* in St. Louis, who "regarded labor only as a commodity and gave his workers no greater attention than the horses who pulled his wagons, or the dogs who chased the rats from his corncribs." When traffic fell during the depression that bottomed in 1876 and 1877, railroad owners bowed to the market. They fired some workers, and they slashed the wages and withheld the paychecks of those they retained. Missourians believed that competition was no excuse for employers to abandon workers and their families. Sharing the Sedalia *Democrat*'s anger at the "grinding selfishness too often manifested by soulless corporations" that put market ahead of obligation, the *St. Louis Times* reported Missourians' "popular conviction that there are real and deep-seated wrongs to be righted." The Hannibal *Clipper* agreed that "never before has the cause of justice been so thoroughly on the workingman's side."[41]

The knowledge that tradition-minded neighbors believed in the justice of their cause encouraged railroad workers to consider taking action to challenge the owners' use of the new competition and hierarchy to foster resignation among workers. Workers had acquiesced in layoffs, wage cuts, and deferred paychecks because they could see no way to empower themselves against their employers' economic power to fire them, the police's military power to suppress them, and the editors' interpretive power to discredit them with their neighbors. They feared, too, that employers would exploit the antagonisms between crafts and cultures that had traditionally prevented workers from uniting in resistance.

The strike by railroad workers that broke out in West Virginia on July 16 inspired Missouri workers. The strike flashed across the East. Workers stopped trains, seized railroad property, and battled military forces in bloody struggles at Baltimore and Pittsburgh. President Rutherford B. Hayes enraged railroad workers by calling out federal troops to suppress a worker uprising for the first time in forty-three years. In Missouri railroad workers began meeting to decide how to join the mushrooming revolt. The time for Missouri workers to turn talk to action came on Sunday, July 22, when strikers in the huge East St. Louis yards brought the strike to Missouri by refusing to allow freight trains to cross the Mississippi to St. Louis.[42]

Emboldened by their eastern brothers, Missouri's railroad workers quickly turned commitment to action. To enforce their insistence that the tradition of a "living wage" be restored in place of the new idea of competition, workers projected a democratic alternative to formal law and authority. In place of the law, whose function seemed more and more to protect economic investments with military force, workers sought to guide conduct by the moral and physical authority of collective participation. In Sedalia, strikers on the Missouri, Kansas, and Texas Railroad each signed a formal pledge to support the group's demands and decisions. Since the group was the source of authority, Missouri Pacific strikers at St. Louis insisted that a mass meeting of all strikers retain the final decision on bargains between the workers' representatives and their employers.[43] Strikers could only hope to challenge the new order's pervasive individualism by first securing the pledge of workers to place the group ahead of the individual.

Driven onward by the heady feeling of collective participation, strikers dramatically asserted the group's power. In communities across Missouri they took possession of the railroad yards, stations, and equipment. They insisted that the group, not the owners of tools or guns, would determine how property would be used and how people would behave. So long as fellow workers accepted the group's authority, strikers could use their undisputed possession of railroad property and their knowledge of how to throw switches, fire engines, and spike cars to force their employers to accept their control. By July 25 strikers at St. Louis, Hannibal, Kansas City, Sedalia, Boonville, and St. Joseph determined which, if any, trains would be permitted to run. Conceding the strikers' possession of Missouri, Kansas, and Texas property at Sedalia, general manager William Bond prayed that the workers "will protect the property now in their power to protect or destroy."[44]

Railroad workers used their collective power to encourage the timid, restrain the greedy and individualistic, and generally enforce obedience to the group as the highest good. At the Union depot in St. Louis and in railway yards across the state, strikers surrounded locomotives and firmly requested engineers and firemen to honor the local group's orders not to run certain trains. Crewmen almost invariably chose to defy railroad orders and do as the group asked. They either dismounted from their cabs and abandoned their locomotives or returned them to the yards. When Sedalia's strikers located a conductor who had taken out a train in violation of group orders, they staged an impromptu "court-martial" and sentenced the scab to be hanged. They spared his life only when the frightened conductor accepted the group's authority and begged for its mercy. Strikers also disciplined individuals who might be tempted to defy the group by a thirst for alcohol or adventure. At St. Louis, Sedalia, and St. Joseph strikers sought to close saloons that diverted individuals from the common struggle.[45]

By their occupation of railroad property strikers established an alternative form of authority in which they, not owners or lawmen, decided what behavior to tolerate. At Sedalia strikers "have determined to do their own police duty," reported the *Democrat*. They made a box car into a "sweat box" to incarcerate any individual who defied the group. Strikers at St. Joseph reassured their neighbors by proclaiming, "We are peaceable and law-abiding citizens," and "in this struggle for a decent living we will permit no acts of violence." A thousand strikers at Hannibal formally resolved that "we will individually and as a body discountenance any attempt by any person or persons to inaugurate disorder in the community." But they unmistakably possessed the final authority. Sedalia's strikers generally refused to permit economic activity on railroad property, but they did help unload a carload of farm equipment needed by local farmers, and they even granted the railroad's plea to send a wrecking crew to assist a locomotive that had jumped the tracks outside town. When an arsonist set fire to freight cars at Hannibal, strikers uncoupled the burning cars to prevent the fire from spreading, and "loudly denounced" the perpetrator. The superintendent of the Hannibal Stock Yards complimented the strikers' collective discipline when he said that he was confident that the strikers would effectively patrol his property.[46]

Railroad strikers "showed the world that they had certain rights as men, and as men they maintained them with a dignity and self respect that has gained them the good opinion of all," concluded the Sedalia *Democrat*. They relocated authority in the substance of equality and participation, replacing the resignation fed by the new order's competition and employers' orders. They discovered that by participating equally with fellow workers they could achieve their immediate demands, maintain popular support, overcome traditional cultural divisions, and begin to create an unlimited democratic future. The accelerating momentum of collective participation was unstoppable. Across Missouri a "mighty army of dust besmeared firemen and brakemen have suddenly come to the front with a raging demand which startles the country and compels the most respectful attention, and before which the great railroad kings and monied aristocracy heretofore all powerful, are impotent and powerless," concluded the Hannibal *Clipper*.[47]

The railroad strike soon attracted other workers to broaden the movement into a communitywide struggle for popular control of all workplaces. While the railroad strike empowered shopmen and brakemen to construct in the present a tangible alternative form of law and authority by which they could achieve their modest and immediate goals, it soon drew people who believed that they could envision the precise political shape of a democratic future that workers would control. The Marxist Workingmen's party boasted a thousand members at St. Louis—a fourth of the party's national membership—on the eve of the railroad strike. On Sunday, July 22, as the railroad strike neared Missouri, Workingmen's party leader Albert Currlin developed for a St. Louis party audience the theme that would fuse the railroad strike with political radicalism. In antiquity, explained Currlin, society was governed by wise and honest Solons, but in the new competitive order corruption tainted the making and enforcement of laws. St. Louisans knew! Indictments against the St. Louis Whiskey Ring that had begun in 1875 revealed a trail of corruption that led into the inner circles of the Grant administration, and in 1876 the president's private secretary stood trial in St. Louis for his part in the business. By mid-July, 1877, the new order based on money seemed to be collapsing when a series of bank failures swept across St. Louis.[48]

With the market economy grinding to a halt along with the banks and the trains from the East, the St. Louis Workingmen's party became a natural gathering point for workers who were swept along by the strike to demand more organized and political ways of controlling their futures. Several thousand workers attended a party rally at Lucas Market on Monday evening, July 23, many to assess their collective strength and many others to listen to radical political alternatives to the new order. The crowd grew so large that the party had to establish three separate rostrums so that everyone could hear at least one speaker. Audience and speakers encouraged each other to move quicker and reach farther toward a democratic future than they had ever imagined before the strike carried them along. Cooper J. P. Kadell confessed to the audience that he was frightened that the city's businessmen would brand him a traitor for his radical words. The audience roared its desire that he go even further in expressing ideas that he had feared to express before the strike. He did, adding, "I am getting well surrounded and fortified" by audience approval. The audience warmed to the conclusion of party leader James E. Cope, a veteran of the Chartist wars in Britain, that workers should no longer permit lawyers to represent them in legislatures and could only govern themselves fully when they were represented by fellow workers.[49]

On Tuesday, workers in isolated parts of the city spontaneously marched off their jobs. On the levee, boatmen demanded and won higher wages. Gas workers and newsboys struck. Coopers demanded nine cents a barrel and marched from plant to plant to enforce their demand. From all over the city workers convened at Lucas Market for the evening's Workingmen's party rally.

Tuesday night's crowd could only be measured "by acres," according to one newspaper. Ten thousand people—perhaps the largest gathering in the city's history—came together to declare the nation's first general strike. One speaker struck a responsive chord by insisting that workers should not accept a social and legal order in which wealth, not character, measured an individual's worth:

> You are just as law-abiding citizens as those men who rob the public treasury. Just as decent as those lecherous bondholders who derive their revenue by cutting off coupons. Your wives are just as virtuous as the wives of the rich capitalists, who, decked in silks and satins, ride in their carriage with a nigger driver dressed like a monkey, and your children are just as pure and upright as the bastard offspring of these bastards themselves.

Black and white, German and English, skilled and unskilled, St. Louis workers that night roared their approval of a proclamation that had been prepared by an "executive committee" of trade unionists and Workingmen's party leaders: "Resolved, that while we are in favor of law and order and of maintaining the legal rights of property, we are also in favor of bread and meat, and of maintaining the natural rights of man to 'life, liberty, and the pursuit of happiness.'" The fulfillment of these traditional democratic rights might require the public to take possession of private facilities: "As every man willing to perform a use to society is entitled to a living, therefore, if our present system of production and distribution fails to provide for our wants, it then becomes the duty of the government to enact such laws as will insure equal justice to all the people of the nation." Railroads, for example, should be owned by the government. The rally concluded by calling a general strike of all workers to enforce demands for an eight-hour day and the abolition of child labor.[50]

On Wednesday black stevedores from the levee joined white workers from factories and railroad yards in a four-block-long procession of several thousand workers who, under the leadership of the "executive committee," set out to enforce the general strike. On they marched, stopping at bakeries, mills, foundries, bagging companies, chemical works, and shops along the way to call on workers to quit their posts and join the procession and general strike. To the promoters' *Republican* the march was "simply terrifying in the eyes of all who beheld it": "The condition of mind of that vast, impetuous, perspiring mass of men seemed such that there was no suggestion too horrible for them to carry into execution." Workers answered "the sovereign crowd" by leaving their posts. By the day's end the strikers had closed sixty factories and shops. St. Louis was theirs. They decided who worked. Marchers permitted employees at the Dozier, Weyl & Company's Steam Bakery to finish the dough they were preparing to be baked into bread. The march concluded that night with the strike's most enthusiastic meeting at Lucas Market. Workingmen's party leader P. A. Lofgreen brought cheers with his demand that railroad managers resign immediately and give their roads to the people.[51]

The breathtaking sense of collective power built so quickly on Wednesday's and Thursday's marches that strikers tore down even higher obstacles to a democratic future. Black workers terrified the white press by ignoring the racial strictures that had so long confined them to deferential silence in the presence of whites. Black marchers became "yelling demons" as they broke from the procession to scream "wild yells, peculiar to excited negroes," at white female workers who were slow to walk out of the bagging mills. They refused to act as whites expected. Strikers of both races seemed to command all commercial activity. St. Louisans "must get a permit from a committee of rioters before they can be allowed to proceed with their business," editorialized the *Globe-Democrat* on Thursday. The executive committee did indeed issue a two-day permit to the Belcher Sugar Refinery to operate at the peak of the general strike and sent party members to guard its property against undisciplined rioters.[52]

By this point the strikers had terrified champions of progress. By enshrining the authority of collective participation over that of formal law, general strikers struck the new order at its core. The principle of a competitive labor market was "sacred," explained the St. Louis *Dispatch*: "It gives to each citizen and corporation the right to name the terms upon which it is willing to furnish employment." By subordinating individual bargaining to collective power, the strike was "nothing more than a colossal scheme of intimidation," wrote the St. Louis *Republican*. It "would, if carried to its logical consequences, derange all the operations of civilized society," declared the *Dispatch*. It was bad enough that "an armed mob cannot reason" in the competitive style of individual bargaining, but, continued the St. Joseph *Herald*, "a mob takes the law into its own hands." The issue was clear. General manager John E. Simpson of the Vandalia railroad complained that Workingmen's party spokesmen "make it appear that there is a conflict between labor and capital, when such is not the case; it is simply a conflict between law and order, lawlessness and disorder," or, as the *Herald* put it, between "law or anarchy, peace or war, civilization or barbarism." To believers in individualism, competition, and growth, the strike was "nothing but organized highwaymanism" based on "the art of the armed robber," the *Republican* put it. It was "the application of lynch law to the railroad corporation," concluded the St. Louis *Times*.[53]

To promoters the solution was as obvious as it was when Jesse James had challenged their authority. When elected public officials and the police "kept in the background" at St. Louis, as the *Times* wrote, because a majority of local residents sided with the strikers, champions of growth rushed to use their familiar military solutions to maintain their power and their law. St. Louis businessmen formed their own military force, in the same way that railroads had hired private military forces to impose their view of law. The city's merchants raised $20,000 to arm this militia, which they recruited from among the "best educated classes" with their "fashionable clothes." The Merchants' Exchange shut down its commercial activities so that its employees could join this military force to suppress the strike. Facing the probability that the merchants would put down the strike on their own, Mayor Overstolz and Governor John Phelps reluctantly authorized the police on Friday to send out a procession of law enforcers, whose largest contingent came from the merchants' militia, to arrest leaders of the Workingmen's party. As the procession approached the Workingmen's headquarters most of the party leaders escaped out the windows, but the enforcers took seventy prisoners, whom the city refused to prosecute. The St. Louis general strike disintegrated before this military force. For good measure the merchants' militia four days later "gave to the late turbulent classes a wholesome lesson that will not be forgotten in this generation," the *Republican* wrote hopefully, by parading through the city in their military uniforms.[54]

But the real defeat for the St. Louis Workingmen's party came not when the merchants' troops stormed their headquarters, but when they lost the battle over ownership of law. Strikers had agreed with merchants that laws against disorder ought to be enforced, but they had insisted that they owned the law as much as the merchants' hirelings did, and that they ought to be permitted to discipline their own members. The general strikers had established the capacity of the collective whole to control its individual members as the present reality on which to build their future dreams. The Workingmen's party repeatedly insisted at its nightly rallies and at its daily meetings with Mayor Overstolz that it, not businessmen or police, ought to preserve order: "We, the unfortunate toiling citizens, desire to faithfully maintain the majesty of the law whilst we are contending for our alienable rights." When the city's authorities refused to let the strikers patrol the streets and protect employers' property and thus uphold "the majesty of the law," party leaders felt that they had lost the basic battle over law and that there was little point in continuing the merely economic facets of the strike. "We are united in purpose, but are undecided what course to pursue," the party confessed in a handbill that circulated Wednesday night. The party decided not even to send speakers to mass meetings on Thursday, much to the disgust of those who had come to expect the party to lead. The only law left by Thursday for marchers to enforce was Mayor Overstolz's ban on liquor sales.[55]

Workers in other Missouri communities resolved the Great Strike of 1877 in ways that reclaimed from the railroads the values of law and authority for which they went on strike. For one thing, strikers convinced many editors that they had better claims to social authority than did the employers who wanted law to protect their property. "We would not . . . advocate mob law, but 'necessity knows no law.'" argued the Hannibal *Clipper*, "and the men whose necessities have driven them to seek a redress of their wrongs, even through violence, are in our judgment almost guiltless, in comparison with those whose avarice and greed have forged the present contest." For another thing, railroad strikers insisted that law was the common property of all, not the exclusive property of employers. At Hannibal they won both their economic demands and ownership of law. A hundred workers formed a Hannibal and St. Joseph Railroad Employees' Protective Association to claim the right to control behavior on the railroad's property. When the railroads demanded that Mayor Benton Coontz protect their property, the mayor swore in about fifty members of the workers' organization to serve as "special policemen."[56] They won the struggle strikers had lost in St. Louis.

Strikers underscored their complete authority over railroad property at Sedalia by staging a formal conclusion to their occupation of the railroads. During the week of the strike neither railroad nor city officials there dared challenge the strikers' undisputed occupation of railroad property. The railroad hastily rescinded wage cuts and sent a pay car to Sedalia with overdue wages. Finally, on Saturday, July 28, the city's railroad workers covened a solemn but festive meeting where they officially resolved: "After a brief and glorious experience of railroad proprietorship of one long week, we cheerfully surrender the road, right side up, back to the original owners, hoping that they make more money out of it than we have."[57]

The strikers wanted above all to control the rules that governed their lives. In 1877 they still believed that the law belonged to them, and they wanted to control law and authority. They bitterly resisted the railroads' drive to use law to promote the new order. In St. Louis the authorities deemed them outlaws. In Hannibal the authorities made them law enforcers. But the theme was the same. The railroads and businessmen were pretenders to social and political legitimacy, and the workers believed that they, not the railroads, were preserving the community's tradition of using rules to enforce locally determined standards of conduct. They would not accept a new order that judged them outlaws.

5

Communities, Economic Development, and Vigilantes

Missourians rooted their expectations about how to relate to each other and the land in their families, cultures, religions, and economic activities. They expected that formal law, if operative at all, would merely supplement discipline by families and churches and perhaps inform newcomers of a community's traditions. Communities elected the local law enforcers, the sheriffs, who, in turn, knew that their political futures depended on letting local custom dictate which laws to enforce and how to enforce them.

Promoters of the new order soon learned that each local community was determined to protect its unique traditions of social regulation against new production methods, new cultural groups, and new uses of formal law that threatened the community's control over behavior. Missourians had asserted popular sovereignty when formal law failed to protect life and property after the war. They would build from their recent experiences of collective direct action to preserve their capacity to regulate conduct.

Champions of growth and defenders of old ways underscored the supremacy of local traditions of community control over formal law when both sides turned to vigilante methods. Developers became vigilantes when their dreams were blocked by local traditions and lawmen who heeded local opinion over law. Traditional people defied formal law when they concluded that developers were using it to change the standards for regulating behavior. The reluctance of elected officials to interfere in the struggle between old and new orders encouraged vigilantes to settle the war.

Missourians became vigilantes at those times and places where the new order first and most profoundly challenged old ways. Rapid economic development came first to the southwestern Ozarks in the 1880s and to the bootheel swamps in the 1910s. In both cases vigilantes filled the huge gap between formal law and social authority created by the collision between old and new.

1. The Bald Knobbers of the 1880s

The clash between the old and new orders overwhelmed formal law in the steep Ozark mountains and valleys of southwestern Missouri. For several years in the 1880s hooded vigilantes imposed by terror what passed for social discipline. While the first vigilantes were newcomers who hoped to secure their new investments against attack by hill people, soon hill people adopted vigilante methods to resist the new order.

Before the Civil War the Ozarks' isolation attracted people from the southern Appalachians who sought refuge from development in their old homes. They built cabins on lands they only sometimes bothered to purchase. They survived by fishing the streams and hunting the deer, wild turkey, and razorback hogs that lived in the forests. Some kept a pig and a cow and grew small patches of corn for food, cane for sweetening.

They built a self-sufficient society in which kinship ties governed conduct more tightly than did law or property. They felt deep loyalty to their own clans, and feuds between families regulated behavior. They created a religion that merged hill traditions with a deeply felt piety. Fiercely independent, they never doubted the rightness of anything they did, as artist Thomas Hart Benton observed. But they stopped even the most violent feud to rally together against strangers with alien values.[1]

During the Civil War the very remoteness of the Ozarks attracted individuals and bands who were trying to escape military or civilian authorities. Guerrillas and criminals sought refuge in the hills. Soon the gun became the law, and many original settlers fled.[2]

After the war the original hill people and the new outlaws drew on their different circumstances and traditions to create a common approach to crime, law, and discipline that accepted unprecedented violence. Between 1832 and 1860 there had been only three murders in Taney County, but there were thirty murders between 1860 and 1886. The authorities bowed to local sentiment and abdicated. Only one murderer was sentenced in the quarter-century after the war.[3] This pattern continued without local complaints until the 1880s. For one thing, the crimes were parts of feuds that, like formal vendettas in places such as Corsica, were the time-honored way to enforce discipline. Punishment came from rival clans, not the state. For another, both groups wanted to preserve the region against outsiders. The original settlers resisted appeals for outsiders to impose formal law because they feared the outsiders would destroy the way of life of the hills. None of the five counties south of Springfield gave a penny to railroads. They wanted isolation.

Outsiders eventually did bring their dreams of growth to the Ozarks. To champions of the new market society, land should be converted into pastures for livestock to graze before shipment to market, and trees should be converted from wildlife habitat into railroad ties and fences. During the 1880s the railroad penetrated the region with a spur from Springfield to Chadwick in Christian County that created a local railroad-tie industry. By the 1870s the Ozarks began to grow faster than the rest of the state. Between 1880 and

1890 Christian, Taney, Douglas, and Ozark counties grew by 60 percent while the state grew by only 24 percent.[4]

Many newcomers believed that economic growth would be impossible in the area until the formal rule of law replaced discipline based on kinship and friendship. When newcomers introduced stores and blooded livestock, many young hill people preyed on them. They attacked merchants who did not accept the local custom of advancing credit. They slashed out the tongues of the fancy new cattle. And, as local opinion dictated, they went free. After the case of Al Layton, Taney County's prosperous newcomers could stand for this no longer. On September 22, 1883, this young hill man killed James Everett, a merchant at Forsyth, in plain view of many witnesses, but the jury acquitted Layton. Businessmen and large farmers began holding meetings to explore ways of compelling hill people to obey formal law.[5]

Captain Nathaniel N. Kinney, at six-feet-six and 260 pounds, towered over these meetings. Coming to Taney County in 1883, he built an elegant house along the White River and imported Red Durham cattle and the county's first merino sheep to graze his 700 acres. Soon he tried to change his neighbors' rough ways by promoting Sunday schools. But Kinney's background set him apart from other promoters of the new order. A one-time Union soldier, frontier post office agent, railroad detective, and saloon keeper, Kinney believed that direct action was the best course against lawbreakers.

Kinney rallied other newcomers. "The best men in the county gradually drifted to my side," he told a reporter, "and it became a war between civilization and barbarism." Kinney's vigilance committee quietly enlisted supporters to help secure prosecutions and convictions in the mountains. By the winter of 1884-85 the group had grown so large it took to meeting on a treeless mountain south of Forsyth that offered members a clear view of approaching strangers. From this meeting place the group would soon acquire its nickname, the Bald Knobbers.[6]

The Bald Knobbers first rode one April night in 1885. Their victims, Frank and Tubal Taylor, typified the young ruffians of the hills. Tubal Taylor maimed livestock and stole chickens and hid in the homes of his family. Frank Taylor, often drunk, rode his horse through schools, churches, and stores, and shot off his revolvers around the town square at Forsyth. On April 7, 1885, Frank Taylor went to John T. Dickenson's store north of Forsyth and demanded boots for his fugitive brother. Dickenson refused to advance Taylor credit. Taylor took the boots and threatened to kill Dickenson if he reported the crime. The next day Dickenson testified before the grand jury. Frank and Tubal Taylor went to the store and shot and seriously wounded Mr. and Mrs. Dickenson. This assault galvanized the Bald Knobbers. Several hundred strong, they scoured the hills, determined to capture, try, and convict the Taylors. Upon learning that the Dickensons were expected to live, the Taylors surrendered. That night a hundred crudely disguised Bald Knobbers broke down the jail door at Forsyth and marched the Taylors to a large oak tree where the vigilantes tried, convicted, and hanged the young terrorists. The vigilantes went unpunished.

The lynching of the Taylors inaugurated a year-long campaign by the Taney County Bald Knobbers to banish or intimidate the hill people who resisted the newcomers' ways. Organized by districts and with military ranks, groups of Bald Knobbers whipped or threatened to whip their victims until they left the county. Nightfall became a time of terror, as signal fires flashed between the hills to herald a new assault by the hooded vigilantes. As champions of growth, the Taney County Bald Knobbers tried to compel people to pay taxes so that the county could maintain the roads, schools, and legal machinery of the new order. They began another round of night riding when a gang of mountain men burned the county's courthouse and its tax records on December 19, 1885. This convinced Bald Knobbers that established residents were depraved people who would do anything to resist progress. More whippings were needed.[7]

But the Bald Knobbers soon drew harsh criticism from more prominent champions of growth, who maintained that the vigilantes had undermined their original objective by discouraging wealthy investors and settlers from entering Taney County for fear their lives and property would be unsafe. Proclaiming "Mob Law in Taney County," for example, the Jefferson City *Tribune* in 1885 headlined the charge that the Bald Knobbers were "A Ku-Klux Organization . . . Retarding the Progress . . . of One of the Best Counties in Missouri."[8]

Kinney himself committed the act that finally provoked other agents of progress to intervene. On March 12, 1886, he shot and killed Andrew Cogburn, a young hill man and anti-Knobber, outside the Oak Grove Church before several witnesses. An intimidated jury ruled it justifiable homicide. To others, however, the incident proved the need to organize to halt the Bald Knobbers. How could murder be permitted to go unpunished when it was committed by the vigilante chieftain but be the justification for terrorism when committed by hill men? The anti-Knobbers hastily formed a company of militia and petitioned Goveror Marmaduke to activate them. Marmaduke sent Adjutant General J. C. Jamison to investigate. Jamison's arrival frightened Kinney and other Knobbers with the prospect that the state might forcibly break up their group. But Jamison appealed to their desire for growth by declaring that an end to vigilante methods "would soon remove the very unfavorable impression prevailing abroad in regard to the social conditions in the county." The Taney County Bald Knobbers disbanded, and boasted in a letter to the Springfield *Herald* that they had achieved their goal: "The wheels of justice have been thoroughly lubricated by a free application of the determination of the citizens to see the law enforced and full justice done to all, and are now running smoothly." A young hill man, Billy Miles, soon ensured that the Taney County vigilantes would no longer threaten either hill people or the region's large developers by killing Kinney and winning a jury's acquittal for his service.[9]

The Taney County vigilantes inspired hill people from neighboring counties who feared the "ruffians" but feared even more the alien and secularizing transformation that growth introduced to their communities. The railroad spur from Springfield to Chadwick transformed Christian County overnight. Local residents could suddenly earn cash by turning trees into ties. A new class of people followed the railroad into Chadwick, offering new and exciting ways for the hill people to convert that cash into fun and adventure. Gamblers, prostitutes, and illegal saloon keepers opened for business. After delivering a wagonload of ties to Chadwick, young men often returned home drunk and broke. Parents began to brood that "the agents of the devil—the saloon keepers—set their snares for the boys." The new industry seemed to be destroying parents' moral authority and the bonds of kinship that regulated mountain life.[10]

Christian County residents formed their own secret organization in September 1885 to preserve the moral fabric of the family. Unlike Kinney's followers, they came from poor cabins where men boasted of their characters, not their possessions. David Walker and his seventeen-year-old son William lived a subsistence life in their cabin along Bull Creek. Horrified by what they saw at Chadwick when they delivered a load of ties, they discussed remedies with their friend, John Matthews, a deacon of the Chadwick Baptist Church. Many of the organizers were Masons, who cherished that order's fraternal spirit of brotherhood and the barrier of secrecy and ritual it erected to keep out strangers, an important hill virtue. But Masonry was purely defensive, whereas what they wanted was something that could counterattack. Kinney, they concluded, had discovered a perfect way to direct the fraternal spirit in offensive directions. Reflecting their Masonic roots, the Christian County Bald Knobbers developed elaborate rituals and distinctive costumes, colorful hoods with horns that pointed heavenward.[11]

The Christian County Bald Knobbers first appeared one summer night in 1886, when 300 masked men rode into Chadwick and attacked the saloons, pouring out 180 gallons of whiskey and beer. Lawmen had too long winked at the illegal saloons. Now the Bald Knobbers took over. Liquor, the destroyer of the family, was a favorite target, and the vigilantes raided saloons repeatedly. They also wanted to compel people to follow time-honored obligations between husband and wife, children and parents. In September 1886 they whipped Horace Johnson for not supporting his family. They swept down at night and beat husbands known to beat their wives. Soon younger and wilder men donned masks and rode at night to settle private grievances. Terrified people began an exodus from the county.[12]

While many hill people applauded the attacks on saloons, they feared the night riders were out of control. On the night of March 11, 1887, two companies of young Bald Knobbers confirmed that fear. They attacked a poor cabin in Smelter Hollow where an old couple lived with their married children. The vigilantes murdered the two young husbands, Charles Greene and William Edens. Next morning neighbors discovered the horrible scene. Apparently the two men had been killed for no reason other than a desire for sport. As word of the massacre spread, the people of Christian County demanded that Bald Knobbism cease. They were joined by regional promoters, such as the Springfield newspapers, which once again charged that vigilantes were retarding the area's growth. In April 1887 the Christian County grand jury indicted eighty persons on about 250 charges of murder, whippings, intimidations, and destruction of whiskey.[13] Most of the eighty were imprisoned awaiting trial.

The trials, which began at Ozark later in the summer of 1887, attracted nationwide attention. Newspaper correspondents descended on the mountain village to report the deeds of the evil vigilantes. But Ozark also attracted the families of the prisoners, who came down from the hills and set up tents so that they could talk with their loved ones and pray for deliverance. Nightfall in Christian County no longer generated fears of vigilantes; now it echoed with the muffled cries from the prisoners' families and the singing from their candlelit prayer meetings. Relieved that family bonds seemed once again stronger than the love of sport and carnage, and angered by the patronizing outsiders who were making money off the community's anguish, many Christian County residents now wanted to halt the court proceedings that had seemed so urgently necessary back in March. A jury acquitted the first prisoner. Finally, the judge freed most of the prisoners after making them pay nominal fines into the school fund. But he ordered nine to stand trial in April 1888 for the murders in Smelter Hollow. That jury sentenced Bald Knobber leaders David and William Walker and John and Wiley Matthews to be hanged and the others to prison terms.[14]

Soon after his conviction David Walker explained the central issue that would determine his fate over the next year: "Well, Ozark is trying to get even with Chicago. Chicago hung four anarchists [after the Haymarket Riot] and some people here think if that many Bald Knobbers were strung up it would give the town a boom." As the hill people observed the grief of the Matthews and Walker families, they began increasingly to hope that the state supreme court would reverse the verdict. When that failed, they deluged Governor David R. Francis with delegations and petitions begging him to commute the sentence to life imprisonment. The judge and prosecutor at the trial reflected the feeling of nine-tenths of the community by joining the appeal. A majority of state legislators signed. The jailer at Ozark left the door open for the men to escape. Wiley Matthews fled and was never seen again, but the other three awaited their fates in prison. But to Governor Francis, a former president of the St. Louis Merchants' Exchange, the primary purpose of law was to encourage investment and growth, not to reflect community or majority sentiment. National press coverage that interpreted the massive campaign for leniency as further evidence of Missourians' depravity concerned Francis more deeply than did democratic or local appeals. "The people of the East," declared Francis, "have an idea that lawlessness prevails here, and profess to believe that their lives and property would be unsafe within our borders." That was reason enough for Francis to lead a delegation of 340 militiamen in a show of Missouri's military might in a New York parade on April 29, 1889, and reason enough two weeks later for him to order the other three Balk Knobbers to be hanged. Word of Francis's order "cast a gloom on every face" at Ozark and inspired "murmurs of dissatisfaction . . . from nearly every lip," reported the Springfield *Leader's* correspondent. The "universal sentiment" opposed the governor, observed the reporter for the Springfield *Express*. And the Springfield *Republican* maintained that the hangings had appeased national sentiment but offended "the local sense of justice."[15]

Although the Bald Knobbers of Christian and Taney counties attracted very different followers, their primitive bonds were rooted deeply in the old order. Both groups drew on secrecy, ritual, costume, pageantry, and the fraternal ideal of mutual protection. Both groups projected alternatives to the new order's isolation and individualism as they swore in their oaths to "answer all signs of fellowship properly made by a brother member, and render him such aid as he may be in need of if not inconsistent with the interests of yourself and family." The penalty for divulging the order's secrets or violating the oath was death.[16] Both groups believed that conflicts between the old and new orders could not be contained within formal legal institutions.

2. Race and Class War in the Bootheel

Poor whites turned to terrorism and lynching as their weapons for trying to gain control over the rapid economic development that wealthy landowners imposed on Missouri's bootheel in the early twentieth century. But the region's traditions deflected the poor whites' vigilanteism into race war, not class war.

Traditional relationships of people to land lasted longer in the six southeastern lowland counties than in any other part of the state. Although nature had endowed the bootheel with rich soil, heavy rains, and a long growing season, nature had also created major barriers to its exploitation. Frequent floods from Ozark rivers to the west and the Mississippi to the east lay forever on this flat delta land, creating huge cypress swamps. Dense oak, gum, and poplar forests also blocked development. By 1890 the bootheel's six counties, although they covered 4.8 percent of the state's area, included only 2.3 percent of its improved farmland and 2.6 percent of its population.[17]

Several traditions intertwined to create the region's unique pattern of racial and class antagonism. Slaveholders worked about four thousand slaves on the bootheel's choicest lands on the eve of the Civil War, leaving the dense swamps and forests to poor whites. The large landowners regarded blacks, first as slaves and then as free agricultural workers, as the best workers. The poor whites, a growing majority, grew to hate both the landowners and their blacks. Poor whites were determined to prevent blacks from living or working among them. The region's unique form of white tenancy reinforced their determination. Tenancy was twice as common on bootheel farms (reaching 49 percent of those farms in 1890) as in the rest of the state, but white bootheel tenants more closely resembled black farm workers than did white tenants in the Deep South, because they were hired only for a single year and had to find new employers each year. Finally, the bootheel had been a center for vigilante terrorists after the Civil War. In 1866 alone white gangs shot blacks in Mississippi and New Madrid counties and white Republicans in Stoddard County. Blacks fled these mobs. As late as 1887 New Madrid blacks complained that "it seems to be the inclination of some parties to take law into their own hands, . . . whereupon we are publicly beaten and sometimes taken from our place of abode to be whipped, mobbed or otherwise maltreated."[18]

The challenge to these traditions was shaped by large landowners, lumber and real estate companies, and outside investors who together promoted transportation, lumbering, swamp drainage, and commercial agriculture. The lumber industry was the key, since its owners were the largest landowners and drainage promoters and its activities attracted thousands of new settlers. Formed in 1895, the Himmelberger-Luce Land and Lumber Company alone owned 200,000 acres in the bootheel. The American Sugar Refining Company and International Harvester bought tens of thousands of acres of timberland to ensure supplies of wood for sugar barrels and farm implements.

The forests fell. By 1899 Pemiscot County ranked second in the state in lumbering, and by 1906 Dunklin, New Madrid, and Butler were Missouri's three leading lumbering counties. The peak annual production for a bootheel county came in 1912, when lumbermen sheared 117,133,500 feet of lumber off New Madrid County. With lumbering came sawmill towns, Parma, Gideon, and Deering, and thousands looking for work in the mills and forests.[19]

The lumber industry spearheaded the draining of swamp and cutover lands, in a process that created huge local debts while concentrating land into fewer hands. The method was to create drainage districts wherever landowners representing a majority of the affected acres wanted them. Petitioners representing only 58.5 percent of the acres to be drained created the Little River Drainage District in the early twentieth century, but four individuals and corporations owned four-fifths of the petitioners' land in New Madrid and Dunklin counties. Since reclamation debts averaged $14.50 per acre, the process of drainage forced small farmers to sell out to wealthy landowners who could afford the new assessments.[20]

Bootheel governments saddled their taxpayers with unprecedented taxes to pay for drainage, in the same way that other local governments had earlier incurred huge debts for railroads. By 1920, 77 percent of the region's 2.1 million acres were included in drainage enterprises. The per capita debt of local bootheel governments skyrocketed from $.77 in 1890 to $14.33 in 1913, over a period when the per capita debt of all Missouri local governments rose by only 14 percent.[21]

Lumbering and drainage brought growth. From 1890 to 1910 the bootheel's population rose 95 percent, from 69,066 to 134,111, four times faster than the state average. Caruthersville leaped from 230 in 1890 to 3,655 in 1910, and Kennett from 302 to 3,033. The percentage of the region's land in improved farms rose from 21.6 in 1890 to 51.0 in 1920. The boom drove up the value of land. From 1900 to 1910 land values rose by 227 percent in New Madrid County and 264 percent in Pemiscot County.[22]

To fulfill the potential unleashed by lumbering and drainage, large land-owners needed cheap labor to chop trees, remove stumps, dig drainage ditches, plant corn, pick cotton. They resorted to the familiar one-year contracts with white tenants to clear, plant, and harvest lands, and the percentage of bootheel farms operated by tenants rose from 49 in 1890 to 65 in 1910. But many of the wealthiest landowners believed that white workers "will work no longer than they can get a sack of flour and a piece of meat, and then they spend their spare time loafing and raising 'Hell' in the country," as Marston landowner-merchant Seth S. Barnes complained in 1911. By the 1910s the large landowners increasingly imported blacks to solve their labor problems.[23]

The sudden transformation of the bootheel threatened the precarious independence of the region's poor whites. The first casualty was their land. When lumbering and drainage made once-undesirable lands suddenly valu-able, large landowners drove off squatters. Unable to afford the new drainage taxes, other small farmers sold out to wealthier ones. The second casualty was their livelihood, for the new black workers would work for lower wages. Worse, landowners no longer honored the traditional geographic barriers, like the Little River and Big Ditch, beyond which blacks had never before been permitted to live or work. The landowners imported them everywhere.[24]

Many poor whites feared that they were slipping to the level of the new black workers. The landowners seemed to want to use them, like the blacks, as a huge army of landless and cheap workers who would wander from lumbering to agriculture as labor needs developed. They would gradually fall into the ranks of migratory farm workers, whom the Charleston *Enterprise* had condemned, black as well as white, in 1910 as "the scum of the lowest class of humanity." Many of the imported blacks seemed to imbibe the new individualistic atmosphere and to learn from the landowners to treat poor whites with none of the old-time deference the poor whites believed to be due them. Blacks even shared the landowners' preference for the hated Republi-can party.[25] Their jobs, politics, homes, and lands threatened to the core, poor whites concluded that large landowners and their black workers had leagued together to destroy their world. As they felt themselves sliding, they grasped ever more desperately onto race as the one unchangeable badge of their worth and independence that landowners and blacks could not destroy.

Formal law, they concluded, had contributed to their problems and cer-tainly could not help them. The large landowners used legal machinery to create drainage districts, evict squatters, force small farmers to sell out. Under Dunklin County's tax assessments, "the rich property holders pay about one-third what the poor pay in taxes on their small holdings," concluded the Kennett *Justice*. When unsafe machinery mangled Albert Waltrip's foot at the Richmond Cotton Oil Mill in 1914, the *Justice* demanded, "Can't this company be taught a severe lesson by the law, or are they stronger than the law and the courts?" Many poor whites agreed with the *Justice* that "jails, prisons, laws, and constitutions are made chiefly to prevent those who have too little from helping themselves from the supply they have created of those who have too much."[26]

At the same time, however, many poor whites knew that local officials shared their prejudices, wanted their votes, and would ignore their acts if they took the offensive against unpopular and defenseless victims. "There is a deep settled purpose on the part of probably ¾ of the population in this town and section generally to keep the colored people away," wrote C. G. Post from Parma in 1911. Parma's constable informed Adjutant General Rumbold that same year that "90 percent opposed the introduction of negro labor" and that he would resign rather than defy local opinion. "It will be political suicide for anyone to oppose the sentiment against negro labor," added the town marshal.[27]

Many poor whites concluded that the region's tradition of vigilante terror offered the best way to deprive large landowners of their cheap labor and assert the last remaining proof of their own worth. At Marston in 1902 white railroad crews drove off a new black crew. A gang fired 500 shots into the home of a mill owner who had imported blacks to a traditionally white-only area of New Madrid County in 1905 and forced a neighbor to abandon farming because white mobs continually frightened away his black workers.[28]

In the summer of 1910 this tradition of vigilante incidents erupted into a massive campaign of terror. Poor whites launched a ferocious drive to expel the imported black workers. The region seemed suddenly overrun by strange blacks who failed to show proper deference. Late in May one black newcomer quarreled with New Madrid Marshall Richards so vehemently that the argument attracted a crowd, and the crowd was horrified to see the marshal receive so much disrespect from a black man. Richards jailed him. The next morning residents found the black stranger hanging dead from a pecan tree. No one was prosecuted, but the New Madrid *Record* assured readers that the victim had been both dangerous and a stranger.[29]

The same explosive setting existed in neighboring Mississippi County, particularly in towns where landowners imported blacks for the first time that summer. By early July the county seat of Charleston was "thronged by strangers," and the *Enterprise* reported a growing "pent-up feeling of resentment" toward the new blacks. On July 3 poor whites were terrified when they learned that two itinerant black workers had robbed and killed a popular white farmer, William Fox, as he was driving home from Charleston. The two were promptly jailed, and they must have foreseen their fate when a thousand people descended on Charleston, many of them from the area's formerly all-white communities. The mob seized the two suspects and immediately hanged one in the courthouse square. This act intensified the mob's determination to give a clear warning to absentee landowners and imported blacks. Its members dragged the second suspect to the black Bad Lands section of Charleston and, locating the clearest symbol of anger toward outsiders, used a railroad crossing sign to lynch him. "The mob hung two highway robbers and murderers," applauded the *Enterprise*.[30]

Newspapers from St. Louis joined Governor Herbert Hadley in condemning this brutal act for tarnishing Missouri's reputation and discouraging
outsiders from investing in the booming bootheel. Hadley warned Mississippi
County officials that it would be a "disgrace" if the lynchers went unpunished,
and he offered a reward for their capture. Prosecuting attorney J. M. Haw
confided that he was afraid to investigate because the lynching had been
popular and local whites were angry enough to take more victims. He had
just barely succeeded in getting a black accused of rape out of a mob's hands.
To appease the governor, however, Haw called a grand jury, which arbitrarily
singled our four whites for reasons no one understood. A mob now threatened to storm the jail and free the four arrested whites, so Haw recommended
bail—and freedom. At their trial in 1911 the judge won "the approval of most
every person in the county" by giving a directed verdict of not guilty for those
charged with the murders.[31]

The New Madrid and Charleston lynchings of 1910 were only the beginning. By the summer of 1911 white tenants and millhands had formed a well-
organized "conspiracy to drive negro cotton pickers out" of New Madrid and
Pemiscot counties, wrote landowner-merchant Seth Barnes to the governor.
Pleading "for some protection from the roving mobs over our county who are
intimidating the negroes," Pemiscot County prosecuting attorney J. S. Gossom told Hadley that the mobs "are composed of tenants and laborers, who
think if the negroes were out of the county they could get better wages for
picking cotton and get cheaper rent." In September whites posted signs
warning blacks to leave. When landowners ignored the warnings, poor whites
turned to organized terror. On the night of September 11 they attacked black
farm workers at two separate places in southern New Madrid County,
wounding four and terrifying the rest into leaving. In October they drove
black cotton pickers off Bud Killian's Pemiscot County plantation.[32]

The climax of the 1911 terrorism came at Caruthersville in October. The
influx of white and black itinerants had brought with it crime and drunkenness, part of the price of economic growth. In the first nine months of 1911
there were nine murders in Pemiscot County, but only one person was caught
and punished. "If we have no State law that will reach the tough element,
both white and black," urged the Caruthersville *Democrat*, townspeople
should invoke a "higher law" to create order. Early in October lawmen
arrested a black man for stabbing two whites during a street fight outside a
saloon, and foiled a gathering lynch mob by moving the prisoner. But the
opportunity for action soon came.[33]

On October 10 police arrested two blacks in separate incidents that kindled
poor whites' fears that blacks were refusing to show traditional deference. A
nervous white woman charged that Ben Woods had pestered her as she
walked home, and Woods was arrested. That same evening police arrested
A. B. Richardson, who enjoyed insulting whites during his frequent drunks,
for stealing dress goods. A mob of three hundred gathered and dragged the
two prisoners from the jail. First they whipped Woods and might have killed
him except that Richardson began insulting them. They then turned on

Richardson. The mob left a fifty-yard trail of its brutality before throwing Richardson's body into the Mississippi. Still not content, the mob burned a black boarding house which, the Caruthersville *Democrat* assured its readers, was an "immoral incubus, too deep-seated for the probes of the law to eradicate." Many blacks caught the first boats and trains out of Caruthersville, and the coroner's jury solemnly reported that Richardson had died of "causes unknown to this jury."[34]

The large landowners demanded that formal law punish those who had intimidated their workers into leaving. Governor Hadley offered rewards and prodded Pemiscot and New Madrid lawmen to prosecute the lynchers. The large landowners finally turned to the grand jury as their method to discover the perpetrators and turn law into a way to protect their labor force in defiance of public opinion. Seth Barnes, a railroad promoter, mill owner, and large landowner, passionately believed that his interest in the region's growth—and his investments—gave him a special obligation to bring the mobs within the reach of formal law. As foreman of the grand jury, Barnes tried to secure indictments, but he was stymied when one of the jurors alerted the vigilantes to the grand jury proceedings, and the vigilantes convinced local lawmen not to cooperate. Undaunted, he persuaded the state attorney general's office to assist him in empaneling a new grand jury at the November 1911 term. This jury indicted twenty-seven alleged vigilantes. Both sides agreed that the March 1912 trial of the first two cases, Jay Alley and Robert Crosser, would determine whether New Madrid juries wanted law to control vigilantism. The trial jury hastily acquitted the two defendants and forced prosecutors to drop the other cases.[35]

The landowners were even less successful in Caruthersville, where a grand jury investigated for several weeks before deciding to return no indictment in December 1911. "If the purpose of the recent grand jury was to gloss over anything that has occurred here, it certainly seems that the purpose was faithfully performed," commented the *Pemiscot Argus*.[36]

"This is a matter that can not be controlled by the local authorities for the reason there are so many in sympathy with the marauders," complained Pemiscot County prosecuting attorney J. S. Gossom to Hadley. The vigilantes, he said, "usually succeed in getting a jury that will acquit them." Hadley sent Adjutant General F. M. Rumbold in December 1911 to investigate why no one had been punished for vigilante terrorism in the bootheel. The vigilantes, he reported, intimidated even most landowners into silence. But the basic reason was stated by the Caruthersville *Democrat:* when "the power of the law becomes impotent" in the face of social conflict, "only the righteous indignation of the community" remained to "overthrow evil." After the Caruthersville lynching, added the *Democrat*, "the future portends a higher and better regime."[37]

Many poor whites in the bootheel hoped to supplement vigilantism with solutions that would bring the landowners under political control by the community. They joined the Socialist party and supported two local Socialist papers, the *Scott County Kicker* and the Kennett *Justice*. "Socialism alone will rid our country of the curse of landlordism," declared the Dunklin County Socialist convention of 1914, which demanded lower rents "so that tenants may better secure the product of their toil." The *Justice* appealed:

> A landlord . . . says "pay me a fourth, or a third, or a half of what God and you produce." . . . We don't pay any earthly rain-lord or air-lord or sunshine-lord so why pay a land-lord? . . . Let's unite and possess the lands of Dunklin Co. for ourselves, for God made it, not for the Shelton's, Ely's, Byrd's, Hunter's, Douglass' and other big landlords, but for the common people to use and enjoy.[38]

Bootheel socialism appealed to poor whites' feelings of ebbing independence and morality. Socialist revival meetings, sometimes conducted by holiness and pentecostal preachers, rocked with the enthusiastic message that Socialism fulfilled Jesus' historic mission of helping the poor and the sick. "Vote Like You Pray," a popular Socialist anthem, put words by a Stoddard County Socialist to the melody of "Sweet Bye and Bye." A poor Dunklin County widow reported that the Bible and the Kennett *Justice* were her favorite reading.[39]

White tenants and mill hands turned the bootheel into the state's leading Socialist stronghold for a brief season. The number of Socialist voters for president in these six counties rose from 207 (1.1 percent of the region's voters) in 1904 to 1,291 (5.5 percent) in 1908, to a peak of 3,240 (12.9 percent) in 1912. With less than 4 percent of the state's voters, these counties gave Socialist presidential candidate Eugene Debs 8.4 percent of his Missouri total in 1908 and 11.4 percent in 1912. At the local level Socialists in 1912 elected all the town officers in Cardwell, a Dunklin County village of nearly a thousand people.[40]

But the threats were too immediate and the votes for the Socialist party too ineffectual for poor whites to rely on the formal political process to solve their problems. By 1916 two-thirds of the Socialists' 3,240 voters of 1912 had abandoned the party.[41]

Poor whites returned to the proven method of vigilante terror. But clearly the Socialist experience had influenced them. This time they began with a Socialist-sponsored renters' union. The mill hands and tenants around Sikeston organized to compel mill owners to grant an eight-hour day and compel landlords to charge lower rents. White tenants around New Madrid demanded that landowners lower rents and raise wages for clearing stumps. They threatened to boycott landowners who rejected their demands. They appealed to blacks to join them in a biracial tenants' movement, but blacks, understandably suspicious, did not become involved.[42]

The tenants' movement buttressed its economic demands by mailing threats to large landowners, and followed up the threats with familiar night-riding terrorism. Most of the local newspapers concluded that these new night riders were Socialist voters using older methods. One gang was composed of the old "Scott County Socialists," observed as Sikeston *Standard*. To prevent blacks from stopping their drive against landowners, the gang posted warnings telling blacks to leave. After planter John Clarahan rejected their demands to dismiss his 125 black farm workers, they fired shots at night into the cabins that housed the blacks. Three hundred blacks immediately left the area. In early November another mob attacked a landowner who had rejected tenants' demands for higher wages and lower rents. And they frightened both landowners and blacks with the new class consciousness that accompanied their traditional vigilantism.[43]

The landowners organized to fight back. No longer trusting local lawmen to enforce formal law, they decided in 1915 to hire their own army of private detectives to protect their property from poor white mobs. The detectives, unlike elected sheriffs, would obey their orders. On November 22, 1915, the detectives fought a pitched battle with night-riding tenants. The owners of a total of 200,000 acres, who, together employed 5,000 workers, raised a huge fund to prosecute the gangs. In contrast to earlier trials, this time the landowners delivered evidence. And they won. At the January 1916 trials eight defendants were sentenced to the state penitentiary for two to five years for their vigilante activities, and the landowners allowed forty-two other defendants to be paroled on their promise not to participate in vigilante gangs in the future.[44] But for a decade bootheel poor whites had demonstrated that vigilante terrorism was more effective than formal law as they desperately tried to turn the remaining shreds of their traditional independence into bases for popular restraint of the onrushing transformation of their communities.

IV

The Cultural War

Champions of the new order soon learned that the struggle to impose their values required greater resources, imagination, and persistence than did their drive to secure their property against popular bandits and vigilantes. Traditional Missourians, determined to protect their innermost values as well as their outward patterns of life and work, countered each of the promoters' new impositions in ways that increasingly frustrated the promoters. No sooner did the promoters develop a way to compel obedience to one of their new values than traditional Missourians opened a new front, or suddenly changed from regular troops into guerrillas. What made the cultural war so different from the attempts to secure property against popular outlaws was that the promoters' new order could not be fully realized until they had converted the hearts and minds of Missourians. That, they discovered, was impossible.

Traditional integrations of life and work threatened the new order at every turn. Although differences of place, culture, and occupation separated Ozark mountain farmers from German artisans, Missourians from all traditional cultures worked to accomplish tasks. Then they relaxed. Holidays and festivals, hunting and fishing trips, a long beer with co-workers, all were ways of relaxing. "The town was addicted to celebrations," recalled artist Thomas Hart Benton of his Neosho childhood in the 1890s. A funeral in a black community or a wedding in a Polish neighborhood measured rhythms of life far more important than any work. Missourians further expected the times of work to be controlled by nature and God. The drought of 1911, explained Presbyterian minister J. E. Cortner to Governor Herbert Hadley, was "God's effort to bring His people back to a more righteous observance of His commandments."[1] They expected to learn what mattered from their families, from the clergy, and from people with such skills as homemaking, carpentry, fishing, and shoemaking.

Believing that deference grew from bonds of mutual obligation, not from economic power, each of the state's traditional cultures had evolved its own form of independence. Missourians broke or simply ignored new rules that violated their traditions, and did so with the same enthusiasm with which they had supported outlaws. Economic power did not confer the right to order people around. "The highly strung individualism of the mountain man, his utter faith in the rightness of his personal will," wrote Thomas Hart Benton of his southwest Missouri neighbors, "functions pretty satisfactorily in a simple agricultural background where certain ways, beliefs, and restrictions are regarded, because of their long standing, as manifestations of the will of God." Although they inhabited a different world from the mountain people, urban workers shared the same conviction that traditional obligations and aspirations, not economic power, ought to shape patterns of deference. To John Niblock, a worker at Lexington in 1892, the new leaders' attempts to change familiar values and habits were despotic and unpatriotic:

> Are we politically . . . capable of self-government, or is it to be conceded that henceforth we are tied to the chariot wheels of those innumerable despotisms and have no recourse but submission? . . . In the name of all that is American, let us put a stop to these monstrous abuses. . . . Let the humble toiler be restored to his primitive rights. We have wandered from the old path. Let us try to regain it. . . . The chief end of man should not be in the accumulation of wealth. He ought to have a nobler purpose . . . in life.[2]

The state's leading artists painted powerful portraits of the dignity and resourcefulness that Missourians drew upon as they dug in for the cultural war against the new economic leaders. In novels as different as *The Gilded Age*, *Tom Sawyer*, and *Huckleberry Finn*, Mark Twain made heroes of those who lived their lives by traditional codes of honesty, democracy, simplicity, love, nature, and self-sufficiency while he pilloried people who embraced the new order. Growing up in the home of a congressman but surrounded by mountain life, young painter Thomas Hart Benton felt that the basic difference between the old and new orders was between the qualitative and the quantitative. Describing the promoters of change as "parvenus," Benton explained that "the psychology of the parvenu is destructive of the appreciation of the qualities of things. His is a quantitative mind. He is intent on expansion rather than on cultivation and preservation of value in things. Things—all things—are, for his kind, merely instruments expanding areas of control and promoting his wealth and power." Defending the aesthetic values of skilled, self-sufficient craftspeople who made the "fine old patchwork quilts" and "solid hickory chairs" against "the shrewd and narrow practicality of the dominant classes," Benton proudly recalled that in the 1890s "we of southwest Missouri were lagging in the headlong race of commercial modernism."[3]

Missouri's "parvenus" faced a herculean task when they sought to compel the obedience, let alone win the support, of people like Benton's hill neighbors or young villagers like Huckleberry Finn. Traditional Missourians were determined to preserve their ways in the face of compulsions and inducements to accede to the new values. Even when the promoters succeeded in fixing some of the externals of their lives, traditional values inspired their hearts as they created vibrant popular cultures of defiance.

6

Discipline and Self-Discipline

Armed policemen and moral teachers patrolled the no-man's-land between the old and new orders. Both performed vital functions in the cultural war.

Champions of growth developed a two-pronged approach to transforming the behavior and values of traditional Missourians to conform to their own dreams and demands. The first challenge was to compel people to change the ways they behaved. But promoters quickly concluded that changes in values were even more important. The key to victory in the cultural war was somehow to lead Missourians to turn external discipline into internal self-discipline.

1. Economic and Military Compulsions

The new economic leaders soon concluded that workers' traditions were the most formidable barrier to their control over production, and they used basic economic compulsions to get workers to abandon their traditional ways of working. As employers replaced skilled workers with ever more complex and expensive machines, they increasingly demanded punctual, sober, and disciplined workers. They turned to the most basic economic pressure—workers' need for income to support their families—to compel workers to abandon the traditional pattern of performing a task and then relaxing, a pattern that had given workers real control over the job. In its place they imposed a new pattern of routinized work regulated by a time clock that the employer controlled. Workers now had to work at a steady pace throughout the day and week. Time became money as work became timed. In the company town of Grandin in the 1890s the Missouri Lumber and Mining Company blew the mill's whistle for five solid minutes at 4:00 each morning so that employees would have time to wake up, dress, and eat breakfast before reporting to work punctually at 6:00 A.M. When cabinetmakers adopted a relaxed attitude toward the starting time of the Beattie Manufacturing Company in St. Louis, the company retaliated by requiring, after January 2, 1891, that all workers report to the watchman by 7:00 A.M. sharp or lose a full hour's pay. The cabinetmakers won this particular struggle against the alien new imposition of punctuality when the forty-one members of Local 12 of the Furniture Workers' Union struck the company until it retreated from the new rule.[1] Few workers were as indispensable as skilled cabinetmakers, however, and employers frequently won the war over punctuality when they made it a simple condition of employment.

Workers' traditional thirst for a drink before, during, and after the performance of tasks likewise seemed to employers to menace their investments. Workers who came to work drunk or hung over or those who drank on the job were careless with the expensive new machines and failed to give their employers full productivity. Desperate employers used everything from external disciplines to movements that fostered self-discipline in their long and frequently unsuccessful battle to impose the new discipline of sobriety. Methods of control that worked in one occupation failed in others, since each occupation had its own traditions of alternating drink with the performance of tasks. In dock work, railroading, and brewing, workers traditionally took advantage of slack periods to drink. Brewery workers, for example, clung to the "sternewirth" privilege, which gave them access to free beer from the brewery taproom when they felt thirsty, but the St. Louis breweries increasingly limited the sternewirth privilege in the late nineteenth century. In their zeal for profits the brewers would soon become so contemptuous of workers' traditional habits, a brewery worker predicted in the *Arbeiter Zeitung* in 1903, that his own recurrent nightmare would become reality. Employers would require workers "to stop drinking beer in the brewery; that takes too much time. Each worker must drink through a water meter, which would show how much he drank each day. On pay day the water would be deducted from his pay."[2]

Employers used their ability to define the terms of employment to try to impose sobriety as well as punctuality. The St. Louis and San Francisco Railroad announced in 1883 that it would fire any employees who were drunk on the job or found in saloons during working hours, and that temperate workers would receive preference in employment. By 1907 St. Louis mail carriers were forbidden from even "loitering" in saloons. But the tradition of combining drink with work persisted. After creating Grandin as a company town in 1888, the Missouri Lumber and Mining Company over the next twenty years fired employees who drank and prohibited saloons and gambling in town. It assisted federal marshals in locating and prosecuting distilleries in the surrounding hills. But the company failed to prevent workers from drinking, for bootleggers furnished the town with illegal liquor. The company encouraged churches, where they hoped workers would learn to internalize the values of sobriety and self-control, but in 1909, after twenty years, the town of 3,000 contained only 200 church members. When economic pressure proved inadequate to compel sobriety, some employers embraced prohibition in the early twentieth century, with equally unsuccessful results.[3]

By eroding older means of social control, the new order actually intensified the search for new compulsions. Church discipline, once a powerful way to discipline rebellious individuals, lost its force as secularism undermined religion and the separation of churches along class lines took poor members beyond the disciplinary reach of elites.[4] By bringing isolated and antagonistic traditional cultures into competition and proximity, employers themselves accelerated the social explosions that seemed increasingly out of control. And the new economic leaders guaranteed that traditional Missourians would be less willing than in the past to obey laws by using law in new, expensive, and corrupting ways. The widening gulf between old and new conceptions of proper behavior spawned not only social outlawry but a larger pattern of "crime" that was popular among traditional peoples but beyond the reach of the new leaders.

The surest way to force people to obey their orders, the promoters reasoned, was through military force. But they had to develop new forms of military force, because popular tradition dominated older forms. Since the law enforcement officers with military powers, the sheriffs, were popularly elected and frequently sided with grass-roots resistance to the new order, promoters could only insure the loyalty of military forces by directly hiring Pinkertons or other private police forces.

As they tried to develop military means to curtail rowdyism, gang fights, arson, train robberies, slave revolts, and murder, the developers began in the 1870s to perceive a new menace from traditional Missourians. The nationwide railroad strike of 1877 and the accompanying general strike in St. Louis gave a razor's edge to fears of popular rebellion, fears already sharpened six years earlier when workers in Paris had overthrown the government and established the Commune. By the late 1870s it seemed possible, even likely, that workers might mobilize their superior numbers into an organization that would attempt to seize power. The new business elite had to be ready with loyal military forces. "No state is safe for one day without" loyal troops, proclaimed the businessmen's political ally, Governor Thomas T. Crittenden, in 1885. "In this respect, the present and future are not like the past. Times have changed and so have the minds of men. There are many turbulent spirits constantly engaged in stirring or attempting to stir up strife and disobedience to law among the wage workers of the country."[5]

St. Louis businessmen learned during the strike of 1877 that the best way to insure the loyalty of military forces was to rely on, and pay for, volunteers. Unable to trust former Confederates, blacks, Germans, or the police to protect their property and quell the strikers, businessmen recruited their army from employees of the citadels of the new order, the city's commercial exchanges. Refusing to copy other governors who had called out federal troops to suppress the railroad strike in their states, Governor John Phelps simply gave federal muskets to the businessmen's troops. Soon after the strike, merchants spearheaded the St. Louis Police Reserve. Early in 1878 they created the St. Louis National Guard Battalion, which became a regiment the next year. This pattern evolved into the militia and National Guard as the new leaders' military solution. By 1881 thirty-five militia companies were armed and ready, and two years later Governor Crittenden pointed to "the commodiuous [*sic*] armory hall erected by the foresight and liberality of a few of the prudent property-holders of the city of St. Louis." To insure the troops' loyalty Crittenden insisted that they be volunteers. For the rest of the 1880s the military force maintained its independence from popular control by remaining a volunteer corps financed by private and federal appropriations earmarked for national guards. For their part, Missouri taxpayers remained skeptical of supporting a state military primarily for employers to use against their workers, and as late as 1891 they refused to give state funds to the guard. Although the legislature did begin to appropriate public funds to the national guard in the 1890s, it limited the guard's size to the federal minimum requirement, because legislators knew that traditional Missourians agreed with Governor William J. Stone's 1897 observation that "our people should not be accustomed to the habit of using or relying upon the military." During the Spanish-American War in 1898 individual members of the guard contributed more to their organization than the state did. With the guard, promoters had created a military force dependent on them and relatively independent of public opinion. But even this force had limits. As late as 1900 Governor Lon Stephens was reluctant to use military forces to resolve a strike because of "the prejudice existing in the State against the Militia."[6]

While the militia and guard stood ready to act in the event of major strikes or riots, promoters also sought military forces that could suppress the day-to-day disturbances that threatened individual promoters or that could escalate at any moment into violent mass challenges. The new forces had to be visible at all times in all parts of the community so that they could respond quickly and prevent isolated conflicts from becoming general ones. They were needed to perform the traditional function of church discipline. They were needed to reassure the new leaders that traditional people would defer to the new leaders' authority on the street as well as on the job. The larger challenge came on the streets, where new leaders lacked direct economic power over the rebellious. The St. Louis police commissioners confessed their failure by 1869 "to prevent the obstruction of sidewalks and thoroughfares, by gamblers and idlers, who congregate on the corners of important streets, and by words, gestures, looks and suggestive demonstrations offend the eyes and ears of all decent people, and often make such places impassable for virtuous and modest women." The commissioners were "practically powerless" to prevent such confrontations on the streets, since "the real offense is so obscure that proof of guilt is hardly attainable."[7] "The real offense" was hard to punish, of course, because it was the failure to defer to "decent people" who did not deserve respect by traditional yardsticks. For this reason, the new military force, unlike sheriffs, needed to be independent of public opinion.

In the 1860s and 1870s the new economic leaders began relying on appointive police departments to replace elected sheriffs as the enforcers of social control and public order. Although St. Louis had a patrolman as early as 1808 and uniformed police by 1854, the real development of police to protect the city's growth and its promoters against rebellious acts by traditional people came after the Civil War. Over the half-century after 1861 the number of patrolmen grew twice as fast as the city's population, from one patrolman for each 1,022 citizens in 1860 to one for each 491 citizens by 1910. Four of the seven police stations at the turn of the century were built during the military boom that accompanied the economic bust of the 1870s. Reaching into every corner of city life, the patrolmen moved quickly to deter the poor from robbing or insulting the new leaders. But they strove hardest to prevent individual acts that reflected a lack of proper deference from turning into more general or deeper threats. In the fiscal year 1871, for example, 65 percent of arrests by the St. Louis police were either for disturbing the peace or for public drunkenness. Even as late as 1899 the St. Louis police arrested 2,267 people for committing or attempting to commit such direct criminal challenges as robbery, burglary, and the destruction of property. But they arrested 13,432 people for "loafing," disturbing the peace, "loitering," public drunkenness, vagrancy, discharging firearms, begging, and similar acts reflecting a failure to internalize the new values and threatening at any moment explode into a riot or worse.[8]

Lexington appointed its first regular police officers in the mid-1880s, and they soon demonstrated why promoters wanted them. The city's Methodist, Disciples of Christ, and Presbyterian churches had repeatedly disciplined members for drinking and gambling in the old order, and as late as 1887 the Presbyterian Session threatened to employ the traditional "discipline by the Church" to stop a wave of gambling. When neither the Presbyterians nor other churches disciplined gamblers in subsequent years, promotors feared that drinking and gambling might turn into social explosions that would threaten their property and lives. They turned to the police to punish public drinkers and gamblers. In 1888 Lexington's new police force arrested and fined sixteen gamblers in a single raid. By 1904 the Henry County village of Montrose conceded the inability of church or family to restrain rowdy young people by enacting a curfew for military forces to enforce.[9]

The new police inspired fear and hatred in traditional Missourians, who found them to be beyond traditional or popular control. Traditional cultures knew that the new military discipline fell most heavily on them. Blacks and immigrants accounted for 74 percent of the arrests at St. Louis in 1871, even though they made up only 43 percent of the population. Blacks were less than 10 percent of Kansas City's population in 1911, but more than a quarter of that city's arrests. Many workers refused to accept the new military discipline. When Lexington policemen attempted to arrest some of that city's workers for drinking in 1890, the workers resisted. In the ensuing struggle they threw rocks at policeman William Golightly and shot policeman T. C. Young.[10]

Farseeing promoters like Governor Herbert Hadley recognized that the military deterrent had to be used with restraint and that overzealous, independent police would undermine the developers' larger dreams. Hadley was particularly alarmed by police violence in his hometown of Kansas City. On one occasion in 1910 a patrolman tried to arrest two blacks for the "crime" of cooking a chicken and, in the struggle that ensued, shot an innocent woman. From May 1 to September 1, 1910, Kansas City police shot fourteen citizens, four of whom died. "I fear that the sense of authority incident to the wearing of a uniform and the carrying of a club and a pistol has caused some of the police officers to become too truculent and belligerent," Hadley complained to Kansas City police commissioner Thomas Marks in 1910. Hadley warned another commissioner that "this promiscuous practice of shooting people must be vigorously dealt with, or else public sentiment is going to become very justly aroused."[11]

Employers tried to instill punctuality and sobriety by making them conditions of employment while the new military forces tried to compel outward obedience to the codes of the new order as they supplanted older forms of social discipline. They were only moderately successful for, as the *St. Louis Times* concluded, "against public opinion the military arm is unavailing."[12] And few developers expected that external compulsions would permanently secure the full transformation they desired, in the face of resistance by traditional cultures. The real solution was to try to persuade traditional Missourians to internalize the new values.

2. The Battle for the Hearts and Minds of the Children

Defenders of tradition and champions of growth agreed that education was the major battleground in the cultural war, because the values and habits that children acquired in their formative years would be hard to obliterate in adulthood. The most important thing that parents did was to raise their children with values, habits, and skills that reflected their own values, needs, and aspirations. Each traditional culture developed its own forms of education, formal and informal, to assist parents in passing the culture's values on to the next generation.

Parents assumed major responsibility for the education of their children in the old order. The most common pattern of formal schooling before the Civil War was the subscription school, in which groups of parents retained a teacher for their children. In Taney County, for example, parents determined the teacher's qualifications, examined candidates, and arranged the school calendar so that it did not conflict with the times when children were needed at home. These schools sometimes evolved into private schools. From 1825 to 1866 the legislature assumed that parents, not the state, were responsible for education by assessing school taxes according to the number of children parents sent to the local schools. In the sectarian old order the most important alternative was some form of religious instruction. In either case, however, parents controlled the values children learned and the ways they learned them.[13]

The Unionist victories of the 1860s created a unique opportunity at the state level for the champions of change to impose an educational revolution by which they would circumvent traditional parents' resistance to the new order by reaching their children and persuading them to internalize the new values. A new public school system would spearhead a cultural revolution.

From a base in St. Louis, William Torrey Harris became a national leader of the educational revolution. Born to wealthy parents on a Connecticut farm in 1835, Harris moved west with his family in search of profits from land speculation. He landed in St. Louis in 1857 with a thirst for opportunities. Taking a job in the new public schools, Harris rose rapidly to become a principal and, in 1867, superintendent of the St. Louis public schools. His reports as superintendent, from 1868 to 1880, created his reputation as the nation's leading schoolman, and he became U. S. commissioner of education from 1889 to 1907. By shaping Missouri's largest public school system, Harris formed the model for the rest of the state.[14]

Harris began with boundless enthusiasm for the new order. "Civil society . . . exists for the creation and distribution of material resources. . . . Property is its ultimate object and aim," he told St. Louis teachers in 1872. The purpose of education was "the creation and preservation of property," proclaimed Harris. "Wherever the great mills and shops shall rise, there also shall arise the school house, equally a symbol of an industrial civilization," wrote Harris, a sentiment that echoed through his reports. Advising school administrators that "the conservative businessman" was their best ally, Harris explained that public school children ought to learn "first of all to respect the rights of organized industry."[15]

Harris wanted the new schools to stamp out traditional work patterns, impose the industrialists' work values, and get children to internalize the new values as their own. "The utmost energy of the teacher is expended in securing for all his pupils that formation of correct habits. Industry, punctuality, regularity, respect for the rights of others, and obedience to established authority—these are the cardinal virtues of the schoolroom and the foundation of his orders," he declared in 1872. In a society whose rhythms were increasingly dictated by new machinery, "punctuality becomes a moral virtue" and "discipline is quite essential, and must be carried out with great minuteness." Harris never tired of explaining how the new public schools were the best agency to teach the new values of the workplace:

> The discipline of our Public Schools, wherein punctuality and regularity are enforced and the pupils are continually taught to suppress mere self-will and inclination, is the best school of morality. Self-control is the basis of all moral virtues, and industrious and studious habits are the highest qualities we can form in our children.[16]

To those who complained that he had weakened the traditional educational objective of imparting knowledge, Harris repeated that "the reason why more stress is placed upon discipline than upon instruction here in America is plain. In our society and government we aim to place as few safe-guards as possible around the individual from without, and therefore our system of education must make the character strong and self-determined from within."[17] If schoolchildren were constantly forced to suppress their instincts, to obey orders, to be regular and punctual, they would internalize these values by the time they entered the workplace.

Factories provided the models of how schools could accomplish these goals. Traditional schooling, Harris wrote scornfully, was like the "antiquated process by which the gun was made throughout—lock, stock, and barrel—by one gunsmith." Modern schooling applied to schools "the division-of-labor systems . . . where each manipulation has a different workman to perform it."[18] The new guiding principles would be specialization, hierarchy, certification, uniformity, discipline, and classification, in schools as in industry.

The developers who came to power in the 1860s with the temporary post–Civil War disfranchisement of many traditional voters shared Harris's vision of how the schools should be changed. State school superintendent T. A. Parker explained in 1870 how economic growth required public schools to forge an official culture that would break down the resistance of traditional cultures to the new ways:

> Until our lands are occupied and our manufacturing interests properly represented, we shall continue to have communities composed of those who speak a different language, and whose views of society and government differ widely from our own. To assimilate [*sic*] these discordant elements and bring them into harmony with our institutions is the business of the public school. Were the representatives of the different nationalities left to establish their own schools, and to transmit their own peculiar views to their children, we should soon present the spectacle of a people bound together, not in bonds of sympathy, but by the strong arm of the law. . . . Our form of government is such, that in order to perpetuate it, some means must be used to disseminate its principles. . . . In an economic point of view the public school stands preeminent. . . . It is a safeguard to society, and our country's only hope.[19]

The purpose of the educational revolution, explained Parker's successor, John Monteith, was to create an official culture based on economic growth. Education fostered "virtue, truth, submission to authority, enterprise and thrift and thereby promotes national prosperity," declared Monteith, while ignorance encouraged "laziness, poverty, vice, crime, and riot." By increasing an individual's wants, education encouraged people to buy goods and thus stimulated markets for the new machines.[20]

The promoters concluded that the central battle in the war over education was over whether parents or the state had the largest claim to the values children learned. Superintendent Parker concluded that traditional Missourians resisted public schools because of "their understanding of the relation existing between the parent and the child, by virtue of which education is a domestic duty, with which the public has no concern whatever." To the developers, on the other hand, "the children are the hope of the State, and the latter should provide the best guarantees for its safety and security, in the education of the former." The public schools would instill in Missourians values that would restrain them from using their right to vote to challenge the powerful.[21]

Developers proceeded with a kind of frantic energy born of the fear that their political opportunity would be brief and that they had to reach every corner of the state before parents, taxpayers, and communities could mobilize effective opposition. Fearful that they could lose the war over education at any moment, they hastily abolished popular votes on school taxes. Elections provided the easiest way for traditional Missourians to overturn the promoters' plans, as taxpayers were proving by voting against railroad bonds. In place of traditions that had given power over education to parents and a majority of local taxpayers, the Radicals used their power over state government to establish local school boards across the state, which were managed by the Radicals' allies among business and professional men. These boards were empowered to levy taxes for schools without calling for popular votes. Because education's new role was to protect the new economic order and the state, and because they feared opposition from parents, Radicals required all taxpayers, not just parents of schoolchildren, to pay school taxes. By 1875 the Radicals had created the structures for the new education. More than half the state's children between five and twenty-one were enrolled in the 7,325 public schoolhouses across the state, where 9,651 teachers taught 394,780 students. When more conservative politicians did indeed return to political power in the mid-1870s, as the Radicals had feared, they created more decentralized school administration, limited the amount that local communities could spend on public education, and established a two-thirds vote as a requirement for local school taxes, but these changes did not undo the developers' basic achievement.[22]

Building from the Radicals' base, and inspired by Harris, champions of progress worked closely with schoolmen to make public schools into the most important cultural agency of the new order. Some promoters, like state superintendent John Monteith in 1872, enlisted support from businessmen by promising that public schools would weaken the appeal of labor unions and strikes, while others, like Governor Thomas Crittenden in 1881, appealed to fears of rowdyism and unrest from below by declaring that "parsimony towards education is liberality towards crime." "The best thing to be taught in our public schools is obedience to law and order," declared Principal Henry A. White of Kansas City's Franklin School in 1876. Superintendents like Monteith and T. A. Parker repeatedly maintained that the new public schools were an essential partner of the new railroads in erasing traditional values. The railroads eroded isolation and created a competitive order, while the public schools created the common values and disciplines, the unified, common culture, that would replace the diversity that isolation had nurtured. The turning point for the Bollinger County public schools, wrote county superintendent I. H. Sample in 1869, was the arrival of the railroad: "The competition of the St. Louis and Iron Mountain Railroad has inaugurated a new era in nearly every department of improvement. Both capital and intelligence from abroad are being introduced in our midst."[23]

The new public schools taught the new order's cultural values of obedience to authority, punctuality, sobriety, and self-control. The first rule of the St. Louis public schools in 1884 was that "the pupils must, on all occasions, be obedient to their teachers." "Stand straight," "Don't lean against the wall," "Don't talk, but listen," "Speak when you are spoken to" were the predominant lessons in the St. Louis schools, according to J. M. Rice's 1892 report for *Forum* magazine. In smaller communities, too, school leaders insisted that the most important lesson was that "pupils are required to conform cheerfully and promptly to the rules of the school, and to obey promptly and precisely all of its requirements," as at Columbia, and that "No pupil shall 'talk back' to any teacher," as at Lebanon. St. Joseph officials considered their schools a success by 1865 because teachers had "subdued the most unruly and forced them to yield a ready submission to the wholesome laws of the school." Schoolmen across the state believed that the best evidence that students had learned to obey their teachers and others who lacked the familiar authority of family and neighbors was if students sat quietly. At Lexington teachers were required to enforce "the entire suppression of noise and communication among pupils during school hours, and not to proceed with the exercises of the school while there is want of proper order and silence in the school room," while at Richmond, "Pupils are forbidden to study aloud, to make signs, to whisper, or in any way to attract the attention of others during school hours."[24]

School officials struggled heroically to compel youngsters to learn to regulate their lives by the time clocks that would soon regulate their employment. The object was "to inculcate, and, as it were, engraft on the very nature and personality of the child habits of promptness and punctuality," explained St. Joseph school superintendent Edward Neely. In the new order, Kirksville officials reminded students, "Time is money." Schools from elementary grades to the University of Missouri gave awards to encourage punctuality. Punctuality was such an important value in the new world of school and factory that Kansas City superintendent J. M. Greenwood proclaimed that "the thoughtless parent who allows his child to be habitually tardy, is an enemy to his own offspring and a disorganizer in society."[25]

Traditional Missourians, both parents and children, used frontal assaults, alternatives, dodges, and indifference to resist the new public schools. Promoters and school administrators painfully concluded that they could build schools, compel taxes, and require punctuality and obedience without ever persuading parents to accept the state as a substitute for family or church and without ever persuading children to internalize the new values. The basic problem was that "the growth of public education, by the State, has been slow and by forced methods, at times in advance of popular favor," superintendent Parker reluctantly admitted in 1869. As a result, parents encourage their children to rebel against the new schools. "Frequently the child is confirmed in the vilest habits contracted at home before he ever enters the school room and the teacher may exhaust all her skill in trying to eradicate the evil in the child's nature," observed Kansas City's Greenwood. "It is not an unusual occurrence for the parent instead of assisting the teacher, to set up his influence in opposition thereto, thus, encouraging the child to commit offenses aginst the peace and quiet of the school." In the cultural war between the traditional world of parents and the new world of the public school, "the greatest obstacle which our teachers have had to encounter in the way of securing punctual and regular attendance has been the indifference and in many cases decided and willful opposition of the parents themselves," complained Superintendent Neely from St. Joseph.[26]

Members of many of Missouri's traditional cultures escaped the public schools and their official culture by turning to the schools of their religious denominations. Outraged that the new public schools taught obedience to human and secular authority and amoral values, many devout Christians sent their children to sectarian schools. "We would . . . emphasize the importance of having our children educated under Christian influences," the Salt River Baptist Association in northeastern Missouri formally resolved in 1883. "Our people have been fully aware that Christian education, deep and high and thorough, is the bulwark of the church and the safeguard of the Bible. . . . Secular education exclusive of the Bible is the devil's prime factor in the fearful work of human destruction," concluded W. H. Lewis, historian of Missouri Methodism in 1890. "Denominational education," resolved the Polk County Baptist Association in 1879, "is of paramount importance to the efficiency and further growth of our Zion." To many of Missouri's Catholics the "godless public schools" represented the greatest menace from the dominant culture, beckoning Catholics to foresake traditional ways and beliefs.[27]

The rapid spread of public schools only intensified drives by both Catholics and Protestants to offer religious instruction. Protestants capped their denominational schools with academies and colleges that served the additional purpose of training the sect's future spiritual leaders. "Infidelity, and almost every false doctrine and ism ever thought of, are being advocated in our midst. We must have men able to meet and refute them," resolved the Spring River Baptist Association in southwest Missouri in 1876. The solution was to support the Pierce City Baptist College. Similarly, the Salt River Baptist Association founded Louisiana Baptist College in 1869. Beginning with William Jewell College in 1849, Missouri's Baptists created sixteen colleges and seminaries by 1906. By 1909 Missouri's Disciples of Christ had created thirty-three schools and colleges, and the state's Methodists boasted over a hundred schools and colleges. While the percentage of St. Louis schoolchildren in parochial schools declined from 36.5 in 1860 to 19.4 in 1880 and remained at that level until World War I, the number of children in that city's parochial schools rose from 6,972 in 1860 to 12,341 in 1880 and 26,753 in 1920. Secondary education at Cape Girardeau in 1883 was exclusively the province of church and other private schools.[28]

The preference of many traditional Missourians for religious instruction frightened promoters, who feared that church-controlled schools would immunize children from the new official culture. School officials, like the state superintendent in 1870, hoped to meet this opposition and create greater legitimacy for public schools by encouraging public school teachers to read the Bible regularly in their classes.[29] But the gesture did not convince traditional Missourians, who retained their distrust of secular schools.

Many other parents concluded that the new public schools threatened their traditional independence in several ways. County school superintendents in the 1860s and 1870s complained that parents "who cling to the time-honored ways of their fathers, and refuse to advance," retarded public education in St. Charles County, while local "prejudice against all innovations" was a problem in Linn County. The "old fogyism" of local residents was the chief obstacle to the public schools of Barry, Marion, Saline, and Wayne counties. Many old fogies resented the economic fact that higher taxes forced them to participate more in market activities in order to pay the new school taxes. Many others resisted the loss of physical and cultural control over their children that came when the state replaced the family as the shaper of children's education. Critics in Cole County lambasted the new public schools as "an offshoot of monarchial government" that subordinated citizens to the state. Still others resented the new disciplines of the public schools, which clearly favored children who had earlier acquired the new order's values at home. Madison County superintendent Daniel Peterson attacked the "injustice to the poor children" that resulted from "a one-sided course of discipline imposed by an aristocratic teacher."[30]

Parents and children resisted by refusing to enroll their children in the local public schools or, once they were enrolled, refusing to attend classes. While many parents refused at first to enroll their children, that form of resistance died out in many communties within decades after the establishment of local schools. By 1872 three-fifths of school-aged children in the typical county were enrolled in local public schools, and that proportion reached three-fourths by the mid-1880s, and four-fifths by the early 1890s. In many of the new cities, however, parents did not enroll their children. As late as 1886 less than half the school-aged youth of St. Joseph attended any school—public, private, or parochial—estimated Superintendent Neely. The majority of children "receive their education on the street, in the society of the vicious and in the haunts of iniquity. . . . They are the street gamins who spend their days in idleness and mischief, and their nights in petty depredations and incipient debauchery."[31]

The more typical and persistent way that traditional Missourians resisted the new schools was by enrolling but not attending. Among about half of all parents the desire for schooling was deeply felt, and their children attended regularly from the day the local schools opened. This was particularly true for the children of newly freed slaves, for whom the new schools were also the most obvious badge of their freedom. But the other half of Missouri's schoolchildren simply did not attend the schools in which they were formally enrolled. And this resistance continued unchanged for decades. The percentage of enrolled students who actually attended classes on a typical day in a typical county rose only from 56 in 1872 to 63 in 1903. By the turn of the century, the average daily attendance reached only 36 percent in the Kansas City public schools, 42 percent in St. Louis, and 58 percent in Chillicothe. Since some counties reported patently inaccurate statistics, the accompanying table includes only counties with reliable reports.

Percentage of Enrolled Students Attending School on Average Day

	1872	1884	1892	1903	1913
Average County	56%	64%	60%	63%	69%
Median County	58%	62%	60%	64%	71%

The champions of progress could create public schools, but they could not effectively compel students to attend. About two-fifths of enrolled students simply stayed home on any typical day from the early 1870s to the early 1900s. School administrators revealed their desperation and failure when they encroached further on parental prerogatives with compulsory school attendance laws in 1905, 1909, and 1911.[32] Even these laws failed to force a third of students to attend.

Missouri's school administrators despaired of compelling punctuality or regularity or even attendance. And even when they could compel attendance they could not compel students to pay attention, let alone to respect or internalize the new values. As workers from traditional cultures had vented their fury at employers' new and expensive machines by sabotaging them, their children showed their lack of respect for the new schools by attacking school property. Although respect for school property was a cardinal tenet in the new schools, the state superintendent gloomily reported in 1892 that 71,330 of the 97,912 desks in the state's public schools had been defaced by students. At Kansas City students covered school walls and fences with "silly, vulgar drawings, and too frequently the most obscene language."[33]

While many children from traditional backgrounds hoped that schools would help them gain greater control over their lives, they clearly failed to internalize many of the values the promoters wanted to instill. Black parents across the state showed more initial enthusiasm for the new schools than did whites, for example, but they found time clocks to be particularly alien, and by 1887 their children were four times more likely to be tardy in the St. Joseph schools than were whites. Other traditional parents believed that their children should skip school to participate in religious occasions, with the result at St. Joseph that "whole divisions [were] broken up in consequence of pupils being absent . . . to attend the religious instructions of their church." Missourians had oriented their lives around the weather far longer than around the new schools, and school officials at Carthage lamented that "with the near approach of Spring," many children "become affected with a malady known in school circles as 'Spring Fever' under the influence of which they will use extraordinary effort to become exempt from confinement." But perhaps the most common way they resisted was to gaze out the window at the more interesting things outside the school's confining walls. Principal

Lizzie Gunn complained to the St. Joseph school board that trains passing near her Mitchell Avenue School "have a tendency to keep the children distracted and inattentive to their studies." Principal J. W. Perkins of Kansas City's Washington School captured the general frustration experienced by teachers as they battled for the hearts and minds of the next generation by simply observing that "much difficulty is experienced by teachers in gaining the attention of pupils."[34]

The developers knew they had lost the cultural war over values.

7

The Democratic Culture of
Escape and Ragtime

Many traditional Missourians could not stand the strain of conforming to unfamiliar disciplines. Rather than directly attack the new economic leaders, however, they sought escape from the new disciplines by creating new, supportive cultures. By the early twentieth century these vibrant forms of release and escape would come to appeal even to many promoters of the new order, thus demonstrating that those with economic power had lost the cultural war. By providing the social settings that encouraged isolated groups to build a common culture, Missouri won national prominence for the popular and creative ways its traditional peoples proved that the economic losers were the cultural winners.

Traditional Missourians had long resisted new disciplines through escapes rooted in their occupations and cultures. Sometimes they turned the traditional task orientation of work into a new pattern in which they obeyed edicts for punctuality and sobriety on the job and then cut completely loose at the end of the workday or week. Pay day in the Lafayette County coal mines in the late 1880s, complained many miners' wives, meant "the beginning of a two days' carousal." Blacks sought release from new work disciplines by celebrating older ones. From all over Henry County blacks thronged to Clinton's Artesian Park to celebrate Emancipation Day in 1892, not by celebrating wages or freedom but by dressing as slaves, singing plantation melodies, and reenacting traditional cotton-ginning, corn-shucking, and to-bacco-stemming parties. Artist Thomas Hart Benton observed that gambling, drinking, and prostitution accompanied rapid economic growth in traditional communities because they offered the instant release people wanted when they first encountered the new disciplines. In the new sawmill town of Parma, Tobe Oller made his living in 1911 by shooting craps with drunken mill hands from the new lumber industry. In 1914 workers in the bootheel's boomtown of Kennett spent their last dimes at the new movie houses instead of paying their debts to local merchants, complained businessmen. As employers turned Sunday into the workers' only day of freedom, traditional Missourians turned it from a day of rest into a day of hard play that revolved around excursions, picnics, baseball, newspapers, and, frequently, drink.[1] Many Missourians now wanted release, not rest.

By the late nineteenth century many traditional Missourians began to see a clear pattern in what had at first appeared to be isolated encroachments. Temperance, Sunday closing, public schools, time clocks, police forces, job competition all seemed battlegrounds in the same war to replace traditional ways of life and work and force people to defer to the new demands for punctuality, sobriety, regularity, and obedience to authority. Employers, schoolmen, policemen, clergymen, and other leaders seemed to be forging a single, official, and alien culture. Once traditional Missourians perceived a narrowing war between themselves and the new leaders, they developed patterns of release and escape with collective, even political dimensions. At a Saturday-night opening in 1877 of a new resort in Sedalia, for example, Bessie Dunham "brought forth tumultuous applause" with a biting portrayal of railroad magnate Jim Fisk.[2] The audience's loud cheers combined politics with release.

Missourians wanted refuges where they could find both release from the new tensions and preservation of old values. Saloons were perfect. They offered companionship in place of competition and democracy in place of hierarchy. Whiskey and beer were stimulating and relaxing releases from the new tensions. Saloons were havens from the official culture: employers and schoolmen rarely entered. The saloon's companionship was more important than its liquor. Only one out of ten patrons of Kansas City's black saloons in the 1910s actually drank; the rest socialized. With the enemy so clear and friends so abundant, saloons became places where escape turned to resistance and politics. Nearby brothels likewise offered physical release from tension, along with love and intimacy, if only briefly and for a price. Gambling was an exciting way to try to buy instant independence from the new order. Players matched skills in an atmosphere of equality in which the best or the luckiest, not the richest, won. Joplin's saloons and brothels fulfilled "an unconscious yearning for sympathetic companionship" for young artist Thomas Hart Benton, as he sought escape from the competition, conspicuous consumption, and discipline of his middle-class home.[3]

Ethnic groups had their own beer gardens, pubs, and taverns. The wealthy might like polo, the poor baseball, the Scots curling, and the Italians bocce, but the fondness for some kind of sport was universal. Building from traditions of hard play, democracy, sociability, skill, and strength, these new gathering places were traditional in the frequent segregation of their patrons by ethnic and occupational backgrounds.

But there was one place where Missourians from different cultures mingled on equal terms, where the drive for release broke down the barriers between groups and encouraged people to build a common culture that incorporated strands from all backgrounds: the so-called sporting districts. The emotional yearning to escape from the new disciplines and the guilt that sometimes accompanied that escape created widespread demand for an underside in most communities. This was the part of town where, at least at night, disciplines, taboos, cultural divisions, and pressures to conform could be thrown aside. Here black and white, immigrant and native-born, rich and poor came together on clandestine terms of intimacy to celebrate their common release. Sharing with Thomas Hart Benton "the inability to conform to accepted behavior patterns," they joined him in patronizing those parts of their towns, which served, as Benton recalled, as an "asylum" where they could "get away from contact with respectability." Benton found his refuge in the sporting district of Joplin, where miners rubbed shoulders with businessmen. He quickly lost his virginity to a prostitute. As a refuge from Victorian morality as well as capitalism, the sporting belt enjoyed immunity, because the creators of the new order recognized that it was an essential safety valve and the enforcers of the new order, the police, frequently shared its profits and pleasures in exchange for immunity from arrest and prosecution. Governor Herbert Hadley, typically, urged the Kansas City police in 1910 not to close brothels but to move them out of residential areas so "they can be segregated in their natural habitat."[4]

To help attract customers from varied backgrounds, merchants in the sporting belt wanted a new culture that took familiar elements from those varied backgrounds and melded them into entertainment for all. And indeed, the sporting districts of several Missouri communities spawned a popular culture for the whole nation. The tenderloins of St. Louis and Sedalia earned national reputations as places where cultural barriers fell, where the common pursuit of escape outweighed even racial prejudice. In St. Louis's red-light district saloons, brothels, cafes, gambling parlors, and boarding houses sprawled from the boisterous Mississippi River levee toward the notorious Chestnut Valley and the Union Railroad Station. In the new railroad city of Sedalia in west central Missouri people sought release from the railroad yards and repair shops, from the processing and packing plants, in the saloons, honky-tonks, clubs, and brothels around East Main Street, which jumped to life when night fell on respectable Sedalia.

In 1900 the building at 121 East Main Street became a national symbol of the new popular culture that thrived on illicit release from disciplined respectability. The first floor housed the Blocher Seed Company, where Pettis County farmers purchased their needs. Upstairs was a social club where whites and blacks used rehearsal rooms, a corner piano, and a large bar for everything from political meetings to entertainment. In December 1898 a group of Sedalians formally incorporated a social club that using the second floor rooms. They called themselves the Maple Leaf Club. Soon the city's black ministers petitioned city officials to close the Maple Leaf and another club in order to "stop a great source of vice" and "create a better moral atmosphere for our young people." Out of this tension between demands for conformity and yearnings for release the thirty-year-old black musician who played the corner piano as the club's official "entertainer" created the *Maple Leaf Rag*. It brought national fame to its composer, Scott Joplin.[5]

Sporting belts like East Main Street and the Chestnut Valley, by providing the income, training, popular support, and merging of isolated cultures, allowed composers and performers to create in ragtime a new, popular, and profoundly democratic music. Ragtime's rhythms and melodies fairly pulsed with the desire for release from the new order and its disciplines.

Ragtime drew on the black experience in ways that spoke with eloquence and relevance to most Missourians by the late nineteenth century. For centuries blacks had turned to music to express daily protests and accommodations as well as a constant yearning for release. In their shouts, spirituals, cakewalks, and dances, accompanied by stamping and clapping, blacks developed syncopated rhythms in which the clapping and stamping were not strictly tied to formal beats. When, after emancipation, blacks began to acquire pianos, they replaced the clapping accompaniment with the piano's left hand and let the right hand carry the melody that had traditionally been carried by banjo, violin, and voice. Black folk dances directly inspired ragtime, for the rags' melodies were frequently dance tunes and the musicians intended the new music to accompany dancing. The call-and-response pattern between leader and chorus in black work songs inspired the unique bridges in ragtime. Originating in the ancient slave quest for release, black musical traditions fitted the needs of other cultures in the late nineteenth century.

The new ragtimers sought to project black musical traditions into a popular music that would free them from the limitations of both the growing commercial music industry and racial prejudice. The popular minstrel shows of the late nineteenth century, in which white performers caricatured black songs and dances, led directly to the popular "coon songs," in which whites, combining bigotry and envy, stereotyped blacks as uninhibited, fun-loving, lazy, musical, and promiscuous, as primitives who rejected the new disciplines. The coon songs led directly to a dance equivalent, the cakewalk, which provided the formal link between ragtime and the nineteenth-century European tradition of brass bands and marches. John Philip Sousa's *Washington Post March* (1899) introduced the two-step dance, and Sousa also played the closely related cakewalks while encouraging his trombone soloist, Missourian Arthur Pryor, to develop syncopated arrangements based on Pryor's deep familiarity with Missouri's folk rhythms. Soon marches, two-steps, cakewalks, and slow drags overlapped, to provide the structure and flexibility for syncopation on which ragtime musicians built.

The explosion of musical fads in the 1890s reflected the rapid emergence of a popular music publishing industry. Tin Pan Alley, as it came to be known, created mass markets for the new dances, but it also determined what was published and heard in the new markets for sheet music and piano rolls. Paralleling other industries, the Alley's publishers tried to produce the largest number of goods at the lowest price by cheapening the music so that it could be played by large numbers of potential buyers.

The black musicians whose work burst into the new markets from its spawning ground in Missouri's tenderloins had spent years developing the music that would soon be called ragtime. Coming from homes with strong musical backgrounds, they had begun with the black music they heard at work, at church, at home. In segregated America they could only earn a living at music by working in the sporting districts, where the pursuit of pleasure knew no color line. They traveled from place to place. At each stop they absorbed the folk music of the cultures around them. They congregated where there were jobs, in the tenderloins and at the edges of national attractions, such as the world's fairs at Chicago in 1893 and St. Louis in 1904. They recognized each other as members of a common fraternity, and they freely exchanged tunes, ideas, and skills.[6]

"Honest John" Turpin and his son, Thomas, made St. Louis into a ragtime center. A former slave from Georgia, Turpin moved his family to St. Louis and in the early 1880s established the Silver Dollar Saloon in the Chestnut Valley so that he would never again have to work for another man. From all over the Mississippi Valley black pianists headed toward the Silver Dollar. Soon their syncopated rhythms emanated from saloons and brothels throughout the Chestnut Valley. John's son, Thomas, continued his father's reputation as a leader of ragtime. In 1897 he persuaded a St. Louis firm to publish one of his pieces, *Harlem Rag*, the first rag by a black composer to be published, and he followed it with *Bowery Buck* (1899), *St. Louis Rag* (1903), and *Buffalo Rag* (1904). He opened his own establishments, the Rosebud and the Harrah Sporting Club, where other young pianists served their apprenticeships. From St. Louis itself came Sam Patterson and the legendary Louis Chauvin, from Ohio came Joe Jordan, and from Tennessee, Charlie Warfield. They exchanged ideas, experimented with syncopating a folk tune, staged piano-playing contests, and formed groups that traveled the Mississippi Valley from their St. Louis base. Caught up in the rhythms of the sporting district, they alternated hard work and hard play. "Lots of players didn't even bother to work except when they felt in the mood or needed a few dollars," recalled Patterson.[7]

By the late 1890s Scott Joplin had drawn on several local features to turn Sedalia into ragtime's creative equal to St. Louis. Born in Texarkana in 1868, Joplin absorbed in his childhood the musical traditions that he would later fuse. From his violin-playing father, a railroad laborer and former slave, Joplin learned respect for Western European musical dance forms such as the waltz, schottisch, and polka. His mother, a cleaning lady and church caretaker, was a good singer and banjo player who taught him the syncopated style of plantation dances and songs. From the church, to which his mother took him several times a week, he absorbed melodies and syncopation. From Julius Weiss, the German "professor" who gave him formal piano lessons, he absorbed a faith that classical music, particularly opera, created a kind of immortality for its composers. Joplin soon enjoyed local fame as a precocious pianist, and he played at churches and social gatherings. After his parents separated, his father urged him to take a railroad job, but his mother, who needed his income, encouraged him to continue his performances as an increasingly itinerant musician. By the late 1880s he left home for good and made St. Louis the initial base for his tours around the Mississippi Valley.

From his travels Joplin absorbed the sounds of America's traditional cultures. His music echoed with the sounds and rhythms of a brass band as it marched, a merry-go-round at a circus, a song from a church or saloon, and, above all, the exuberant mixture of song and dance that came together in sporting districts like the Chestnut Valley.

But Joplin differed from other musicians. He wanted the pieces he was creating to last beyond the immediate performance. And so around 1894 he moved to Sedalia to study at the Methodists' George R. Smith College for Negroes. He enrolled in composition and advanced harmony classes and supported his studies by playing the piano on East Main Street and the cornet in the black Queen City Concert Band, and by creating a touring group. In 1895 and 1896 he published five waltzes and marches. In *The Great Crush Collision March* (1896) he revealed his sympathy for victims of the new order. As a resident of the railroad town of Sedalia, with its frequent strikes, as the son and brother of railroad workers, as a pianist in bars where railroad workers came to unwind after a tense day manipulating dangerous machinery, Joplin knew why railroads were unpopular. With irony that appealed to his audience, he wrote on the top of this march, which depicted the collision of two fast-moving trains, "Dedicated to M.K.&T. Ry."

Joplin earned a reputation in Sedalia, however, for his pieces that united folklike melodies into a syncopated whole whose rhythms expressed the feeling for dance that attracted customers. He won local piano-playing contests. He attracted young musicians who wanted to learn ragtime. Two black Sedalians, Arthur Marshall and Scott Hayden, studied with him, and as his reputation grew, black pianist Joe Jordan came from Cincinnati and white pianist Brun Campbell from Oklahoma to work with him. Tom Turpin even came from St. Louis to hear for himself why Sedalia was becoming so famous.[8]

Viewing himself as a composer with a mission, Joplin began his search for a publisher who knew good from bad music, shared his vision of uniting musical traditions, and was unafraid of complex music that was hard to play—and to sell. That person, Joplin discovered in the summer of 1899, ran a music store only a few blocks from the places where Joplin had worked for five years. During his boyhood in Kentucky and Indiana, the fifty-eight-year-old John Stark had learned both white and black folk songs, which he loved to sing to his family. Before entering the music business in Sedalia in the 1880s he had been a traveling salesman for products as different as pianos and ice cream. With a salesman's enthusiasm, Stark soon saw himself as an apostle of music. He embraced European classics. Combining a love for both folk and classical music with a flair for promotion, Stark was more interested in producing for a local market than in cheapening products for mass markets. He was the ideal publisher to introduce white, middle-class purchasers of sheet music to the new ragtime that had originated in the forbidden tenderloins.

The partnership between Joplin and Stark that shaped what both soon envisioned as classical ragtime began late in the summer of 1899, when Stark agreed to publish *The Maple Leaf Rag*. Within six months Stark had sold 75,000 copies, and it ultimately sold over a million copies. It was the first ragtime hit and, in fact, the largest-selling piece of popular music in America up to that time. As late as World War I it remained the most frequently recorded piano roll. And it became a standard for amateur pianists in their middle-class homes and for professional musicians in saloons and honky-tonks. *The Maple Leaf Rag* popularized the musical conventions of the Missouri style of ragtime, sometimes known as "folk" or "classical" ragtime.[9]

Joplin quickly became "The King of Ragtime Writers," a label Stark placed with pride (and a keen eye for promotion) on Joplin's rags. Joplin went on to publish another thirty-eight rags, along with a ragtime instruction book for painists (1908), two syncopated concert waltzes, an opera (1911), nine songs, and seven other compositions. Stark used his profits from *The Maple Leaf Rag* to move to St. Louis and expand. Joplin soon followed him. Maintaining his commitment to the difficult Missouri style, Stark published twenty-four more of Joplin's compositions. Joplin influenced James Scott, a young musician from Neosho, Missouri, and Stark published twenty-five of Scott's thirty piano rags, including his popular *Frog Legs Rag* (1906), *Grace and Beauty* (1910), *Hilarity Rag* (1910), *The Ragtime Oriole* (1911) and *Climax Rag* (1914). Joplin also persuaded Stark to publish Joseph Lamb, widely hailed as the third of the major ragtime composers, whose major hit was *American Beauty Rag* (1913). Joplin and Stark collaborated on classical ragtime in other ways. Musicians at the time regarded Louis Chauvin as Joplin's only creative equal, but Chauvin had no desire to record his ideas. Joplin helped to preserve Chauvin's music by locating the dying pianist in a Chicago bar, persuading him to transcribe two of his themes, adding two of his own, and convincing Stark to publish their collaboration as *Heliotrope Bouquet*. Stark advertised it as "the audible poetry of motion." Joplin encouraged his Sedalia apprentices by collaborating with them on six piano rags, including *Swipesy Cake Walk* (1900) with Arthur Marshall and *Sunflower Slow Drag* (1901) and *Something Doing* (1903) with Scott Hayden.[10]

The Missouri style of ragtime was uniquely democratic. It came from the bottom up, as the first time that popular audiences heard unadulterated black music composed and played by blacks. Instead of feeling a competitive sense of possession about their compositions, the musicians regarded their music as common property to be exchanged, shared, built upon. The music was democratic, too, because it came from the one place in American society where a common objective—the pursuit of escape and release—lowered the barriers between social, racial, and cultural groups. It was popular with all groups.

Missouri ragtime fused sounds, melodies, and rhythms from many cultures and places into a common popular art. Joplin, for instance, turned a New Orleans bawdyhouse song, *Bucket's Got a Hole in It—Can't Get No Beer*, into the second theme of his *Paragon Rag* (1909). A ribald folk song of Mississippi River roustabouts was echoed in Ben Harney's *Cakewalk in the*

Sky; in a hit rag, *The St. Louis Tickle*; and even in Joplin's song, *Sarah Dear* (1905). From his home in Columbia the black virtuoso pianist, J. W. "Blind" Boone, began a forty-year career on the concert stage in 1880 by playing programs that included familiar hymns like *Nearer My God to Thee*, classics by Liszt and Chopin, popular songs like *Dixie*, and syncopated black folk songs. In his *Southern Rag Medley No. Two: Strains from the Flat Branch* (1909), Boone directly quoted such songs as *I'm Alabama Bound*, *Carrie's Gone to Kansas City*, and *Honey, Ain't You Sorry*. The titles of Boone's own songs reflected the surrounding folk world: *Dinah's Barbecue*, *You Can't Go to Glory Dat Way*, and *That Little German Band*. The folklike quality of the Missouri style in creative hands such as Joplin's lay not in the literal transcription of a particular song, but in the original incorporation of many folk materials into a single rag.[11]

Joplin himself wanted to extend even further the unique Missouri merger of folk and classical music. Encouraged by Weiss back in Texarkana, by his work at George R. Smith College, and by his study in the early twentieth century with Alfred Ernst, director of the St. Louis Choral Symphony Society, Joplin dreamed of transforming classical music to embrace American folk, particularly black, music. European composers encouraged the incorporation of folk materials into classical music, and Joplin may have known of Anton Dvořak's 1895 challenge to American composers to use folk and especially black music and of Dvořak's *From the New World Symphony* and *American Quartet*, which attempted to point the way.

Joplin began by trying to stage a ragtime ballet suite, *The Ragtime Dance*, in the hope that Stark would publish it. He worked for several weeks on the orchestration, then rented Sedalia's Woods Opera House for a single night late in 1899, drew an orchestra from his old Queen City Concert Band, persuaded his brother Will to introduce the four dancing couples, and conducted the performance from the piano. In this suite Joplin incorporated ragtime's origins in formal dance, and he showcased a succession of popular dance steps. The audience loved it. Overwhelmed by the cost of selling music for a twenty-minute suite, Stark waited until 1902 to publish it and then did so mainly out of a sense of obligation to the composer of *The Maple Leaf Rag*.

Following his move to St. Louis in 1900, Joplin concentrated on composing and staging a ragtime opera, *A Guest of Honor*. Although Joplin published such rags as *The Entertainer* and *Elite Syncopations* soon after coming to St. Louis, Morris H. Rosenfeld, a composer of popular hits, told the *St. Louis Globe-Democrat* in 1903 that Joplin "affirms that it is only a pastime for him to compose syncopated music and he longs for more arduous work. To this end he is assiduously toiling upon an opera, nearly a score of the numbers of which he has already composed." Joplin staged at least one performance of *A Guest of Honor* in St. Louis in 1903, and a company that he organized to tour the Midwest late in 1903 may have performed some or all of it, along with *The Ragtime Dance*. Although people who heard its songs considered it beautiful, no one has located a copy of this opera since its few performances in 1903.[12]

Joplin joined Stark in New York, where he hoped to find support for a second opera. But publishers wanted ragtime. Joplin published twenty more numbers, including many of his most classical rags. *Bethena—A Concert Waltz* (1905) was followed by *Gladiolus Rag, Searchlight Rag*, and *Rose Leaf Rag*, all in 1907, then by *Euphonic Sounds* (1909) and, finally, in 1914, *Magnetic Rag*, with the subtitle "Syncopations classiques."

As he concentrated more and more on fulfilling his dream of incorporating folk ragtime into the classical tradition, Joplin worried that trends in playing and publishing ragtime were running against the folk strands and high standards he and Stark had promoted as the Missouri style. He was appalled that pianists had become obsessed with displaying their speed, and that this increase in tempo was leading performers to abandon the original dance component in ragtime in favor of encouraging audiences to listen in silence. In reaction, he began with *Leola* in 1905 to instruct pianists: "Don't play this piece fast. It is never right to play 'rag-time' fast." He hoped to counter the shoddy schools of ragtime that were appearing everywhere by publishing his own complex exercises, *The School of Ragtime*, in 1908. "That real ragtime of the higher class is rather difficult to play is a painful truth which most pianists have discovered," he wrote. Joplin's real enemy was the tendency toward cheapened production that buried quality and skill, as publishers cashed in on the ragtime fad. By 1910 the large publishers of Tin Pan Alley had virtually driven out smaller and regional publishers by controlling the distribution system and placing their own music racks in the large retail outlets. Unable to compete, John Stark returned to St. Louis in 1910, where he continued to publish what he called "classic rags" and to taunt the Alley from his old base on the Mississippi: "As Pike's Peak to a mole hill, so are our rag classics to the slush that fills the jobber's bulletins. . . . St. Louis is the Galileo of classic rags."[13]

As Joplin concentrated on his opera *Treemonisha*, he, too, learned that New York was not Missouri. Although blacks, from editors to entertainers, welcomed the illustrious newcomer from the West, and although his various residences became virtual boarding houses for musicians, Joplin lacked the encouragement for fusing folk with classical forms that he had found in Missouri. In New York, the center of commercialized vaudeville, where rigid lines of color and class drew tight distinctions between popular and classical music, the *New York Age*, a black paper, explained Joplin's problem in 1908: "From ragtime to grand opera is certainly a big jump." Popular musicians lacked the respect for folk materials that he had found in the Midwest. Publishers were uninterested in Joplin's difficult pieces and new forms. And the classical music community lacked people like St. Louisan Alfred Ernst, who believed that Joplin could contribute to classical music. At the height of his creative abilities, Joplin could only find publishers when he confined his classical experiments to the piano rag form and could only find promoters when he toured vaudeville as the "King of Ragtime."

But *Treemonisha* was his love and ambition and, after about 1909, obsession. One publisher after another rejected it. Finally, in 1911, he mortgaged his family's security by paying to publish the entire score for piano, soloists, and chorus, over two hundred pages, under his own imprint. "He has created an entirely new phase of musical art and has produced a thoroughly American opera. . . ," ran the review in *American Musician*:

> He has created an original type of music in which he employs syncopation in a most artistic and original manner. . . . Its composer has focused his mind upon a single object, and with a nature wholly in sympathy with it has hewn an entirely new form of operatic art. Its production would prove an interesting and potent achievement. . . .

It was the only notice inspired by *Treemonisha's* publication.

Joplin pressed on to find a producer, orchestrate the score, and stage a performance. After producers rejected it and a change of theater management aborted a planned 1913 performance, Joplin decided to stage it himself. He trained a cast of singers and dancers for a single performance in 1915 at the Lincoln Theater on 135th Street in Harlem. A small audience watched as the cast, without scenery or costumes, ran through the songs and dances while Joplin accompanied them from the piano. The polite applause of the audience at the end was the only notice anyone took of the only performance of *Treemonisha* until its revival in the 1970s. Joplin despaired, and his physical and mental health deteriorated from the terminal stages of the occupational disease of syphilis until he died on April 1, 1917.[14]

Treemonisha remains as Joplin's democratic vision. Its lyrical use of musical inheritances from many traditional cultures, along with a decidedly popular flavor that climaxes in the three major ragtime numbers, contribute to the opera's democratic structure and message. Joplin's use of folk language, song, rhythms, myths, and dances, particularly of blacks, has led many musicologists to hail it as America's first folk opera.

Joplin underscored *Treemonisha's* democratic thrust by starring the chorus instead of the soloists. The central dramatic issue in the opera is whether the chorus will finally side with Treemonisha, who represents education as a way to control community life, or with superstitious conjurers. The chorus directs Treemonisha to follow her mother's advice and orders Remus to rescue her. Exchanges between chorus, on the one hand, and conjurors and preachers, on the other, legitimate the worlds of both religion and superstition. The chorus orders Treemonisha's death with the words "Go on an' count." The chorus climaxes the opera in the long song, "We Will Trust You as Our Leader," in which the people accepted Treemonisha's message, and then celebrate by dancing "A Real Slow Drag," the concluding ragtime number. By giving unprecedented attention to the chorus, Joplin underlined his democratic message that communities, after all, possess the power to determine the values and leaders they wanted to govern themselves.[15]

In *Treemonisha* the chorus concludes that education will save blacks, but by education its members mean not the disciplines of the public schools, but the traditional ways communities had controlled life. In fact, the opera repeatedly celebrates the traditional pattern of hard work and hard play while rejecting the new disciplines of sobriety, punctuality, and obedience. Treemonisha's father, Ned, defiantly defends his habit of drinking while he farms: "I'm going to drink an' work my crop,/'Cause I think it is no sin." The cornhuskers announce that they have arrived to husk the corn, but first they decide to do a rousing ragtime folk dance. In the same vein the cotton pickers sing "We Will Rest Awhile."

Joplin saw education as the way blacks could escape superstition and acquire the ability to control their own lives and guide them by traditional values. While Harris and the public school leaders encouraged the individual to aspire to be better than the group, Joplin maintained the classic black faith that there was no individual salvation without community salvation. Treemonisha had acquired her education from a white lady, not a schoolhouse, and her new converts saw education as the traditional master-apprentice relationship. The community, not some outside economic power or certifying agent, determined the qualifications for its teacher-leader.

Treemonisha and her first apprentice, Remus, repeatedly demonstrate that the purposes of education are to defend traditional moral principles. He affirms the traditional values of obeying God's commandments, of acting like good neighbors, of fulfilling the duty of the strong to care for the weak, in short, of traditional moral tenets:

> Never treat your neighbors wrong,
> By causing them to grieve.
> Help the weak if you are strong,
> And never again deceive.
> Your deeds should please heaven's throng,
> For you are in their sight;
> You should never think of wrong,
> For wrong is never right.

Parson Alltalk receives the congregation's affirmation to his traditional moral challenges: "Does yer feel lak you've been redeemed?" "Does yer always aim ter speak de truth?" "Does yer love all yo' neighbors too?"

The clash between Joplin's use of folk musical materials to affirm traditional values, on the one hand, and the schoolmen's new purposes, values, and disciplines, established a basic pattern for the twentieth century. Out of the tenderloin districts of Missouri came a new musical art whose infectious folk exuberance and rhythms pulsed defiance of the rigid rhythms of life that the promoters of the new order hoped to impose. Ragtime liberated the singer, player, or dancer to accent whatever beat or note the performer wanted, to escape regimentation and express feelings. Ragtime's basic rhythmic impulse of releasing tension from regularized discipline saturated American popular music, from the classic piano rags to the songs and dances that emanated from vaudeville and the new commercial music industry. It lasted longer than earlier fads, from the late 1890s until the mid-1910s, because its folk materials and rhythmic tension directly answered a popular yearning for release and escape. "In fact people generally are beginning to think and talk and act in ragtime," reported one newspaper. "Everything is being syncopated, even conversation and political speeches." A new hit explained:

> I got a ragtime dog and a ragtime cat,
> A ragtime piano in my ragtime flat.
> I'm wearing ragtime clothes from hat to shoes.
> I read a paper called "The Ragtime News."
> I got ragtime habits and I talk that way.
> I sleep in ragtime and rag all day.
> Got ragtime troubles with my ragtime wife.
> I'm certainly leading a ragtime life![16]

Building from the longest experience of any culture in developing ways to escape external disciplines, black musicians developed ragtime in the one environment where a common yearning for release overcame social barriers. Scott Joplin observed that ragtime offered that release in a description for his *Wall Street Rag* (1909): "Listening to the strains of genuine negro ragtime, brokers forget their cares." The *Howard County News* explained how the music freed listeners from the new competition in its 1904 account of a concert by "Blind" Boone: "Not from the time when Boone first touched the keyboard . . . until the last mellifluent sound of the finale spent its force did his hearers realize that they were real living beings located on a dull old prosy world run on the principal [*sic*] of 'dog eat dog,' and the dog with the largest stomach gets the most dog."[17]

Ragtime's popularity filled creators of the new order with the fear that they could not dominate the hearts and minds of people. Like other Americans, Missourians not only refused to internalize the new disciplines, but they sang, danced, and played that refusal to embrace regularized discipline and competition in their musical culture of release. Leaders of the official culture complained that ragtime "savors too much of the primeval conception of music, whose basis was a rhythm that appealed to the physical rather than to the mental senses," or that, more bluntly, ragtime "overstimulates" passions. "Symbolic of the primitive morality" that tended to "lower moral standards" and subvert the new disciplines, ragtime originated "in the dens of vice and in the vilest of cabarets," among undisciplined, lazy blacks. The purpose of music ought to be to "pacify" people, but ragtime created "physical and mental disturbance," complained a leading businessman. "The chief law of ragtime," explained another critic with horror, "is to be lawless." Fearing unleashed emotion and despising its social origins, defenders of capitalism and Victorian morality tried vainly to suppress ragtime. In New York, for example, the commissioner of docks in 1902 banned ragtime from free summer pier concerts and the superintendent of vacation schools banned it from school music programs in 1914.[18] The persistence of ragtime, the forging of a culture of release and escape that united people from different cultures, reminded the promoters that they had lost the cultural war.

Ragtime's sense of throwing off discipline also offended traditional people. Religious traditionalists feared that the new forms of escape reflected an erosion of traditional moral authority in both their secularism and their commercialized vice. They weakened people's traditional responsibility to assist each other. Drink, for example, weakened the family. Associating ragtime with brothels and saloons, Eubie Blake's mother stopped him from playing the new music, saying, "Take that ragtime out of my house." While bitterly condemning the new order, some traditionalists made common cause with the promoters in seeking to close the sporting districts that had been the creative wellsprings of ragtime.[19]

Other traditionalists protested that the culture of escape was, after all, escape, pure and simple. However enjoyable the drinking, gambling, sex, or music, however strongly the culture of escape preserved traditional values in their forms of release, that culture did nothing to challenge the new order directly. The black *New York Age* complained that ragtime inspired interest in folk songs that went back to slavery, while doing nothing to improve the conditions of blacks in 1913.[20] After releasing the tensions built up by their chafing at the new order's disciplines, Missourians still faced the same factories and schools.

The central fact remained, however, that in ragtime Missourians created their own world, one with a fundamentally different vision than that of the promoters. As the promoters tried to make them obey new disciplines, traditional Missourians struck back in the least expected place, by pushing aside the new schools and official culture to lay claim to the whole field of popular culture. And they did it with such profound mockery and contempt for the new leaders and their values that they stripped those leaders' claims to popular legitimacy. They built the experience of democracy by proving that traditional cultures could be united in democratic ways.

V

Mutual Aid

To combat the growing insecurities in their daily lives traditional Missourians needed more substantial and permanent help than outlawry or escape provided. They wanted relief, not release, and they found it by expanding the paternal and fraternal bonds of the old order into new patterns of mutual assistance. Missourians tried to cling to traditional supports when huge new markets eroded the ability of local markets and personal networks to control economic activity, and when the new competition increasingly left families unable to protect themselves. Around their familiar religious, racial, and ethnic groups they expanded an earlier pattern of mutual aid. They gave new meaning and force to traditional family obligations by creating fraternal orders and cooperatives that assisted their members in fulfilling those obligations while projecting an alternative vision of and giving an alternative form to the pursuit of profit that dominated the surrounding new order. These new forms of mutual aid extended the experience of kinship beyond the traditional bonds of blood relations and broadened the meaning of community beyond the traditional limits of geography.

8

The Protections of Church, Race, and Language

The new order transformed the ways that Missourians used their ethnic, racial, and religious cultures to give meaning and control to their lives. In the old order that meaning had come from the integration of culture, economic activity, and place. Religion or race or language were simply pieces of a larger whole. When competition shattered this traditional unity of life, Missourians had to choose whether they could best find security by building from their cultures, their workplaces, or their communities.

The challenges of the new order drove many Missourians to identify more with and build from their religious, ethnic, and racial backgrounds. For one thing, the new order placed special strains on the family's capacity to direct life by encouraging individualism and secularism, by bringing traditional cultures into proximity and competition, and by placing fathers into competition with their children. Church, race, and nationality had long supported family life, and many Missourians hoped they could be used to restrengthen the family.

The increasing competition and contact with peoples from different races, religions, and nations drove many traditional Missourians to identify more deeply with their own backgrounds. Being a white Irish Catholic meant little in County Cork, but it became a defining feature, one to defend, in St. Louis as one competed and interacted with Italian Catholics, evangelical white Protestants, and blacks. Proximity to strangers raised all manner of economic, social, and sexual anxieties, while it fueled conflict between generations within the same cultures. With increased proximity, many Missourians believed that their traditions and sometimes their very lives required the tolerance or at least indifference of people with greater numbers, wealth, or power. Knowing that their culture would be judged by the behavior of its most unusual members, they tried to maintain control over all members. And

133

they developed a heightened sense of their cultures as they worried about defection of members through opportunity, intimidation, and intermarriage. Missourians came to belive that they had found security and friendship when they heard the same language, saw the same race, and worshipped the same God. Here they found people who shared their sense of what was right and wrong.

By linking Missourians across time to a common heritage, however tragic, of mutual concern, these cultures initially provided the most reassuring defense against the new order. From a common past they refashioned their ethnic, racial, and religious cultures into forms of mutual assistance that projected a vision of the proper relationships between people different than the law of the jungle to which the market seemed to be dooming them. From birth to death, from one generation backward to the last and forward to the next, each culture gave its members the faith that others would come to their aid. Their cultures offered material assistance, spiritual and psychological solace, companionship, familiar ways of understanding unfamiliar behavior, and, most importantly, the feeling that they belonged to something larger than themselves, that they could escape their isolating workplaces when they were with their own people. They were not alone.

Although particular patterns of mutual aid varied from one culture to another, they reflected common themes that defied the new economic thrust. Members related to each other as brothers and sisters, parents and children, cousins and aunts, in a sort of expanded kinship, not as competitors. Each member's duties toward others and the larger culture were moral, not economic. Members expected that strong individuals or the culture as a whole would aid them in times of trouble. They banished the pursuit of profit from the workings of mutual aid. Their traditions, languages, rituals, institutions, and disciplines bound members together against outsiders and their values. Even as they modified their ways of assisting and controlling their members, Missourians found the defenses of nationality, race, and religion attractive and powerful precisely because they seemed relatively unchanging, even eternal, in a world that change seemed to dominate.

1. Immigrant Cultures and Mutual Aid

Immigrant cultures retained a large core from the old order. Their members frequently had come to Missouri, after all, to protect that core from turmoil in their homelands. The very familiarity of that core in the face of a strange, sometimes hostile environment convinced Missourians that their ethnic cultures could be enlarged and reshaped to provide mutal aid and security. Although differences between groups, generations of the same group, locations in Missouri, and economic and social settings of particular periods led to differences in the ways ethnic groups created their cultures in Missouri, the search for mutual aid of some kind continued at all times.

At the center for most were the religious beliefs and activities that had guided their families since time beyond memory. But as they assisted troubled members in their new environment they came increasingly to emphasize the common language and nationality that they had taken for granted in their homelands. They turned to nationality because they needed enough members from a variety of occupations and regions to form cultural institutions in Missouri. Over the nineteenth century nationality increasingly united their homelands behind a common language, and in Missouri other people identified them by the language they spoke. Over time immigrant cultures would subtly extend their traditional concern with family preservation.

From this core immigrants created patterns of mutual aid that mobilized their traditions to bring relief from the new insecurities. For some it was a short step from their cultures' traditional unity of family, religion, and economics to a new form of mutual aid. Croats brought to St. Louis a belief in the Old Slavonic Rite of Catholicism and an almost tribal conception of economic and religious unity based on their governing institution, the *zadruga*, whose motto was "all for one and one for all." When they moved to St. Louis, they recreated traditional mutual aid by establishing zadruga-inspired boarding houses in which all boarders contributed equally to the rent and, after 1902, by creating St. Joseph's Church with Old Slavonic services in Croatian.[1] For other immigrants the promotion of ethnic solidarity and mutual aid served the aspirations of some members toward mobility and of others toward group cohesion.

Many Catholic Missourians created fraternal and benevolent societies in their local parishes through which parishioners aided members in distress, rejected profit as an objective, and shielded themselves from assimilative pressures. Bohemians founded the Checkho-Slavonic Benevolent Society at the same time as they founded their St. Louis church, in 1854, and by 1900 had established eleven other Bohemian benevolent societies. German Catholics aided each other in their parish benevolent societies and, after 1900, in the statewide Catholic Union of Missouri. In St. Louis, Irish Catholics established the Erin Benevolent Society in 1818, but after 1870 they concentrated in local chapters of the fraternal Ancient Order of Hibernians in their parishes. Inspired by their homeland's struggles for unity and independence, St. Louisans created the first Italian society in the United States in 1866. The new Societá d'Unione e Fratellanza Italiana rasied money to help impoverished countrymen in St. Louis as well as independence fighters in Italy. St. Louis Italians had created twenty mutual benefit societies by 1913. Syrians formed the Maronite Catholic Benevolent Society in St. Louis in 1901, while Hungarians and Poles joined national fraternal insurance bodies founded by their countrymen. By 1907 the St. Vincent de Paul Society had recruited St. Louis Catholics from forty-six parishes and all national backgrounds to aid Catholics in distress.[2]

Missouri's Jews also shared a belief in assisting members in times of trouble. Joining other German refugees, Reformed Jews established mutual aid organizations in St. Louis by 1844 and in Kansas City by 1864. The test of Jewish charity began in the 1880s when poor Orthodox Jews began seeking refuge in Missouri from the pogroms in Eastern Europe. Reform Jews created agencies to help these impoverished victims of repression while also encouraging them to erase their more embarrassing Orthodox habits from the sight of gentile Missourians. Beginning in 1886, Kansas City's Reform Jewish women established a school to help the poor newcomers find jobs, and then a free kindergarten, bath, savings bank, night school, and mission school.

As Orthodox Jews accumulated the means and experience they established their own organizations and increasingly assumed control over all Jewish charities. To care for their elderly members Orthodox Jews in St. Louis mounted their largest charitable effort up to that point to create an old folks' home that opened in 1907. Sensing their loss of control to the more numerous Orthodox, Reform Jews led the campaign to pool the charitable resources of both groups as the United Jewish Charities in Kansas City in 1901 and the Jewish Charitable and Educational Union in St. Louis that same year. Over its first decade the United Jewish Charities established a day nursery, an employment bureau, a settlement house, a library, a camp for children, and series of concerts and lectures in Kansas City. Implementing the tradition that strong individuals and the group cared for weak members, St. Louis Jews "have by their own efforts almost banished extreme poverty among people of their faith," observed the *Globe-Democrat* in 1911.[3]

By participating in activities that aided their suffering members, Missouri's immigrants and their children gave new meaning and strength to traditional moral and religious doctrines that resisted the values and leaders of the new order. Reform Jews emphasized the ethical bases of brotherhood, and Catholics defended the moral character of work. "If all men are indeed beasts and if their destination is not preparation for eternity, but simply the struggle for their own good," argued the German Catholic *Amerika* from St. Louis in 1886, "then they should proceed after the model of the hyena and the tiger." The new order "has cut the working-man to the quick" by replacing "Christian labor for the love of God" with "modern labor for the mere sake of wages and sensual gratification," lamented the Catholic St. Louis *Review*. "When all the strata of society once more consider labor as *a moral calling*, as *a God-given office*, then, in place of commercialism and competition we shall have a noble rivalry to do one's best in the service of the whole community," wrote the *Review* in 1902.[4] The church battled zealously against the competitive and secularizing ideals of what was, in the end, an ungodly new order.

The moral base of protecting families, of resisting secularism and individualism, gradually evolved into a unity based more on language and nationality. In Ste. Genevieve 95 percent of Germans married other Germans between 1885 and 1889. By the outbreak of World War I St. Louis Germans had created over three hundred secular clubs. The Catholic church tried to respect the ethnicity of parishioners, because clerical leaders knew that Catholics would reject a church that ignored their ethnicity. Protesting against "Germanizing" in the St. Louis churches, the East St. Louis parish of St. Patrick's grew restive with the priest provided by the diocese. Demanding a recent Irish immigrant as priest, parishioners in 1899 threatened the incumbent with clubs and revolvers and hissed at the Sacraments. Appalled that a congregation would so blatantly challenge church authority in order to follow its ethnic traditions, the pope finally excommunicated the entire parish in 1899. By 1914, 34 of St. Louis's 89 Roman Catholic parishes officially used two languages.[5]

German immigrants to Washington in Franklin County built around their *Turnverein* a social world that shielded them against the isolating social order around them while encouraging a new nationalism. Emerging in early nineteenth-century German states to resist French influence and unite Germans across geographical and religious barriers, the *Turnverein* movement emphasized a common German culture. The *Turnverein* at Washington united Germans from all religious sects, and by 1866 the Turners build their own hall. They sang German songs and staged German plays. They doubly offended their native-born Protestant neighbors by following German custom and holding celebrations on Sundays at which they drank beer.[6]

Many immigrants feared that their cultures would only survive in Missouri as alternatives to the new order if their languages survived. Newspapers like *Il Pensiero* and *Le Lega* for St. Louis Italians and *Westliche Post* and *Amerika* for Germans helped to preserve those languages as they aided readers to interpret the outside world in familiar terms. Many parents passed on their languages to their children by speaking them at home, and they hoped to preserve their ethnicity by sending their children to schools conducted in their languages. In 1906, 256,953 churchgoers, or 21.4 percent of the state's church members, attended religious services that were conducted in a language other than English.[7]

Members of Missouri's ethnic cultures staged frequent celebrations to remind their children and their neighbors of their nationality's unique contributions. To perpetuate the Italian tradition of expressing religious faith through military processions, St. Louis Italians formed the Cavalleria Italo-Americana in 1892 to "increase the prestige of the Italian name before the American nation." Some 40,000 people gathered at St. Louis Park on May 7, 1906, to honor writer Friedrich von Schiller in a ceremony of German speeches and music that ended with a moving rendition of "The True German Heart." Irish immigrants reminded Missourians of a common hereditary enemy, Great Britain, when they celebrated St. Patrick's Day.[8]

As immigrant cultures evolved increasingly from defense of family to encouragement for emerging nationalisms, they became more responsive to events in Europe than to those in their own Missouri communities. As their relatives in Europe became more nationalistic, many immigrants faced horrible new fears when their adopted country for the first time in a century prepared for a war against their homelands.

Most Missourians had long sympathized with the Irish desire for freedom from British rule. As the movement for independence grew in Ireland, Missouri's Irish citizens felt compelled to prove their commitment in new ways and to intensify their Irishness. No longer could they merely raise money for the revolution and entertain its visiting leaders. As Irish nationalism spread, Missouri's Irish became embarrassed that they spoke English instead of their ancestral Gaelic. A Gaelic revival spread rapidly in the first decade of the twentieth century among St. Louisans of Irish ancestry, some of them removed by two generations from Ireland. "The town is Gaelic-mad," reported a St. Louis Irish Catholic newspaper in 1906. "People of Celtic stock are alleging hardness of hearing as an excuse for their taciturnity these days; the fact being that they cannot talk their native tongue, and for the first time in their life they are heartily ashamed of it."⁹

Missouri's Jews underwent a similar transformation. Instead of limiting mutual aid to care for their own young, old, and sick, many Jews increasingly focused their lives on events in remote places. Although physically removed for centuries from a national homeland, many Jews, particularly those from Eastern Europe, became zealous Zionists. In St. Louis the Daughters of Zion formed in 1900 with two hundred members, and in 1901 Beth Hamedrosh Hagodol formed the first congregational Zionist society. By 1904 St. Louis had eight Zionist groups. Russian immigrants formed Kansas City's first Ladies Zion Club in 1901. As Missouri's Irish felt increasingly bound to the revolutionary movement in Ireland, Missouri's Jews increasingly tied their identities to events in Europe that would lead to the Balfour Declaration in 1917.¹⁰

Between the outbreak of war in 1914 and American participation in 1917 Missouri's ethnic communities faced their greatest crisis. They organized massive campaigns to aid their countrymen while desperately fearing what their new government in Washington would do. The largest organized charity effort in the history of St. Louis occurred in October 1915, when over 100,000 people visited booths at a bazaar to raise money for wounded and imprisoned German and Austrian soldiers. By 1915 William M. Reedy believed that "the solidity of German-American sentiment is astounding." Soon the United States government and many citizen groups branded Germans, Irish, and others as enemies for the first time in their many generations of residing in America. Not only could they no longer publicly display their heightened sense of cultural nationalism, but they had to sacrifice their lives and treasure to a war against their homelands. And in their hearts the real war was between their culture and their adopted land. At a time when the *St. Louis Globe-Democrat* proclaimed that "for the first time America celebrates St. Patrick's Day with a mental reservation," St. Louis Mayor Henry Kiel, once proud of his German heritage, supported a police decision to cancel a concert by Austrian musician Fritz Kreisler, as though the Kreutzer Sonata were the Iron Cross.¹¹

The very cultural pride that had kept alive a tradition of mutual assistance amid the terrifying insecurities of the new order turned out to threaten the survival of those cultures. Before the events that led up to World War I, however, those cultures had nurtured relief from the new order's insecurities.

2. Segregation, Racial Control, and Mutual Aid

Black Missourians, some 6 percent of the state's population, created their patterns of mutual assistance in a more hostile environment than white immigrants faced. Their fight for freedom coincided with the drive by champions of progress to create a new order in which individuals could compete without prejudice of caste or place. Encountering the fierce resistance and, soon, the political power of traditional white Missourians arrayed against their hopes to compete as individuals, Missouri's newly freed slaves hoped to use their new freedom to fulfill old dreams. When large landowners and other employers turned to blacks as a source of cheap labor at the turn of the century, Missouri's blacks had developed such patterns of mutual assistance and race pride that they refused to accept the new order on their employers' terms. By then successful blacks had attained their success from the patronage of fellow blacks and, as a result, believed that the strong had deep obligations to the weak. The welfare of the individual was the welfare of the race in a world circumscribed by whites.

The patterns of racial segregation that evolved in Missouri after the Civil War never strayed from the fundamental fact that the white majority was determined to preserve the inferior status of blacks. The Constitution of 1875 mandated the separation of the races in marriages and schools. In 1889 the legislature enacted custom by formally prohibiting blacks from attending white public schools. The state segregated colleges and institutions for the blind, deaf, consumptive, and feeble-minded. Local governments cut blacks off from most public hospitals, parks, playgrounds, and swimming pools. Racial prejudice forced blacks to enter the St. Louis Coliseum by the rear door and to sit in the rear seats of Kansas City's theaters. Confining blacks to inferior housing, public authorities rarely enforced public health regulations against white owners of black living quarters. Hotels, bars, restaurants, barber shops, and other commercial establishments were often segregated. Whites organized to keep blacks from competing with them for jobs. Racial prejudice and its institutional form, segregation, pervaded every encounter between members of the two races. As the Clinton *Eye* observed in rebuking Theodore Roosevelt for violating its strictures, "This is a white man's country and President Roosevelt nor no other man or nation can make it aught else. His recent dining with Booker T. Washington has toppled Teddy from the pinnacle to which he was rapidly being accorded in the public eye and all classes regret it."[12]

Determined to express their newly won freedom and preserve their pride in the face of a hostile white majority, Missouri's blacks created new patterns of mutual aid to free themselves from the dependence on whites that had been their lot under slavery. They simply refused to accept the white contention that white skin conferred higher status. "I regret the color of our skin makes it necessary for us to thus serve God," declared St. Louis Baptist preacher J. L. Cohron to fellow black clergymen. Missouri's blacks organized, sometimes with white allies, to resist each new proposal for segregation, and thereby saved their communities from the patterns of segregation that existed in other southern and border areas. St. Louis blacks in the late nineteenth century blocked the adoption of segregated streetcars. When other cities in the 1910s copied Baltimore's example of enacting ordinances to segregate housing, Missouri's blacks repeatedly halted similar ordinances in the city councils of Kansas City and St. Louis, and when St. Louis voters enacted one in 1916 they blocked its enforcement in the courts. They persuaded the legislature not to enact bills in 1907 and 1913 that would have extended segregation to such new areas as trains. And they preserved the right to vote at a time when southern states were disenfranchising black voters. In fact, St. Louisan Charles H. Turpin became the state's first elected black officeholder in 1911 when he was chosen constable.[13]

Missouri's blacks tried to preserve their pride further by turning segregation into a weapon for independence and solidarity. They insisted that white authorities create parallel institutions for blacks. By fighting to create and control their own schools, churches, hospitals, and fraternal orders, they developed means for mutual aid that measured their independence from their former white masters.

Denied education before the Civil War by state law, Missouri's blacks believed that the most concrete evidence of their new freedom would be the establishment of public schools where they could translate their freedom into knowledge and power. They wanted the state to make a full commitment to educate black children in ways that met their concerns. In implementing the right to education in the 1865 constitution, blacks and their Radical allies relied at first on strong state supervision to overcome local prejudice against both blacks and public schools. Led by St. Louis and Kansas City, the state's public school system by 1875 enrolled 35.4 percent of black children between five and twenty-one and 56.0 percent of white children. Although many school boards tried subterfuges to escape their legal obligation to create schools for blacks in the era of greater decentralization that began in the mid-1870s, black parents increasingly won their battle. By 1901 the state's public schools enrolled 65 percent of black children between six and twenty and 73 percent of white children. By 1915 the proportions reached 76 percent for blacks and 87 percent for whites.[14]

Missouri's blacks were more effective in compelling public authorities to create schools for their children than were blacks in the Deep South. Less than half of black children were enrolled in the public schools of eight southern states in 1912, a time when 73 percent of Missouri's black youngsters attended public schools. By 1917 Missouri spent more money for each black student than did any other state with segregated schools.[15]

After fighting to secure public schools, Missouri's black parents tried to compel the authorities to equalize black and white schools. In the 1910s Kansas City's black schools simply received equipment discarded by white schools. At the same time across the state in rural Pike County three scholars had to cram together at two-person desks in one black school, and at the other students sat on five log benches hewn by slaves before the Civil War and brought to the black school when their original lodging, a white school, had been torn down forty years earlier. In 1890 seventy-six black students crammed into a one-room schoolhouse with only sixty seats at Sturgeon in Boone County.[16]

Black parents were more successful in some areas than others. In two former slaveholding counties bordering the Missouri River in 1890, Boone and Howard counties, for example, the student-teacher ratios were approximately the same for both races. But there were 62 black students and only 39 whites for each teacher in Chariton County and 65 black and 49 white students for each Lafayette County teacher. By the 1910s even the reputedly fair Kansas City schools had 39 black and 35 white students to an average classroom. In 1898 Missouri had 203 public high schools for whites and only 2 for blacks, but by 1902 black parents had forced establishment of new "high schools" for their children in Boonville, Chillicothe, Columbia, Fulton, Hannibal, Louisiana, Macon, Marshall, Sedalia and Springfield, as well as those already established in St. Louis and Kansas City.[17]

Even though white school boards held formal power over black schools, black parents soon learned how to veto school policies and personnel, at least. Concluding that administrators would be unable to control anything if black children refused to attend schools, they made the boycott into their major weapon. In Boone County in the early 1890s black parents boycotted the Hayden school because the teacher was a hated Democrat and the Centralia school because they disliked the school board's choice of location. Columbia's black parents in 1901–2 forced the board to dismiss the black principal of Douglass School because they disapproved of both his morals and his politics.[18]

Missouri's blacks fought to make public education meet their unique concerns. Many black parents felt deeply suspicious toward the patronizing and ill-trained white teachers who taught their children in the years immediately following emancipation. They demanded black teachers for their children. "There is a prejudice among both whites and blacks against white teachers for colored schools," wrote state school superintendent R. D. Shannon in 1875, and that prejudice blocked white teachers from understanding black children and black parents from accepting them. By the fall of 1877 black parents in St. Louis mobilized a boycott of the schools until the board of education hired black teachers. Attacking the "false and wicked ideas" of white teachers, the Colored Educational Council that fall insisted that black teachers, by associating with black parents, "know better the wants of their pupils and how to supply them," and argued that "by example and intercourse" they could better serve their race's needs. The school board promptly began to hire black teachers, and black parents ended their boycott. Black attendance in the city's schools jumped from 1,500 in 1876, before the hiring of black teachers, to 3,600 by 1880. St. Louis pointed the way for the rest of the state. By 1891 there were 722 black teachers employed in eighty-five Missouri counties. Black parents had won this battle.[19]

The successful campaign for black teachers created community leaders whose personal welfare was intimately tied to that of their race. By 1914 St. Louis's black male educators, mostly principals and high school teachers, were the best-paid blacks in the city. Some of the nation's leading black scholars taught in Missouri's black high schools, notably Sumner High in St. Louis and Lincoln High in Kansas City. With better instructors than many of the state's white high schools, Missouri's black high schools were a source of enormous race pride and aspiration. "In equipment, quality of work, and educational opportunities," wrote the inspector for the United States Bureau of Education in 1917, Sumner High "stands first among the public high schools for colored people in the United States." That year over a thousand students enrolled at Sumner. St. Louis blacks measured their progress since emancipation as their children studied with such Sumner High teachers as biologist Charles H. Turner. Turner, who had a doctorate from the University of Chicago, contributed research papers to leading scientific journals and international conferences and was one of the few scientists elected to the academies of science of both Illinois and St. Louis. As leaders in their communities, high school teachers assumed special responsibilities to aid other blacks in distress. In 1911, for example, at least one teacher from Kansas City's Lincoln High visited each student's home.[20]

The demand for black teachers led to institutions to train them, and these institutions, in turn, became the major black opportunities for public higher education. Black soldiers and white philanthropists had founded Lincoln Institute in Jefferson City shortly after the Civil War to teach former slaves competitive methods of farming. By the 1870s, as blacks demanded black teachers and rallied behind the Lincoln Institute, the state government began to appropriate annual sums for training black teachers and finally took over full responsibility for Lincoln in 1879. Managed and taught by blacks since the 1870s, Lincoln shifted its mission as jobs for blacks changed. Its primary emphasis on teacher training faded about 1900 as teaching opportunities declined with the completion of the system of segregated schools. Steering a middle ground in the fierce controversy over the desirability of academic or industrial education by offering both, Lincoln expanded its industrial departments after 1900, when its students for the first time began to find jobs in skilled trades. The need for black teachers likewise led to the establishment of what became the major black public college in St. Louis. In 1889 the city's school board added a teacher-training department to Sumner High School, and this department gradually expanded until it became Harriet Beecher Stowe Teachers' College in the 1920s.[21]

By both choice and necessity segregated schools meant that blacks retained their racial heritage at the same time that public education attempted to socialize them into the values of the new order. More importantly, blacks came to believe that education would fulfill the promise of emancipation and that the most successful members of the race had obligations to advance the welfare of all local blacks. In this way segregated schools gave blacks a real measure of control over socialization, even as they nurtured a special form of mutual assistance.

Missouri's blacks fought to establish and control other public institutions that eased the insecurities fostered by emancipation, competition, and prejudice. Slavery had forced them to humiliate themselves to get basic services from their white masters. Now they insisted that government owed them the same services that it provided for whites as a matter of right, not charity. Promoting an industrial school for black girls to parallel an existing one for whites, the black St. Louis *Advance* explained in 1912, "Education in literary and practical directions is a duty of the State and not a charity of the citizens." Forced into jobs and housing that made them more vulnerable than whites to disease, black Missourians worried especially about health care. They felt at first skeptical about the ability of black doctors and, as a result, patronized white doctors and did not press the state to train black doctors as it did black teachers. By the turn of the century, however, they concluded that medical care ought to meet the unique needs of the black community. Blacks began to patronize black doctors to an extent that reached 50 percent in St. Louis by World War I, and they campaigned to compel public authorities to set up black-operated hospitals and centers for training black nurses. With a death rate twice that of local whites, Kansas City blacks forced the Hospital and Health Board in 1911 to turn over City Hospital to the management of black physicians and surgeons for black health care and the training of black nurses.[22]

Since religion had served as a basic defense during slavery, Missouri's blacks turned to it after emancipation to express their traditional faith in ways that proved their newfound freedom. While their masters had wanted slaves to internalize obedience from Christianity, slaves had converted Christianity into spiritual resistance that emphasized the dignity and equality of souls, redemption for personal suffering, eternal damnation for oppressors, and, above all, collective deliverance through faith. The call and response between individual and chorus, for example, reflected the traditional dependence of individuals on the support of the community.

After emancipation, blacks throughout Missouri broke from their masters' churches to form churches of their own as the most immediate badge of their freedom. From 1865 to 1867 alone black Baptists formed congregations at Fulton, Webster Groves, LaGrange, New Salem, Boonville, Rocheport, Columbia, Huntsville, Lexington, Mexico, Moberly, and Springfield. By 1880 Missouri's black Baptists had created 150 churches with 10,000 members, at a time when the state's white Baptists had 1,300 churches and 80,000 members. By 1906 the federal census identified 655 black congregations in Missouri with a total of 600 church buildings. Although the only clergymen they ever saw were intinerants who preached irregularly for what they could coax from their audiences, 100 sparsely-settled families of black farm workers in rural Pike County in the late 1910s maintained two separate churches in and around Paynesville.[23]

Blacks turned the new churches into social centers, emblems of freedom, and reinforcers of community values. St. Louis blacks in 1914 owned churches worth two-and-a-half times more than all black businesses. Church property was one-fourth the value of all black property in Columbia in 1900 and one-fifth of all black wealth, real and personal, in Kansas City in 1911.[24]

Around the new churches sprang up a network of associations that structured Missouri's black communities around the ethic of mutual assistance. Learning the desirability of mutual over individual effort from building churches, church members led crusades to care for individuals in bad times by means of fraternal organizations that frequently met in church buildings until they could afford lodge halls. Church members likewise created Sunday schools and young people's clubs at their churches to pass their culture and pride on to their children. By 1906, 22,912 blacks attended Sunday schools. Granted the legal right to form families for the first time with emancipation, Missouri blacks centered their family lives on churches, the sense of rituals such as marriage and baptism and informal community functions such as church suppers that abounded from St. Louis to rural Pike County. Shortly after emancipation only three of every five Boone County black couples used clergymen to perform their marriages, but by 1900 ministers married virtually all Boone County black couples, as churches became increasingly central to family life.[25] In churches Missouri's blacks could completely govern their lives.

Churches assumed the responsibility for aiding distressed members of the race. Kansas City's black Episcopal Church created Saint Simon's Nursery House in 1910 in the heart of the Hick's Hollow district to care for neglected children. That city's largest African Methodist Episcopal church, Allen Chapel, provided by the 1910s free baths, a swimming pool, a basketball court, a gymnasium, a library, and a day care center, as Dr. S. W. Bacote won national prominence as a leader in making churches into community centers. Pressured by his black parishioners, Father John McGuire established a settlement house for black working girls in St. Louis in 1913. The blacks' campaigns to create their own Young Men's and Young Women's Christian Associations in St. Louis and Kansas City in the 1910s reflected the same pride that their parents had expressed in building the first black churches a half-century earlier. Kansas City's blacks subscribed over $25,000 in ten days to create a Y.M.C.A. building. Concerned about friendless black girls who migrated to St. Louis, black women there opened the Phyllis Wheatley House in 1912, which soon became a branch of the Central Y.W.C.A. of St. Louis.[26]

The churches created the pattern of black support for black mutual enterprises. A guaranteed local market of black patrons insulated blacks' economic activities from the larger marketplace. Churches stimulated this process by providing meeting places for fraternal insurance groups and encouraging race enterprises. The Economic Club of Kansas City's black

Vine Street Baptist Church in the 1910s required its members to invest in black enterprises, for, as Asa Martin observed, "the churches are teaching their people to be proud of their race; to care for and support each other." Black churches operated colleges to train their sects' future clergymen at Western Baptist Bible College at Macon, Campbell-Stringer College for African Methodist Episcopal students at Jackson, and George R. Smith College for Methodists at Sedalia. Black Baptist and Methodist newspapers like the Jefferson City *Western Messenger*, the *Macon Messenger*, and the Sedalia *Times* repeatedly encouraged cooperative black enterprises. By the 1890s sixteen black newspapers flourished, encouraging racial solidarity as they followed the trail blazed by the pioneering St. Louis *Negro World* in 1875. Kansas City's Afro-American Investment and Employment Company found jobs for 2,700 men and 3,600 women in 1911 alone. Black patronage assured the survival in Kansas City by 1912 of four drugstores, four undertakers, a shoe store, a dry goods store, twenty-five cleaning and pressing establishments, seven saloons, eighty-five tailor shops, seventy-five pool halls, two newspapers, and several restaurants. Sedalia's blacks combined to build a theater in 1913. At St. Louis black patronage created a culturally united island in the competitive ocean, as the number of black businesses rose from 75 in 1902 to 288 by 1913.[27]

While the family was the source of resistance in other cultures, many blacks hoped that the new churches would fulfill the ancient dream, denied by law until the Civil War, of having stable families. Since slave families potentially undermined the slaveholders' power and investment, slaveholders had dispensed with marriage, separated families, assigned wives to other husbands, and generally "supervised" sexual and family relationships among slaves. Emancipation placed an enormous burden on black mothers, who had to perform their traditional function of providing for their children without the security of guaranteed food, clothes, and shelter for the children that had come with slavery. At St. Louis in 1880 nearly half of black mothers had to work to support their children, while only 13 percent of white mothers did. After emancipation many black churchgoers, particularly women, hoped that the new churches would nurture an inner sense of control to replace the external discipline that slaveholders had exercised.[28] They hoped that religion could rally those blacks who favored stable families.

Black women shared with white women the hope that churches could instill communal and moral values and disciplines as alternatives to the new secular and individualistic ones. While the new pressures for personal escape affected both races, black women in Missouri were even more determined than whites to use churches in this way. In 1906, 67 percent of the state's black Baptist and Methodist churchgoers were women, while 61 percent of white Baptists and Methodists were women. Black churches frequently became the earliest crusaders against secular and "immoral" escapes. Black churchwomen spearheaded a Woman's Christian Temperance Union at Jefferson City in 1890 in a local crusade that white women did not join until 1892. Black churchwomen likewise provided the margin of difference when

Ray County voters decided to make their country dry in 1887, by convincing their husbands, brothers, fathers and sons. Black women merged concern for family and moral uplift in such organizations as the F. E. W. Harper Leagues of St. Joseph and St. Louis, the Woman's Club of Jefferson City, and the Phyllis Wheatley Club of St. Louis. They fulfilled a special mission that combined race and sex by forming the National Association of Colored Women in the 1890s.[29] By encouraging family activities, by providing formal pressures, such as marriage and church discipline, and by seeking to teach internal moral constraints, black churches stimulated the family to become a source for resistance to the new order.

Racial segregation created black communities that were focused inward around traditions of mutual aid and race pride. Completely dependent on whites for their physical needs during slavery, now blacks developed schools, churches, and fraternal orders that gave them control over their lives that had been impossible before emancipation. The most successful felt special obligations, because they knew that their success depended on the support of other blacks. When individuals sought better jobs or homes, they confronted a recalcitrant white society. "The modern fight for human freedom is the fight of the individual man to be judged on his own merits and not saddled with the sins of a class for which he is not responsible," editorialized *The Crisis* against a 1913 Missouri segregation bill. But the plain truth was that white Missourians would not let them escape that responsibility. When black teachers and Pullman porters bought houses on Cook Avenue in St. Louis and Montgall Avenue in Kansas City in the 1910s, their white neighbors greeted them with rocks, dynamite, and arson. White labor unions tried to block them from taking better jobs.[30] The fight for the individual, then, was not to escape responsibility for the rest of the culture, but to help wage a collective fight for the whole race.

3. White Protestants and the Crises of Conduct and Control

The new order posed a desperate challenge to Missouri's white, English-speaking Protestants. The Protestant tradition of individualism attracted many to the new order's opportunities for individuals to transcend ancient restraints, while the traditions of moral conduct and of fervent hatred of secular intrusion into spiritual matters profoundly alienated many from the greed and secularism that rose around them. Evangelical Protestantism contained within it further contradictory traditions of submission and defiance, equality of souls and deference to rulers, that created excruciating conflicts within congregations and, indeed, within individual Protestants as they sought relief from the new insecurities. Even their position as a political majority created dilemmas. Unlike other traditional cultures, they were not forced by language, skin color, or religious practices to band together in defense against the majority's opportunities and intimidations. A tradition of regulating others' behavior collided with a militant belief in the separation of church and state. The result of that collision was profound ambivalence toward government regulation of behavior.

A quest for relief drove traditional Missourians in unprecedented numbers to churches and their contradictory appeals. Church membership rose from 735,839, or 27 percent of the state's population, in 1890, when comprehensive and comparable statistics were first compiled, to 1,370,551, or 41 percent of all Missourians, in 1916. The state's population grew less than 25 percent over this period, but the number of native-born, English-speaking Baptists grew 69 percent, Methodists 57 percent, Disciples of Christ 49 percent, and Presbyterians 45 percent.[31] Some of these members had simply followed their parents into their churches, but many others converted from unchurched backgrounds, concluding that religion might offer new help.

Evangelical Protestantism appealed most dramatically to Missourians in older parts of the state where the market economy had most thoroughly transformed familiar ways. By 1890 the more settled counties were twice as likely to have heavy concentrations of Baptists, Methodists, Disciples of Christ, and Presbyterians as were the newer, less-developed ones. Between 1890 and 1916, for example, while the population of the five north central counties of Harrison, Mercer, Putnam, Grundy, and Sullivan declined by 8 percent, Disciples of Christ membership rose by 78 percent, Baptists by 66 percent, and Methodists by 58 percent. The most prosperous counties in 1902 were six times more likely than the least prosperous ones to have a high proportion of residents who were members of the four leading Protestant denominations. These sects appealed particularly to residents in rural areas, where farming was changing from a way of life to a business. By 1916 the rural counties with the highest proportion of residents who belonged to evangelical sects were five times more likely also to be the most market-oriented of the agricultural counties.[32]

Overwhelmed by the transformation of their communities, established residents embraced evangelical Protestantism because it directly, passionately, and yet ambivalently addressed the central dichotomies in the new order, individual control versus moral restraint, this world or the next. On the one hand they shared with other traditional cultures an intense uneasiness at the new order's emerging secularism and competition, and they resembled others in the ways they drew on their traditions to protect members. They expected that the brotherhood and sisterhood of their sect and congregation would last for eternity. A Disciples of Christ primer told young members, "souls that loved here [will be] reunited and bound together in everlasting friendship." Methodists divided each congregation into classes, in the words of the 1892 discipline, in order "to secure the sub-pastoral oversight made necessary by our itinerant economy." As with other cultures, "the strong must help the weak," proclaimed *The Christian* of Sedalia in 1899, while Sedalia's *Harmony Baptist* instructed readers in 1898 to help people in need.[33]

Each sect and congregation developed its own forms of mutual aid. At Lexington in the 1870s, members of the Christian Church gave $25 to the Robinsons because the couple was too ill to work. The Methodists staged a play and donated the proceeds to their poor, and the Ladies' Guild of the Christ Church Episcopal visited sick members, reported their needs to the congregation, and gave them aid. Protestant denominations operated institutions to care for needy members. Methodists founded a children's home at St. Louis in 1865 and the Missouri Methodist Hospital at St. Joseph in 1897. Baptists opened the Missouri Baptist Orphans' Home at St. Louis in 1886 and the Missouri Home for Aged Baptists at Ironton in 1913. In the first decade of the twentieth century Methodists founded the Kingdom House in St. Louis and the Wesley House in South St. Joseph to provide day care, pure milk, recreation, and job training for their urban poor.[34]

Fearful of the corrosive influences of the secular knowledge and amoral values that many of them associated with the new order's materialism, they established clubs and publishing ventures as religious alternatives to secularism. Young people's clubs grew up on the 1870s to create fellowship within the denomination and to offer alternatives to the secular amusements that beckoned from outside the church. Methodists believed they were following John Wesley's injunction: "I desire to form a league, offensive and defensive, with every soldier of Jesus Christ." In 1889 they merged the youth groups into the Epworth League, and in 1891 Missouri's Southern Methodists officially adopted the Epworth League. Bitterly hostile toward cheap, secular, sensational newspapers and eager for methods of communication that would bind members together, native Protestants published hundreds of newspapers, magazines, tracts, and primers for their members. The Shoal Creek Baptist Association, for example, repeatedly urged southwest Missouri Baptists to read Baptist literature. Early in the twentieth century the Disciples of Christ founded a Board of Publication in Missouri as the base from which to send *The Christian Evangelist*, books, Sunday school supplies, young people's literature, and other tracts to Disciples across the country.[35]

Missourians carried their denominations with them as protection when the new order threw them into competition with people from other backgrounds. In rural Missouri Protestants encountered fierce resistance from established churches and from haters of religion. Pleasant Hill in Cass County was anything but pleasant for the Baptists who tried to organize a church there in 1881. Hostile toward religion and unwilling to give up the tradition of hunting and fishing on Sundays, local residents repeatedly threatened to kill the new Baptist preacher. Baptists found an equally hostile environment when they organized the Clear Creek Church in a Presbyterian area near Pierce City in 1882 and the Mount Zion Church in a Holiness and Christian area near Newtonia.[36]

They felt even a greater dependence on their religion for guidance when they moved to cities. "God made the country and man made the town," summarized the Methodist St. Louis *Central Christian Advocate* in 1890. Cities were particularly dangerous, warned the *Advocate*, because they threw native-born whites into competition with people from different backgrounds, particularly immigrants, while offering such secular temptations as saloons, newspapers, gambling, and Sabbath violations, which too often led people to foresake their families and their faith. Many were so eager to transplant their country churches onto city street corners that they were accused of ignoring urban realities. Many urban holiness sects revived the traditional Methodist camp meetings, as farmers and artisans brought their rural ways to the cities. The son of a Methodist preacher, Aura Clay Watkins formed a branch of the Church of God (Holiness) in Kansas City in 1914 patterned directly on his old church in Macon County. All but one of the new congregation's members came from the Macon area. In its membership, personal religion, and conservative theology, the new urban church was a copy of the old rural one.[37]

They clung so tenaciously to the old religious core because the new secularism and individualism were rapidly eroding traditional guides of conduct. Evengelical Protestantism, like social outlawry, grew directly from the erosion of traditional patterns of law and authority. In the natural order God gave the laws through the Bible for all time, according to the evangelicals, and it was each Christian's duty to obey those laws. But their eagerness for more wealth led Christians to violate God's commandments. Liberty, license, rebellion were the villains of the new order, and could only be banished by discipline, order, and obedience to ancient laws. "The purpose of God [is] to have the earth as free from the spirit of rebellion as the heavens now are," in the words of the Macon *Messenger of Peace* in 1882. Protestants echoed the Sedalia *Harmony Baptist*'s 1897 complaint that "everything seems to have gone wrong all at once and refuses to submit, be controlled or, to return to 'law and order.'" "How are we to maintain the family and civil relations if personal independence is to be accounted the first virtue?" demanded the Methodist *Central Christian Advocate* in 1886. "We shall have to retrace our steps, and learn that obedience . . . is an ennobling quality which lets men into the highest experiences of true freedom." Too many Protestants in the new order redefined liberty as "unhindered opportunity to do as they please," lamented Sedalia's Baptist editor in 1898. They had forgotten, warned a Primitive Baptist editor at Marceline, that all things of this world "are perishable and passeth away," while "the word of the Lord endureth forever."[38]

Even as they struggled to preserve the traditional supremacy of church over state, of moral over economic concerns, of congregational discipline over individual advancement, many evangelical Protestants feared that religion's power to control life in familiar ways was fading even as their numbers grew. Polling fifty Missouri Baptist preachers in 1906 on changes over the previous quarter-century, Reverend H. E. Truex found that the universal lament was that the new thrust was toward "bigness, not fitness" and that "discipline was a lost art." The more preachers became fund raisers, they noted, the less church trials and disciplines regulated conduct. "We are in danger of ignoring or neglecting the indispensable necessity of regeneration— of Christian experience—of deep-felt, genuine, vital religion; and in its place substituting formal profession—mere outward conformity to certain forms and ceremonies and ordinances—*formality* instead of *spirituality*," lamented Baptist preacher W. H. Burnham in 1906. Another Baptist minister observed in 1898 that his revivals no longer attracted people as in the past because "a generation has come into our churches which seems not to understand" traditional religion.[39]

Fear of declining spirituality resulted from accelerating pressures that encouraged simultaneous resistance and accommodation. Some evangelicals believed that the pressures originated completely outside religion and that "our intense commercialism is the thing which prevents a profound revival of religion," as a speaker told a Methodist congress in St. Louis in 1899. At the other extreme, some maintained that Protestantism had created the new order by encouraging "industrial habits, without which one may not hope to obtain the best in any of the walks of life," according to the historian of the Salt River Baptist Association in 1909. But there was little disagreement that the new order had unleashed new forces—industrialization, secularization, urbanization, immigration—that severely eroded traditional religious practices by eroding the traditional control and authority of the family. Blaming the decline of religiosity on "the decline of family life," the Methodist *Central Christian Advocate* complained in 1886 that "home is no longer home; the house is more like a hotel in which people are constantly coming and going" to work, to meetings, to concerts, and that, as a result, families now depended on external excitement for the happiness they had once derived from common prayer and Bible reading.[40]

Evangelical Protestants were divided in their advice to workers in the new order, even while they spoke with one voice on the proper nature of work. The Sedalia *Harmony Baptist* in 1899, agreed with the Catholics that "work is not the mere doing of one's tasks, the getting through with so much drudgery for the sake of wages at the end of the week." Instead, work "is an expression of one's spiritual energy." Too often "wealthy capitalists" shunned their moral responsibility to treat their workers with dignity because they succumbed to "competition," "greed," and "avarice," according to Methodist Reverend D. Marquett in 1886. Concerned above all to protect the family's role as the center of religious life, pietists frequently condemned child labor. The Methodist *Central Christian Advocate* cheered in 1890 when the American Sabbath Union proclaimed its goal of compelling employers to let workers rest on Sundays. Some evangelicals counseled workers to resist their immoral employers. Others believed that "a man's work is not done upon earth so long as God has anything for him to suffer; the greatest of our victories is to be won in passive endurance." Upholding the separation of church and state, many agreed with one Methodist preacher that "the difficulty is a moral one, and the remedy must be sought in the moral and religious realm rather than in the regions of legislation and political economy."[41]

It was this very recognition that the struggle between old and new order took place within the hearts and souls of individual Missourians that attracted so many troubled people to the evangelical sects. Some found churches that reinforced their rise to the top. Others, like bootheel tenants, confortably mixed evangelical religion and socialism. But for most Missourians evangelical Portestant traditions probably translated on a day-to-day basis less into militant rejection or acceptance of the new order than into feelings of guilt when they attended church or when they pursued individual gain or other secular "vices." Since "we are indebted to our noble mothers for the learning of Christianity which they infused into the rising generations," according to Methodist Thomas Shackelford in 1910,[42] many evangelical families probably resolved the tension by assuming that husbands and fathers would make the necessary secular compromises to provide food and shelter while wives and mothers transmitted traditional religious beliefs to the children.

When Protestants resolved their conflicts by forming churches that reflected the economic divisions in the secular world, and when churches lost their traditional power to discipline individual behavior, many Protestants concluded that the state was not, after all, such a bad alternative source of discipline. Loyalty to sect and congregation had been the highest loyalties in the old order, and people from all backgrounds had belonged to all churches. The wealthy had tended also to run the church tribunals that meted out church discipline. With the widespread competition and weakening of denominational ties that came with spreading secularism, Missourians increasingly formed churches with people who shared their economic positions. Since rich and poor now worshipped in different churches, and the poor were thus outside the reach of church discipline by economic leaders, many wealthy Protestants turned to the state to control behavior.

Many workers, for their part, concluded that the new economic leaders violated moral and religious traditions in their secular activities and were worthy neither to be members of their congregations nor dispensers of discipline. Slaves measured their freedom by immediately leaving their former masters' churches. Many white Protestant workers similarly bolted the churches of the new economic leaders, and turned instead to sects that emphasized the tradition of the equality and dignity of souls rather than submission. They concluded that fraternal support of other workers and ancient moral traditions offered greater promise of everlasting salvation than submission to the orders of businessmen. Marcus Pomeroy, an author popular with the state's workers, captured in *Our Saturday Nights* the special promise of dignity and brotherhood that evangelical religion encouraged: "Thank God the rich . . . cannot . . . keep the ones who labor from loving each other truly."[43]

Evangelical Protestants drew on their traditional ways of guiding conduct as they grappled with the paramount issue of alcohol. Their resolution of this issue over the half-century after the Civil War would lead them to ferocious struggles with other traditional religions equally dedicated to preserving the sanctity of family, community, and moral values. These struggles would show how completely the evangelicals had altered their approach to conduct.

Liquor became the paramount issue because evangelicals believed that victims of the new order turned to it for escape and, in so doing, robbed their families of economic and psychological support. Liquor, explained the Methodist *Central Christian Advocate* in 1886, was "the enemy of the home." The religious press repeatedly told of fathers who, crazed with drink, had killed their children or allowed their families to starve.[44] New saloons posed other threats. They served the new immigrants, who undermined the economic security of native-born Protestants. They corrupted politics. Drunkenness caused the loss of control and discipline that so haunted evangelicals. The struggle over liquor was a struggle to reconvert Protestants to older obligations.

Believing that the way to restore moral discipline was for the drinker to renounce sin and honor his traditional obligations, temperance advocates originally focused on the drinker's behavior rather than the saloon's temptation, on individual conversion, not state regulation. Temperance advocates grafted their goal onto the new fraternal orders. Although organized before the Civil War, the Independent Order of Good Templars grew most rapidly in the 1870s. Formed as "a 'Fraternal Union' of every friend to moral reform; to establish order in more perfect tranquility," the Sedalians who united in 1867 to establish Olive Leaf Lodge Number 91 publicly vowed neither to drink nor sell alcohol, "the source of so much crime, poverty, and sorrow in our community." By 1874 countrywide chapters of the I.O.G.T. had formed in Saline, Adair, McDonald and Pettis counties.[45]

Evangelical churches used traditional revivals to win private conversions and public commitments. Temperance revivals swept across Missouri in 1877 and 1878, appealing to workers and businessmen alike. Over two weeks in July 1877, two revivalists from the Murphy Temperance Movement convinced 1,700 Sedalians, mostly workers, to sign pledges of abstinence. Beginning in the new mining and industrial cities of Joplin and Carthage, the Red Ribbon and Blue Ribbon movements secured pledges of abstinence as they kindled feelings of personal responsibility by appealing to drinkers' guilt for destroying their families and giving in to temptations that deprived them of control over their lives. By 1878 one statewide temperance organization reported that 28,000 Missourians had signed pledges. Temperance swept through Protestant churches. As late as 1876 at least one Baptist church in the southwestern Shoal Creek association excluded members of temperance societies from church membership, but by the mid-1880s every church in the association was, in effect, a temperance society.[46]

Fired by the desire to preserve the traditional family, groups of angry Protestant women in the 1870s turned to direct action to remind males of the evils of drink. Denied the ballot, they asserted popular sovereignty after male politicians ignored it in order to cater to a few saloon keepers. Although voters had banned alcohol from Lathrop in Clinton County, city officials allowed two bars to continue to do business in 1890. There, temperance advocates charged, young men learned to drink for the first time, and older men, once abstinent, "were tempted back to their cups." Three boys had to be carried home "dead drunk." A drunken fight between a mechanic and a farmer only ended when the farmer stabbed the mechanic. The mechanic's wife led a drive to close the saloons. Infuriated because "wretchedness was coming to their homes," a band of praying women marched to the saloons and demanded that the saloon keepers leave town. The saloon keepers nervously locked their doors. The women stormed the saloons, breaking the windows, demolishing the fixtures, and pouring out the liquor. Amen, cried the Methodist *Advocate* from St. Louis. Protestant discipline had filled the void left by the civil authorities.[47]

Desperate Protestant women became the earliest temperance forces to focus on the saloon, not the drinker, and to ask the state to do the work of regulating behavior that churches had traditionally done. Temperance pledges simply could not protect their children, they argued. Women first brought in the state to assume the traditional responsibility of moral reformers when they campaigned successfully for legislation to bar saloons from the neighborhood of schools and colleges. St. Louis women formed a local chapter of the Women's Christian Temperance Union in 1875, and by 1883 the W.C.T.U. had some eighty chapters in Missouri and had become the most effective anti-saloon group. After watching male politicians repeatedly refuse to enforce licensing and regulatory measures, the W.C.T.U. concluded in the mid-1880s that outright prohibition was the only permanent solution. When legislators heeded the money and votes of the saloons instead of the voice of conscience, the W.C.T.U. accepted a compromise: each community would decide, by popular vote—of males—whether to prohibit liquor sales. The Wood Local Option Law of 1887 thus shaped the framework for the crusade against liquor for the next generation. Having abandoned the crusade to convert individual drinkers, by the late 1880s temperance reformers were devoting their energies to campaigning to persuade voters to ban drink in their communities.[48]

In their campaigns for local prohibition, enemies of liquor frequently assumed that workers would more naturally fight to preserve the old moral bonds than would businessmen. Businessmen had created the new order that had caused the problem. Arguing that "the plutocrats, accustomed only to the dolls of fashion, cannot understand us," while "the working men need us and we need them," the Missouri W.C.T.U.'s committee on temperance and labor reported in 1890 that it "would be well for" the W.C.T.U. and the Knights of Labor "to double teams for awhile." Demanding an end to laws that favored "the few against the many" in 1893, the state W.C.T.U. resolved in 1896 that workers were entitled to a just reward for their labor. It was true that the huge St. Joseph and Doe Run lead-mining companies had long prohibited saloons on company lands. But other businessmen defended saloons out of ideological opposition to any popular or governmental regulation of any business. At a time when saloon licenses brought in sufficient revenue to run entire city governments, as at Glasgow in the early 1880s, many businessmen supported saloons because they favored the public improvements that were paid for by saloon licenses. The 1880 campaign to persuade employers in St. Louis to impose abstinence on their employees originated with the Women's Christian Temperance Union, not employers. Businessmen and bankers supported the wets in local elections at Moberly in the 1880s and Nevada in the 1900s. During the 1910s most St. Louis businessmen opposed prohibition.[49]

As temperance gave way to prohibition, the liquor issue evolved into a bitter battleground between traditional cultures which were developing increasingly different ways of fulfilling their traditional goals. Native-born white evangelicals and immigrant liturgicals began by agreeing on the need to preserve family, moral discipline, and separation of church and state. Between 1861 and 1867, after all, Baptist and Methodist ministers had repeatedly gone to jail rather than obey the oaths of obedience to the state that secular authorities enforced. Drunkenness threatened all sects. In its 1886 lament that the liquor issue was leading the state to do the traditional disciplining job of the church, the Methodist *Central Christian Advocate* of St. Louis sounded much like the Catholics and Lutherans. The Young Men's Total Abstinence and Benevolent Society for St. Louis Catholics in 1870 was strikingly similar to the temperance-oriented fraternal orders of native-born Protestants.[50]

Liturgicals brought different traditions to the liquor issue than did evangelicals. Coming from places where beer and wine were accepted beverages, believing that salvation came from following a traditional ritual, Catholics, Lutherans and other liturgicals recognized that they were minorities and that state interference with behavior would almost certainly cost them their freedom to live and worship in traditional ways. They could best preserve their cultures by keeping church and state apart. Evangelical Protestants, on the other hand, proved their salvation by following proscribed patterns of conduct, not belief. A drinker was damned by definition.

But the crisis that led evangelicals to embrace state discipline came not from different traditions but from the new order itself. As Missourians lost control over their lives to market and secular pressures in workplace, school, and government, they felt a greater need to escape. By 1890 there was a church for every 438 Missourians and a saloon for every 318. The saloon came to epitomize secularism, greed, competition, and corruption. By eroding the traditional moral authority of churches and the economic and psychological survival of the family as preservers of traditional values, drinking epitomized how things had got out of control in the new order. Protestant women took the lead in fighting to restore family and moral discipline. Concerned for their children as well as their husbands, sons, fathers, and brothers, they embraced any means to save their families. Most evangelical groups followed them in turning to the state in the last two decades of the nineteenth century. The Anti-Liquor League of Sedalia typified the change when it changed its name in 1894 to the Anti-Saloon League.[51]

When Protestants shifted the crusade from drinker and church to saloon and state, when they tried to legislate the morality of all Missourians, members of liturgical churches felt that their cultures were under attack. Denouncing the Methodist church for abandoning its traditions by supporting prohibition in 1916, the Catholic Kansas City *Register* explained, "We Catholics cannot afford to lend a hand in transplanting private morality from the rich soil of moral suasion to the arid wastes of the police club. And instead of assisting in unwarranted interference of religion in state matters, it would prove to our advantage to catch the boomerang which Protestants are making for themselves." Seven-eighths of the counties voting most heavily for prohibition in 1916 were counties with the heaviest concentrations of Baptists, Methodists, Disciples of Christ, and Presbyterians, while none of the most prohibitionist counties contained large numbers of liturgical Catholics, Lutherans, and German Evangelicals.[52] The intertwined crises of control and conduct truly drove a wedge between the state's traditional cultures.

9

The Fraternal and Cooperative Ethic of Mutual Aid

Traditional Missourians broadened the family relationships of the old order into a fraternal ethic that protected them from the new order's insecurities while nurturing an alternative economic and cultural vision. By seeking to preserve families and local communities in the face of a loss of autonomy that accompanied the new competition, Missourians placed the new fraternal ethic at the core of their efforts to regain control over their lives. The fraternal ethic inspired fraternal lodges and labor unions, vigilante bands and economic cooperatives. It came to dominate alternatives to the new order.

The fraternal ethic originated in the primitive, almost sociobiological drive of families to insure that husband, wife, and children could survive the drastic new consequences of the sickness, injury, unemployment, or death of the male family head. In an increasingly impersonal world the fraternal movement created barriers of ritual and secrecy behind which members immediately knew that they were among "brothers" and "sisters" in an expanded network of mutual protection, a new kind of family. They kept alive the family's traditional function of supporting and disciplining its members while escaping the new order's hierarchical agencies regulating conduct. Since neighbors shared the same fate when national markets eroded the community's capacity to shape its members' lives, traditional Missourians turned to neighbors to forge the most natural bond for self-protection and resistance. Finally, on an economic level the fraternal ethic encouraged Missourians to create their own alternatives to the new middlemen who intervened between production and consumption. Rejecting the competitive doctrine that a few individuals should own and profit from an economic activity, fraternal movements required each member to contribute and share equally in the organization.

Although Missourians had created fraternal organizations before the Civil War, they greatly expanded the fraternal movement after the war, as part of a wider search for new forms of mutual aid. The secret fraternal orders grew spectacularly. The Masonic orders had the deepest roots in Missouri before the Civil War. The number of white Missouri Masons rose from less than 10,000 in 1865 to 60,000 in 1914. The Odd Fellows grew even more dramatically among white Missourians, rising from 4,000 in 1866 to 93,000 by 1914. The Knights of Pythias formed in 1871 and boasted 20,960 white members by 1895. Organized in Missouri in 1870, the United Brothers of Friendship became the state's leading black fraternal order, with 15,320 members by 1914. By 1900 one-sixth of Columbia's black families belonged to fraternal orders, and by 1922 two-thirds of black rural Pike County residents did. In 1912, 23.6 percent of blacks who died in Kansas City were fraternal members. Women of both races joined Missouri's fraternal orders for the first time after Appomattox, forming such adjuncts to male organizations as the Order of the Eastern Star, Daughters of Rebekah, Ladies of the Maccabees, and Sisters of the Mysterious Seven. Beginning with the founding of the Ancient Order of United Workmen (A.O.U.W.) in 1868, fraternal insurance groups grew to number 349,148 Missouri members by 1913.[1]

Other Missourians joined fraternal orders that were based on shared backgrounds, such as religion, ethnicity, or community, or shared commitments, as to the cause of temperance. In addition to national organizations, such as the Ancient Order of Hibernians and the Catholic Knights of America, St. Joseph's Catholics in the 1880s belonged to congregational benevolent societies associated with St. Patrick's, St. Stephen's, and St. Francis Xavier's church parishes. Columbia's blacks formed a Colored Benevolent Society in 1867. The German Order of Harugari claimed 3,000 Missouri members by the mid-1880s. A small group of artisans, laborers, merchants and professionals organized a Mutual Benefit and Burial Union at Hannibal in 1885. Local residents formed the Boone County Mutual Aid Society in 1896, and by 1903 it had 630 members, while similar groups in Howard, Lewis, and Scotland counties each had several hundred members by the early twentieth century. The fraternal movement attracted the temperance-minded because its cohesion and benefits could prevent members from backsliding. In addition to the Good Templars movement that swept Missouri in the 1870s, temperance-minded Catholics formed Father Mathew's Young Men's Total Abstinence and Benevolent Society in 1870 and Troy residents formed a Temperance Benevolent Association in 1884.[2]

The fraternal movement grew in small towns and big cities. The lumber of fraternal lodges at St. Joseph jumped from 10 in 1868 to 128 in 1908. By 1895 St. Louis boasted 751 fraternal lodges for its white residents alone. In the Bollinger County village of Lutesville, the 235 local residents in 1885 could choose among local lodges of the Masons, Odd Fellows, and A.O.U.W., while that same year Farmington's 1394 residents could choose among the Knights of Pythias, Knights of Honor, Masons, Odd Fellows, and A.O.U.W.[3]

   The impulses of mutual aid, exclusive membership, group discipline, and cooperative ownership extended beyond the fraternal orders. The Bald Knobbers and Ku Klux Klan, for example, shared with the fraternal orders the themes of secrecy, pageantry, mutual defense and aid, exclusive membership, and group discipline. The Patrons of Husbandry attracted 80,000 Missouri farmers to form two thousand granges in the 1870s by appealing to their fraternal yearnings. Patterning the Grange after the Masons, its founders relied on fraternal secrecy, mutual aid, and graded degrees of membership to attract members. No fraternal order guarded its secret rituals more zealously than the Noble and Holy Order of the Knights of Labor, who also fought for cooperation over competition. Many craft unions that formed after the Civil War shared with Hannibal's Local 76 of the Cigar-Makers' Union the "chief aim" of assisting their members' families in sickness and death.[4]

   Missourians applied the fraternal ethic to cultural as well as economic challenges. Fearful that Eastern boys might acquire too much influence at the University of Missouri, Missouri's sons banded together in a single residence house to form the school's first fraternity in 1869. Even veterans' organizations, such as the Grand Army of the Republic, appealed to brothers in a common cause who yearned for mutual aid as they faced a world that no longer honored their sacrifices.[5]

   Incorporating ethnic and religious traditions of mutual protection along with craft traditions of artisan control, the fraternal movement for mutual assistance covered Missouri's landscape from the Civil War to World War I. By 1914, 712,032 Missourians belonged to purely fraternal bodies, while hundreds of thousands of others belonged to member-owned cooperatives.[6]

The fraternal movement offered a collective ethic of mutual aid to project an alternative to the new order's competition and impersonality and particularly to protect their members' families from the devastation that now accompanied accident, illness, loss of job, or death. Until the black Knights of Pythias was formed in the mid-1880s, "hundreds of my people" were "fighting the battle of life single-handed . . . ," recalled Grand Chancellor A. W. Lloyd in 1915. "Prejudice, jealousy, malice and hatred usurped the place of social, brotherly feeling, and made us enemies of each other instead of friends," until the Patrons of Husbandry emerged in the mid-1870s to bring Missourians "together in mutual friendship and confidence; . . . an identity of interest recognized, and a fraternal feeling enjoyed . . . ," declared Missouri Grange leader T. R. Allen. Hannibal Cigar-Makers' Union Local 76 proposed in 1890 to "unite, fraternally, all acceptable persons working at cigar making" and "to give all moral and pecuniary aid in its power, to members of the Union, encouraging and assisting each other in the hour of trial." The Knights of Pythias explained:

   Misfortune, misery and death being written in fearful characters on the broad face of creation, our noble Order was instituted to uplift the fallen; to champion humanity; to be his guide and hope; his refuge, shelter and defense . . . and by the sweet and powerful attractions of the glorious trinity of Friendship, Charity and Benevolence to bind in one harmonious brotherhood men of all classes and all opinions.[7]

Through the new fraternal orders Missourians hoped to supplant the doctrine of competition with one of mutual assistance and brotherhood. Fraternal members chose mottoes proclaiming their vision of fraternity over individualism: "Friendship, Unity and True Christian Charity" (Ancient Order of Hibernians); "Charity, Hope, Protection" (Ancient Order of United Workmen); and, most succinctly, "United to Assist" (United Ancient Order of Druids). Many Missourians, like founder Moses Dickson of the Knights and Daughters of Tabor, believed that fraternal orders would one day evolve into a single fraternal and benevolent association that would embrace all humanity with its ethic of mutual aid.[8]

The appeal and strength of the fraternal movement came from the concrete aid offered to specific members rather than abstract ideas of universal brotherhood. The fraternal vision originated in the paternal and fraternal obligations of male family heads toward their dependents and brothers. The Knights of Pythias pledged to extend the traditional obligations from their own families to families of brother members: "The brightest jewels which it garners are the tears of widows and orphans, and its imperative commands are to visit the homes where lacerated hearts are bleeding; to assuage the sufferings of a brother; bury the dead; care for the widow, and educate the orphan." Fraternalism, in the end, drew its strength from the assistance it gave to particular families of fellow members. "We promise to care for the sick, to bury the dead, to protect the widow, to educate the orphan, and to see that the last days of our aged and infirm members should not be spent in darkness and misery, poverty, disease and want," pledged Missouri's leader of the black Knights of Tabor in 1894. "If a brother be naked and destitute of daily food and one of you say to him, 'Depart in peace, be ye warmed and filled,' notwithstanding ye give him not the things which are needful for the body," ran the Odd Fellows' ritual, the unfeeling brother "is wedded to selfishness and greed." The Knights of Labor was more succinct: "An injury to one is the concern of all."[9]

Since the most basic responsibility was to insure that a father's children would survive his death to live healthy lives, fraternal orders enacted formal obligations to require members to fulfill that responsibility. After 1879 the Ancient Order of United Workmen required the Master Workman to ask the assembled lodge: "Does any member know of a Sick Brother, or of a Brother's family in need of any assistance, or of a Brother wanting employment?" Each 1880 meeting of Sedalia Lodge 27, Knights of Pythias, included the question, "Does any brother know of a sick brother or a brother's family in distress?" Women's auxiliaries allowed wives and sisters to join the fraternal family of their husbands. The black Grand United Order of Odd Fellows created the Sojourna Household of Ruth so that the women could "unite with their fathers, husbands, sons, and brothers in one great, happy, and prosperous family" of Odd Fellowship.[10]

Fraternalists created economic forms of mutual aid as alternatives to the new order. Instead of permitting stockholders to make a profit from mutual aid, or allowing wealthy policyholders to purchase more insurance than poorer ones, the fraternal orders required each member to contribute equally to the fraternity's resources and allowed each to share equally in its benefits in times of distress. They paid benefits to members or their survivors at times of death, illness, accident, or unemployment. The death and burial benefit developed by classic orders such as the Odd Fellows, Knights of Pythias, and A.O.U.W. was adopted by temperance benevolent societies, by immigrant orders such as the Societá d'Unione e Fratellanza Italiana, and by local unions, such as the brewery workers, journeyman bricklayers, paperhangers, and printers in St. Louis. Most paid automatic benefits when members became sick or disabled. Some, like the white Masons and Knights of Pythias and the black Odd Fellows, provided homes in Missouri for aged members.

Since fraternalism organized Missourians as neighbors and the local lodge shaped each fraternal community, the lodges determined the amount of assessments and benefits. Among the Knights of Pythias lodges in the 1880s, for example, Sedalia Lodge 27 paid fifty dollar death benefits and five dollars weekly for sickness and disability, while Coeur De Leon Lodge 11, at Hannibal, paid twenty dollars for deaths and two dollars weekly for disability.[11]

Missourians extended the basic fraternal economic vision of banishing profit and pooling the group's resources beyond the life, health, and employment insurance provided by fraternal orders. Thirty German immigrants in Kansas City in 1868 created an alternative to bank mortgages by pooling their savings and lending money to their members to buy homes. This building-and-loan movement soon spread to Germans in Washington in 1871 and St. Louis in 1872, and by 1892 there were 313 building-and-loan associations in Missouri. Two-thirds of the state's 71,578 members in 1892 were laborers and mechanics, and their pooled resources equaled nearly a third of the banks'. As part of their crusade to wrest economic control from profit-oriented middlemen, Grangers created consumer-owned mutual companies in the 1870s that insured their members for a third the cost of private companies. The Patrons' Home Protection of Clay County (1873) and Patrons Mutual Insurance Company of Lafayette (1875) launched a local mutual insurance drive that by 1898 included sixty Missouri companies with almost 63,000 members and by 1906 included 120 companies with 100,000 members insuring risks of over $200 million.[12]

As they explored structures through which to apply the traditional household's integration of production and consumption to the new brotherhoods, Missourians hoped that cooperative ownership and distribution—sharing ownership, risks, and benefits equally among members—would replace both profit and the growing layers of middlemen. Cooperative ownership increasingly became the most popular alternative to competition as resisters formed self-contained groups to share resources and benefits. Confining their concerns to the needs of a particular group, cooperators expected to wrest local and personal control—over price and quality of goods, over terms of work—from the remote and impersonal market.

Many Missourians concluded that the purest way to merge self-sufficiency with cooperative ownership was to establish brand new communities whose inhabitants would all share the cooperative faith. Several members of the Knights of Labor founded Eglinton in Taney County in the early 1880s as an "absolutely independent community" guided by the cooperative dream: "Do not produce to sell, do not buy to consume. Be independent of capital, independent of markets and of the price of labor. Work for yourselves." Other groups built cooperative alternative communities at Reunion in Jasper County in 1868, Friendship in Dallas County in 1872, and Mutual Aid in Bollinger County in 1883. As late as 1900 Missourians maintained cooperative communities at Long Lane, Kerrigan, and Cabool.[13]

Farmers and workers frequently created consumer cooperatives as important parts of their efforts to recover control over the marketplace. Missouri's Grangers tried to bring "the producers and consumers of agricultural implements and products together" by establishing cooperative stores where members of local lodges could buy goods, and by operating a cooperative tannery at California and a cheese factory at Mapleton. As local lodges established cooperative stores, the State Grange maintained a wholesale store in St. Louis that did a million dollars in business within two years. By 1880 two-thirds of Missouri's consumer cooperatives were Granger stores. At Hannibal, Knights of Labor members tried to supplant capitalism with cooperatives, by creating a Workingmen's Co-operative Company in 1886 to sell food and clothes exclusively to Knights' members, who owned the store.[14]

When farmers organized again in the late 1880s they again turned to consumer cooperatives as an important "defense of God-given rights which the toiling masses should defend to the bitter end" against monopoly, middlemen, and competition, declared Phil Chew in the Farmers' and Laborers' Union's official *Journal of Agriculture* in 1890. Farmers' and Laborers' Union members created three member-owned cooperative stores in the bootheel's Mississippi County in the late 1880s to free themselves from the region's hated landowners and merchants. In the city of Macon the Farmers' and Laborers' Union operated a cooperative flour mill, packing house, and hotel in 1890, while that organization's Grubville Cooperative Store saved its Jefferson County members 20 percent on provisions in its first year, 1889–90.[15]

"The middleman is the vermiform appendix attached to the bowels of civilization and . . . he should be cut out," declared H. J. Bowen, manager of the Producers and Consumers Co-operative Market at St. Joseph, in 1913. By cooperatively furnishing themselves with the family's provisions, cooperators reached out to retake territory claimed by the new economic leaders. Believing that consumer cooperatives permitted consumers to regain control over the quality and price of products, the Knights of Labor store at Hannibal in 1886 required its board of directors to investigate any complaint by any member about any product sold in the store.[16]

Many Missouri workers challenged both their employers and the market system by pooling resources. Appealing to the yearning for the self-contained family, Sedalian G. B. DeBernardi in 1889 and 1890 launched a plan to supplant the competitive wage system with worker-controlled barter. "Cooperation will prove the salvation of labor," proclaimed DeBernardi when he set up the Labor Exchange in Sedalia. Workers exchanged their own goods and services for those of others with different skills through a system of deposit certificates based on the amount of labor, not its money value, each member contributed to the exchange. "The Association is their market place," announced DeBernardi, for members could meet their needs within the self-contained system of barter. By 1898 the labor exchange operated centers in five Missouri communities and had plans for running brickyards, sawmills, tanneries, canneries, and factories for furniture, boots, shoes, brooms, and hats to provide jobs for unemployed members. At St. Louis in 1884 and Kansas City in 1889 women developed exchanges where they traded goods made in their homes for goods made by other women.[17] The fraternal passion to enlarge traditional family self-sufficiency so as to embrace the fraternity's entire membership found most striking expression in the labor exchanges that gave the fruits of labor to worker-members, not employers, that replaced money with labor as the basis for exchange, that supplanted middlemen with member-owned cooperatives, and that cared for members in distress by providing them jobs.

Some Missouri workers tried to regain control over their workplaces by pooling their resources to acquire ownership of their plants. St. Louis furniture workers provided a stunningly successful national example of producers' cooperatives with their member-owned factories. Striking workers created the cooperatively owned St. Louis Furniture Workers' Association in 1878 to employ themselves, and workers at two other furniture plants acquired their own factories in 1881 and 1885. Furious at the mine owners' increasing use of unskilled workers from other cultures, imposition of seasonal work, and introduction of wage cuts, skilled British coal miners struck the mines of Macon and Randolph counties in 1885 and for five months refused to work. Finally, the desperate owners agreed to allow the workers to acquire ownership of the mines by paying the company a royalty (of a penny a bushel at Huntsville) on the coal they mined. At Bevier 150 miners bought ten-dollar shares in the new Summit Cooperative Coal and Mining Company, and the cooperative company proposed to remove the insecurity of seasonal employment by using its lands for farming and brick making in the off-season. Striking female workers at a St. Louis knitting mill created a short-lived factory in 1885, and striking garment workers in Sedalia created a longer-lived factory there in 1910.[18]

Cooperatives grew from the strong fraternal feeling of familylike cohesion that bonded particular Missourians as equal contributors, that brought together local residents who wanted new ways to recover the old sense of community control over production and consumption. They grew only from the bottom up and could not be imposed on unwilling communities. Eastern philanthropists tried to create a massive cooperative system in Grundy County. Seeking an American center for the English Ruskin Hall movement, Walter Vrooman and others purchased an ailing college at Trenton in 1900 and renamed it Ruskin College. By 1902 they had poured hundreds of thousands of dollars into Ruskin College and its associated cooperatives, the Western Co-operative Association and Multitude, Incorporated. The empire embraced a cannery, a woodworking plant, an 1800-acre farm, a chemical factory, five stores in Trenton, fourteen businesses in Independence and Kansas City, and facilities for lumbering, fishing, and raising fruit, rice, and sugar. Ruskin College students paid for their educations by working in the cooperative factories. In 1904 the whole network collapsed, due to bad weather that destroyed crops, poor management, and a shift in public sentiment in Trenton, for local residents came to resent the college president's indiscretions, the strange theories of the outsiders, and the cooperative's practices.[19] The spectacular failure of Multitude, Incorporated proved that the large amounts of capital that encouraged success under private ownership were less important to cooperative success. The fraternal ethic of mutual aid derived its vitality from the ways that local residents drew on community traditions to intertwine economic cooperation with social fraternity.

The fundamental attraction and unit of every fraternal organization was the local lodge. Each local unit determined whom to admit to membership. Each local unit determined the rules for members to follow, whether rules of work or conduct, and enforced those rules.

Since the fraternal movement appealed to Missourians precisely because it defied the thrust of the new order by preserving local control within the brotherhood of members, the movement recruited members by the traditional criteria of their social and moral qualities. Even craft unions excluded people who practiced the craft but lacked social, moral, or "fraternal" qualities deemed important to the local's members.

The preservation of local communities and personal networks was too important a mission for the economic distinctions of the new order to disrupt. In their extended families of mutual assistance and group discipline Missourians were interested mainly in the social and personal, not the economic, characteristics of their prospective brothers. At St. Joseph in 1887 members of the Catholic Knights of America elected as their officers a laborer and a hotel owner, a mason and a manufacturer. Twenty years later in the same city the Odd Fellows chose for their leaders three foremen, three janitors, three carpenters, and three contractors, along with two grocers, two lawyers, a lather, a laborer, a bookkeeper, a teamster, a traveling salesman, and a painter. Sedalia's Russell Camp 2065, Modern Woodmen of American, included among its 1901 members Mayor Walter C. Overstreet, laborer James D. Creegan, butcher Joseph Paradis, architect E. A. Strong, machinist George R. Fletcher, Baptist preacher James M. Plunnett, clerk Joseph

Kraus, grocer Sol Rosenthal, mason James Wilkerson, teacher Charles Deppe, driver Perry C. Huntsman, and shoemaker Thomas Solon. In 1880 the Odd Fellows' Itaska Encampment Number 6 at Lexington counted as fraternal brothers day laborers like Garret Etherton and Richard Charlton, lawyers like Amos Green and George S. Rathburn, farmers like W. H. Ewing and George W. Mullinix, teamsters like James Edelen and N. W. Bullard, saloon keepers like Joseph W. Homer, bricklayers like W. W. Lamborn, tinsmiths like Henry Gelzer, machinists like Charles Taubman, and traveling salesmen like W. R. Bolton.[20]

Since the fraternal movement was intensely local and each lodge chose its members for their traditional personal qualities there were great differences in occupational composition from one lodge and community to another. Unskilled laborers and artisans formed a majority of some lodges, while business and professional men formed a majority of others, but most lodges included brothers who represented all occcupations. The accompanying table on page 165 shows the occupational background for 1,525 fraternal Missourians from seven orders and seven communities.

The fraternal movement broke through the traditional sectarian barriers of belief and ritual that separated religious denominations to forge a common ethical approach and local focus that attracted Missourians from all religious backgrounds. Catholics found it particularly difficult to join nonsectarian fraternal orders, since their leaders discouraged them from joining orders that were "made to take the place of religion and not to work in harmony with it" by replacing traditional religious guides to conduct. The orders were "an infallible symptom of the reversion of Protestantism to paganism," warned the Catholic church's *Review* of St. Louis. Church leaders hoped to prevent Catholics from associating with others in organizations designed to regulate conduct by creating their own fraternal orders, such as the Catholic Knights and Knights of Columbus. But Catholic Missourians expressed their fraternal yearnings by also joining with sympathetic neighbors who happened to be Protestants and Jews. In St. Francois County in the late 1880s Catholics belonged to the A.O.U.W., Odd Fellows, Knights of Pythias, and Knights of honor. Their fraternal brothers included southern Methodists, Congregationalists, and Presbyterians in the A.O.U.W., as well as Epsicopalians and Lutherans in the A.O.U.W. and Odd Fellows, Baptists in the Odd Fellows and Knights of Pythias, and northern Methodists in the A.O.U.W. and Pythians. Fearful that Catholics would lose their faith through such associations, Archbishop Peter Richard Kenrick of St. Louis singled out the Knights of Labor for particular censure, but Father Cornelius O'Leary defied the church ban to work closely with the Knights during the 1886 railroad strike at St. Louis. For his efforts O'Leary won the lifelong gratitude of Terrence V. Powderly, Grand Master Workman of the Knights, and ouster from his parish by Archbishop Kenrick.[22] Religious loyalties restrained some Missourians from following the fraternal thrust across those traditional barriers.

Although many Missourians had first formed strong political loyalties in the 1820s and 1830s, when the interrelated issues of Freemasonry and Catho-

Occupations of White Fraternal Members, 1874–1912[21]

	Laborer	Artisan	Farmer	Merchant	Manufacturer and Manager	Sales and Clerical	Professional	Number of Members
Masons								
Clinton, 548, 1892	0%	6%	0%	28%	16%	15%	34%	32
Lexington, 149, 1880	4	13	8	35	0	25	17	24
St. Joseph, 78, 1901	2	35	0	18	10	22	13	96
St. Joseph, 189, 1901	2	12	0	24	16	25	20	99
St. Joseph, 331, 1901	10	14	0	10	29	24	14	21
Sedalia, 272, 1896	3	57	1	19	0	5	13	67
Sedalia, 236, 1905	1	19	0	25	12	23	20	91
Kansas City, sample, all lodges, 1912	1	10	0	15	27	27	20	143
Odd Fellows								
Hannibal, 41, 1897	6	39	0	19	11	25	0	36
Hannibal, 26, 1901	26	42	0	13	5	8	5	38
Lexington, 323, 1874	19	50	6	13	0	13	0	16
Lexington, 6, 1881	10	25	4	20	5	8	25	51
Knights of Pythias								
Hannibal, 11, 1893	4	25	0	34	13	16	9	126
Sedalia, 27, 1880	0	49	1	6	16	11	16	77
St. Louis, all dead members, 1892–95	0	30	0	23	9	34	5	66
Ancient Order of United Workmen								
Hannibal, 161, 1885	14	50	0	11	14	6	5	64
Hannibal, 23, 1895	8	30	0	6	21	27	8	63
Lexington, 87, 1878	20	35	0	20	5	10	10	20
Knights of Honor								
Lexington, 1880	6	13	9	28	3	16	25	32
Knights of Maccabees								
Sedalia, 4, 1898	15	48	0	13	10	9	5	177
Modern Woodmen of America								
Sedalia, 2065, 1901	11	33	1	18	9	18	11	186
Total, All Lodges	6.8%	31.3%	0.5%	18.8%	12.6%	18.0%	12.0%	1525

licism divided them, fraternal Missourians by the 1880s tried to bury traditional partisan divisions. Knowing that ancient ethnic, racial, and religious
conflicts, as well as more recent passions from the Civil War, formed the
bases of partisanship, the fraternal movement specifically banned political
partisanship from lodge meetings. Local lodges attracted Democrats, Republicans, Prohibitionists, Populists, and independents in roughly their local
proportions. In overwhelmingly Democratic St. Francois County in the late
1880s, for example, Democrats constituted 65 percent of the Odd Fellows
and Knights of Pythias, 75 percent of the A.O.U.W., 79 percent of the
Masons, and 80 percent of the Knights of Honor.[23]

The fraternal lodge was, first and foremost, an extension of the member's
family. Members were expected to relate to each other as blood brothers
would and to view the lodge's relationship to the outside world as they viewed
their family's. In creating organizational forms to reinforce familylike feelings
that the lodge was a haven from the jungle outside, fraternal Missourians
strengthened their orders' economic function as an alternative to middlemen,
one that protected members and their families. They viewed these familylike
bonds as so central to the fraternal ethic that the Odd Fellows, for example,
warned new members before their initiation to quit the order if they had
conceived of it as "a mere beneficiary society."[24]

Fraternal forms encouraged members to think of the lodge as an extended
family and to subordinate their personal wishes to the lodge's welfare. At
Hannibal in the 1890s, for example, the Odd Fellows, A.O.U.W., Typographical Union, and Iron Molders' Union threatened expulsion to "any member
who shall wantonly disturb the harmony of the lodge," in the Odd Fellows'
words. The oath of the Hannibal Typographical Union encouraged members
to think of each other as blood brothers: "I will not wrong a brother member,
or see a brother member wronged if in my power to prevent."[25]

The key to the lodge's capacity to serve as an extended family was the
selection of new members. "We should guard, with vigilance, the entrance to
our mystic temple," proclaimed Grand Master Willis N. Brent of the Colored
Masons in 1880. In addition to requirements of race, age (twenty-one to fifty
for Pythians, for example), and apprenticeship, fraternal and union lodges
tried to preserve traditional criteria by insisting that members be "of good
moral character." But the real determinant of admission was a screening
process designed to preserve fraternal harmony. Any two or three members
of each lodge had the unquestioned right to veto any applicant whose
fraternal qualities they questioned. Committees investigated each applicant,
reported to the lodge, and the lodge voted, frequently by placing anonymous
black or white balls in a "ballot box." At Lexington twelve black balls denied
admission to the United Mine Workers. The Hannibal printers' union and all
local branches of the Farmers' and Laborers' Union rejected any applicant
whose name inspired three black balls, and the Sedalia Pythians rejected any
applicant who received two black balls at two successive elections. The St.
Joseph Masons and Hannibal Order of Railway Conductors rejected those
who received even one black ball at two successive elections. To embolden

members to exercise their ability to keep out people they regarded as unfraternal for whatever reason, the printers and the Pythians provided penalties for revealing the names of those who had opposed a candidate's admission. The Pythians explained that "no one has a right to inquire who cast [a black ball] or why."[26]

Initiation into the order represented a coming of age. The new member pledged to honor the brotherhood's bonds and codes, often in dramatic terms. Apprentices to each of the seven Masonic degrees bound themselves "under no less a penalty than that of having my throat cut across, my tongue torn out by its roots, . . . should I ever knowingly violate this my entered apprentice obligation."[27]

Each order developed elaborate rules and rituals that distanced the fraternal family from other Missourians, on the one hand, and that empowered the lodge to regulate its members' conduct, on the other. State Grange leader T. R. Allen explained that the Grange's secret rituals gave members "a language of their own, by which they may recognize each other when they meet." At Hannibal the Cigar-Makers' Union and Odd Fellows threatened severe penalties to any member who revealed the fraternity's secret proceedings to outsiders. Secrecy heightened members' dependence on brothers, to give access to the further secrets that meant advancement within the order and to not betray the order to outsiders. Behind the barrier of secrecy members could build the experiences and ideologies to challenge the new order. Founder Uriah S. Stephens rooted the Knights of Labor in the secret rituals of the Masons, for, as he explained, "Nothing can remedy this evil but a purely and deeply secret organization of workingmen that will imbue its membership with ideas ultimately subversive of the present wage system."[28] To preserve their secrecy against outsiders the Knights of Pythias maintained official Inner and Outer Guards.

Each order developed forms and rituals that projected traditional values and social relationships against the new order. Fraternal traditions instilled reverence for a past in which reciprocal bonds of obligation, not competition, had guided relationships between people and when possession of skill and knowledge, not money, had determined status. Since the new order seemed to erode these moral values, fraternal orders developed rituals that made traditional values seem eternal. "No institution, merely human, is altogether free from the danger of innovation, nor is Freemasonry," warned Grand Master Willis N. Brent of the state's black Masons. "It must depend on . . . our steadfast adherance [*sic*] to 'ancient landmarks,' for its future usefulness and permanency." The historical or mythological settings that inspired each order's rituals emphasized how fraternal feeling and possession of skill permitted their predecessors to control their lives. Many orders of foresters and woodmen built their rituals and imagery around forest life, where the skills and mutual aid of the foresters assured their survival and independence. Hundreds of fraternal "foresters" and "woodmen" gathered for a two-day festival at Deepwater in August 1902, for example, to compete in games of wood chopping and log rolling.[29] The Masons celebrated their link through medieval guilds of stone masons to more ancient roots by laying ceremonial cornerstones for churches and public buildings in their communities. In July 1880, for example, Masonic lodges laid cornerstones for a Baptist church in Dalton and a Methodist church in Kansas City.[30]

By basing rank within the fraternity on knowledge of craft secrets, fraternal orders challenged the new order. Within the fraternity Missourians could rise from apprentice to master in the time-honored way, by acquiring knowledge. Higher ranks went to those who had learned more of the craft's traditions and skills. Freemasonry established thirty-three ranks, while the Odd Fellows and Grange had seven grades, United Brothers of Friendship six, Knights of Columbus four, and Knights of Pythias three. By building rituals around the tradition of craft acquisition, fraternal orders insured that their members would view each other as comrades while maintaining a system of deference based on knowledge, not wealth. Each member of the Hannibal Lodge of Odd Fellows could only speak or vote at lodge meeting when "clothed in regalia appropriate to his rank and station."[31] The fraternal traditions of craftsmenship and mutual aid thus challenged the new doctrine that wealth ought to determine mobility and status. Recognizing that members were incapable of insuring their children's survival by passing on their skills, the fraternal orders provided economic and social aid to their dependents as the modern equivalent of the tradition of passing crafts from one generation to the next.

Concluding that law and authority were increasingly remote and corrupt, and rejecting the legitimacy of orders from policemen and employers, fraternal Missourians preferred to trust the guidance of their conduct to those with whom they shared a fraternal commitment to care for each other in times of need. They feared that money had replaced the popular will in the making of laws and that the costs and delays of the court system had eroded the system of judgment by a jury of one's peers. The passion to replace the regulation of conduct by legislatures and policemen with familylike discipline by brothers who shared fraternal vows, to settle conflicts within the fraternal movement rather than by turning to lawyers or the courts, became a hallmark of the fraternal ethic that measured rejection of the new order's disciplines. "Freemasonry is a law unto itself," summarized a masonic leader in 1881. The *Missouri Granger* reported in 1874 that "Grangers don't like lawsuits" and "prefer to have their differences settled by their friends and brothers." Fifteen years later the Missouri Farmers' and Laborers' Union officially declared that it was "contrary to the spirit of the order for brothers to go to law with each other." Both orders commanded members to try to settle disputes among themselves and, if that failed, to accept arbitration by special fraternal courts.[32]

Fraternal Missourians created methods for making and enforcing rules that combined the sense of family and fraternal obligation with forms that were more just than those of the courts and more representative than those of the legislatures. They incorporated traditions such as representative government and trial by jury. Each lodge established its own rules for conduct and elected representatives to enact state and national rules. When a member was charged with violating rules, advocates presented evidence and the lodge, acting as a jury, determined the accused's fate. Five-person committees called witnesses and took testimony that the lodge weighed in both Sedalia Lodge 27, Knights of Pythias, in 1880, and Local 142, Iron Molders' Union, in Hannibal in 1896.[33]

Since they yearned to preserve families and moral, not secular, yardsticks, the lodges used fraternal discipline to punish members who strayed from the strictures of family and church. The primary goal of Freemasonry was "the propagation of the correct principles of morality and the application of these precepts to the conduct of life," Grand Master Robert Smith told the state's black Masons in 1883. The A.O.U.W. and Knights of Labor at Hannibal and the Knights of Pythias and Modern Woodmen of America at Sedalia severely punished inebriated members who tried to enter the lodge hall. In an unusual case of biracial cooperation, black and white Masons joined forces in 1888 for a major crusade against drunkenness and gambling, the wreckers of the family.[34]

Missouri's fraternal orders used strong discipline to compel brothers to honor traditional obligations toward their families. Fraternal feelings would only be strong enough to resist challenges from the new order and members would only develop strong attachment to their lodge brothers if they possessed a deep sense of their traditional responsibilities to care for their own families. At Sedalia the Modern Woodmen of America and the Knights of Pythias convened the entire lodge to investigate and punish any member charged with the fraternal crime of "neglecting his family." Among the Knights of Pythias, Palmyra's Amicitia Lodge 32 dismissed James S. Spear for neglecting his family, and Springfield Lodge 85 suspended J. H. Fishpool in 1891 for a year because he had assaulted his wife. In Kansas City, Brother George Root "alienated the affections" of Brother Henry Keeling's wife and, on April 10, 1894, Keeling shot Root as he entered the Forest Lodge hall. Since Keeling had acted to protect his family, Forest Lodge acquitted him and expelled the offending Root. The State Grand Lodge, on appeal, upheld Root's expulsion but, embarrassed that the Kansas City lodge had winked at an attempted murder in its lodge hall, suspended Keeling for a nominal ten days.[35]

But the fraternal movement saved its strongest sanctions to insure that brothers would come to the aid of a suffering member or his family. Members had joined the fraternity out of fear that they or their families would be ignored in the impersonal individualism of the new order. When word reached the lodge that a brother of his family was in distress, the lodge mobilized elaborate machinery to bring relief. It hired nurses. It required brothers to sit with the sick. It dispatched financial benefits to the family. It used fraternal punishments to insure that members honored their obligations. Most lodges followed Iron Molders' Union Local 142 in fining members who failed to visit sick brothers on their assigned days.[36]

Fraternal Missourians viewed the fraternal funeral and subsequent memorial services and the survivor benefit to dependents as the most important ways that the lodge provided dignity and even a measure of immortality in an increasingly impersonal and insecure world. For many of the state's blacks death had long held a special significance, sorrow mixing with joy at relief from life's pains, and fraternal funerals were major events in black communities. Following their orders' rituals and attired in uniforms that their orders traced to earlier times when societies cherished bonds of mutual obligation, fraternal lodges called out all their members for the funeral of a brother. The Odd Fellows' Hannibal Lodge held members in contempt of the order if they failed to take their turns at sitting with the remains of a deceased brother or to attend the funeral of any brother in "proper regalia." The state's black Masons punished members who failed to attend a masonic funeral. And brothers were not just buried and forgotten. The ritual for black Masons included a prayer for all dead members, and the Knights of Pythias and Knights and Daughters of Tabor held annual memorial services for all dead members. Fraternal Missourians honored a spirit of brotherhood that challenged the new order when they participated in funerals by singing songs like the anthem of the Woodmen of the World:

> Huge pillars of marble may mark the last spot
>   Where lie the remains of the rich.
> Mausoleums may tower o'er the tombs of the great
>   Or their statues be placed in a niche.
>
> But over the grave where the Woodman lies sleeping,
>   A shaft is erected, remembrance keeping,
> That he who lies there, to his neighbor lived true.
>   Hence 'Dum tacit clamat,' this stone as his due.[37]

The fraternal movement successfully filled the new gaps in the tradition of mutual aid created when the new order eroded church discipline and charity. Many clergymen believed that fraternal orders more effectively performed the traditional religious duty of mobilizing assistance in times of trouble. The official Catholic *Review* of St. Louis lamented in 1900 that "when a member of their church became ill the other church members did not come voluntarily to 'watch' with him, to provide for his daily needs, while the members of fraternal societies in which he held membership came nightly to his bedside and daily provided for the necessities of his family." Church members rarely brought "even a rosebud" to honor a deceased member, while his fraternal brothers "sent in wreaths of flowers to garland the casket and relieve the darkness of the grave."[38]

Although the fraternal movement inspired the survival of traditional brotherhood and discipline in the new order by uniting people across the new divisions of job and class, it remained rooted so deeply in the old order that it usually failed to transcend traditional loyalties based on race, ethnicity, and religion. All traditional cultures embraced the fraternal ethic, but it was precisely each order's roots in the experiences of its culture that made it familiar and attractive to traditional Missourians. Fraternal orders divided Missourians along racial, ethnic, and religious lines. The fraternal German Order of Harugari, for example, had as a major objective to preserve the German language. The Catholic Knights recruited members across ethnic barriers, but they erected a religious hurdle. All fraternal orders, even those that united workers at the same trade, drew the color line, so that in late nineteenth-century St. Louis there were separate unions for English-speaking white printers, English-speaking black printers, and German-speaking printers. Black lodges of the Masons, Odd Fellows, or Pythians were more part of the local black community than of a fraternal community. White lodges in the same communities sometimes divided along ethnic lines. At Lexington in 1874, for example, the Odd Fellows' Guttenberg Lodge 323 attracted members with names like Sinauer, Schaefermeyer, Winkler, Goehner, Fritz, Sigwalt, Schneider, and Fischer; thirteen of the sixteen members had been born in Germany. At the same time Lexington's other Odd Fellows' lodges included members with names like Green, Price, Lemborn, Fleet, McKean, Bolton, Johnson, Taylor, and Thompson.[39]

When forced to choose between fraternal and ethnic allegiances, traditional Missourians retained their primary ethnic loyalties. For many years the Grand Lodge of the Knights of Pythias permitted predominantly German lodges in Kansas City and Hermann to conduct their meetings and rituals in German, but when the Grand Lodge developed a new ritual in the 1890s it refused to print the new ritual in German, despite protests from the German lodges. In response, the German lodges broke away to form their own Improved Order of the Knights of Pythias.[40] The very appeal to traditional values that made the fraternal movement so attractive to traditional Missourians limited its capacity to transcend ancient cultural barriers.

Many Missourians hoped that the fraternal movement would broaden its mutual aid to unite and mobilize workers to gain control over their workplaces. After all, craft unions and the Knights of Labor had long combined fraternal discipline with workers' control. Many other workers expected that fraternal discipline could be used to forge worker solidarity. In the coal-mining community of Bevier, Benton Lodge 71, Knights of Pythias, dismissed Brothers Issac and Keith for siding with employers during a labor struggle in 1885. It was unfraternal to support management. But the State Grand Lodge ruled that this was an improper use of fraternal discipline and overturned the dismissal.[41]

Fraternal Missourians repeatedly tested the limits of the fraternal movement's readiness to mobilize workers against the new order. Since most fraternal orders assumed that a brother who needed a worker would give first preference to a brother who needed a job, local lodges frequently required brothers to report job openings to fraternal employment bureaus, such as those maintained by the Knights of Pythias, to help unemployed brothers. Since the lodge helped in times of need, many workers assumed that the order would join them in buying only union-made products or in boycotting employers when members were on strike. Arguing that the Knights of Pythias was "largely composed of men who labor daily in the different vocations of the industrial field" and that "through the introduction of labor-saving machinery thousands of mechanics have been thrown out of employment and this is especially true of the printers, many of whom are members of this Order," ten local lodges persuaded the state Grand Lodge in 1898 to require the union label on Grand Lodge printing. Two years later, however, the Grand Lodge rejected a resolution that required local lodges to employ only union printers for lodge business, and in 1906 the Grand Lodge tabled a resolution from ten local lodges requiring the union label on Grand Lodge printing.[42]

Missouri's workers learned that fraternal discipline could not be used to compel members to boycott employers and was only sometimes effective in helping brothers whose jobs were threatened by labor-saving machinery. Workers who at first hoped to turn the fraternal movement into an aggressive weapon against employers would later develop unions that maintained fraternal spirit and discipline but dropped elaborate rituals, graded membership, and cooperative ownership, as they replaced mutual assistance based on local families from all occupations with unity based on members' jobs.

Even when they created labor unions, however, many Missouri workers continued to believe that purely fraternal orders served needs that unions never could. Unions united workers across geographic lines as people who worked at the same job, but many workers continued to share with Missourians of all classes the dream that fraternal orders projected of preserving family and community. Still suspicious of law and competition in the new order, they wanted the kind of familylike discipline that fraternal orders provided. Even as they turned to organizations that aided families by improving their purchasing power rather than relieving them in times of distress, they continued to seek the kind of personal control over life that had in the past revolved around their communities and families. John Bour, Sedalia's 1905 leader of the Brotherhood of Locomotive Engineers, for example, was also a member of the local Masons' Granite Lodge 272.[43] The fraternal ethic of mutual aid preserved and extended family and community discipline.

VI

The Search for Security in the New Workplaces

Many Missourians hoped to find security in the new order by organizing relief in their workplaces, the source of the most immediate challenges to their lives. As they formed new occupational groups, businessmen, professionals, artisans, and farmers concluded that the underlying challenge was a crisis of discipline. In the old order individual producers had felt restrained by a concern with reputation in transactions that had been ordered by face-to-face exchanges and personal networks, by their crafts' or professions' traditions, by community moral standards of conduct. The new order burst these restraints, and its ideology exalted competition and encouraged individual producers to discard and ignore anything that prevented them from producing more goods at lower prices. In fact, the new order seemed to reward individuals who reached for the businesses or jobs of already established producers by curtailing expensive training and other traditional ways of doing things. Traditional Missourians struggled frantically to restrain "greedy or "cut-throat" individuals.

Missouri's producers hoped at first that family, community, church, and craft could be broadened, as with the fraternal ethic, to refashion local, craft, and moral controls over production and over individuals. As they tried to restrain competition, however, many tradition-minded producers encountered others in their own trades who hated competition not because it eroded tradition but because it subverted the new order's promise of growth, profits, and higher incomes. To these producers group action was the means to advance growth. In contrast to the old values of skill, reputation, democracy, community, and morality that inspired traditional Missourians to restrain competition, corporate-minded producers argued that concentration, specialization, hierarchy, uniformity, and freedom from popular control were the best ways to insure stable growth.

Creators of goods and services struggled between competitive, traditional, and corporatist solutions. They formed groups to suppress both greedy individuals within their own ranks and producers of goods and services who

173

competed in their markets. They lurched between an enthusiasm for government, because it could limit competition by granting monopolistic franchises, imposing certification requirements, and banning child labor, on the one hand, and a fear that voters might mobilize to assert new public restraints over their own groups' activities, on the other.

New economic groups reshaped the conflict between the old and new orders. The new organizations of businessmen, professionals and workers simultaneously escalated, concentrated, and narrowed the fundamental issues of power and control that the new order had set in motion. But as these organizations adapted traditional values to new economic imperatives, they frequently transformed those values beyond easy recognition. When they grafted the new fear of popular restraint onto the ancient artisan traditions of controlling craft access and regulating members' conduct, for example, what emerged was a new kind of group-defining elitism that revolved around certification, among other things. Although producers frequently started out with the traditional moral revulsion against competition, their groups often narrowed the solution into the creation of economic monopolies of producers that subordinated everything else to growth. By limiting the conflict to particular issues of production, the new groups narrowed the conflict and conceded defeat in many areas that traditional Missourians had claimed as theirs.

10

The Economic Organization
of the New Order

Missouri's businessmen, professionals, and workers saw the new order's challenge in remarkably similar terms. They groped for ways to restrain the individual whose dreams or greed refused to be bound by traditional expectations or restraints of skill, conduct, and practice. Somewhere between traditional restraints and new corporatist pressures they sought to find new controls.

1. The Organization of Business

The most enthusiastic creators of the new order soon saw their deepest hopes and ambitions threatened, in fact, by large-scale market production that swamped the local economies and personal networks that had shaped economic activity in the old order. As they scurried to create new organizations to discipline and even escape the very competitive pressures they had unleashed, they frequently felt that their individual dreams and the new ideology of competition were in conflict with the ways that competition actually affected their economic lives.

The new order shaped the ways businessmen resolved the tension between competition and consolidation. The markets that widened between producers and consumers created more and more middlemen for shipping, transporting, credit, insurance, processing, and marketing. The resulting economic specialization encouraged firms and individuals engaged in the same activities to cooperate in the face of common problems and enemies.

Businessmen also sought members of their industry as allies because they shared a common fear of the next counterattack by traditional cultures against their newest innovations. Workers might strike a plant over a new

175

rule, or strike a businessman in the street. The real issue in the new order increasingly became one of power and control, not the ability to defeat a competitor. And that was a chronic issue of political significance in a society in which workers held the right to vote and government had the authority to restrain businessmen. Businessmen looked increasingly to other businessmen for help as workers, consumers, and farmers entered politics to defend their traditional values and rights. In trying to assert control, businessmen cared little whether their opponents rallied behind the solidarity of the working class or the traditions of German Catholics or carpenters. Businessmen measured their failures across a wide battleground, from saloons to machine wrecking, from tardiness and absenteeism to unionization. But fear of action by traditional Missourians focused their sense of mission.

Promoters had dreamed of a new order because they had chafed at the traditional restraints that had limited individual enterprise and initiative. In the face-to-face world a businessman's success depended less on how cheaply he made a product than on how well his methods, products, and character satisfied individual consumers. The concern for reputation, even when not supplemented by traditional governmental regulations, strictly limited the ways businessmen treated consumers, employees, and competitors. The new order eroded personal discipline when its huge, faceless markets and large-scale corporations drowned individual responsibility in a sea of impersonality. Competition drove prices so relentlessly downward that most producers faced the probability that they would fail. With survival based on cheapened production, many producers desperately tried to escape spiraling pressures by innovating in the new realms of technology, marketing, management, and labor. Suddenly there were no limits either to market imperatives to produce more goods at lower prices or to the greed and drive of particular businessmen to prevent the adoption of business practices that seemed immoral by traditional standards.

As unprecedented markets combined with the lifting of external and internal restraints, businessmen searched for new ways to assert order and discipline. Kansas City department store owner Thomas B. Bullene was appalled to discover that the First National Bank, on whose board he served, had engaged in such shady practices that it was forced to suspend payments on January 28, 1878. Believing in the old tradition that "some may have had additional confidence in the Bank on account of my identity with it," he confided to his diary: "It is my determination to never accept such a position in the future, if unable to discharge its duties more faithfully toward the stock holders and depositors than I have in this case."[1] Resignation was the only solution that the tradition-minded Bullene could imagine, but in the new world competitive pressures led other businessmen to abandon the traditional concern with reputation.

Some promoters began to see how the new order itself contained the potential for restoring discipline over both impersonal competition and unscrupulous individuals. The new markets that united unprecedented numbers of buyers and sellers of particular commodities created inherent pressures for group consciousness and discipline. Real estate agents in Fulton or livestock traders in Kansas City shared a common interest that turned the promotion of the individual into the promotion of the group. But they also shared a double-edged fear that uninhibited colleagues might do things that either threatened their own economic survival or inspired popular pressures to restrain the entire group. The desire to expand the producers' market, as with earlier agricultural promoters, combined with a yearning to escape both competition and popular regulation, led businessmen to organize the markets themselves into new organizations that simultaneously promoted the group and restrained its members from harming the group's reputation.

Businessmen organized to define and regulate acceptable business practices that would both stimulate the group's growth and advance its members' ability to limit competition. Sedalia's grocers came together in 1882 to form a Retail Grocers' Association so that they, not the uncertain market or particular consumers, would establish operating hours, prices, and credit practices for all grocers "to the end that extortion and unbusinesslike competition may be discouraged and eventually prohibited." Through organization they hoped to abolish such costly consumer traditions as credit purchases. The rapid growth of cities likewise created a new group of middlemen, real estate agents, who intervened between buyers and sellers of land and homes. In 1877 all twenty-five real estate agents in St. Louis met to form the Real Estate Exchange to establish uniform business practices. By 1887 the drive to organize real estate agents even reached the Henry County village of Clinton.[2]

The new middlemen organized the markets that developed between farmers and processors of agricultural products such as meat packers and millers. St. Louis merchants had pointed the way by creating the nation's oldest trading organization. In 1836 twenty-five merchants founded the Chamber of Commerce, which in turn established a Millers' Exchange in 1849 and finally a Merchants' Exchange in 1854, to create standards for the inspection, buying, and selling of grains and flour. In Kansas City the Commercial Club, formed in 1857 to attract railroads, evolved into a Commercial Exchange in 1869 and then a Board of Trade to regulate grain sales. Both groups developed over the next half-century into major markets, with the St. Louis Merchants' Exchange the nation's third largest primary grain market and the Kansas City Board of Trade the third leading market for futures trading.

The St. Louis Merchants' Exchange and Kansas City Board of Trade strove to impose uniform practices on their members. They established standard grades and weights of grains and displayed samples of each so that buyers and sellers could agree on the quality and amount of each transaction. Since both groups assumed responsibility for the transactions of individual members and recognized that farmers and consumers were suspicious of the traders' new activities, particularly futures trading, they created elaborate mechanisms to discipline members who might attract unwelcome publicity.

The St. Louis group maintained committees on arbitration and appeals with power to examine witnesses and documents and to adjust differences between members. Both groups had the power to suspend or expel members who refused to follow the exchanges' rules for inspection, grading, weighing, storing, and shipping of grains. Both groups insisted that they promoted stability by equalizing prices across the entire year, by discounting the impact of changes in weather in advance of actual harvests, by using their storage facilities to meet the year-round demand, and by leveling prices between one geographic market and another.[3]

Other middlemen copied the grain traders and organized to escape competition by extending their new operations while also imposing uniformity. Eager for more business, railroad officials joined stock traders to build the first stockyard at Kansas City in 1870. The rapid growth of the new Kansas City livestock market unleashed competitive pressures that led traders, in turn, to adopt new, dishonest, and unhealthy practices. In response, livestock producers, shippers, meat packers, commission merchants, and bankers created a livestock exchange to discipline buyers and sellers and to prohibit practices that discredited the entire market, such as the sale of diseased animals for human consumption. The Kansas City livestock exchange used its collective economic power to secure favorable rates from railroads and its political power to secure favorable laws.[4]

While traders organized to discipline competition by identifying and policing a line between acceptable and cutthroat practices, other producers tried to escape competition by dividing among themselves the territory, freight, or income that had been the source of competition. The very creators of the new market economy, the railroads, led the retreat from price competition by pooling traffic among competing lines. Railroads in the cattle trade began as early as 1871 to meet in St. Louis to divide traffic. But these agreements soon collapsed when one road, eager for greater business, cut rates to attract traffic assigned to another. Searching for a more formal structure, freight agents and superintendents from the seven major railroads serving the area between Chicago and St. Louis to the east and Omaha and Kansas City to the west met in 1876 to form the Southwestern Railway Rate Association. The board of directors set rates and determined earnings for each road. Although the greed of a particular road or a new competitive situation sometimes led to temporary colapses, the Southwestern pool continued to divide up traffic until it merged in 1888 with other regional pools to form the Western Freight Association, in 1889 with the Interstate Commerce Railway Association, and in 1891 with the Western Traffic Association. In its period of greatest success, from 1881 to 1887, the pool proved the advantages of setting prices with other firms. The Missouri Pacific, for example, began to make a profit for the first time in the early 1880s as its surplus rose from $1,156,000 in 1880 to $4,284,750 by 1884. The pool's very successes inspired shippers to organize against it, and in 1887 Congress weakened it with the Interstate Commerce Act. In 1897 the Supreme Court killed it by prohibiting such rate agreements.[5]

Missouri's lumber firms likewise preserved their individual identities while they shrank from the competition caused by their large-scale Ozark activities, combining to form a central selling agency. John Barber White, head of the Missouri Lumber and Mining Company, first organized pools among yellow pine firms in 1882, but his early efforts failed because other manufacturers preferred competition to stable prices. By the late 1880s and early 1890s yellow pine manufacturers began to set prices effectively. In 1897 White moved his firm's sales offices from the Ozark mill to a Kansas City office building which also housed his competitors. The manufacturers soon incorporated the Missouri Lumber and Land Exchange Company for "the purpose of holding us together on price," as White declared in 1897. Soon the exchange's higher prices brought profits, for the first time for some members. With annual sales of 260 million feet in 1903, the exchange was the largest central selling agency in the lumber trade and covered almost half the nation's yellow pine. By 1904 the exchange created standardized grades of lumber in an attempt to retard competition. It forced the region's railroads to grant rate concessions to its members. Although the exchange ran afoul of the antitrust laws by 1907, it successfully insulated its members from competition for more than a decade.[6]

In their retreat from competition, businessmen sought organizational forms that maintained high prices in ways that prevented aggressive firms from withdrawing from the pool. During the 1870s and 1880s large meat packers formed the American Pork Packers' Association to maintain high prices by dividing up the market and establishing standardized products. From 1893 to 1902 Armour, Swift, and Morris maintained a similar pool in beef products by determining the number and prices of products that each would ship each week and fining companies whose overshipments depressed prices. Fire insurance companies maintained high rates and avoided competition through two bureaus that set rates for most communities and types of property in the state. Fire insurance agents in St. Louis formed the St. Louis Board of Underwriters in 1872, and this organization evolved into the St. Louis Inspection Department in 1883, which set rates for St. Louis city and county. In 1891 William J. Fetter established a similar bureau for Kansas City and, by the mid-1890s, for some fifty other Missouri communities. In the late 1890s seventy companies created the St. Joseph Underwriters' Social Club to set and maintain rates.[7]

But the railroad, lumber, insurance, and packing companies that cooperated to escape competition faced a double-edged challenge, and it was a formidable one. Defining competition as the means to create economic growth, the new order's ideology, culture, and laws encouraged individual producers to seek wider markets and prohibited them from combining with other firms to stifle competition. At the same time, traditional Missourians organized as voters to force elected officials to restrain the new commercial organizations. Popular pressure and competitive law were too much. In all four industries public officials broke up the companies' price-maintaining combinations.

Missouri businessmen who preferred stability to competition continued to search for ways to escape the greed of competitors and the wrath of public officials. The most effective solution was for competing companies to merge. A larger company frequently took advantage of its size or a competitor's weakness to acquire the competitor. Frustrated by the collapse of pools, the Missouri Pacific's Jay Gould set out in the late 1870s to acquire Southwestern railroads. In the 1890s a syndicate of English investors tried to acquire and merge American breweries, and by 1895 it had bought eighteen St. Louis breweries, including Cherokee, Excelsior, Green Tree, and Hyde Park. By the turn of the century Standard Oil kept oil prices 50 percent above the market by owning three companies in Missouri that pretended to be separate and competitive but all responded to orders from 26 Broadway in New York. Early in the twentieth century J. P. Morgan's investment bankers merged a half-dozen of the agricultural implement maufacturers that had competed for the business of Missouri's farmers into a single monopoly, the International Harvester Company.[8]

Private utilities led the push toward monopoly in many communities. Investors merged separate companies that provided the same services and then added others until, by the early twentieth century, only one or two companies provided the lighting, transportation, electricity, and water services for most communities. In the late 1880s and early 1890s an Eastern syndicate merged St. Joseph's half-dozen street railways and electric lighting companies into a monopoly that they named the St. Joseph Railway, Light, Heat, and Power Company in 1895. In 1899 another Eastern syndicate acquired what over the past forty years had been seventy-one separate street railway companies and in 1906 absorbed its last competitor to create a street railway monopoly in St. Louis. Investors created the Union Electric Light and Power Company in the early twentieth century to incorporate what had been twenty-one separate companies that either built electric generating equipment or delivered electricity to St. Louis and eastern Missouri.[9]

In their drive for stability and domination businesses took advantage of the new competitive cycles of boom and bust that encouraged monopoly by destroying weak competitors. The depression of the 1870s drove small packing houses in Kansas City out of business and left Armour with a monopoly. St. Louis entered the same depression with sixty banks and emerged in 1879 with twenty-five. The depression killed the Bank of the State of Missouri, with more capital than any other in the state, because the bank had speculated too freely and got caught short. As a result, the Boatmen's Bank, which had 8 percent of St. Louis deposits and 11 percent of capital in 1874, became the city's largest bank, with 12 percent of deposits and 17 percent of capital.[10]

While the drive for stable profits that underlay the merger movement inspired businessmen to form new organizations, that drive was never their sole focus, precisely because mergers effectively ended competition. Mergers might indeed be the most secure route to stable profits, but mergers also dampened the individualistic dreams that had inspired the new order's creation. The vacillation between competition and combination led individual

Springfield insurance agents, Ozark lumber mills, and Missouri railroads to form pools one moment and withdraw from them the next.

Missouri businessmen overcame their ambivalence by building their organizational response to the new order as much around competition between communities as around competition between producers. From the start they had promoted population and economic growth for their communities, and they increasingly believed that growth offered the best resolution to the conflict between competition and consolidation. A community's growth insured more customers for all local businessmen.

Growth for the whole community insured the survival of individual firms better than could either competition or merger. Many businessmen made growth the foundation of their organizations, even when they embraced stability. A group of businessmen formed the Lexington Business Association in 1885 to attract railroads and the accompanying economic boom to their community. Within a year the dry goods merchants in the new association used the group's meetings to agree among themselves to close their stores at seven instead of competing for nighttime shoppers.[11]

Local business groups sprouted across the state to try to reshape communities around the gospel of growth. Businessmen fought to convince traditional Missourians that growth solved all problems. In 1919, for example, Sedalia's Chamber of Commerce fulfilled its motto, "For a Bigger, Better, More Prosperous Sedalia and Pettis County," by initiating and securing voter approval for major bond issues that encouraged that city's development.[12]

Although businessmen had long derived a sense of purpose from promoting growth in the midst of indifferent or hostile Missourians, they implemented that vision differently as they came to depend on growth to solve the new order's problems. Facing traditional resistance in many forms, businessmen increasingly insisted that other businessmen shun their traditional identities in favor of creating a united new class. With their identities based increasingly on the new criterion of income rather than the old ones of ethnic, church, or partisan affiliation, businessmen created new educational, cultural, and religious institutions to give their members a sense of superiority over traditional Missourians. Businessmen had attended all of Lexington's churches in the 1870s, a majority in none, but during the 1880s and 1890s they turned the Presbyterian and Episcopalian churches into religious bastions of the wealthy, as they became 67 percent of Lexington's Presbyterians and 63 percent of Episcopalians. In the 1880s local businessmen insured that their children would only associate with those of other worthies by sending their daughters to the new Elizabeth Aull Seminary and their sons to the Wentworth Academy.[13]

Missouri's most famous agency of elite formation was the Veiled Prophet celebration at St. Louis. Charles S. Slayback, a grain merchant from New Orleans, helped to found this event, which both advertised the economic achievements of St. Louis businessmen and gave them a sense of cultural superiority. Slayback and other businessmen created a secret Order of the Veiled Prophet, derived in part from the New Orleans Mardi Gras and incorporating fraternal imagery, with substantial wealth the major basis for admission. Beginning in 1878, the Veiled Prophet every year led a huge parade of floats that advertised the city's growth and wound through city streets to the Merchants' Exchange, where the Veiled Prophet opened the Court of Love and Beauty, declaring that "there should be no jealousy, or business or social rivalry to mar the friendliness at the Court of Love and Beauty." The parade was followed by an exclusive ball which inaugurated the social season. Each guest received a special gift from the Veiled Prophet, which could be displayed throughout the year to advertise his or her admission to the uppermost levels of St. Louis society. The elaborate parade and ball gave leading businessmen the opportunity to identify their peers at the top of the new social pyramid as they marched and danced the rituals of the new class consciousness, while the secrecy, pageantry, and fun became ways of trying to persuade traditional Missourians that wealth ought to confer status.[14]

Businessmen hoped that their new commercial and cultural organizations and associations would both establish their authority over other groups and contain conflicts within narrow enough bounds so that the basic thrust of the new order toward growth could be preserved. When shippers and railroads organized to battle over freight rates, for example, both sides never questioned that growth was the ideal or that corporate power over other groups had to be retained. At the Veiled Prophet Ball or the Wentworth Academy they were reminded of their common interests and common foes. Growth was enough to unite businessmen, but the basic issue was whether they could persuade others.

2. The Organization of the Professions

Members of Missouri's professions drew on standards of craft autonomy, conduct, and training that they had shared with other artisans. As they organized to control their crafts, to limit competition and restrain individuals, however, they developed increasingly distinctive forms of organization.

Since their training and skills established their ability and authority to practice their crafts, professionals traditionally resembled other artisans. They had learned medicine, law, education, or journalism by apprenticing with a skilled practitioner. Apprentice attorneys first learned to sweep the office, then to read law books, prepare briefs, and argue in court. I. N. Love recalled that he had learned medicine at St. Louis in the 1860s under the "tutelage" of Dr. John T. Hogden, whom he came to regard as "my patron saint" in a city where the leading practitioners had "loyal followings." The old order's restraints on professional conduct included master-apprentice training, and face-to-face relationships with clients, and admission to practice was dependent on traditional associations and loyalties, such as those that frequently motivated local school boards and judges when they decided whom to admit to the bar and the classroom. E. W. Moore, a Bunceton banker, expressed the faith that traditional associations retained their power when he asked his friend, Governor Lon Stephens, in 1899 for the "personal favor" of assisting his brother to get a teaching certificate from the state school superintendent, W. T. Carrington. Traditional Missourians had accorded professionals higher status than other artisans or businessmen because they were the interpreters of the rules that guided both individual behavior and interactions between people, the judgers and healers of weakened bodies, souls, minds, and relationships. Although they acted with the independent authority of their learning, they depended for their livelihood on individual consumers who expected to participate with the professional in shaping the treatment, whether it was a religious conversion, a medical cure, or a lesson.[15]

The new order transformed the functions, crafts, and clients of the professions. Developers turned to the professions to buttress the new order by legitimating its values and mediating its conflicts. In order to overcome the resistance of traditional parents and churches to their new values, developers agreed with pedagogy professor J. P. Blanton of the University of Missouri in 1896 that "the crying need of the day" was "an army of trained teachers." The spectacular growth in the size and complexity of business transactions led to a growing demand for corporate lawyers. Pressures for cheapened production called for specialized engineers to design new technologies. Professionals contributed to their own competition. Charles B. McAfee recalled that standards for admission to the bar in southwest Missouri were only nominal because "lawyers were in demand and we 'created' them" by admitting all applicants.

The resulting changes troubled many professionals deeply. Competition from untrained practitioners "has done more to discredit the bench and bar and to create unfavorable criticism and distrust of both and to commercialize and lower the standards of the bar than any other cause," lamented Kansas City attorney William H. Piatt to the Missouri Bar Association as late as 1915. Qualified teachers could not win high wages because there were "plenty of teachers who will underbid the good teachers," reported the state school superintendent in 1904. Doctors, lawyers, journalists, and engineers desperately tried to restrain competition because competition's cheapening tendencies eroded competence, its lifting of restraints attracted people whose methods produced popular pressures to regulate the whole profession, and its commercialization undermined the integrity that had been the professionals' chief pride. Worrying that "in our pushing day and generation the lawyer comes to look upon the law more as a business than a profession," St. Louis attorney W. C. Marshall warned the state bar to establish restraints before the courtroom became simply a battlefield between "gladiators who acknowledge no law but success, and seek no honor but riches." Commercialization, reported distinguished St. Louis editor William Marion Reedy in 1908, destroyed both the competence and integrity of journalism. Doctors had to reach to rise "above the commercialism of today," warned President W. G. Moore of the Missouri State Medical Association in 1904.[16]

At first they hoped that the methods used in fraternal and artisan orders could be extended to restrain competition and commercialism in the professions. The doctors who formed the St. Louis Medical Society in 1836, the Missouri Medical Association in 1850, the Kansas City Medical Society in 1869, and the St. Joseph Medical Society in the 1880s aimed at "the promotion of kindly feeling and harmonious action among its members," in the words of the St. Joseph group, by holding their members to a code of ethics that the American Medical Association first developed in 1847. Fear of the fraternal discipline of expulsion restrained members from cooperating with competitors of the medical societies. In a similarly fraternal vein, the St. Louis Bar Association in 1874 denied admission to candidates who failed to receive support from at least 80 percent of members of the group formed "to maintain the honor and dignity of the profession of law" and "to cultivate social intercourse among its members."[17]

The practitioners who led the drive for professionalization soon sought an alternative to fraternal discipline, because they concluded that under the new order interpretive crafts such as medicine, law, and education were being transformed in ways diametrically opposite to the changes in production crafts such as butchering and shoemaking. The growing complexity of relationships in the new order meant that knowledge increasingly followed the new corporate values of stability, specialization, and growth, while cheap production supplanted artisans' skills with complex machines and unskilled operators. The bar associations and medical societies turned into places where professionals could explore the frontiers of the new "medical science" and "legal science." Doctors who campaigned to professionalize medicine based their ideology and practice on the model of industrial production. The new science of medicine subdivided the human body into small, specialized units and functions and developed drugs to cure a particular malady in a specialized part. School administrators organized the Missouri State Teachers Association in 1856 in the hope of persuading teachers to replace their traditional desire to satisfy parents with a new commitment to increasingly specialized knowledge. To lead the campaign for professionalism, the Missouri State Teachers' Association chose as its presidents the school superintendent of St. Joseph (1867), the state school superintendent (1868), the president of the University of Missouri (1869), a Washington Unversity professor (1870), and then, successively, the presidents of the three state normal schools. To all these leaders specialization was the key to professionalization.[18]

Putting the acquisition of specialized knowledge at the center of the professions, Missouri's professionalizers concluded, would limit competition while giving professionals greater autonomy than they had enjoyed in the more democratic past. The professionalizers called for formal schooling to replace apprenticeships, which had insured neither uniformity nor specialization. Both the new St. Louis Law School in 1867 and the Kansas City School of Law in 1895 conceded the difficulty of their new mission as they acknowledged the persistence of apprenticeship by scheduling their formal classes in the evenings and early mornings, so that students could also serve apprenticeships. Physicians began to give formal training in specialized medicine at St.

Louis's Missouri Medical College in 1840 and St. Louis Medical College in 1842, at the Kansas City College of Physicians and Surgeons in 1869, and at the Ensworth Medical College of St. Joseph in 1877. To staff the new public schools with teachers, developers established state-funded normal schools for whites at Kirksville and Warrensburg in 1870 and Cape Girardeau in 1873 and for blacks at Lincoln University in the 1870s. Each new group turned to the University of Missouri to establish professional schools providing formal, systematic training, and the university responded with branches in Columbia for teachers (1867), lawyers (1872), physicians (1873), and engineers (1860), and another for engineers at the School of Mines and Metallurgy at Rolla in 1871. Concluding that "professional and vocational schools have taken the place of the individual training of the past," Columbia editor Walter Williams helped found the world's first school for jounalists at the University of Missouri in 1908.[19]

Promoters of the new professionalism tried to steer aspiring teachers, doctors, and lawyers to the new schools by rewarding graduates with an automatic right to practice. In 1874 the legislature established the policy that graduation from a law school conferred the right to practice law. During the 1880s graduates of normal schools received an automatic and unconditional license to teach. In 1874 the state medical association tried to strengthen the new schools further by persuading the legislature to limit the right to practice medicine to graduates of medical schools. But this rule only sparked new competition among medical schools, encouraging new schools to compete for students by charging lower and lower fees for shorter and shorter courses of study. In 1882 the medical association estimated that barely half of Missouri's 4,834 doctors had graduated from "reputable" medical schools. During the 1880s and 1890s the association campaigned for minimum entrance and graduation requirements and longer courses of study, but the state supreme court finally blocked this approach in 1896, reaffirming the new order's thrust toward competition, by denying the state the power to regulate medical schools. The state bar association protested as early as 1884 against automatic admission for all law school graduates.[20]

As professionals increasingly defined themselves in terms of the acquisition of specialized knowledge, they came to base their professional self-consciousness on the conviction that traditional Missourians were ignorant resisters of progress whose potential power to discipline the professions, as consumers or voters, threatened the professionals' legitimacy. The indifference, if not outright resistance, of traditional Missourians to the new missions of the law and the public schools was painfully obvious. Looking at his organization's long struggle to shift control over schools from parents and elected school boards to professional—and unelected—administrators, the president of the Missouri State Teachers' Association, state superintendent William P. Evans, concluded in 1913 that "a false notion of democracy has hindered the development of the public schools." Too many traditional Missourians likewise seemed to cling to the old belief that the law ought to be accessible to all. University of Missouri Law Professor Manley O. Hudson argued that the legal profession could only advance when people jettisoned the "obsolete" democratic notion that "the privilege of practising law was deemed a part of the birthright of every young man."[21]

Professionals were outraged when Missourians rejected specialized knowledge as the basis for interpreting and treating their problems in favor of traditional values and controls. A great many Missourians resisted the application of industrial practices to health and retained the traditional focus on the whole patient. Building on traditional religious concern with individuals, faith healers won great popularity in the late nineteenth century with their insistence that individuals could heal themselves through their own faith. Christian Scientists were particularly successful in blocking the medical association's attempts in the 1890s to assume the exclusive right to define medical practice.[22]

Missouri's medical association faced additional resistance because the state was home to a popular therapy that emphasized the body's integration and rejected the use of drugs. Coming from a family of doctors and Methodist missionaries, Andrew T. Still merged both traditions in 1874 to create osteopathy. He soon moved to Kirksville, which served as his base while he traveled around the state as a "faith cure doctor." Maintaining that "all the remedies necessary to health are compounded within the human body," Still insisted that illness was the result of a breakdown in the normal immune mechanisms and could be cured by adjusting the body to restore the normal flow of the blood and lymph systems. Rejecting drugs and emphasizing integration, Still's therapy proved so popular that he established at Kirksville in the early 1890s what became the American School of Osteopathy to train disciples in his alternative approach to illness.[23]

Missouri's ambitious professionals seized on certification as the best way to limit competition, suppress alternative ways of teaching school or healing the sick, and "elevate the profession" by establishing its practioners' superiority over those they called amateurs. The popularity of osteopathy galvanized physicians in the Missouri Medical Association because they regarded it as quackery. Residents of northern Missouri astonished the physicians by aborting their drive to outlaw osteopathy, burying the legislature in expressions of support for Still's therapy. When Governor Lon Stephens seemed to legitimate an alternative therapy by appointing a homeopath to head the State Hospital for the Insane at Fulton, the doctors pushed even harder for certification. Finally, after exempting osteopathy, the 1901 legislature gave the doctors what they had sought and created a board to examine applicants for medical practice in Missouri. The doctors who dominated the new state board received the power to license other doctors. They quickly used that power to suppress competition and establish their authority, failing 36 percent of the applicants who appeared before the board in its first two years.[24]

Missouri's profession-minded attorneys also crusaded for state certification as the best way to enshrine specialized knowledge ahead of either the traditional concerns that had motivated judges or the fact of attendance at something that called itself a law school. Forming in 1880, the Missouri Bar

Association began its aggressive campaign to base admission to the bar on a competitive examination in 1899. In 1905 the legislature enacted this method for barring "incompetent and badly prepared men, whereby the dignity and high character of the profession has gravely suffered." In 1908, 18 candidates failed the new bar examination among the 135 who took it.[25]

Educational administrators likewise hoped that certification would transform schools and attract teachers with a professional self-consciousness similar to that of doctors and lawyers. "Unless teaching takes its place beside law, medicine and theology as one of the learned professions, it cannot hope to attract the best and most capable men and women," explained President W. S. Dearmont of the Cape Girardeau Normal School in 1906. Since the purpose of the new schools was to instill the new values, administrators sought to change teaching itself so that practitioners would be loyal to the "profession," not to parents or taxpayers, whom they frequently regarded as ignorant and hostile. To do this administrators tried to make teaching less seasonal and more important in their students' lives by lengthening the school year from four months (1874) to five (1877), six (1889), seven (1899), and eight months (1909). They set up graded and high schools in another application of the new order's specialization. They established competitive grades so that youngsters would learn the new way, in which advancement was based on approval from authorities other than parents. They tried to break resistance from local traditions of community control by consolidating local schools into large, specialized schools that met their professional standards. They created teachers' institutes where teachers learned the new approaches to education. In 1891 the state required each county to establish institutes whose directors certified achievements, and in 1903 the legislature encouraged county teachers' associations to instill professional consciousness. They persuaded the legislature to raise steadily the requirements for various grades of teaching certificates. The major new 1911 certification law, for example, led immediately to an increase of 25 percent in the number of rural teachers who had attended high school or normal school.[26]

In these ways administrators dramatically changed the kinds of people who became teachers and thereby encouraged loyalty to profession, not to parents or taxpayers. Teaching had traditionally attracted young men who took this low-paid seasonal work before they began their "real" jobs. By extending the season and raising the status without raising the salaries of teachers, the professionalizers changed the composition of the teaching force from transient young men to young women who were willing to make a longer commitment to a job that had traditionally been an unpaid responsibility of women. Female students rose from 36 percent of Kirksville Normal's students in 1879 to 59 percent in 1908, from 49 percent at Warrensburg in 1875 to 74 percent in 1908, and from 40 percent at Cape Girardeau in 1877 to 60 percent in 1908. Males declined from 83 percent of Missouri's teachers in 1858 to 38 percent by 1900. The mission of teaching new values under these conditions failed to attract Missourians from homes that were committed to the new order. Between 1881 and 1892 the children of merchants and professionals made up between 12 and 16 percent of Warrensburg's students, while children of farmers made up between 69 and 74 percent of future teachers at that school. The administrators' real triumph was to make teachers into full-time practitioners with teaching as their vocation. Beginning in the late 1870s the state normal schools required their students to teach in Missouri's public schools after graduation. In response to these changes President William Evans of the state teachers' association detected by 1913 a "growing sense of professional spirit," as members "come to feel the increased security of a scarcity value" that resulted from limited access to the vocation and led members "to assert prerogative."[27]

Professionals used their expensive training to justify concerted attempts to escape competition by setting rates in ways that closely paralleled businessmen's pools and artisans' union scales. Physicians formed the Lafayette County Medical Association in 1879 to set fees for office visits, fractures, and medicine. Ten years later the St. Joseph Medical Society published an elaborate scale of the fees its members were permitted to charge. On May 13, 1903, the Henry County Medical Society established a $10 fine for any member who treated a patient with a record of failing to pay a previous medical bill or who charged less than the society's rates of $5 for an ordinary consultation and at least $1.50 for a housecall. To keep members from undercutting each other the Bar Association of St. Louis reminded members that "the profession . . . is not a mere money-getting trade" and that they should base their fees partially on "the customary charges of the Bar for similar services."[28]

As examinations, certificates, and formal schooling replaced the artisan-apprenticeship system at the entrance to interpretive crafts, professionals came to share a growing number of values with businessmen. Their specialization, for example, paralleled the new order's. As secularism eroded traditional sectarian loyalties, clergymen formed local ministerial alliances with people from different denominations. Journalists shunned moral and partisan commitments in favor of "objectivity." Professionals formed groups to escape competition by setting rates, establishing standardized practices, and disciplining violators. They embraced growth as a sure way to insure stability and limit competition. By turning to the state to license practitioners, the professions moved away from the old order's moral, sectarian, democratic, partisan, and artisan traditions. To the new professionals those traditions were the province of "amateurs." Professionalizers believed that certification and training proved their superiority over traditional Missourians because they taught how to adapt to the new order's values and disciplines. In the new order engineers would design the technologies, lawyers settle differences to minimize conflicts, doctors and clergymen give people the physical and mental capacities to tolerate the new changes, and teachers try to instill the new values. The escape from competition ended in a new elitism.

Yet to many teachers, lawyers, and doctors, as to their clients, the professionalizers had moved their crafts too far beyond their roots. While they welcomed relief from competition in any form, they held back from the professionalizers' narrow campaigns for specialization, standardization, centralization, and certification. The Moniteau County Teachers' Institute de-nounced the state school superintendent's professionalizing measures in 1892 because they tended "to a centralization of power that is calculated to prevent . . . the placing of the teacher on a par with other professionals," leading teachers to develop not a democratic sense of pride but merely a willingness to "pander to [the superintendent's] wishes" and the wishes of "those high in authority." Teachers shunned the Missouri State Teachers' Association. After fifty years, in 1906, it still had only 395 members. Only coercive membership policies sparked a growth in its numbers; it reached 11,036 in 1917. Although the Missouri Bar Association appealed three times more to lawyers in the new cities than to those in rural Missouri, it still included only 357 members among the state's 5,500 attorneys after its first twenty-five years, in 1905. Even worse, attorneys led the fight that retarded the state bar association's campaign for competitive examinations. Indifferent, if not hostile, to the direction of the professionalizers, many teachers, lawyers, and clergymen preferred to draw on other traditions and ally with Missourians from other occupations to preserve a different vision.[29]

3. The Organization of Labor

Missouri's workers felt torn between their fraternal and craft traditions and the new trends toward consolidation as they organized to resist the new competition's ravages. They hoped at first to broaden the fraternal ethic of mutual aid to cover their workplaces. But they soon concluded that national markets and cheapened production had unleashed new challenges. The fra-ternal ethic drew strength from workers' ethnic, craft, and local origins, but the new national markets and corporate employers eroded that strength by throwing workers from different ethnic groups, crafts, and communities into competition. Market pressures constantly encouraged workers to find secu-rity not by defending traditional values, but by accepting the new order's thrust toward growth and contesting the amount of wages, not the wage system. Each new organization wrestled with the temptation to accept some loss of control and independence in exchange for higher wages. Although some organizations came to accept the corporate emphasis on stability and growth by World War I, most Missouri workers preserved traditions of fraternal and craft control.

Missouri workers built their first labor unions on the fraternal tradition of assisting fellow members in times of need. They were a natural extension of workers' traditional ways of seeking relief, for in 1884 more workers polled by the state labor commissioner belonged to benevolent societies than belonged to labor unions.[30] The first unions differed from fraternal orders mainly by limiting membership to a particular trade. They screened new members, staged elaborate initiations, enacted rules and disciplined members who violated them, conducted business in secrecy, and assisted members and their families in times of individual need.

The first unions incorporated the fraternal pattern of assessing members for a common fund from which they or their families could draw in case of sickness, death, accident, or unemployment. In St. Louis, for example, labor unions began by offering death benefits for journeymen bricklayers (1865), German printers (1873), English-speaking printers (1877), boilermakers (1878), and paperhangers (1880). In classic fraternal form the St. Louis Typographical Union in 1869 required members to sit up with its sick members and fined those who shunned this obligation. As late as 1901, 119 of Missouri's 409 local unions had sick benefits and 244 had death benefits. In 1903 local unions in Missouri paid $7,193 to members who failed to find jobs, $65,346 to members who lost wages because they were on strike, and $39,134 to those who suffered illnesses or accidents.[31]

The new unions also followed the fraternal tradition of trying to control their lives by collectively adopting rules all were required to obey. They hoped those rules would control the trade by uniting all its members into a single union held together by benefits, social events, group discipline, and sole possession of the craft's knowledge and apprenticeship. The willingness of members to obey union rules meant that employees had no choice but to hire union members. In Hannibal in the 1890s, for example, the Iron Molders Union, Local 142, decreed the hours of work at stove shops by ordering its members to work from 7:00 A.M. until noon and from 1:00 P.M. until 3:00 P.M. It set the minimum wage for stove plate molders by prohibiting its members from working for less than three dollars a day. In St. Louis and Hannibal the typographical union fixed the scale of wages for printers. In turn-of-the-century Sedalia, Local 333 of the Amalgamated Sheet Metal Workers and Local 1792 of the United Brotherhood of Carpenters and Joiners fixed the work day at nine hours, while Local 14 of the Bricklayers' and Masons' Union enforced an eight-hour day on its members and, therefore, on the trade. In St. Louis the Carpenters' District Council, similarly, prohibited members from working Saturday afternoons after Aug. 19, 1899, and established a minimum wage for St. Louis carpenters of forty-five cents an hour on April 3, 1900, sixty cents on April 1, 1907, and sixty-five cents on April 4, 1911.[32]

Local unions maintained their control over work rules by severely disciplining members who violated those rules. Hannibal's Iron Molders automatically fined members five dollars for working outside the prescribed hours. Sedalia's carpenters' local expelled members for their second violation of its scale of wages and hours. The Carpenters' District Council in St. Louis fined members five dollars for working during an 1896 strike and two dollars for working on Saturday afternoons in 1899, and suspended business agent Paul Wilms for using nonunion mill work in his home in 1911. At Kansas City in 1907 the Carpenters' District Council fined Brother A. W. Dixon $100 for "violation of obligation" when he worked during a strike, fined Brother A. J. Lyman $150 and expelled him from the union for acting as a spy for the Fuller Construction Company, and fined Brother Q. S. Custer $5 for the unfraternal act of hitting a brother member. Depending on secrecy to preserve their fraternal roots and their capacity to organize against their employers, St. Louis Local 2 of the machine woodworkers severely fined Joseph Gunson in 1902 for "carrying tails [*sic*] to the bosses," a contemptible crime that showed his fundamental unfitness for a movement that hoped to supplant a hierarchical present with a democratic future.[33]

Decade after decade the St. Louis Typographical Union hoped that tight fraternal discipline would prevent printers from working in nonunion shops that undercut the union scale. The union called such workers "rats," and it periodically compiled and distributed a list of "rats" that it exchanged with printers in other cities, in what amounted to a national blacklist of printers who had "ratted" on their brothers. Union printers in St. Louis assumed that concern for fraternal reputation would deter members from acting in ways that would lead their names to be "published to the world at large" as "rats." During the newspaper strike of 1864 the union created a Rat Committee and a Sub Rat Committee to act as a "detective force" to identify strikebreaking members. The union expelled members for ratting in 1866, 1887, and 1893. Since rats threatened to the core the union's capacity to control the shop, by reinforcing competitive against fraternal pressures, the union worried about even rumors of friendship between members and rats. In 1877 it set up a special committee to discover which union member had introduced particular "rats" to other people as "nice fellows." Concerned in 1886 that the "rodent element" associated in "too easy a manner" with union members, it legislated a five dollar fine for each offense in which a union member was found associating with a "rat" on any terms "except in Battle Royal."[34]

If rules, discipline, and knowledge reinforced the fraternal ethic within the union, members claimed the outer limits of mutuality by striking employers who refused to abide by the union's rules. The double risks in a strike—that all members might not honor the strike and that employers might not rehire strikers—strengthened the fraternal sense of mutual sacrifice and craft control. In 1883 and 1884 St. Louis boot and shoe workers struck over the refusal of employers to honor union work rules. Employees at the St. Louis Rolling Mill walked off the job when the company announced it would no longer pay the scale of wages established by the Amalgamated Association of Iron and Steel Workers in 1888. In St. Louis the typographical union ordered union printers away from the *Times* in 1880 when the paper broke a work rule, from all city newspapers in 1887 when the union was trying to enforce a shorter work week, and from the *Evening Call* in 1891 when it tried to undercut the union scale. In 1900 and 1911 the carpenters' union struck St. Louis contractors who refused to abide by the new hourly wage scale adopted by the Carpenters' District Council.[35]

The unions used fraternal discipline and strikes to assert their control over crafts against constant cheapening pressures. Skilled lasters struck in 1894 to block the Hamilton-Brown Shoe Company in St. Louis from introducing machines and unskilled workers. Electrical workers walked out of the same city's Wagner Electric Company in 1899 when it introduced two machine systems. Sedalia's bricklayers' union required workers to serve a four-year apprenticeship to learn the whole craft before they could become journeymen. Considering the boys that newspapers hired to run the power presses to be merely "half-fledged pressmen," the St. Louis Typographical Union sought to limit their numbers in 1864. The same union required workers from rural areas in 1873 to present certificates to prove "their competency to fill the place of journeymen." Members of Carpenters' locals in St. Louis refused to allow unskilled workers to handle their tools or do their traditional jobs for fear that the laborers might learn enough of the trade to do their work at lower wages. The St. Louis District Council refused in 1901 to aid in creating a building laborers' union because "it would result in a kind of kindergarten [sic] for carpenters." Fearing that both piecework and time cards permitted employers to subdivide the craft and thus gain control over its pace, the District Council on August 23, 1910, prohibited members from signing time cards and a week later ordered carpenters away from the Chamberlain Weatherstrip Company until it abandoned piecework.[36]

With their group consciousness defined by control over their craft, members of craft unions perceived other crafts as threats. The new technologies constantly transformed work processes, materials, and tools and left in their wake rivalries over which union's traditional responsibility applied to the new process. In St. Louis carpenters battled with elevator constructors in 1899 over which trade had jurisdiction over the cutting and finishing of elevator hatchways and gates, with painters in 1905 over scaffolds, with iron workers in 1908 over metal sash and fire doors, with lathers in 1911 over metal corner beads, with sheet metal workers in 1913 over hollow metal work.[37]

Since craft loyalties overlapped with the ethnic and religious affiliations that inspired the fraternal ethic, the new unions frequently had a distinctive ethnic cast. Drawing on the fraternal and benevolent German societies of the 1850s, the St. Louis brewery workers union of the 1880s and 1890s still reflected their German heritage. Since the original craftsman members had given preference in apprenticeships, in characteristic fraternal way, to their own sons and other relatives, Germans formed 90 percent of the members of Local 6 of the United Brewery Workers. The local conducted its business and published its journal in German. With strong ethnic roots in the fraternal ethic, many unionists viewed people from different backgrounds who increasingly competed with them for the same jobs as enemies and excluded them from their unions. In 1892 St. Louis's 1,200 organized hod carriers belonged to three separate unions, one for white English speakers, one for German speakers, and one for black English speakers. The same divisions separated the city's three waiters' unions. The printers were divided into German and English unions. Although German and English printers agreed to honor each other's working cards in 1873 and to work at the same scale and charge the same dues in 1883, the English-speaking union overwhelmingly voted against amalgamation with the Germans as late as 1893. St. Louis marine firemen were also divided by race. By the mid-1880s German-speaking locals in St. Louis put ethnicity before class or craft by organizing a citywide Arbeiter-Verband.[38]

As Missouri workers broadened the fraternal impulse, they incorporated its intensely local orientation along with its traditions of ethnicity and craft. Inheriting the fraternal heritage that had united people across occupational divisions to protect their families and communities, the new unions revolved around their local lodges and they expected support from the community when outside corporations imposed changes on local workers. During the 1877 railroad strike newspapers in Hannibal, Moberly, St. Joseph, and Sedalia did indeed report that local residents from all backgrounds had sided with local workers, whom they labeled "defenceless labor," against what the Moberly *Enterprise Monitor* called "organized and domineering capital."[39]

Missouri workers also drew heavily on patriotic traditions. It was the desire to assert "American citizenship" against the new menace of "corporate greed," resolved coal miners from Randolph City in 1888, that had led workers to form unions "to preserve their sacred rights guaranteed to them as American citizens."[40]

Many Missouri workers tried to transcend the craft and ethnic loyalties that had originally inspired the fraternal impulse of the new unions. "Oh, ye workingmen of America, who love your liberty and your native land; ye great creators of wealth," began a Knights of Labor appeal from St. Louis in 1886, "the great question of the age" was "shall we . . . be a nation of free men or a nation of slaves?"[41] They tried to organize workers, skilled and unskilled, from all backgrounds into a united class. They expressed their dream of empowering workers in the mass in the St. Louis general strike of 1877, in the Knights of Labor's plans for a single union of skilled and unskilled, and in the Socialist party's hopes for the political overthrow of capitalism. Each of these attracted massive support from workers, who glimpsed in them how the fraternal impulse could be broadened to a whole class. But their moments were either brief or narrow, in the end, because the fraternal impulse constantly pushed up against and was restrained by craft and ethnic limits, and because in the marketplace unskilled workers were, finally, desperate competitors.

Missouri's workers built much deeper alliances with other workers when craft, community, or ethnic loyalties reinforced those alliances. When news of the 1871 Chicago fire reached St. Louis, the typographical union convened a special meeting at which they sent $300 to their fellow printers in distress and agreed to donate a day's wages each to the Chicagoans. Craft unions never doubted that they shared more with other craft unions than with employers. They created building trades councils so that unionists, not employers, would resolve jurisdictional disputes. In 1881 the St. Louis Trades and Labor Assembly created a Resistance Fund in which each constituent union contributed a nickel for each of its members to a common pool for use in strikes. Community loyalty led nine English-speaking and four German-speaking local unions to form the St. Louis Central Labor Union in 1885, and by 1904 six Missouri communities had citywide labor councils. The St. Louis Typographical Union extended "our brotherly and fraternal sympathy" and $300 to striking telegraphers in 1883, and the district council of St. Louis carpenters donate $500 to help their community's striking telephone operators in 1913.[42] Many workers united across craft lines to elect political candidates and promote public policies that would aid workers against employers. Workers in St. Louis formed a Workingmen's party in 1877, and they formed workers' tickets in several Missouri communities in the mid-1880s.

The most profound and effective way that Missouri workers broadened the fraternal impulse into a consciousness of class grew from a merger of two old traditions: the tradition of face-to-face discipline by consumers over producers, and the fraternal yearning to escape competition by reintegrating production with consumption around the family. Workers developed the boycott into an instrument of moral solidarity and discipline that best expressed the possibilities, as well as the limits, of collective working-class action.

Missouri workers developed the boycott into a means to unite workers across craft and ethnic lines in their roles as consumers so as to force employers to respect workers' unions. Union members and their families pledged to boycott products made by anti-union employers and to purchase only from employers who had the support of the union in that craft. Although unions had occasionally urged their members not to patronize anti-union firms in other trades as early as the 1860s, the boycott did not develop into a formal and major weapon until the 1880s. During strikes against the *Times* in 1880 and the *Post-Dispatch* in 1881, the St. Louis Typographical Union forged the methods for turning the consumer power of the city's unionized workers into a major organizing force. They sent delegations to other St. Louis unions and to the new Central Trades and Labor Assembly to urge their members to cancel their subscriptions to the *Times* and *Post-Dispatch* and to refuse to patronize merchants who advertised in those papers. Then they warned advertisers that they would lose business if they advertised in "unfair" papers. On April 24, 1881, the union was cheered to learn that the *Post-Dispatch* had suffered deeply from the boycott by subscribers and advertisers.[43]

The development in the 1880s of citywide and national federations of craft unions, of the Knights of Labor, and of union label leagues provided a more formal mechanism for boycotts by unionist consumers to reinforce direct appeals from striking unions to those in other trades. At Sedalia in the mid-1880s, for example, the barbers' union urged consumers to boycott a new nonunion shop, while the printers imposed boycotts on two nonunion newspapers and the cigarmakers asked consumers not to patronize nonunion dealers. The local Knights of Labor urged all Sedalians to honor these boycotts. St. Louis brewery workers persuaded the St. Louis Trades and Labor Union, the American Federation of Labor, and the Knights of Labor in the late 1880s and early 1890s to boycott the major brewers. Early in 1891 two major breweries, Anheuser-Busch and Lemp's, bowed to the boycott by working-class consumers and became union shops. At its first meeting in 1891 the new Missouri State Federation of Labor established a Committee on Strikes and Boycotts, as though one automatically implied the other.

Individual unions also continued to organize boycotts directly. At St. Louis the Carpenters' District Council used a two-month boycott fo force William Barr's Dry Goods Company to hire only union carpenters. The most spectacular of the state's boycotts came during the 1900 strike by the Amalgamated Association of Street Railway Employees against the St. Louis streetcars, when for several months passengers refused to ride the scab cars.[44]

Boycotts became such a powerful expression of solidarity precisely because they drew so heavily on Missourians' traditional and fraternal disciplines. They were a new way for workers to express the old tradition of trading on bonds of reputation between consumers and producers. Workers proved the depth of their commitment to the boycott by using the full weight of fraternal discipline against members who broke boycotts by other unions. The St. Louis Typographical Union formally informed the brewery workers' union in 1889 that "members of this union drink none but union beer," and it fined member Charles Beatty fifteen dollars in 1888 when it learned that he had broken a musicians' union boycott. The St. Louis Carpenters' District Council pledged to discipline two members if it turned out that they had in fact violated a 1913 teamsters' union boycott of the St. Louis and Pevely Dairy.[45]

Many workers hoped to extend fraternal craft pride across craft barriers to express before all Missourians the same kind of class solidarity and pride that business and professional leaders demonstrated through activities like the Veiled Prophet festival in St. Louis. Although they had long marched proudly in civic parades with the banners and uniforms of their crafts, Missouri's workers in the 1880s increasingly shunned civic parades and reserved their full attention to Labor Day. By parading along some of the same St. Louis streets that the Veiled Prophet had followed, they sought to project fraternal unity among their different crafts as they asserted their shared democratic heritage. In St. Louis in 1903 the machine woodworkers quietly "filed" a request from civic leaders that they participate in a civic parade to celebrate the World's Fair, while they took pains to organize and compel their members' participation in that year's Labor Day parade.[46]

In the course of their efforts to broaden the fraternal tradition in their new organizations, Missouri's workers concluded that the great strength and great weakness of the fraternal ethic was that, fundamentally, it rejected the market. And fraternal workers received popular support for that rejection. Other newspapers agreed with the *Sedalia Daily Bazoo's* 1877 attack on the "mistaken belief of railroad officials that when industry is glutted, the price of labor should come down to starvation prices."[47] Fraternal-minded workers denied the very legitimacy of the market because its competition eroded the craft, ethnic, community, and moral sources of the fraternal movement.

Relentless competitive pressures, however, drove some workers to the painful conclusion that they could not abolish the market and that, instead of resisting it, they should follow the businessmen's example of organizing to control it. By uniting workers across crafts, communities, and ethnic groups, they could hope to fix the price of their labor. Only through national organization could Missouri workers hope to escape competition with workers elsewhere, since the new corporations sold products throughout the country from plants in many communities. To combat Jay Gould's railroad network, Missouri's railroad workers in the 1880s joined others throughout the Southwest in locals of the Knights of Labor, to negotiate on equal terms with Gould's companies.

National unions and bargaining meant acceptance of the basic terms of the new order. Workers' new organizations sought wages based not on traditional local needs but on how much they could win from employers. And that generally depended on their employers' financial health. Four St. Louis boiler manufacturers rejected the union's 1893 request for higher wages because their Eastern competitors already paid lower wages. On the other hand, Eastern iron and steel mills threatened to bust the Amalgamated Association of Iron and Steel Workers if it failed to compel the St. Louis Rolling Mill to pay the same wage scale that the union had extracted from Eastern mills. In the same spirit, Missouri's coal operators urged the United Mine Workers in 1910 to organize the nonunion Western coalfields in order to raise the price of Western competition to Missouri coal.[48]

As St. Louis printers tried to control the price for their labor in the face of the new order's cheapening pressures, the market imposed painful limits on the demands they placed on their employers and the ways they sought to win collective control. As early as 1864 the typographical union wrote the city's newspaper proprietors that it considered "your interests as forming to a great extent our own," and agreed to discuss with them a scale that would allow St. Louis to maintain a competitive position. On this occasion the union preferred to strike rather than permit an employer's financial condition to determine its members' wages. During the depression of the 1870s the union adopted new and lower scales each few months as its members tried to restrain the market. By 1875 the *Globe-Democrat* was the city's only "square" shop. In the summer of 1877 members faced the reality that only one or two proprietors paid any attention to the union scale, and the fraternal prohibition against working below scale simply meant that loyal union men could not take printing jobs in St. Louis, where most paid less than scale. Finally, on July 25, 1877, members gathered to declare that the union "lacked power to enforce any authority" and dissolved it. With the return of good times two years later printers recreated the union, but this time they were even more sensitive to the financial health of their employers. In 1887 they consulted with international union officers as well as those from Cincinnati and Chicago about the regional printing market before setting the St. Louis scale.[49]

The new commitment to national bargaining left Missouri workers dependent on their employers' profits and on the business cycle—in short, on economic growth. Once they embraced growth as the basis for their new organizations, they came to cooperate with employers in promoting their industries and communities so that their employers could afford better wages. When St. Louis promoters formed a Million Population Club in the early twentieth century to boost that city, the local typographical union was one of the first organizations to affiliate. Boasting that it was "a thorough business organization," the union claimed that affiliation with the boosters showed "the civic pride and alertness" of its membership. Unions came to base their demands less on their members' needs than on the commercial position of employers. In the 1910s the St. Louis Building Trades Council even joined the Chamber of Commerce in order to keep abreast of the city's business outlook.[50]

As unions accommodated themselves to the new order, many Missouri workers lamented the decline of the fraternal ethic. The local tradition of mutual aid did not extend well to faceless people from different ethnic backgrounds in remote communities who simply happened to work for the same employer or in the same industry. The new national unions sometimes provided the economic form of mutual aid but not its underlying spirit of assisting people from the same craft, ethnic group, or community to aid each other and control the dimensions of their lives that were most important to them. The new unions demanded that each local community surrender a measure of autonomy in exchange for the union's power to bargain for all its members in all communities. Accustomed to local control, many workers deeply resented having to commit themselves above all to the national organization.

Sedalia's railroad workers felt the clash between the fraternal tradition and the new labor organizations when they struck the huge Gould empire. Organized in lodges of the fraternal Ancient Order of United Workmen, Sedalia's railroad workers struck the Gould railroads on March 7, 1885, to protest drastic wage cuts, longer hours, and arbitrary dismissals of local workers. They remained solid and disciplined. Lacking national organization, the strikers appealed to their neighbors' anger at the economic and political power of the Gould system and to their general antimonopoly sentiments. To most townspeople the issue was whether a huge external institution could trample over the rights of Sedalians, and local merchants and city officials joined the strikers in asserting the value of community control. The strike's only arrest was of Gould's superintendent, A. M. Hager, for shouting profanities when city officials hired railroad workers instead of Pinkertons to police the Gould company's property. The strikers won when railroad officials agreed to restore wages and consider shortening hours.

Inspired by the victory, nearly a thousand Sedalians soon joined the Knights of Labor. When representatives of the five locals came together to form District Assembly 101 and selected Martin Irons to chair its executive committee, they expected that fraternal and organizational appeals could coexist. Irons soon explained, however, that he wanted to build a "broad and comprehensive union for labor on a basis that would counterbalance the power of aggregated and incorporated wealth." Since the basic struggle was between two centralized economic organizations, the railroad and the union, he wanted above all for the Gould system to recognize the Knights as the workers' bargaining agent. When the Texas and Pacific Railroad discharged a Knights delegate in March 1886, Irons saw his chance. He called out all the workers along the Gould lines to show their commitment to the union. The workers promptly struck, but they soon began to wonder why. The cause of the 1885 strike had been immediate grievances, and its thrust had been the desire to preserve community control. But in 1886 the grievance—discharge of a union official in Texas—was neither local nor immediate. Most Sedalians blamed the union in the 1886 strike, for now the union seemed to be the outsider preying on the community. As the weeks dragged on, local merchants blamed the union for the shortages that resulted from disrupted rail service. The strikers themselves could do nothing, for the power to call or halt the strike rested with Irons and remote Knights officials. Since loyalty to the organization was the issue in 1886, the strikers could only wait, with a growing feeling of powerlessness, for orders from the Knights. Agreeing with an official of the Brotherhood of Locomotive Firemen, Eugene V. Debs, that the strike had been "hasty and rash," and increasingly desperate, some strikers broke ranks and straggled back to work. Others, angry and uncertain in purpose, engaged in violence against railroad property and nonstriking workers. Finally, two months after the Knights had called the strike, Grand Master Workman Terrence V. Powderly ended the disaster by ordering the workers back to work.[51]

Workers throughout Missouri shared the Sedalians' skepticism that labor relations could or ought to be reduced to a struggle between two huge rival organizations, both of which accepted the new order and, what was worse, sought to subordinate everything else to the claims of their organizations for loyalty. Missouri workers wanted to preserve fraternal mutual aid amid the thrust toward economic bargaining, to maintain local control amid the national focus, to assert the defense of democracy and community above institutional loyalty. When union printers at St. Louis reestablished the typographical union in 1879, they hoped to escape their earlier dependence on powerful executive committees that conducted their bargaining. On August 24, 1879, they abolished the executive committee, explaining that they feared it would destroy community and democracy by creating "distrust among members" and that it "would gradually become a star-chamber power." Although by the early twentieth century machine woodworkers at St. Louis believed that business agents could conduct the union's commercial activities more effectively than could local meetings, they feared that the business agents would threaten their fraternal base. They insisted on frequent elections to keep the business agents responsive to the local, and they rejected a request to extend the agents' term from six months to a year.[52]

Many of the state's workers saw that they received more support from other Missourians when they fought for traditional fraternal values than when they organized to parallel the new corporations. "The mass of the people of Sedalia are neither capitalists nor Knights of Labor, and they do not propose to be tyrannized over by either without our urgent protest," proclaimed an 1886 mass meeting. Contrasting the popular support for railroad workers in 1885 with the opposition to the strike in 1886, the Jefferson City *Tribune* explained that "when it comes to a question of power between the Knights of Labor and the railway company . . . , the strikers lost the sympathy they would otherwise have."[53]

Many Missouri workers tried to support the national union while preserving local control. Carpenters from St. Louis spearheaded the formation in 1880–81 of the national United Brotherhood of Carpenters and Joiners. Within a decade the national union ordered locals to form Carpenters' District Councils in order to enhance carpenters' bargaining power with citywide contractors. But the district councils recognized that they threatened the tradition of local control. In the St. Louis district some locals were predominantly German, and the council allowed them to preserve the ethnic basis of their unionism by voting in 1897 to publish a thousand copies of the union's trade rules in German and to translate the council's proceedings into German. Other locals were rooted in the specialized carpentry crafts of cabinetmaker and millwright, and in the early twentieth century the district council allowed these locals to use business agents in different ways than outdoor carpenters did and to set their own wage scales. When the business agents tried to centralize power in 1914 by promoting a state council of carpenters, the locals voted down the proposal by a three-to-one margin.

The Carpenters' District Council defended its community and craft traditions against more centralized bodies. When the St. Louis Building Trades Council permitted other unions to do jobs carpenters regarded as theirs, the St. Louis carpenters' council withdrew from the trades council. This occurred in 1908 and again in 1915, when the trades council ruled in favor of machinists and iron workers, respectively, in jurisdictional battles. Likewise, St. Louis carpenters defended a local tradition by furiously, and successfully, protesting an 1899 proposal by the national union and the American Federation of Labor to issue a charter to organize carpenters' helpers. When the United States entered World War I and unprecedented pressures for economic consolidation were unleashed, Carpenters' president William Hutcheson issued unprecedented commands to the St. Louis District Council. He urged them to consolidate locals into fewer and larger ones, which they did. He told them to stop blocking laborers and hod carriers from building hoists and scaffolds, which they refused to do. And he ordered them to reaffiliate with the Building Trades Council, which they postponed doing.[54]

Even as they tried to maintain the fraternal content, Missouri workers adopted the new economic form of organizing in order to try to control the market. The state's coal miners first organized in local fraternal bodies that aided members in the 1870s and 1880s, and later moved to a national union, the United Mine Workers. U.M.W. organizers created eighteen locals in the state's coalfields in the single year of 1899. On April 1, 1910, the national United Mine Workers convention ordered all soft-coal workers in the nation to strike their employers. The strike lasted nearly six months. As the new unions focused on bargaining, more and more Missouri workers called their strikes to win for a national union the right to be the exclusive bargaining agent in Missouri workplaces. In 1899 thirteen of the twenty-six strikes and walkouts in Kansas City were over the issue of union recognition. By 1910 the state's workers were organized primarily in geographically dispersed locals whose major function was to support the national union's efforts to bargain with employers over the price workers received for their labor. In 1911 workers in 47 Missouri locals owed primary loyalty to the United Mine Workers and in 44 Missouri locals to the United Brotherhood of Carpenters and Joiners. Missouri's workers that year belonged to 29 locals of the railroad trainmen and locomotive firemen, 28 of machinists, 27 of locomotive engineers, 24 of railway carmen and railway conductors, 21 of painters, 17 of boilermakers, and 16 of the national brewery workers.[55]

While the ethnic, craft, and community loyalties that had undergirded the fraternal tradition kept Missouri workers from becoming part of the class-conscious proletariat that Karl Marx had expected to be the form of economic organization in the new order, the fraternal tradition also prevented them from accepting the competitive values and disciplines of the new order. Like their employers, they wanted a more secure price for what they sold, but unlike their employers, they wanted at the same time to preserve the fraternal traditions of mutual assistance, local control, and the vision of the fraternal family as the alternative to competition.

VII

Political Resistance in
the New Order

Resisters increasingly entered the world of politics and government as Missourians organized in response to the new order. Politics concentrated and narrowed the patterns of resistance.

Politics at first appeared familiar and inviting to Missourians as they organized to regain control over their lives. The nation's republican heritage and its avenue of political involvement reached back, after all, to long before the birth of the new order. Politics seemed the natural way to turn the guerrilla skirmishes and private struggles that were endemic in the new order into all-out war to redistribute power. Only after bitter experience did Missourians conclude that the new order had dramatically reshaped the core of politics, leaving only its outward appearance unchanged. Familiar patterns of mobilization turned into actual barriers to fundamental change.

Missourians soon discovered that the champions of growth used structures and traditions of politics and government as tools to secure the new order and block popular resistance. The mass-based political parties, in particular, attracted the new, far-flung corporations with markets and plants throughout Missouri. The parties united representatives from across the state in loyalty to a single organization that had the means to compel most of its members to follow the party line. Since politicians subordinated policies to the winning of office, corporations could persuade politicians to adopt favorable policies by providing parties and candidates with the money and troops to win elections. Governor Lon Stephens explained in 1900, for example, that the Democrats had to cater to the Missouri Pacific Railroad's concerns because "we must have" the railroad's support "in order to carry Missouri."[1]

Since their basic expectations about how politics could help them control their lives had been formed before the development of the new order, traditional Missourians themselves created major obstacles to successful political resistance. Possession of the ballot gave them the feeling that they already controlled their fates more substantially than did people in other lands. They had long exercised the right to vote as a way to defend their personal and

201

cultural networks against attack by people from different racial, ethnic, religious, and sectional backgrounds. They had formed their major political parties around those defenses. Even after the new order introduced new threats, many traditional Missourians continued to see politics in its traditional form, as a battleground for cultural, not economic, war. So long as Missourians confined their view of political control and partisan attachment to the traditional defense of church, language, race, and party, and limited their activity to the election of friends and party, not the making of policy, they made it easier for the new economic leaders to advance their own policies and to deflect popular resistance.

In the late nineteenth century traditional Missourians further weakened their capacity for political resistance by the strong suspicion and even hostility they developed toward law and government. Government had become the enemy. Immediately following the crisis of law and authority in the Civil War, governments of unprecedented power and scope had propelled Missouri to the center of the new national market economy and imposed new compulsions that were eroding the familiar ways Missourians had regulated their lives. Infuriated by developers' expansion of the size and cost of government, traditional Missourians wanted a state that was less, not more, powerful and creative. They fought back with a new constitution in 1875.

Missourians used the 1875 constitution as the framework to slash the scope and costs of government. By 1903 they had completely liquidated a state bonded debt of $21.8 million from the 1870s, and over the same period they cut the state property tax rate in half. Reflecting the new restraints on local governments, the tax rate in St. Louis fell from $3.49 on each $100 of property in 1875 by $1.90 in 1901. Promoters tried to remove these constitutional restraints by permitting local governments to raise taxes for such public improvements as bridges, roads, and public buildings, but the state's voters rejected their proposals in 1884, 1886, 1894, and 1896.[2]

Missouri's political leaders accepted, sometimes regretfully, the limitations that popular hatred for government placed on them. Governor Joseph Folk told the legislature in 1909 that Missouri's state tax rate was half that of neighboring Iowa and one-third that of neighboring Kansas and Illinois. In 1917 Governor Elliott Major boasted that Missouri conducted its public business at the lowest per capita cost in the nation. Believing that "the opportunities for development here . . . are unlimited," Governor Herbert Hadley lamented in 1912 that "for too long have we been prone to glory in a system of low taxes" based on the "theory that that government was best which governed least."[3]

Lingering popular suspicion of the powers and costs of government, and the enshrinement of that suspicion in the 1875 constitution, fundamentally limited the forms of relief that Missourians could expect from political action. Fearful that a powerful state would severely limit their own actions, corporations continually tried to rekindle popular suspicion of government whenever resisters challenged their power. Popular suspicion combined with corporate intransigence to form a formidable barrier to the political imagination and mobilization of resistance.

Traditional Missourians persisted in searching for ways to turn their resistance into effective political action. Resisters developed two different patterns, because they entered the world of politics from two different paths.

The earliest movements began as cooperative campaigns by groups to help their own members in fraternal ways. Groups turned to politics and the state, sometimes reluctantly, only after they had built a solid and independent base of members in earlier participatory mutual aid activities. Labor unions and farmers' alliances are classic examples.

The second group of resistance movements sprouted by the turn of the century around the initial objective not of helping members but of direct political action to change the state or at least its laws. Bound together more by a common political program or temper than by shared activities, the second group leapfrogged the more traditional and defensive origins of resistance in mutual aid, and started out by taking the political offensive against concentrated wealth and power.

The two kinds of political resistance developed different approaches to the same challenge. Both confronted, however, political structures and traditions that had revolved around officeholding to respond to their policy concerns. Those traditions and structures, resisters learned, had deep roots in Missouri life and were hard to change.

11

Traditional Resistance, Populism, and the Limits of Politics

To traditional resisters the arena of politics seemed a natural one in which to broaden their fraternal quest for control in the new order. They soon discovered profound limits to politics as their farm, worker, and temperance groups turned to the state for help.

1. Traditional Resistance and the Limits of Politics

Traditional resistance movements began in cooperative activities to assist members in preserving familiar patterns of security. They began by assuming that the best way to reunite production with consumption and to discipline competitive, secular pressures with the authority of moral tradition, was to form defensive groups in which members could aid each other and live by alternative values and mutual assistance.

Traditional movements at first viewed politics as alien to their resistance. Partisan loyalties subverted these movements' goals by dividing members along irrelevant lines. Growing from a fraternal movement that assisted members through consumer cooperatives and mutual aid, the Granger movement of the 1870s specifically prohibited even discussion of partisan politics. The farm protest movements of the 1880s also followed cooperative and fraternal, not political, lines. When the Farmers' Alliance merged with the Agricultural Wheel in 1889 to form the Farmers' and Laborers' Union of Missouri, Wheel president H. W. Hickman hailed the new group as "a great fraternal brotherhood." Its member-owned network of producer and consumer cooperatives would free members from the new middlemen. Members could keep uncongenial strangers out, because any applicant for membership who received three black balls would be denied admission. Fearful that its

205

members would be "blinded by partisanship," in the words of the Sedalia *Harmony Baptist* in 1898, the temperance movement was likewise nonpartisan. Agreeing with St. Louis *Labor* in 1903 that "the Democrats and Republicans are feathers of the same bird of prey," labor unions also scrupulously banned divisive partisan politics as they built from their defensive and fraternal origins into groups to challenge employers.[1]

When the new economic leaders used government and the courts to knock down Missourians' traditional protections, resisters concluded that they had to enter politics, if only to maintain their defensive and alternative character. When employers' legal injunctions in the courts denied unions the power to strike, when farmers had to repay their loans in currency whose value rose with the political power of their creditors in Washington, when railroads and bondholders preyed on taxpayers, when the state licensed growing numbers of saloons to encourage secularism and rebelliousness, traditional resisters entered politics. Fearing that the growing political power of saloons and breweries paralleled the ebbing moral authority of church and family, the Salt River Baptist Association in 1882 broke its tradition of resistance to the state by demanding that the state adopt prohibition. Although the St. Louis Typographical Union resisted political action more than most of that city's unions, the printers organized and raised money in 1890 to block their anti-union nemesis, proprietor Charles Gitchell of the St. Louis *Star-Sayings*, in his bid for election to the city's House of Delegates. The Grange, Farmers' Alliance, and Knights of Labor went into politics to protect their cooperatives from political and economic annihilation by middlemen, landowners, and employers. The Missouri Farmers' Alliance was finally driven to politics, explained Vice-President A. B. Johnson, because politics had robbed its members of everything.[2]

The spectacular explosion in the 1880s of monopolistic middlemen, which separated production even further from consumption, gave increasingly sharp political focus to a single isue that rallied many of the state's resistance movements to enter politics. Around that issue they began to formulate a political ideology. "God hates monopoly," cried a crusader for the Farmers' Alliance. Alliance and Agricultural Wheel lecturers traced farmers' problems to "a monopoly that wants to buy the earth, and with it the souls and bodies of the people who inhabit it" and thus "wring from labor its true reward." The grievance that angered Missouri coal miners most in the 1880s was the requirement that they buy all their food, clothing, shelter, and medical care from a single monopolistic middleman who was also their employer. "Gould and his monopolies must go down, or your children must be slaves," the Knights of Labor warned in its appeal to St. Louis workers in 1886. Farmers and workers hoped to keep more of the wealth they produced by using the state to remove the monopolistic middlemen who intervened between what they produced and what they consumed. The new Missouri State Federation of Labor aimed "to secure to the toilers a proper share of the wealth they create."[3]

By the end of the 1880s farmers and workers had given an antimonopoly thrust to their fraternal movements and were entering politics to try to keep more of the wealth they produced. When rural Missourians launched the Farmers' and Laborers' Union of Missouri in 1889, the new group proposed laws against monopolistic middlemen. It called for government ownership of transportation, communication, and bank notes, to replace the huge private railroads, telegraph companies, and banks. It demanded laws that would restrain middlemen who speculated in land and farm commodities by allowing only actual settlers to purchase lands and by prohibiting speculation in agricultural futures. Less than two years later the state's labor unions launched a similar attack on middlemen when they came together to create the Missouri State Federation of Labor. The unionists, too, demanded government-owned banks to replace private ones and called for a single tax that would encourage the use of land by producers, not by speculators.[4] These demands were part of a larger and more general movement for a strong antitrust law and for prosecutions that would smash the new monopolies that intervened between producers and consumers. Fired on by their vision of a future in which they could keep more of what they created, resistance movements concluded that politics was essential to their salvation, even as they retained many of their traditional suspicions.

As they tried to turn their hopes and programs into policies, they found new confirmation of their fears that the world of politics was an alien one full of hazards and barriers. They immediately ran into the same barrier that historically had kept them out of politics: that "the only government that we know in this country is party government," as Governor Herbert Hadley concluded in 1912. The death grip of partisanship forced resisters to adapt their programs to the parties' tradition of subordinating both issues and candidates to the all-consuming goal of officeholding. Compounding this problem was the widespread expectation that parties were the only agencies to mobilize voting majorities and that every voter possessed a nearly hereditary commitment to support one of the two major parties. Many despaired of finding solutions, and lapsed into growling their old hatred for partisanship. "Stick to your party! . . . Yes, stick till the last cow is mortgaged and the sheriff gets the harness on you and shows you over the hills to the poorhouse," spat the Memphis *Farmers' Union* from northeastern Missouri in 1891. In the late 1880s temperance advocates charged that Democrats and Republicans were so obsessed by officeholding that they would never make a full commitment to prohibition. Although some Democratic and Republican officeholders did "their very best for organized labor," observed Reuben Wood, longtime president of the state labor federation, "their good work is limited by the Capitalist influences of the political parties that elected them to office."[5]

The problem was somehow to turn a system that pivoted on officeholding into one that could pivot on policy. Since political parties were the most familiar vehicle for mobilizing voters, resisters generally answered the challenge of unresponsive existing parties by creating new parties more committed to policy than office. The Republican party's history gave them hope. That party had emerged within a single decade to focus the national agenda on slavery, elect a president, control Congress, and win a civil war. Trying to escape uncertain employment and competition from children "caused by the monopoly in the hands of the capitalists," St. Louis trade unionists in 1877 turned to the Workingmen's party. Pursuing policy, not office, the new party called a general strike, not an election, to pressure the Missouri legislature to enact eight-hour and child labor laws.[6]

Resisters usually confined their third-party activites to the more conventional partisan goal of trying to win elections. Angered by the Democrats' extravagant spending and subservience to railroads, many Grangers eagerly joined a new People's party in 1874 that pledged to regulate railroads, reduce taxes, and "be under the control of the people, and not partisan tricksters and wire pullers." During the late 1870s and 1880s resisters hoping to widen the political arena created the Greenback and Union Labor parties. Temperance advocates assumed at first that politicians would act as soon as they were convinced of public opinion. They collected signatures on 47 prohibition petitions to the 1881 state legislature. In 1883 they sent 245 petitions. At their peak in 1887 they buried major party politicians under 761 petitions. Democratic and Republican officials alike ignored this proof of public support.[7] The solution was to create and support a Prohibition party.

Many of the state's workers concluded that they could best turn their fraternal and craft traditions into political relief in the new order by creating their own independent political party. In St. Louis, unionists in the 1880s combined craft autonomy, ethnic pride, and community loyalty into a special kind of political action. After calling for "a complete severance of all political connection with the two ruling parties by whom" workers "have been so long and so persistently deceived," the new St. Louis Trades Assembly officially urged in 1882 "that steps shall be taken for a union of producers at the ballot-box." Soon the demand for an independent third party began to coalesce around an ideology. The unionists who came together in 1887 to form the St. Louis Central Trades and Labor Union combined their German tradition of strong governmental protection against economic insecurity with the American republican tradition of rejecting capitalism itself for fixing "the bonds of wage slavery" on workers. They helped steer the new Missouri State Federation of Labor toward the Socialist party. "What is urgently needed in Missouri . . . is a powerful working class [political] organization which will be a natural ally of the trade union movement," declared State Federation president Reuben Wood in his first report to Missouri unionists, who had selected him president in part because he was a Socialist. The St. Louis Central Trades urged workers to embrace the Socialists, insisting that there was "no issue between" Republicans and Democrats "which concerns labor's interest."[8] Missouri attracted national attention in the early twentieth century because its labor movement was particularly committed to the Socialist party and political action.

Maintaining that "the ruling class" controlled both Democrats and Republicans, Missouri Socialists formally called for "abolition of the wage and profit system, and for the introduction of the co-operative system of production and distribution which will guarantee to the working people the full fruits of their labor" in their 1908 state platform. They proceeded to nominate candidates, set up county and state party committees to elect them, and make promises that sometimes echoed those of the major parties. A leading Socialist newspaper, the Kennett *Justice*, captured the new party's traditional faith that parties best mobilized voters for radical action with the slogan, "Workers of the world unite at the Ballot Box." At its peak in 1912 the Socialist party polled 4 percent of Missouri's voters, appealing as strongly to tenants along the Oklahoma and Arkansas borders as to urban workers. Traditional cultural loyalties led workers, as well as farmers, to reject the new party. Socialists carried an additional cultural burden, for the Catholic church officially forbade its members to join the new party, which, it charged, "denies the existence of God, the immortality of the soul, eternal punishment, the right of private ownership, the rightful existence of our present social organization, and the independence of the Church as a society complete in itself and founded by God," according to the official Catholic St. Louis *Review* in 1902.[9]

Concluding that third parties would never break through the two-party barrier, many resisters tried to turn the major parties' concern with office-holding into pressure for political change. They hoped that thirst for their members' votes would lead the major party politicians to support their programs. They made it easier for those politicians by adopting a strictly nonpartisan stance. The St. Louis Typographical Union donated $50 in 1885 to pay expenses for a lobbyist to convince legislators that workers wanted them to vote to end child and convict labor. The State Federation of Labor, which was founded in 1891, soon was organizing a new labor lobby that sought to mobilize legislators, not voters. In 1893 the federation appointed a three-person committee to coordinate labor lobbying, and by 1907 its new Joint Labor Legislative Board was working with the railroad labor unions to influence legislation. The labor lobby hunted sponsors for bills, recruited testimony, sought friendly committees and chairs for its measures, and reminded legislators that their members' votes could make the difference at reelection time. During the early twentieth century the federation concentrated on eliminating convict labor and introducing workmen's compensation, with discouraging results. Labor lobbyists secured a law to phase out convict labor in 1911, but in both 1911 and 1913 the legislature refused to fund its implementation and in 1915 and 1917 administrators balked at implementing it. The long drive for workmen's compensation began in 1911. The legislature created successive commissions to "study"—and bury—the proposal. Having exhausted the legislative process, which seemed designed to thwart the passage of popular bills when powerful interests opposed them, the Federation appealed directly to voters by placing the measure on the 1926 ballot by initiative process. Voters enacted what legislators had rejected.[10]

Other traditional resistance movements had the same limited results when they tried to hurdle the partisan barrier by forming nonpartisan pressure groups. Early in 1894, for example, the St. Louis Ministers' Alliance created a group that within a few months evolved into the Missouri branch of the Anti-Saloon League. The league tried to pledge major party candidates to support its causes and then pressure those who won elections to honor their pledges. Only when St. Louis officials believed that voters backed the league's spectacular crusade against downtown wine rooms, as in 1899–1900 and 1903–5, did they close the illegal rooms.[11]

As they encountered the severe limitations of both third parties and nonpartisan pressure groups, resistance movements learned that the fundamental problem was the great distance in time, space, and function between a voter's ballot in the election booth and a representative's vote in the legislature. It was a distance that encouraged representatives to tell voters what they wanted to hear at election time but to listen to campaign contributors and party leaders when they voted on legislation. Legislators followed the thrust of law in the new order toward encouraging investment, opportunity, and growth. While defenders of tradition had viewed government as an enemy and remained aloof, promoters of growth had exuberantly used the political system to create the new order. The legislature attracted people whose experience favored compromise on or indifference to issues posed by a growth-oriented world. The 1909 legislature, for example, included 66 attorneys, 38 other professional men, 28 businessmen, 21 farmers, mostly with large operations, and 1 clerk.[12]

Experience tempered the resisters' vision, and they became resigned to narrow limits for serious debate. Missouri's labor lobbyists dreamed of an alternative order where workers had the power and there was no incentive to use dangerous machinery, but they discovered that they had trouble winning political support for something as minimal as a proposal for automatic compensation for injured workers. St. Louis unionists abandoned the hope of local political control and sought relief instead by following the market and forming national unions that would bargain with employers within the wage system. Although they had entered politics for policy, not office, resisters came reluctantly to adjust their demands and finally their vision itself to the distance between voter and policy.

For many traditional resisters the relentless imperative of officeholding had its most corrosive effect on their leaders. Time and again resisters watched the partisan and officeholding features of politics transform their own leaders into politicians. They watched politics divert their leaders from an initial determination to secure the movement's program into a quest for office for themselves. Leverett Leonard tried to show that resistance movements did not have to follow the all-too-familiar pattern when he decided to resign as president of the Missouri Farmers' and Laborers' Union in 1892 when the Populists nominated him for governor. Labor leaders Henry Blackmore and C. P. Connolly in 1892 led the successful drive to block the St. Louis Central Trades and Labor Union from formally affiliating with the

Socialists, and a few months later a grateful Democratic governor appointed
them state labor commissioner and factory inspector, respectively. Next, the
Central Trades' president declared that the group was supporting the Democratic mayoral candidate in 1893. Infuriated at the Democrats and their
leaders for diverting their organization into office seeking and partisanship,
Central Trades members ousted the president. They turned increasingly to
Socialists as leaders. When a new Central Trades president in 1901 accepted
the Democratic nomination for city inspector of weights and measures, the
group demanded that he resign as a union leader. E. H. Behrens knew that he
was expected to resign as president of the state Federation of Labor in 1904
when he accepted the Socialist party's nomination for the governorship.[13]
Trade unionists deeply feared that thirst for public office, even on the
Socialist ticket, could lead their leaders to betray the group's programs.

2. Populism and the Limits of Politics

The largest mass movement in late nineteenth-century Missouri, the farm
protest movement, faced the most subtle challenges from partisanship and
office seeking. From the start Democrats hoped to prevent the movement
from following earlier farm protests in diverting voters from the Democrats.
Beginning with the People's ticket of 1874, farm protest leaders had shared
nominations with the Republicans. Through this cooperation Missouri
Greenbackers had elected one congressman in 1878 and four in 1880. Democrats watched anxiously as a new farm movement, beginning in 1886, grew to
100,000 members when several groups merged in 1889 to form the Farmers'
and Laborers' Union (or Missouri Farmers' Alliance). Worse, the new movement grew increasingly radical in its demands for fundamental changes in the
areas of land, transportation, and money, changes that would reshape power
relations in the new order. For the 1890 election it listed thirty demands and
warned the two major parties that "we will not support any man for a
legislative office, of any political party, who will not pledge himself in writing
to use his influence for the formulation of these demands into laws."[14]

  Democrats hoped to tame the movement to their own purposes by combining promises, rhetoric, and proposals appealing to Alliance members with
offers of offices to leaders of the new movement. Democrat David Francis
rode antimonopoly rhetoric into the governorship in 1888. During the election he promised voters an antitrust law. At his inaugural he proclaimed that
the law would encourage "healthy competition." Once in office Francis
backed a measure that took farmer and worker desires to keep more of what
they created and turned them into a plan that actually aimed to reinforce the
new order by encouraging a greater number of producers to produce more.
The Democratic legislature followed Francis's lead and enacted an antitrust
law in 1889, but the law remained unenforced until the state supreme court
declared it unconstitutional in 1891. The 1891 legislature enacted a new
antitrust law that passed judicial muster, but large corporations viewed it as a

mere inconvenience they could evade by paying minor fines. Democrats hoped that their antimonopoly rhetoric and the 1889 and 1891 laws would distract Alliance voters from the Democratic party's failure to enact its pledges to that group in 1890 and would stave off more radical proposals. In 1892 Democrats nominated William J. Stone for governor in an attempt to win more Alliance votes. Wearing a floppy hat, issuing vague attacks on concentrated wealth, refusing to campaign in the cities, "Gum-Shoe Bill" Stone won election with a style that implied sympathy with the Alliance. Democratic newspapers, like the Kennett *Clipper* in 1890, tried to reinforce the traditional bonds of party by warning farm protesters that if they "stray off with side issues" raised by their movement, they would "aid the enemy" and only accomplish "the purpose of defeating the democratic party."[15] The Democrats were throwing tough challenges at a resistance movement whose roots were fraternal and cooperative, not political.

When farm protesters entered the unfamiliar world that centered on officeholding, they naturally felt that they could accomplish most by choosing leaders with political experience. For president of the Missouri Farmers' Alliance they selected H. W. Hickman, in part because he had served as a sheriff for seven years and had twice run for the legislature. Secretary J. W. Rogers of the Farmers' and Laborers' Union had served as county assessor. Among farm protest leaders from southeast Missouri, James K. Tubb had been a sheriff and state legislator, Land Lee a state legislator, John M. Allen a county assessor, and Ralph Wammack a probate court clerk. Democratic newspapers, like the Charleston *Enterprise* in 1886, charged with some justice that farmer movements were led "by disappointed office seekers and sore-headed politicians."[16] At the very least, officeholding leaders repeatedly blunted the movement's radical potential by reminding resisters of political "realities."

Alliance members felt the office seekers' restraint on their democratic push when they seriously championed the subtreasury plan that their movement had evolved to free members from the private credit system. The plan called for the government to establish local branches of the Federal treasury that could ease farmers' economic insecurities by making low-interest government loans in inflated paper currency. By proposing to replace bankers, commission merchants, and other money lenders with government, the plan took direct aim at powerful middlemen and sought an unprecedented expansion of government power, in a state where middlemen could easily appeal to popular distrust of government. Missouri's politically minded Alliance leaders recognized immediately that Democrats would reject the plan, and would certainly not advance leaders from a movement that proposed something so radical. Worried that the Alliance was pushing political debate beyond acceptable limits, the Democratic *St. Louis Republic* tried to bar the sub-treasury plan from the Alliance's agenda by charging that it originated with a "communistic organization" of "cranks and demagogues" who formed a "secret order within the Alliance" known as "Anti-Monopolists." This secret order's real goal, the paper warned, was to "freeze out the Democrats." Democratic office seekers within the Alliance set out to keep the movement within safe bounds. Longtime Democrats Uriel S. Hall, state lecturer of the Alliance, and Phil Chew, editor of the Alliance's official Missouri journal, succeeded in keeping the sub-treasury plan out of the official 1890 platform of the Missouri Alliance, although debate "waxed hot and furious" all one night at the convention. In return, the Democrats allowed the Alliance to write the party platform—minus the sub-treasury—and selected Hall as floor leader of the party convention, Alliance president Hickman as party nominee for railroad commissioner, and Alliance member Lloyd F. Wolfe as nominee for state school superintendent. All were elected.[17] In the traditional world of politics the movement's ideas advanced only as far as its leaders' offices.

Many Alliance members concluded that their leaders had sold out the movement's democratic and radical thrust. The sub-treasury plan represented the movement's dream of a democratic future, but Alliance leaders seemed more eager to serve Democratic politicians than their own members' dreams. Alliances in twelve central counties bolted their leaders and nominated third-party slates in county elections in 1890. Hall quashed this revolt by revoking the official charters of the rebellious county alliances by executive order.[18] "Bossism," another feature of traditional politics, thus accompanied the Alliance's entry into politics.

Angry at their own leaders for viewing election to office as the most important reform, infuriated at Democratic officeholders for refusing to make good on their promises to the Alliance, members organized to disentangle their movement from the clutches of office seeking and partisanship. "The air is rife with resistance, and the seeds of revolution are germinating on fertile soil," observed the Alliance journal from St. Louis in 1891. They warned Democrats that the Farmers' Alliance would no longer be "a tail to fly your Democratic kite with," as a central Missouri Alliance editor put it. Concluding that the movement's press shared their commitment to policy above office seeking, members turned to reform editors as their new leaders. They cheered when fifty-six Alliance editors came together in the summer of 1891 to create a Missouri Reform Press Association to explore fresh ways of mobilizing the full ideological thrust of their movement, particularly to use the subtreasury plan to dislodge the "money power." At the Alliance convention that same summer they replaced the Democratic politicians who had led the Alliance with subtreasury supporter Leverett Leonard as the new president.[19]

To maintain their democratic thrust in the face of the political restraints of office and party, Alliance members tried to create a mobilizing agency that would be free from the new order's commercial contamination. Whereas parties had once been "machines to carry out principles and enact them into law," in the new order the major parties had become "fossilized organizations." Wealthy contributors shaped their policies and their "very existence depends on the spoils system." Destroyed by commercialism and bossism, the two major parties had "rejected" the "teachings of Jefferson, Jackson, Lincoln, and Stevens," to whom Alliance editors looked as authorities for reform thought. Instead, the parties reenacted empty and "sham battles" over the Civil War and tariff and no longer permitted discussion of issues of wealth and power.[20]

Members of the Farmers' Alliance concluded that the way to mobilize resistance was not only to follow the path of other traditional resisters and create a new political party, but also to root that party in group experiences that would reinforce members' traditions, forming a democratic alternative to the commercialized parties. Since they hoped their party would reunite production and consumption, they tried to offset the major parties' appeals to ethnicity, sectionalism, and partisanship by activating and harnessing traditions of household control over production and consumption. Farmers followed the "passions and prejudices" of two-party politics because their geographic isolation from each other, together with the competition of the new order, deprived them of the social support on which resistance grew. And "however oppressive this isolated condition may be to the farmer and his sons, it is immeasurably more so to his wife and daughter," noted W. Scott Morgan, an Alliance editor from St. Louis. So to break down the isolation of each farm and to mobilize the full power of household traditions against middlemen, the Alliance held frequent gatherings at which farm husbands and wives participated equally. They believed that "woman's presence exercises a moral influence in all the exercises of the order" and "strengthens right principles," and that participation by women would release political force from the reintegrated household. Through meetings that brought households in the same neighborhood "into a closer connection and sympathy than now exists," they hoped to reactivate the tradition of community along with that of household. As they experienced the democratic power of family and community, Missourians would conclude that they faced a simple decision: "Take your choice between supporting the two old parties and saving the home for your children" by supporting the new party, declared the Alliance editor from Lamar.[21]

Democratic participation would permit the new party to enact principles instead seek offices. Members would take the place of campaign contributors in setting policy. Active participation by equals to "demand" changes would replace the resigned deference of the two major parties, whose bosses told voters to "only be quiet" and merely "petition" their betters for changes. "Dare we do it?" was the only question that mattered. By "maintaining and standing by our principles," declared Missouri Farmers' and Laborers' Union president Leverett Leonard, "we become a party into ourselves." Through active participation based on the experience that "all men are brothers and fellow citizens," members created a democratic present from which they could envision a democratic future whose terms they would shape for themselves. "Things are moving so fast that we can hardly keep up with the procession," panted an Alliance editor from northern Missouri in 1892.[22]

Missouri's delegates joined with other reformers in declaring their independence from the two-party system in 1892 by launching the People's party:

We have witnessed for more than a quarter of a century the struggles of the two great political parties for power and plunder, while grievous wrongs have been inflicted on the suffering people. We charge that the controlling influences dominating both these parties have permitted the existing dreadful conditions to develop without serious effort to prevent or restrain them.

The way to force their agenda into politics was, as ever, to create a new party whose representatives would not subordiante policy to "power and plunder." The Populists' presidential candidate, James Weaver, went on to attract 41,204 votes in Missouri in 1892, 7.6 percent of the state's total. Even though the new party's program appealed to a great many Missourians, the Populists only carried 61 of the state's 2,175 precincts because voters continued to view elections as traditional cultural battlegrounds between Republicans and Democrats, not as the wellspring for policies to restrain the new order.[23]

The new Populists struggled valiantly to preserve their radical vision despite the diversions, temptations, and threats of electoral politics. "The only hope of the people lies in remaining free from entangling alliances with rotten politicians of both old parties," proclaimed the Populist *Free Press* of Butler. The same paper contrasted the Populists' democratic thrust with the parties they wanted to replace by asking a question: "Why does it take lawyers to explain Democratic and Republican principles while farmers explain People's principles?" From the start many Populists felt the pull of election victories that drew them to cooperate with reform Democrats. The real threat to Populism, as one reform editor observed from central Missouri in 1891, was that the Democrats "will accede to just enough of [the third party's] demands to swallow it up, without reaching the vital questions at issue."[24]

Although their new party lost elections, Populists sympathized with Democratic reformers who routed the conservative, commercial wing within the Democratic party. They respected Democratic congressman Richard ("Silver Dick") Bland from Lebanon for his twenty-year crusade to inflate the currency, even while concluding that his proposals to monetize silver failed to address the underlying issues of wealth and power. Reformers agreed with Bland that the Democratic "party can gain no victory in the future without utterly repudiating" their party's reactionary president, Grover Cleveland, on the currency issue. They officially committed Missouri Democrats at an 1895 convention to a program of coining silver currency to relieve debtors without adopting the Populists' subtreasury challenge to the power of private creditors. They completed the rout in 1896 by drafting a reformist national platform and nominating Nebraska silverite William Jennings Bryan for the presidency.[25]

Populists suddenly had to decide whether the Democrats had moved far enough for the Populists to abandon their separate existence. Although thirty-two of Missouri's thirty-eight delegates to the 1896 Populist convention rejected cooperation with Democrats and voted to nominate their own presidential candidate, Missouri Populists accepted their party's nomination of Bryan and worked closely with the Democrats in a common campaign for Bryan. As election day approached, Populists became increasingly indistinguishable from Democrats. In the last week of the campaign the Populist gubernatorial candidate withdrew in favor of Democrat Lon V. Stephens. When Republican William McKinley won the presidency, the Populists realized they had lost all on a desperate gamble. The victorious Stephens repaid the Populists in the familiar way, not enacting their policies but appointing one of their leaders, A. Rozelle, to the prestigious and powerful post of state labor commissioner.[26]

Missouri's traditional resisters failed to translate a system based on office-holding and partisanship into one based on policymaking. Missourians came to regard any farmer movement "as some political movement that, while professing to advance the interest of agriculture, is endeavoring to win their confidence and open up political spoils to a new set of men," observed the State Board of Agriculture in 1898. They expected resistance to be subordinated in politics to "the office-holding and office-seeking class," according to the *St. Louis Republican* in 1875, the "self-seeking, time-serving parasites," as the *Fulton Gazette* characterized politicians in the early twentieth century. When they did enact policies, politicians insisted that their party reap the credit, and the votes. Fearing that Republicans would receive credit if the legislature enacted Republican governor Herbert Hadley's popular reform proposals of 1909, the Democratic Senate killed all the bills, in what the *St. Louis Post-Dispatch* termed "a quagmire of partisan wrangling."[27] To resistance movements politics remained an alien world.

12

The Consumer Revolt and the Grass-Roots Origins of the Missouri Idea

On December 9, 1897, a foggy, chilly day, hairdresser F. De Donato and his family alighted from a Suburban line streetcar at Hamilton and Plymouth avenues near their home in St. Louis. They began picking their way gingerly through the mud. Suddenly a streetcar loomed out of the fog on the opposite track, bearing down on them. Terrified that his own family was about to join the hundreds of streetcar casualities that occurred in St. Louis every year, De Donato pulled out a revolver and ordered the motorman to stop until his family was safe. The company prosecuted, and on January 2, 1898, Police Court Judge John H. Stevenson fined De Donato ten dollars.

Believing that the law should not punish him when he was simply trying to protect his family, De Donato appealed Stevenson's decision. On January 20, 1898, Judge David Murphy reversed the police judge and ringingly upheld De Donato's conception of law: "Even if Mr. De Donato pulled a gun he had a right to do so. Citizens have rights which corporations must respect. If Mr. De Donato thought his life or his family in danger he had a right to protect them. The street railways don't own this court."[1]

From the beginnings of the new order Missourians had fought over whether law existed fundamentally to protect families and traditions or to encourage growth. At first the promoters of growth used the law with such sudden and far-reaching power that traditional Missourians attracted national attention by trying to evade the new law and supporting social outlaws. By the turn of the century resisters made the law itself a battleground again. This time urban consumers used the same popular traditions that had earlier supported Jesse James to build an organized political movement that they hoped would reassert law as a weapon by which communities could restore traditional values and popular control.

The heart of this emerging progressive temper in Missouri was a struggle over law itself: who made it, who enforced it, who obeyed it, and who benefited from it. In this struggle progressives had to overcome the widespread and resigned conclusion by many traditional Missourians that law and the judicial system would be incapable of dispensing justice. "The wheels of justice . . . revolve slowly enough even if their ultimate revolutions produced any actual grist, but what with appeals, reversals, discharged juries, errors and other legal shuffling, the grist is all chaff by the time it comes out," proclaimed the Kansas City *Star*'s William Rockhill Nelson as part of his crusade in the 1910s for popular vetoes over court decisions. Progressives based their drive to reclaim popular control of the law on the conclusion that the developers' new methods were simply crimes against ancient community values. In the new approach they came to call the "Missouri Idea," progressives battled to make law into the major weapon for popular restraint of wealthy and powerful commercial and political leaders. In these progressives' view the new order was fundamentally a result of criminal behavior. The best way to regain popular control, concluded University of Missouri president Richard H. Jesse in 1901, was to discipline its creators and agents as criminals:

> No one can assimilate the prodigious fortunes of our modern plutocrats by honest labor and clean transactions. . . . The man that in any shape or form uses the rules of the commercial exchanges, or the laws of the state or nation . . . for oppressing his employees, or robbing his neighbors, should be sent to the penitentiary as surely as the man, that at the point of the pistol, holds up the wayfarer.[2]

By choosing to contest the new order's appropriation of law itself, progressives turned courtrooms into a major battleground for popular control. A code of simple honesty should guide conduct and define law, they believed. Dishonest acts and relationships should be illegal acts and relationships. Behind that conclusion lay their hope for reasserting community discipline and recapturing law.

Progressivism was capable of using traditions to recapture the law because it entered politics from a very different direction than earlier resistance movements, and that difference led its supporters to perceive political possibilities and challenges differently. In contrast to labor unions, farmers' alliances, or temperance societies, whose members had shared a well-developed and self-conscious sense of mutual aid and community with other members of the group before they entered politics, progressives began by assuming that politics was itself the arena in which to fight for community concerns and forge a common spirit. Even when they encountered many of the same barriers as earlier resisters had, progressives put politics at the center of their fight because they believed that private losses had to be made bases of public combat, rather than bases of private aid from other group members. Earlier resisters were more defensive and slower to take the political offensive because their members gave them a base on which to build an alternative to dominant power. While earlier movements concentrated on building cooperative stores and third parties that paralleled the dominant corporations and political parties, progressives, lacking close-knit private support, concentrated instead on offensive, direct attacks by which the community could either control or replace commercial and political powers. The central thrust of progressivism was to use politics to reassert traditional community, moral, and public control over private and economic activity that was moving far beyond any popular control in the new order.

Progressivism developed its special approach to community and politics because it drew Missourians together around what they shared as community residents and as consumers. In contrast to farmer, worker, business, and professional associations that separated and isolated people on the basis of their occupations and united them only around the desirability of growth, the consumer revolt united people across job, ethnic, and religious lines around what they shared as consumers. Since every consumer was a potential recruit, progressives developed a profound faith that they could control politics if they could mobilize and unleash their real power, the loosely organized majority of consumers, to rule directly.

1. The Consumer Revolt

The sources of the consumer consciousness that reached organized political form in the progressive movement drew on the memory of a time when production was integrated with consumption.[3] Since the central focus of consumption remained the household even as new markets focused production around national producer organizations, consumer-minded Missourians continued to judge economic activity by the traditional values and experiences of family and the larger units in which families naturally combined, neighborhoods and communities. Inspired by family values and the local tradition of community discipline, consumers projected a moral vision of human responsibilities against the secularizing and competitive thrusts of the market economy, of recreating in some form the communitywide public controls over the price and quality of goods and services that had existed in the old order.

When Missouri consumers dreamed of recovering control over production in the late nineteenth century, they incorporated a tradition that had exalted majority rule over minority producers and had included direct action, such as bread riots and tea dumpings. Frustrated by the power of producers in political institutions, consumers had developed the weapons of exposure and publicity to discipline producers. Those weapons implied that the majority, in its capacity as consumers, was rallying to reassert older family and community values, and that producers would be unable to contain community ostracism or direct action.

Missourians frequently cooperated in more formal ways to reclaim ownership of or control over things they needed as consumers but had lost to the
emerging monopolistic middlemen. Fraternal orders and consumer-owned
cooperatives mushroomed after the Civil War as ways for consumers to
supplant the new middlemen or monopolies. Fraternal orders and consumer-
owned cooperatives were an important inspiration for progressivism because
they showed Missourians that they could indeed come together with their
neighbors across occupational lines to help to defend the family, the source of
consumer values, against the new order's insecurities. They were a consumer-
oriented way of extending family protection and mutual support to a larger
number of families.

Angry consumers developed the organized political form of progressivism
as they encountered new challenges. Rapid urban growth created a new social
identity, that of urban consumer, who became increasingly dependent on
huge new corporations to do the daily activities that had traditionally defined
household self-sufficiency. Where once families had raised and butchered
their own meat and poultry, molded candles, baked bread, milked cows,
boiled sorghum for sweetening, chopped and split trees for fences and heat,
and drawn water from a well, now people in the new cities became dependent
on companies to provide these needs. As giant corporations increasingly
came to deliver these services, consumers agreed with the Kansas City *Star* in
1901 that "the trusts and monopolies find their opportunities in the necessities of the people."[4] Streetcars replaced the family's horse and carriage for
transportation. By the early twentieth century urban consumers were completely dependent on monopolistic corporations for transportation, heat,
light, water, and sewage removal. And these utilities maintained their domination by controlling local politics and securing long-term exclusive franchises from local governments. They responded to the depression of 1893–97
by curtailing services, raising fares and rates, and refusing to accommodate consumer's concerns about health and safety. They counted on their
political allies and long-term franchises to shield them from community outrage.

At the turn of the century consumers in communities across the state
battled with their local monopolies for reducing services and menacing public
health and safety. In 1903 typhoid fever swept through Columbia because the
water company refused to dig deep wells, forcing Columbians to drink creek
and surface water that was contaminated by human and animal wastes.
Consumers in Boonville and St. Charles demanded healthful water from
their monopolies at the same time. The new giant streetcar companies formed
from the merger of several smaller ones in St. Louis in the 1890s lengthened
the distance between stops, reduced the number of cars, and ignored the pleas
of pedestrians and passengers for bumpers that would prevent children and
adults from being mangled beneath the cars. In its 1894–95 crusade to force
the street railways to install safety fenders, the *Post-Dispatch* showed how
pedestrians' anger defined economic activities as criminal threats to the
community when it roared that "the managers of our electric roads who run

cars without fenders are nothing less than murderers, and the lowest kind of murderers—those who murder innocent beings for the sake of a few paltry dollars." The street railways brought "horror and dread to the minds of all loving parents" by refusing to install fenders to keep careless children from falling under the cars.[5]

The struggles between outraged consumers and utility managers dominated urban politics in communities across Missouri in the 1890s and 1900s. One-fourth of all *St. Louis Post-Dispatch* stories on local government and public affairs in the late 1890s concerned utility issues. From Columbia in 1903 a citizens' group concluded the same: "At every city election for several years the water and light question has directly or indirectly entered into the determination of who should be the mayor and who should be the councilmen."[6]

St. Louis's struggles between consumers and utilities exploded at the state level in 1899, when corporate lobbyists persuaded elected officials to accept utility money and patronage as the price for abandoning their promises to voters. Over the preceding few years politicians had come to agree with Governor Lon Stephens that "the sentiment throughout the State is so strong against the organization of trusts and the anti-trust agitation is so active" that the dominant Democratic party had to fulfill its increasingly outspoken antitrust promises. The voters were expecting action to follow rhetoric. Instead, the Democratic state legislature further enraged voters in the spring of 1899 by accepting bribes from St. Louis utility promoters and enacting a law permitting promoters to consolidate the city's street railways into a single monopoly. This wholesale bribery of legislators proved "the utter failure of representative lawmaking" to the *St. Louis Post-Dispatch*. In St. Louis the party's leading campaign organization, the Jefferson Club, censured the Democratic legislators who had voted in favor of the merger authorization bill. They had turned party policy into what the *Post-Dispatch* called a "fraud and farce."

From across the state Democrats like Chillicothe lawyer Scott Miller warned Governor Stephens that "you now have it in your power to save the Democracy of Missouri or to permit it to be lost" by vetoing the bill. Stephens stunned voters by signing the bill, placing the utility trust ahead of either voters or the party. Consumers blasted the governor. They agreed with publishers Theodore D. Fisher of the *Farmington Times* and J. T. Bradshaw of the *Chillicothe Constitution* that at a time when "the Democrats of Missouri have taken a stand against trusts of every character," the governor and legislature, by supporting the St. Louis monopoly, "will at least compromise the party's position on the trust question."[7]

To its control over the governor, legislature, and Democratic party the new street railway soon added control over St. Louis consumers. Armed with its new authority from the state, its managers quickly bribed through the Municipal Assembly in 1899 an ordinance that merged all but one of the city's streetcar lines into the new St. Louis Transit Company and soon thereafter tried to absorb the last remaining independent, the Suburban company. The new company took advantage of its monopolistic position to tighten what the St. Louis *Mirror* called "a death grip upon the community" and its consumers. Passengers cursed the "execrable service" that the new monopoly imposed on passengers in 1900 as it cut the number of cars, laid off motormen and conductors, stopped cleaning the cars regularly, and curtailed transfers between routes. Consumers agreed with the *Commonwealth* that "the uncontrolled public service corporation is everywhere a menace to public order."[8]

Stunned at first by the company's arrogance, St. Louis consumers soon asserted their independence by turning a private fight between the company and its workers into a public battle between the company and the whole community. In late April and early May 1900 the Amalgamated Association of Street Railway Employees struck both street railways and urged members of other unions to boycott the cars. The Central Trades and Labor Union and the Building Trades Council endorsed the boycott. St. Louis residents from all social backgrounds seized on the boycott, a weapon that until then had been limited to unions' organizing struggles, as a way for the entire community to punish the monopoly. Consumers boarded furniture vans, traps, sprinkling carts, bicycles, tallyhos, hacks, ice wagons—"every conceivable vehicle . . . excepting balloons and baby buggies"—to participate in common action to protest the company. "Silk Hats and Shirt Waists are Side by Side in Delivery Wagons and Furniture Vans" headlined the *Post-Dispatch*. "Numerous small boys, yet unborn, will boast of the pedestrian records of their grandfathers in the great strike time of 1900," reported the paper. It was what the company deserved for trying to turn the local government into a servant "of monopoly, by monopoly, and for monopoly," exclaimed German *Westliche Post* publisher Emil Preetorius, a sentiment that transcended ethnic lines. Week after week the company refused to negotiate with its workers or to respect its boycotting passengers. Since St. Louis seemed perversely to support the strikers in what he considered "perhaps the greatest industrial upheaval the country has seen in many years," Governor Stephens felt powerless for several weeks to conceive of, let alone execute, a political or a military resolution of "the disgraceful condition of affairs in our chief metropolis." In the end the company won by using strikebreakers and a posse against the strikers, and the union ultimately called off the boycott and strike. In the meantime, the strike catapulted a young lawyer, Joseph W. Folk, to local prominence. Folk tried to arbitrate a settlement by using the worker-consumer alliance to rally the community against "the menace of a monopolization of public utilities," according to the *Post-Dispatch*.[9]

Building from their experience of fighting the company by boycotting its streetcars, St. Louisans next channeled what the *Mirror* called "the intense feeling against the Street Railway Trust" into a crusade for political relief in the mayoral election of 1901. To lead that crusade they wanted a program and a leader that would not be diverted by partisanship or officeholding until the public owned both the company and the government. By 1901 Lee Meriwether had proved his independence. As state labor commissioner, Meriwether had launched the popular crusade against the city's street railways in 1896, when he devoted over eighty pages of his official report to proving that the railways had paid only $47,500 on their local tax bill of $1,478,582. Thousands had cheered Meriwether's 1897 candidacy for the Democratic mayoral nomination and his platform, a promise to make the street railways pay their taxes. Most regular party leaders rejected Meriwether, and he ran as an independent. Although they had long shared his anti-utility sentiments, local papers proved their deeper commitment to partisanship in the 1897 election. The Democratic *Post-Dispatch* attacked Meriwether for the "fatal blunder" of bolting the Democratic party, warning it would make him a "political exile," and the Republican *Globe-Democrat* urged voters "not to leave their party to chase after alleged reforms" and instead "to perpetuate Republican rule in St. Louis." They did.[10]

By 1901, however, St. Louis consumers from all social backgrounds had embraced labor's weapon, the boycott, and had used it to assert community independence. Now they looked to former labor commissioner Meriwether. Casting aside his vague 1897 promises to tax the street railways, Meriwether in 1901 launched a Public Ownership party. Even moderate William Marion Reedy had concluded that the company's contempt for democracy in St. Louis had narrowed the alternatives to a simple choice between "government ownership of [street] railroads or railroad ownership of government." Since the monopoly "has taken the government out of the hands of the people," consumers and taxpayers needed a new party whose success would be measured not by the offices it held but by the spread of public ownership of economic and political activity. Twelve thousand people jammed the campaign's final rally at the Coliseum, the city's largest hall, to hear former Illinois governor John Peter Altgeld champion Meriwether and public ownership. A German-born scourge of Chicago street railways and a hero to workers for his pardoning of the accused Haymarket rioters, Altgeld was popular with the same consumer-oriented, anti-utility movement, with its slight German, artisan, and South Side flavor, here in St. Louis.[11]

Republicans and Democrats were terrified that voters might elect this "pyrotechnically proletarian Mayor," in the words of William Marion Reedy and unseat major party officeholders. The two major parties tried to divert Meriwether's supporters by adopting as their own his party's program of municipal ownership of utilities. Democratic Boss Edward Butler did what came naturally to him: he offered Meriwether $25,000 to withdraw from the race. The daily press once again chose partisanship over its campaigns for utility consumers, ignoring both Meriwether and public ownership.[12]

On election day St. Louis voters from all backgrounds and parties flocked to Meriwether's side. Besieged bosses bribed and intimidated voters on a scale massive even by tolerant St. Louis standards. Meriwether claimed to have received 13,000 more votes than the official Democratic victor, but the state supreme court refused to allow a recount or an inspection of the ballots. The official tally stood at 43,167 (39 percent) for Democrat Rolla Wells, 34,938 (31.5 percent) for Republican Parker, and 29,566 (27 percent) for Meriwether. Meriwether carried 98 precincts to 146 for Wells and 86 for Parker. The Public Ownership party captured six seats in the Municipal Assembly to eighteen for the Republicans and twenty-one for the Democrats. Voters from all ethnic, sectional, and partisan backgrounds supported Public Ownership. The new party in 1901 took 54 percent from both the Republican and Democratic totals of 1900 in the ten precincts the new party won by an absolute majority.

St. Louis Popular Vote in Public Ownership Precincts

	Democrat	Republican	Other	Public Ownership	Total
1900 Governor	1,454	2,097	343	—	3,894
1901 Mayor	611	893	203	1,897	3,604

Meriwether and Public Ownership cut through partisan allegiances when St. Louis residents found a program that promised to restore community authority by mobilizing the people to take possession of the company.[13]

As they grew desperate for relief from unsafe, expensive, tax-dodging, corrupt local utility monopolies, consumers in communities across Missouri duplicated St. Louis's campaign for public ownership. The staggering costs of generating electricity, pumping water to each home, or operating a transportation system and the resulting desirability of having a single operation furnish the service to all consumers in the community led Missourians to broaden the tradition of replacing corporations with consumer-owned co-operatives. They extended the tradition of consumer ownership to utilities by mobilizing all local consumers in their other common capacity, as taxpayers. Through municipal ownership community residents, not a few managers, would control the services on which they all depended, and they would reclaim their local governments by abolishing the single greatest reason that politicians betrayed their constituents.

Columbia's year-long battle in 1903–4 for public ownership originated in popular anger at the private water and light monopoly for its refusal to change its methods, which were poisoning more and more of Columbia's consumers with typhoid fever. The company announced that it would not dig deep wells to replace its contaminated surface ponds. Columbia's water drinkers formed a Municipal Ownership League, proclaiming that "municipal ownership with deep well water furnishes the only safeguard for the public health." Municipal ownership promised consumer and community control in larger ways, wrote President A. C. Talley of the typographical union and Columbia Trades Council, in a League leaflet: "The only way for the people of Columbia to get what they want in the way of water and light is to put in a plant of their own over which they will always have a supervisory control. With a private company we will always be compelled to take what it chooses to give us." Only by voting for municipal ownership could Columbians "retain their independence," declared the League. On February 23, 1904,

Columbians voted 469 to 115 to issue $100,000 in bonds to operate a city-owned water and light plant to replace the private company.[14]

Consumers in other communities turned to municipal ownership to recover control over basic services that had passed to private monopolies in the new order. "Cheaper and better water to the consumer is the result wherever municipal ownership has been tried," concluded the St. Charles *Cosmos* on the eve of that city's 1900 vote on the issue. In 1903 alone, as Columbians fought the water company, Boonville's voters established municipal ownership and city-owned plants first began operating in Marshall, Rich Hill, and Farmington. By 1906 St. Louis, Kansas City, and twelve other Missouri cities had municipally owned waterworks, twenty-five other cities had city-owned electric plants, and twelve more communities operated combination water and light plants.[15]

Through the municipal ownership movement of the early twentieth century Missourians, along with urban consumers elsewhere, created the nation's most widespread adoption of socialism. Missourians' were so angry at local utility monopolies that they overcame their traditional distrust of government and dramatically extended the range of the antimonopoly tradition to include public ownership. By 1912 they had made municipal ownership such an acceptable idea that it was the official debate topic for Missouri's high school students that year.[16]

With public ownership they widened the ways Missourians could cooperate to reclaim territory they had lost to the large corporations that increasingly shaped their economic lives. The consumer revolt broadened possibilities. "I firmly believe that the final victory of the people over monopolies is to be had only in public ownership of public utilities," proclaimed M. H. Pemberton in 1905 to the state Live Stock Breeders' Association. Before the consumer revolt his audience of market-oriented farmers had accepted the new order's basic assumptions and confined their criticisms of monopoly to its limitations on competition and growth. They had viewed both monopoly and government as barriers to private initiative and, therefore, productive enterprise. Pemberton showed how completely the consumer revolt had transformed both the antimonopoly tradition and the traditional suspicion of government when he proclaimed the consumers' new discovery that it was "better to have corrupt public officials occasionally in the public service [and, therefore, in control of city-owned utilities,] where we could get at them and kick them out, than to have them continually in the private concerns where we can't touch them with a forty-foot pole." Finally, Pemberton declared, municipal ownership would restore "public ownership of our law-making bodies."[17]

Driven by their struggles with local utility monopolies for public health and popular sovereignty, Missouri's urban consumers searched for broader ways their communities could discipline new economic activities by traditional moral values. The more they came to judge economic activity by its impact on the health and safety of all community residents as consumers, the more they came to conclude that the fundamental issue was whether law would protect consumer-oriented values of life and health or the producer-oriented value of growth. By making health, not growth, the criterion for law, they brought moral yardsticks that had evolved to judge relationships among people to bear on economic activities. In law they found a means of community discipline that turned many new activities into crimes and new economic leaders into criminals.

The common supply of air and water was the source of life and health in every community, and the community traditionally had the right to prevent anyone from poisoning that common supply. In their common roles as breathers of air and drinkers of water, Missouri's consumers judged polluters as poisoners and murderers just as surely as if their smokestacks and water pipes had been arsenic or pistols. Smoky air and unsafe water became symbols of how producers' greed had come to threaten the very sources of life. As traditional defenders of their families' health, women took the lead in demanding that polluters be treated as criminals for endangering community health. In 1893 the Wednesday Club of St. Louis women proclaimed that "the present condition of our city, enveloped in a continual cloud of smoke" was "no longer to be borne with submission" because it "endangers the health of our families, especially those of weak lungs and delicate throats, impairs the eyesight of our school children, and adds infinitely to our labors and our expenses as housekeepers."[18]

The struggle for pure air was also a struggle over whether the law would encourage growth or punish polluters. Under ancient common law those who polluted the common supply of air and water committed a "nuisance" to the community and were prosecuted. The new order's legal thrust toward growth had created technicalities that masked the actual surrender of this ancient right. To groups like the Wednesday Club the campaign for pure air was also a campaign to recapture law from the judicial sophists who had abandoned ancient protections of community health. The St. Louis Municipal Assembly responded in 1893 by enacting an ordinance that declared "dense black or thick gray smoke" a legal "nuisance" whose creators could be prosecuted. This approach reduced the city's smoke by about three-fourths and provoked a lawsuit. In 1897 the Missouri Supreme Court ruled the smoke ordinance an unconstitutional extension of city police powers because the state had not officially granted cities this power. St. Louis air breathers angrily petitioned the legislature. In 1901 the legislature gave St. Louis, Kansas City, and St. Joseph the authority to declare smoke a "nuisance."[19]

Although St. Louis's new anti-smoke ordinance of 1901 empowered a smoke inspector to prosecute violators, the real prosecutors in the early twentieth century were the hundreds of women who scoured the city, climbing to rooftops if necessary, to collect evidence to prosecute polluters. Determined to defend their families' health, the Women's Organization for Smoke Abatement forced the prosecution of violators. Fearing that the prosecutions interfered with what its members considered the primary duty to "encourage manufacturing industries," champions of growth in the new Million Population Club convened several civic associations on May 14, 1911, to call for education of polluters as a "sane and conservative" alternative to prosecution. The Women's Organization blasted the developers. They accepted philanthropist James Gay Butler's donation and used it to hire lawyers and inspectors to continue prosecuting polluters as criminals. To the women the developers' attempt to preserve growth with technological and educational alternatives to prosecution were an unacceptable compromise with the value of health.[20]

Urban consumers sometimes cooperated with traditional producers of familiar products against competing middlemen and producers of new, less wholesome substances. "In nearly every line of manufacture," concluded G. W. Waters at a 1900 farmers' institute, "the tendency seems to be to cheapen production by deception, substituting a gross imitation and placing it upon the market for the genuine." "There is no class of people more vicious than those who put on the market adulterated food products which steal the health of the public," declared the Kennett *Clipper.* Producers of processed foods and beverages eroded consumer confidence in farm products and even competed with farmers by adding chemicals, colorings, preservatives, and substitutes that at best lowered standards and at worst endangered health with "poisonous and nauseous preparations." The legislature required local boards of health to protect consumers and "honest" producers in 1889 by hiring inspectors to prevent adulteration of milk and cream, and, in 1891, adulteration of other products. In 1895 farmers persuaded the legislature to require oleomargarine manufacturers to label their product as a butter substitute. The state board of agriculture prosecuted violators. St. Louis juries in the late 1890s convicted several manufacturers who had tried to deceive consumers into thinking the new product was butter. Clubwomen in the state's cities spearheaded the movement to enact and then enforce a law prohibiting manufacture or sale of foods, drugs, beverages, or medicines that were adulterated or deceptively labeled. Crusaders for pure foods reflected consumers' growing conviction that cheaper production lowered quality and endangered health. The solution was to replace the market's encouragement of cheapened production with a new drive to define, expose, and prosecute dishonesty and criminality in economic activities.[21]

Outrage at polluted drinking water impelled state officials to take the extraordinary step of filing a lawsuit against another state. Chicago's decision in 1900 to send its sewage down a series of rivers to the Mississippi accounted for an additional hundred deaths each year in St. Louis alone. "All we demand is that Chicago quit taking the lives of our citizens," declared Herbert Hadley, the attorney general and the prosecutor in *Missouri* v. *Illinois.* Nations had gone to war over less than Missouri's complaint against Illinois for poisoning its water, Hadley warned.[22]

The same overriding concern with life and family drove consumers to reshape the antitrust tradition from a means to encourage opportunity and competition into a way the community could restrain economic activity by turning moral traditions into bases for prosecution. When Missouri's fire insurance companies responded to the depression of 1893 by conspiring to raise insurance rates by 20 to 300 percent, homeowners demanded that conspiring agencies, such as the Kansas City Board of Fire Underwriters, be prosecuted as would any other criminal who robbed homeowners. Indignant at what the *Sedalia Gazette* in 1894 called the "extortion of insurance companies," several legislators told the *Kansas City Times* that "their people had been robbed until they had arisen in indignant protest." Responding to the consumer protest, they pushed a bill in 1895 that would have included fire insurance companies under the antitrust law. The insurance lobby weakened the 1895 law to exclude the state's two major cities. The *Kansas City Times* continued the crusade against the insurance monopoly in 1897, charging that it extorted "profits for fire insurance companies in excess of the wildest dreams of avarice." It documented that Kansas City policyholders in 1896 had paid four times more in premiums to the trust than they had received back in payments. Sixteen small-town papers joined the *Times* in demanding prosecution. Attorney General Edward C. Crow brought suit to declare the 1895 loophole unconstitutional, but the state supreme court turned him down in 1898. Consumers mounted such a protest that the 1899 legislature removed the exemption and the Kansas City and St. Louis rate-fixing bureaus were forced to disband. Crow, in turn, prosecuted the St. Joseph Underwriters' Social Club, through which seventy-five fire insurance companies fixed rates. This time the state supreme court convicted the companies for fixing rates and, applauded by consumers, threatened to take away their right to do business in Missouri. The companies responded by paying fines and reducing their rates.[23]

Missouri's urban consumers became even more eager to prosecute monopolies with the arrival of unprecedented inflation after 1897. They gasped as they watched a spectacular increase in the number and scope of corporate mergers, and then saw the new corporations use their concentrated power to raise prices and lower the quality of daily necessities. "Monopoly is invading every home in the country, bringing the question of existence itself home to every housekeeper," observed the *St. Louis Post-Dispatch* in 1899. At the present rate "we may well tremble as we think of the tough, meatless sandwiches, the chicory coffee, the oleo butter, the picnic lemonade, the logwood claret and all the other trust-made articles of diet that a monopoly in food would place before its customers so as to insure dividends for its stockholders," prophesied the paper. Four years later the *Post-Dispatch* attacked the lighting monopoly: "When the power is of such a nature that it may be employed to disturb the most intimate, domestic, and personal interests of life it becomes a menace which must be squarely met and defeated."[24]

Consumers were particularly angered by a conspiracy among the huge new meat-packing firms that had replaced independent butchers and had come to dominate the entire meat business, from livestock ranges to delivery of meat to neighborhood outlets. By the winter of 1901–2 consumers were desperate. The *St. Joseph News* reported that consumers had to replace their families' traditional cuts of meat with cheaper grades or do without, and the St. Louis *Labor Compendium* observed that "the most unpopular man these days is he who tries to prove there is no Meat Trust." The price of eggs in St. Louis jumped from ten cents in 1901 to eighteen cents in 1902 as the major packers tried to extend their control to include eggs and poultry. The *Kansas City Journal* reported consumer fears that they would soon be totally dependent on a Food Trust. Consumer anger transcended class and ethnic lines, according to the St. Louis *Mirror*: "The man who eats broilers and truffles and the man who pampers his family on pot-roast and cabbage, are at one in their grievance against the beef trust."

As they united to resist the beef trust, Missouri's urban consumers turned once again to the boycott as a weapon to fight monopoly. The people of St. Louis "revolted and they stopped eating meat," reported the *Mirror* in May 1902. From St. Joseph and Kansas City to Springfield, Sedalia, and St. Louis, consumers in 1902 banded together and refused to patronize the meat trust. Beef consumption fell.

Attorney General Crow brought cheers from consumers when he appealed to the state supreme court in May, 1902, to oust the major packing firms from the state for violating the antitrust law. He launched an investigation to show that their monopolistic practices were criminal. Butchers testified that the "Big Four" packers—Armour, Swift, Cudahy, and Morris—fixed a uniform meat price and used their control over supply to force butchers to acquiesce. St. Louis dealer T. L. O'Sullivan confirmed consumers' worst fears when he declared that the packers sold decayed meat that had been painted to conceal its color and preserved with ammonia. At this point St. Louis circuit attorney Joseph Folk announced that "this has become a subject for the criminal courts," and asked the grand jury to investigate so that "men who have been selling diseased and decaying meat to St. Louisans will be landed behind the bars of the penitentiary." St. Louis hired three new meat inspectors to keep up with the revelations of the packers' adulterations. And on March 20, 1903, the state supreme court ordered the companies to cease business in Missouri or pay $27,136 in fines and end their conspiracy. They paid.[25]

Kansas City consumers called for criminal and antitrust prosecution in the summer of 1901 when the People's Ice and Fuel Company tightened its monopoly over the supply of ice, which families needed for refrigerated foods. Temperatures rose to record highs, so did prices, and food spoiled. Threatening to arrest ice dealers for not having licenses, city attorney Frank Gordon and Attorney General Crow charged that the "ice trust" had compelled dealers to join the conspiracy. Crow helped the local prosecution prepare a criminal indictment. They brought suit on August 28, 1901. Fear of prosecution drove the People's Ice president to flee Kansas City, his trust collapsing behind him.[26]

Uniting people across traditional occupational and ethnic barriers in their common capacities as breathers of air, drinkers of water, eaters of meat, users of ice, riders of streetcars, angry consumers transformed the antitrust tradition from a producer-oriented spearhead for the competitive new order into a comsumer-oriented weapon to preserve the familiar quality and price of consumer goods and services. In the new popular newspapers consumers found a way to communicate their hopes across the miles of occupational and ethnic distance that had earlier separated them when they entered politics. Exposures of unsafe streetcars in the *St. Louis Post-Dispatch*, of the utilities' bribery of local officials in the *St. Louis Star*, of meat packers' conspiracies in the Kansas City *Star* provided a common language and implicit solutions that helped to unite local consumers. Consumers concluded that their best hope was to recapture law from the promoters of progress and reshape it to punish the new large corporations that deprived consumers of their traditional control over price, safety, and quality. The most basic way was to define economic activities that threatened the community as crimes—extortionate insurance premiums were robbery, polluted air and adulterated meat were poison—and to prosecute their perpetrators just as traditional cultures had long prosecuted robbers and poisoners. Brushing aside as inadequate other methods for asserting public control over monopolies, the *St. Louis Post-Dispatch* concluded in 1904, for example, that "the best way to go after the beef trust . . . is through the courts. . . . Punishment is the corrective demanded now. . . ."[27] By reshaping law to protect and extend traditional moral values, consumers added criminal prosecutions to municipal ownership as parts of their campaign to reassert community control in the new order.

As they watched utilities bribe legislators to ignore their constituents, angry consumers sought new political methods that would make it easier to translate traditional and popular concerns into public policies. They wanted consumers to repossess their governments from corporations. Searching for weapons that would unleash their real power as a loosely organized majority, they turned to a method that traditional resisters had developed to empower voters at the expense of politicians.

The idea of mobilizing voters to enact laws directly had originated in Missouri in the 1890s among many groups that wanted to force policy action on proposals that politicians had hoped to keep outside the legislative arena while keeping the votes of the proposals' supporters. These groups turned to the system of elections whereby voters enacted (initiative) and repealed (referendum) laws directly at the polls, without the intervention of legislators or parties. The issue would automatically be decided directly at the ballot box if enough voters signed petitions to indicate that they wanted to vote on it.

Long blocked by partisanship and officeholding from their political goals, organized workers called for initiative and referendum in the first and all subsequent platforms and declarations of principles of the State Federation of Labor, Socialist Labor, Social Democratic, and Socialist parties. Workers became the most sympathetic supporters of direct legislation. The initiative and referendum system "makes it possible to secure every reform that appeals to the conscience and intelligence of American voters," declared President Thomas Sheridan of the state labor federation. Although Populists thought that an alternative political party would best turn radical proposals into law, they came by painful experience to champion initiative and referendum for the first time at their 1894 state convention. Convinced that the "liquor power" corrupted politics, candidates, and parties, Prohibitionists declared officially for initiative and referendum in order to establish "a more intimate relation between the people and government."[28]

But the group that crusaded most strongly for initiative and referendum was the Single Tax movement. Disciples of Henry George, Missouri's Single Taxers believed that tax laws, utility franchises, and other special governmental privileges siphoned the wealth each community created off to parasites. Taxation offered the way to redistribute wealth and power, to discourage land monopoly and speculation. Single Taxers quickly concluded that politicians would never enact their proposal for a single tax on land and that their only hope rested directly with voters. In 1898 Single Tax Clubs from Hannibal, Fulton, Springfield, St. Louis and Kansas City came together to form a state league. Proclaiming "our belief in the doctrine set forth in the Declaration of Independence, that 'governments derive their just powers from the consent of the governed,'" the new league announced in 1899 that it would promote the initiative and referendum "as the best means of obtaining an expression of the will of the people."[29]

The drive by urban consumers to break the alliance between utilities and political bosses so that popular majorities could once again control their communities generated the mass base and energy for direct legislation that neither traditional resisters nor new pressure groups of producers could provide. With the initiative and the referendum desperate consumers created what supporters called "real self-government by the people," and found a way to use their strength as a majority of local voters to enact policy. Urban consumers supported direct legislation with their votes. In 1904 the state's five most urban counties gave a 53 percent majority to initiative and referendum while it received only 33 percent from the rest of Missouri. In 1908 the five urban areas voted by a 67 percent majority for direct legislation, while remaining areas gave it only 45 percent.[30] Consumers hoped that direct legislation would permit the majority to become the government at the ballot box. It would create public ownership of government so that the community could be guided by a vision of democracy instead of growth, by majorities instead of corporations, in making the rules.

2. Bribery and the Local Origins of the Missouri Idea

Consumers focused on bribery as the most blatant and menacing form and symbol of how corporations blocked community residents from using law to reassert popular traditions. "Of all the byproducts of the Trust the most poisonous is the lobby," concluded a national magazine about Missouri's experience. The battles against local utilities broadened into a movement to expunge the commercial spirit from government, to drive money from election booth, jury room, and legislative hall. "We declare a war of extermination against vote-buying, false-counting and ballot-burning," declared the

Independent Democratic Central Committee of Henry County in 1902. Kansas City's young prosecuting attorney, Herbert Hadley, won popularity at about the same time by indicting agents of the huge Metropolitan Street Railway Company for bribing juries.[31]

But it was in St. Louis in 1902 that the movement to reassert public control through prosecution reached its most dramatic peak. When Democratic political leaders nominated Tennessee-born Southern Baptist Joseph Folk for circuit attorney in 1900 because he was popular with the city's workers, they could never have imagined how Folk would turn his evangelical morality and faith in law into a powerful weapon for the community to discipline new leaders by old values. After the Civic Federation of the 1890s, the boycott of 1900, and the Public Ownership movement of 1901 failed to end monopoly control, many in St. Louis feared that nothing could restrain the utility. The *Mirror, Star,* and *Post-Dispatch* prepared the stage for a fresh approach by attracting readers from all ethnic, class, and partisan backgrounds, creating a common vocabulary and standards describing the pattern, and naming those who had accepted bribes to betray their constituents.[32]

Circuit attorney Folk brought the elements together after reading James Galvin's account of street railways' bribery of city aldermen in the *Star* on January 21, 1902. Within a week Folk used a combination of threats, bluffs, and promises of immunity to force the participants to divulge to a grand jury how street railway promoters had agreed to pay $135,000 to an organized "combine" of city legislators in exchange for their votes on legislation. Within two months Folk had arrested city councilmen, bankers, corporation presidents, and "Boss" Edward Butler, and had revealed the commercialization of St. Louis city government into an elaborate system of laws-for-sale. "No city has ever been so completely at the mercy of faithless public servants," concluded the grand jury. Trial juries listened to public officials like House of Delegates member John Helms confess that "I kept up a continuous course of trafficking and selling my vote." Unlike earlier prosecutors of "boodlers," however, Folk attracted national attention because he followed the bribery to its source. "Mr. Folk has shown St. Louis that its bankers, brokers, corporation officers,—its business men are the sources of evil," concluded Lincoln Steffens in *McClure's*.[33]

Folk caused a national sensation. Over the course of the entire nineteenth century a total of only thirty-four bribery cases had ended up anywhere in American courts. Folk brought forty indictments and secured twenty convictions from trial juries. He soon extended his St. Louis grand jury to investigate bribery in the state legislature as well as the St. Louis city council. Working with Attorney General Crow and a Jefferson City grand jury, Folk and his St. Louis jury soon demonstrated that "during a period of twelve years laws have been sold to the highest bidder." To influence votes on a single bill the baking powder trust had bribed the lieutenant governor (who was forced to resign) and six state senators. By the sheer volume of his indictments Folk proved that legislators from both parties at both state and local levels favored corporate bribes over their constituents' wishes.[34]

Folk's prosecutions struck a deeply popular chord. A 1902 trial jury agreed with Folk's conclusion that

> Under our system of government the power of every official belongs not to him but to the people who gave it. The right to vote franchises and to legislate belongs to an official's constituents, and when he sells it, he sells that which does not belong to him but to the people he represents. . . . It is the greatest offense that can be committed against the people.

Bribery harmed the community more than did violent crimes, Folk told another jury, because "the thief only plunders, while the giver of bribes robs the entire community. The man who murders may take one life against the law, while the giver and taker of bribes poisons the very foundation of law itself." "When the passage of laws become a mere matter of bargain and sale," Folk explained to a third jury, "then there will not be a government of and for the people, but a government for the few and by the few, with wealth enough to purchase official power." The way to restore traditions of democracy and popular control was to prosecute promoters who believed themselves so far beyond the reach of community discipine that they could violate its traditions. In the trial of "Boss" Edward Butler, Folk cried, "They say it is an outrage to bring this man here because he is so great, because he is so powerful. . . . Is the law greater than Edward Butler, or is Edward Butler greater than the law? I think the law is greater than he."[35]

Across ancient cultural divisions St. Louisans applauded Folk's prosecutions. Baptist, Disciples of Christ, Catholic, and other clergyman from central city and suburbs alike found rare common cause in cheering Folk and the grand jury, hailing their campaign, in the words of Webster Groves Congregational minister C. L. Kloss, to "classify these sacrilegious polluters of the temple of justice as felons and outlaws." The socialist-leaning Central Trades and Labor Council joined the German Southwest Turner Society, businessmen, and the daily press in a coalition whose breadth of support for resistance was unprecedented in the city's history.[36]

Folk and his supporters believed that the prosecutions of particular criminals were only the first step and that the community would not finally control the new order until St. Louisans rejected the underlying values that the bribers embodied. The prosecutions, in short, were a political battleground in the cultural war. The most basic new value that bribery reflected and that Folk and his allies wanted to stamp out was the greed that lay at the core of the new order. "Too many men seek wealth without the corresponding inclination to labor for its advancement," maintained Folk. "Political commercialism has taken the place in many men's minds of patriotism." Boss Butler violated traditional restraints because he was motivated too strongly by "the greed for wealth, and in this first part of this century, that principle seems to be the dominant characteristic of the controlling elements of this country," assistant circuit attorney A. C. Maroney told the Butler jury. Political commercialism had come to dominate St. Louis politics, believed influential journalist William M. Reedy, because St. Louisans had been too busy privately making money to act cooperatively to create a "public spirit" or "civic pride" for the city.[37]

Partisan loyalty likewise blocked many voters from seeing how bribery had eroded other traditional values. It had "kept the conscience of Missouri asleep behind the thorn hedge of party bigotry for thirty years," according to one observer. Believing that bribers were terrified of "an aroused public conscience," Folk called on voters to cut through their party loyalties with his 1902 slogan: "One who violates the law is not a Democrat, or a Republican, but a criminal." "There is no magic in a party name to change corruption into innocence," he elaborated. Since Missourians would naturally condemn as a criminal a burglar who invaded their homes, Reedy urged each taxpayer to think of city government as "his larger home" that the boodlers had invaded.[38] United as taxpayers, Missourians could overcome their partisan allegiances and discipline boodlers in traditional terms.

Folk had to fight on several levels to turn the law into an effective weapon for popular control because law's content and procedures had become enmeshed in the new order. First he had to persuade public opinion, in the form of trial juries, that bribery was not an acceptable "business transaction" of the new order, as defense attorney Frederick W. Lehmann had portrayed it in the case of wealthy councilman Emil A. Meysenburg. Lehmann's argument enraged Folk and their clash epitomized the central debate over law's purposes. Folk, speaking to the Meysenburg jury, replied to Lehmann that law should follow the Bible in prescribing moral relationships. Jesus pointed the way: "So there are in the temple in which our laws are made those who are trying to make an unholy profit out of the place, and it is for the jury to do like Christ did and run them out and keep them from making what should be the temple of law, a den of thieves, as it now is." The jury convicted Meysenburg.[39]

During the trial of street railway promoter Robert M. Snyder defense attorney Henry F. Priest argued that "in many advanced communities" bribery "is regarded as a trifling offense." Since the issue was exactly whether law could restrain practices regarded as "trifling" in the new order, Folk emphasized in his final summation that "bribery is treason, and the givers and takers of bribes are the traitors of peace." The jury deliberated for less than an hour before convicting Snyder and recommending a sentence of five years in prison.[40]

The state supreme court posed a formidable barrier to Folk's campaign to recapture the law. It overturned the first eight of his bribery convictions and altogether reversed more than half of them. It threw out one conviction of Boss Butler because the agency Butler had bribed ought not to have had the power it had long possessed to award St. Louis garbage contracts! The court nullified a total of thirteen convictions for reasons "which must sound so absurd when repeated to a layman that it is little wonder that our judiciary has lost the confidence of the people," observed one contemporary legal scholar. "From this distance it seemed an outrage," wrote President Theodore Roosevelt to Folk after the court overturned the Butler conviction.[41]

Folk knew that behind his struggle with the supreme court over legal technicalities was the central issue: would law protect communities and discipline the rich and powerful, or would government bodies become simply additional arenas for "business transactions" that technicalities would shield from restraint by older values. Attacking the supreme court for a "distorted mental vision always hunting for loop holes and technical points to defeat the ends of justice," Folk insisted that the court had "overlooked the purpose of the criminal law which is to protect society. They forget that the public has rights in a criminal prosecutions. . . ." Folk's determined prosecutions tested the outer limits of law because he was trying to strip it from the new order it had come to serve so completely. For law to be remade to restrain the wealthy and powerful, "defenders of home and commonwealth" would have to reach behind court decisions to grasp the source of eroding control in "the soulless corporation which employs a lobby to bribe our legislators; hires creatures to control our courts; carries on its payrolls a corps of attorneys whose principal duty is to harass litigants, retard due process of law and prevent by delay, evasion and trickery" substantial justice, declared the *Henry County Republican* in 1903. Lincoln Steffens explained the supreme court's war on Folk simply: "The whole machinery of justice broke down under the strain of boodle pull."[42]

Although stymied by the court, Folk still had popular support, and he sought new ways to continue his crusade. "A great moral issue was moving among the people." observed William Allen White in *McClure's*. "That issue concerned the enforcement or the annulment of law, and Folk dramatized it." "No other man in the nation today is more fully incarnate with the growing idea of revolt against commercialized ideals of government. . . ," concluded the *Paris Mercury* in northeastern Missouri. Within six months of Folk's first indictment the *Washington Post* suggested that he would make an excellent president, and by mid-1903 editors across Missouri were proposing him for the governorship.[43] The political arena had revolved around officeholding for so long that many Missourians could not envision any other way to translate a mission into policy.

Folk elaborated his crusade into what he called the "Missouri Idea" and sought the governorship. At first he simply meant that Missouri would set an example by becoming "first in civic righteousness" by exposure and prosecution of bribery. Then he promised aggresssive enforcement against anyone or anything that diverted elected representatives from enacting majority sentiment on issues. Great and small alike, he insisted, should obey all laws.[44]

During his 1904 campaign for the governorship Folk turned his crusade against bribery into a direct challenge to the traditional appeal of partisanship. By trying to imprison the very political leaders who had nominated and elected him as circuit attorney, Folk had stunned traditional politicians. He had, after all, convicted his party's boss, forced the Democratic lieutenant governor to resign, and either exposed or indicted over a dozen Democratic members of the St. Louis city council and state legislature. "The time has not yet come in the state of Missouri when a man can get a Democratic nomination for the highest office within the gift of the people by going out and attacking his party," bristled the *Nevada Mail and Lamar Democrat*. Organization Democrats heckled him with their supreme taunt: "Are you a Democrat?" Folk sensed that angry consumers and taxpayers wanted public officials to serve voters, not parties or leaders, and he replied to the charge of party treason by attacking the machine's "new kind of democracy" that condoned bribery and placed party loyalty above honesty.[45]

Each of Folk's rivals for the nomination only helped Folk's campaign for law enforcement to restore community discipline. The first to challenge him was Judge James G. Gantt, one of the state supreme court justices who had kept Folk's boodlers out of prison. Gantt's presence reinforced the urgency of Folk's campaign to recapture the law because, as the *Gallatin Democrat* observed, "The common people . . . are getting mighty tired of technicalities . . . that are pulling open the doors of our penetentiary to convicted boodlers. They want fewer decisions based upon hair-spun theories and brain-bewildering subtleties and more based upon justice."[46] Gantt's candidacy never really started.

A more formidable challenger was former St. Louis Police Board president Harry B. Hawes, who supplemented appeals of partisanship and patronage by sending rowdies and policemen to assault Folk's supporters while recruiting machine voters to vote early and often for their patron. Fourteen policemen and three Democratic central committeemen were indicted by the grand jury for vote fraud in the St. Louis gubernatorial primary. But the very success of the machine in using these methods to secure a nearly unanimous St. Louis delegation for Hawes proved the urgent need for some way to convict thugs who blocked voters from an unintimidated ballot and to imprison officeholders who took bribes to betray the voters' wishes. Democratic voters agreed with the *Fulton Gazette* that "the self-seeking, timeserving parasites in and out of office" had as usual blocked a fair election in St. Louis and with the Kansas City *Star* that politicians were waging the "most astounding, inexcusable and disgraceful fight on Joseph Folk that any political records in Missouri or any other state can show." The Sturgeon *Missouri Leader* echoed the conclusion of most Democratic voters in supporting Folk because "the boodlers are all against him" and "the Democratic party needs to be purged of men who preach morality and hold their hands behind their backs for the dollars of the corporations." Folk's fight, explained the *Post-Dispatch*, was for "popular control over the party."[47]

Once the bribery prosecutions had shown how they might recover law to reassert community control, Missouri voters hoped that Folk's 1904 campaign would create a political future in which politicians would heed voters, not corporations, in which law would finally restrain the powerful. Voters agreed with Frank Tyrell that "never before has there been a campaign waged with such intense earnestness, or with an issue of such great moment" as Folk's campaign for the governorship. Folk's first campaign meeting at St. Louis in 1904 astounded the *Post-Dispatch*'s reporter, because here was a cause that for the first time in memory had attracted "business men, clerks, mechanics and laboring men" to a common crusade. The *Mirror*'s Reedy was troubled that Lee Meriwether's former Public Ownership supporters were "conspicuously numerous" at the Folk rally. But the Pineville *Democrat* best captured the sense of democratic movement among voters when it explained that "Folk is not running for the nomination for governor. The people are running him."[48]

Folk went on to capture 549 of the 709 delegates to the Democratic convention precisely because to voters he embodied what Reedy called "the moral law" in his attacks on commercialized government. "The eradication of bribery from public life in this state" was the "paramount issue" of the 1904 election, declared the Democrats' platform. Folk and his supporters proposed ten planks to hasten that end. They proposed, for example, that "professional lobbying" and solicitation of bribes be made felonies, that immunity be granted witnesses in bribery trials, and that franchises obtained through bribery be nullified. They pledged to "hit corruption, and hit it hard," and even declared that "there is no room in the Democratic Party for boodlers."[49]

Republicans made their own appeal for popular law enforcement by nominating Kansas City's young prosecutor, Herbert Hadley, for attorney general in 1904 and by renominating Theodore Roosevelt to head the ticket. To challenge Folk for the governorship, however, the Republicans picked a representative of the very system Folk attacked, Cyrus P. Walbridge, a former St. Louis councilman and mayor and the president of the Bell Telephone Company of St. Louis. Although Folk hoped that his party would nominate an "untainted ticket from top to bottom in harmony with the Missouri Idea," he was unable to block renomination of the shady Samuel Cook for secretary of state and Albert Allen for state auditor even though Cook had admitted that he had counseled a state employee to bribe a state legislator.[50] The party's choice of conservative Alton B. Parker over the popular William Jennings Bryan likewise underscored the difficulties a resistance movement had in trying to capture major parties.

On election day voters crossed traditional cultural and party lines to support the Missouri Idea. Folk outpolled all other candidates on his way to becoming the only successful Democrat. He led his ticket in urban and rural Missouri, among immigrants and the native-born, Republicans and Democrats. In Kansas City voters dramatically cast off party loyalties by giving Folk a 60–37 margin, while Roosevelt beat Parker 56–39.[51] Even as they cast off the anchor of party loyalty that had so long restrained democratic movements, however, they sought to shorten the distance to a democratic future by placing their faith in a leader.

13

The Missouri Idea and State Politics

1. The Folk Administration and the Flowering of the Missouri Idea

Governor Joseph Folk and Attorney General Herbert Hadley brought a new politics along with a new label, the "Missouri Idea," to their new offices in January 1905. The two young prosecutors from the state's two largest cities both felt acutely that voters were trusting them to reclaim government as an agency for the majority to make the rules to guide conduct.

As Folk and Hadley sought to translate grass-roots yearnings to exalt traditional moral precepts over the gospel of growth into a program at the state level, they had to overcome the divisions created by ethnic, sectional, and partisan allegiances among traditional Missourians. Those traditional allegiances had intensified resistance to the new order, but they had also retarded unified political action. Angry consumers had surmounted these barriers in local struggles, but state politics even more than local politics revolved around officeholding and partisanship, and was remote from the local struggles that set consumers in motion. The very differences in background between the secular Yankee Hadley and the evangelical southerner Folk, the different worlds their relatives had defended on Civil War battlefields, came to help them transcend the political divisions between their different cultures. They could concentrate instead on their common mission to restrain the new order through direct government and law enforcement. In this task they complemented each other. The secular Hadley was a creative prosecutor of corporate activities because he instinctively understood commerce and economics, but his secularism also left him susceptible to the appeal of the gospel of growth. The evangelical Folk was more sympathetic to direct democracy and less sympathetic to the value of growth, but he was also less tolerant of people from other ethnic and religious backgrounds. Hadley was, in short, more "modern in mind" than Folk and "more sympathetic to the joy of living," observed William Marion Reedy.[1] Over time Hadley restrained Folk's intolerance, and Folk restrained Hadley's materialism. Hadley encouraged Folk to broaden his vision to include controls over corporate commercial activities, and Folk encouraged Hadley to appreciate the power of direct democracy.

Proclaiming in his inaugural that bribery "is more fatal to civic life than any other crime, for it pollutes the stream of law at its source," Folk launched the Missouri Idea. He called for a crusade to obliterate bribery, bossism, and partisanship so that the majority could shape the community's rules and the law could be used to restrain the high and mighty. To Folk the community could only regain control when political action by the amateur citizen, who "serves his best interest by promoting the common good," replaced domination by the "professionals," who were "selfish people who would make money at the expense of the common good" and were, therefore, "morally blind."[2]

Folk received bipartisan support for the Missouri Idea. The 1905 legislature extended the statute of limitations on bribery cases from three to five years and added employees to the circuit attorneys' offices in large cities. To show that bribery would not be tolerated, he persuaded the 1905 legislature to repeal an earlier law that the baking powder trust had bribed through the legislature so audaciously that the incident had led to the prosecution of several state senators. Convinced that "professional lobbying should be made a crime," Folk compelled the railroads to stop issuing free travel passes to public officials and warned all lobbyists to conduct their business in public. He required that lobbyists report their business to him before they could approach legislators and that they stay no longer than thirty hours in Jefferson City. Folk pushed through a maximum freight rate law because legislators were afraid that they would be portrayed as recipients of bribes if they sided with the railroads. He used his appointments and administrative powers over municipal boards to stamp out corruption in law enforcement and elections. He took particular pride in the fact that during his term there was not a single complaint of fraud in any of the five elections that occurred in the major cities. Folk even protected the political rights of radicals. When St. Louis Socialists staged a rally in 1905 to protest a municipal ban on Socialist gatherings, Mayor Rolla Wells dispatched fifty policemen, who clubbed the radicals. The Socialists appealed to Folk to permit them to meet, and the governor overturned the mayor's ban and protected their right to assemble.[3]

At the start of his administration Folk was led by his evangelical background into the thick of ethnic and religious battles that divided traditional Missourians and threatened to destroy the Missouri Idea. The demands by religious evangelicals for governmental suppression of drinking and gambling peaked during Folk's term. Nearly two-thirds of all local option elections (in which communities voted whether to be "wet" or "dry") that occurred after the start of local option in 1888 came between 1904 and 1908, as traditional cultures fought it out on this political battlefield. Folk enlisted. He diverted his law enforcement crusade into a crusade to close saloons on Sundays. He used the St. Louis police, whom he controlled, to enforce the Sunday closing law in St. Louis County, where officials had hitherto favored thirsty constituents over the law. Declaring "there is no magic in a license to change moral wrong into innocence," he persuaded the 1905 legislature to replace an 1897 law that licensed race track gambling with an outright prohibition of bookmaking and pool selling. He used the St. Louis police to attempt to close the Delmar Jockey Club, a St. Louis County race track, in a two-year struggle that did not end until 1907, when the legislature passed a new law that effectively ended betting on horse races. Folk urged suppression of winerooms, dance halls, slot machines, and gambling in all forms and even supported prosecutors who tried to turn public opinion against him by enforcing the Sunday ban on livery stables, candy stores, and even picnics by German groups. Evangelicals cheered Folk on in what he called the war between "the Sunday saloon and the Sunday home." In October 1905 the Missouri Women's Christian Temperance Union applauded his crusade because "his faithfulness to duty has turned toward him the eyes of our nation and inspired Governors of other states to emulate his noble example."[4]

Consumer champions and other progressives watched in horror as the liquor and gambling issues diverted the struggle to unite the community against the new economic leaders into fights that divided consumers along traditional cultural lines. The St. Louis *Censor* reflected progressives' disappointment:

> The people voted for Folk because they thought he was a real reformer, that is, an official ready to go after the big crooks and the real criminals instead of raising a fog of dust by trying to suppress various kinds of conduct of which the I-am-better-than-thou element does not approve, and which is nearly always the sole method of all fake reformers. . . . Governor Folk, who as Circuit Attorney, gave the people of Missouri the first real reform they ever had, and refused to allow himself to be pushed into the old rut of a fanatic zeal to moralize people by invading their personal liberties, . . . has fallen into that rut since he became Governor.

Reminding Folk that Missourians had elected him to discipline the wealthy and powerful, the St. Louis *Mirror* declared that "pleasure must not be treated as a crime" and that "bigotry and ultra-puritanical repression" were "crazy reform."[5]

Traditional partisan allegiances likewise diverted Folk's insurance commissioner, W. D. Vandiver, from pursuing what promised at first to be a sensational application of the Missouri Idea to life insurance. In October 1905 Vandiver became the first state official outside New York to respond to revelations that New York Life had used policyholders' money to finance Republican candidates. Vandiver threatened to expel New York Life from Missouri unless its top officers resigned their posts and the company repaid an amount equal to its political contributions, $148,702.50, to policyholders.

But that was it. While New York and other states followed up the disclosures of life insurance corruption with vigorous prosecutions and enactment of stricter regulations, Vandiver held back. He even withdrew his order against New York Life just before the expulsion was to occur. "Old W. D. started off with a bang, but this was about it. Surely our great superintendent of insurance could do much more for the public," lamented the St. Louis *Mirror* in 1907.[6]

Vandiver aborted his crusade because he was a fiercely partisan Democrat less interested in helping policyholders than in criticizing a company that had made contributions to Republican candidates. Vandiver, whose personal motto was "He serves his country best who serves his party best," was a colorful partisan who had been elected to Congress from southeast Missouri in 1896 and consistently reelected until Folk named him to manage his campaign in 1904. Texas insurance commissioner Thomas B. Love expressed the disappointment of those who believed that protecting policyholders, not making partisan points, was the essence of insurance reform. "While I am a loyal Democrat," Love wrote a friend in Missouri, "I cannot agree with Vandiver's seeming belief that life insurance reform is a partisan matter. He has raised the public's expectations only to fail them with his subsequent inaction." Chiding Vandiver for subordinating insurance reform to routine partisanship, the St. Louis *Censor* demanded, "Why is he not watching the crooks of insurance instead of running around telling farmers about the tariff?"[7]

Just when the traditional ethnic and partisan loyalties of the governor and insurance commissioner threatened to blunt the Missouri Idea, Attorney General Hadley turned the campaign for law enforcement into a popular crusade against many of the nation's largest corporations. He reunited consumers and rekindled hope that through the Missouri Idea communities might discipline the powerful. Since the purpose of monopolies was to overcharge consumers, Hadley believed that such "corporations are just as clearly committing the offense of larceny as the burglar who enters your house or the pickpocket who takes your purse." The solution was to "demand that those old-fashioned principles of common honesty apply in large corporate affairs" until "the weak and strong shall stand as equals before the bar of human justice."[8]

Within two months after taking office Hadley launched the proceedings that would catapult him to national prominence as a fearless champion of consumers against big business. He learned that Standard Oil of New Jersey had monopolized the oil business in Missouri through three subsidiaries, Standard of Indiana, Waters-Pierce, and Republic. He petitioned the state supreme court to annul the charters and licenses of the three subsidiaries and to prohibit them from operating in Missouri. He collected testimony in several cities, and in October 1905 the St. Louis *Post-Dispatch* concluded that "no monopoly has been so subtle, so secretive, so successful as the Standard Oil." Many witnesses confirmed that the three companies had rigged the oil price artificially high, but Hadley wanted to prove that this was because they were all owned by Jersey Standard. To do that he needed to take testimony from Standard's leading oficers in a courtroom not far from their Wall Street offices. They resisted. John D. Rockefeller donned a wig as a disguise and fled the country. Another company official, H. M. Telford, evaded subpoenas until a keyman (process server) raced from a hiding place as Telford left his townhouse and entered a car, jumped on the car's running board, and thrust the subpoena into Telford's lap.[9]

In January 1906 national attention turned to the New York courtroom where the earnest young attorney general from the Midwest was trying to force the officers of the nation's most famous corporation to concede that they had illegally monopolized Missouri's oil business. Many earlier prosecutors and journalists had caused sensations by attacking Standard's practices, but lacked legal proof the conspiring subsidiaries were owned by the national Standard empire. Kansas, for example, had abandoned its own investigation precisely because its investigators could not prove ownership.[10]

Hadley repeatedly tried to force corporate officers to admit that Jersey Standard owned Indiana Standard or even to admit that both companies had offices in the Standard Oil Building. For several days the company's officers raised objections and parried Hadley's questions with "tactics, which, though within the law, are said to be without legal precedent in New York," reported the *New York Times*. Hadley "was easily the central figure of the proceedings." Finally, the company's financial architect, Henry H. Rogers took the stand. Onlookers, including the *New York American*'s reporter, were stunned by his sarcastic, "insolent" responses to Hadley. Standard's attorneys had directed their clients not to answer questions about ownership. The climax came when Hadley asked, "Do you wish to say to the Supreme Court of Missouri that you, as a director of the Standard Oil Company of Indiana, don't know where its offices are?" Lawyers and spectators gasped when Rogers replied, "It is quite immaterial to me what the Supreme Court of Missouri desires me to say. . . ."[11]

Hadley's appeal to the Missouri Supreme Court to force Standard Oil officers to disclose the company's financial structure recapitulated the large struggle to make the law into a means by which to discipline new commercial practices. Individuals had an ancient legal right against self-incrimination, but in the new order that right had been extended to permit corporate officials to conceal things about their companies. "Hadley was lost unless the Law . . . upheld him in his contention that an individual cannot skulk behind the cloak of a corporation to hide his misdeeds," explained reporter Sherman Morse. It was Hadley's great good luck that at just this moment the United States Supreme Court ruled that immunity from self-incrimination did not apply to testimony by corporate officials that might convict a corporation of a crime. The Missouri Supreme Court promptly ordered Rogers to answer Hadley's questions. Corporations were not above the law. "It is now up to the trust bandits to elect whether they will take their medicine as individuals or as corporations, and in either case it ought to be made bitter enough to put them out of business forever," declared the Kansas City *World*.[12]

The same actors reassembled in a New York courtroom in late March 1906. This time Rogers quietly answered Hadley's questions, until they reached the question of ownership. Rogers yielded to his attorney, Frank Hagerman, "upon whom again fell the duty of lowering the colors of the great corporation," as a reporter observed. "It is admitted," began a formal statement dictated by Hadley and accepted by Standard's lawyers,

> for the purposes of this case only that now and during the period covered by the information, the majority of the stock of the Standard Oil Company of Indiana and the stock of the Republic Oil Company is held for the Standard Oil Company of New Jersey, and that all stock of the Waters-Pierce Company on the books of the company in the name of M. M. Van Beuren are held for the Standard Oil Company of New Jersey.[13]

"It is more than had been done before in a quarter of a century of conflict to hold the Standard Oil Company within the bounds of the law," cheered Sherman Morse in *American Magazine*. *World To-Day* featured Hadley as one of its "Men of the Month." Back in Missouri the same editors who had condemned Folk's Sunday-closing campaign for its intolerance warmly applauded Hadley's triumph. He "made the greatest law-defying corporation 'knuckle under' to the law," wrote Reedy in the St. Louis *Mirror*. The progressive St. Louis *Censor* hailed Hadley as "the only public official who has ever defeated that wise, criminal and secret aggregation of capital—the Standard Oil Trust."[14]

Although Standard dragged out the final resolution of the case with its own testimony and appeals, Missourians recognized that Hadley had won in New York in 1906. The Missouri Supreme Court in 1909 fined each of the Standard subsidiaries $50,000 and annulled their right to do business in Missouri. Waters-Pierce paid, reorganized independently from Standard, and received the court's blessing to resume business. But Indiana Standard and Republic appealed to the United States Supreme Court, which upheld the Missouri court in 1912. Hadley's case became the basis for antitrust prosecutions of the Standard empire in five states, and of the federal prosecution that led the Supreme Court to dissolve Standard Oil in 1911. Ida Tarbell, a leading student and critic of Standard's commercial activities, termed Hadley's prosecution "the cleanest and completest presentation of a case for conspiracy in restraint of trade that I have ever seen."[15]

In his prosecution of Standard Oil, Hadley gave the Missouri Idea its most popular shape by uniting people across cultural barriers as oil consumers and by drawing on that unity to use traditional moral standards to restrain new commercial practices. Consumers cheered the economic results. No longer fearing Standard's predatory methods, thirty independent oil companies began to do business in Missouri. The price of oil fell from 9½ cents a gallon to 6½ cents a gallon, saving Missouri consumers over a half-million dollars a year. The *Joplin News-Herald* wrote that the real victor in the fight against Standard was "the man who buys his gallon can of coal oil for his lamp or the woman who uses a gasoline stove and pays a needlessly high price for her fuel." Arguing that monopolies like Standard Oil extorted their profits from their consumers, a *St. Louis Post-Dispatch* "Reader" demanded, "Why should such enormous profits go to a few? Why should they not be distributed among the people who, as consumers, give all value to products?" By appealing to a consumer theory of value and control, Hadley found a "moral significance" to his victory that transcended the cultural limits to Folk's moral vision. Hadley vindicated the Missouri Idea's moral heart: "No combination of money and power is above the law, and . . . none will be permitted to violate the law with impunity."[16]

Hadley hurried back into court to restrain the commercial practices of other industries. Farmers complained that the new International Harvester Company had deprived them of their familiar choice of binders, mowers, and reapers at competitive prices when it absorbed five implement companies that had formerly been competitors in Missouri. Responding to an official request from the Missouri House of Representatives, Hadley sued on November 12, 1907, to break up the new company. The state surpreme court agreed in 1911, fining the company $50,000 for violating the antitrust law.[17]

He prosecuted an association of lumber manufacturers that "levied a wrongful and excessive tribute upon every home-builder in Missouri" by limiting output and driving up prices. Although the state supreme court in 1914 fined and revoked the licenses of several of the conspiring companies, Hadley brought immediate relief to lumber consumers, for the companies abandoned their anticompetitive practices and lowered their prices out of fear of additional prosecutions.[18]

Although his predecessor had won a conviction of the state's fire insurance companies for antitrust violations, sixty-nine of the companies had paid nominal $1,000 fines and continued their old practices of setting rates artificially high and ignoring the actual risk of fire to each piece of insured property. Determined to win relief for policyholders, Hadley persuaded the now-frightened companies to negotiate a settlement in which they promised to rerate all the property in the state on the basis of actual risk, to cut rates, and to restore competition. Hadley's settlement saved policyholders about $820,000 a year.[19]

Responding to the anger of meat consumers, Hadley found that the Beef Trust was continuing to fix the price of cattle to farmers and of beef to consumers. He collected evidence and passed it on to federal officials who were leading the legal battle against the Beef Trust. When the federal government lost its suit, Hadley prepared his own case. The state supreme court agreed with Hadley that Kansas City's Traders' Live Stock Exchange violated the antitrust law when it boycotted traders who refused to join their association.[20]

Hadley devoted the most time and energy to his long battle with the railroads because he believed that they harmed the most consumers in the most ways. "Nothing we eat, nothing we wear, no part of the house that shelters us from the winter's cold or the summer's heat . . , but the price of it is affected by freight rates," wrote Hadley. He estimated that freight rates constituted between a third and a fourth of the total cost of everything consumers purchased.[21]

Hadley knew that Missouri's consumers regarded taking on the railroads as the real test for whether the Missouri Idea could bring corporations under popular control. The railroads had left such a trail of corrupted laws and judicial rulings, of compromised governors, legislators, and judges, that many Missourians had concluded that only outlaws could reach them. A spectacular case from Warrensburg in 1903 heightened Missourians' fears that the railroads were beyond the law. Years earlier a Missouri Pacific brakeman, Rube Oglesby, had lost a leg when he was run over by a freight car. He sued the railroad and won damages in the circuit court. The railroad appealed to the state supreme court, which found an error in the trial court record and ordered a retrial. The second jury agreed with the first, ordering the railroad to pay Oglesby $15,000. The supreme court reversed this verdict. Reflecting the conclusion of most Missourians, J. M. Shepherd editorialized in his Warrensburg *Standard-Herald*:

> The victory of the railroad has been complete, and the corruption of the supreme court has been thorough. . . . What hope have the ordinary citizens of Missouri for justice and equitable laws in bodies where such open venality is practiced? . . . The corporations have long owned the legislature, now they own the supreme court. . . . The wheels of the Juggernaut will continue to grind out men's lives, and a crooked court will continue to refuse them and their relatives damages, until the time comes when Missourians, irrespective of politics, rise up in their might and slay at the ballot box the corporation-bought lawmakers of the state.

The supreme court cited Shepherd for contempt, fined him $500, and ordered him to jail until the fine was paid. Outraged by the court's attempt to muzzle a free press, the people of Warrensburg raised the money within two hours and paid Shepherd's fine. When the supreme court arrested the editor of the Sedalia *Capital* for reprinting the *Standard-Herald* editorial, the *Milan Republican* concluded that democracy itself was the defendant: "The crime is that of a free press."[22]

Hadley soon discovered that he would need new methods to reach the railroads. This time the federal judiciary was firmly on the trust's side. Folk and the 1905 legislature set the stage by enacting a maximum freight rate law that spelled out reductions in rates on various commodities, averaging about 25 percent. The railroads sped to the Kansas City federal court, which enjoined Hadley and the railroad commissioners from enforcing the law until its constitutionality was determined. Soon thereafter the railroads provided a private car for the railroad attorneys to use to host a fishing trip for the Kansas City federal judges.[23]

While he prepared to defend the rate law in this hostile arena, Hadley also investigated rate structures and cooperated with Folk and the legislature in formulating a railroad policy for the state. They concluded that Missourians had to pay twice as much to ship products within the state as to ship them beyond its borders, a practice Hadley attacked as an "enormous tribute" the railroads levied on consumers. Hadley and Folk jointly recommended and the 1907 legislature enacted a law that reaffirmed the 1905 rate law with some additions suggested by Hadley, and a law that lowered the passenger fare from three to two cents a mile.[24]

Hadley knew that the federal courts posed the biggest challenge to the state's railroad policy and to his creativity. Knowing that the Kansas City federal court would enjoin the passenger rate law, Hadley beat the railroads to the legal punch by several hours, and persuaded state courts in St. Louis and Kansas City to enjoin the railroads from disobeying the rate laws. The railroads promptly asked the federal courts to find Hadley in contempt. During what everyone assumed would be a perfunctory hearing in Kansas City federal court, since Judge Smith McPherson was expected to censure Hadley and enjoin the passenger law, Hadley suddenly woke everyone up. He warned that if the railroads sought a federal injunction against the passenger law, he would appeal to the Missouri Supreme Court to take away the railroads' right to operate in Missouri because they were refusing to obey the criminal provisions he had inserted into the rate law. Next, he proposed a dramatic plan for using criminal law enforcement to compel the railroads to accept the two-cent law. He warned that the trains would have to lock their doors as they passed through Missouri, and that he would post a militia guard on each train to enforce this rule. The state would arrest any station agents or conductors who tried to make passengers pay more than two cents a mile and charge them with violating the criminal provision of the law.[25]

The railroads backed down. They withdrew the contempt charge against Hadley and consented to charge two cents a mile until the court ruled on the law. The Kansas City federal circuit court ultimately ruled that both the freight and passenger laws were confiscatory, but the United States Supreme Court overturned that decision in 1913.[26]

In a state where law had been the new order's handmaiden, where traditional Missourians had regarded lawbreaking as their only alternative to submission, Folk and Hadley had shown how law enforcement could impose popular control on huge corporations. By redefining new corporate practices as traditional crimes, Missouri's prosecutors pointed toward a future in which the community could again control behavior. Instead of serving primarily to encourage growth and competition, law became, through corporate prosecutions, "the reflection of the moral sense of the people," concluded the Kansas City *World*: "The way to enforce the moral sense of the people is to enforce the law."[27]

Hoping that prosecutions could compel the new impersonal corporations to submit to popular discipline, Folk, Hadley, and their supporters concluded that the corporate fines specified by Missouri law were ineffective deterrents. Lawbreaking corporations simply passed the fines along to consumers. Corporations, in addition, could avoid the traditional penal methods of conviction, imprisonment, and rehabilitation because, as Folk put it, they "have no material existence." If corporations had existed in the Garden of Eden, Folk told legislators in 1907, Adam and Eve would have justified their act by saying, "We have formed a corporation; we did not eat the apple, the corporation did." Under Missouri law the corporation could have been driven from the Garden but "Adam and Eve would have been permitted to remain, form new corporations, and continue to eat the apples as long as they pleased."[28]

The way to control the soulless corporation therefore was to reach behind its legal facade and hold its individual officers personally liable to prison sentences when they violated "the moral sense of the people." Corporate officers could not pass prison sentences on to consumers. "The only real and effective way to punish a trust is by punishing the individual responsible for illegal transactions," concluded the *St. Louis Post-Dispatch* in 1907. "Give a trust magnate a striped suit and . . . the next time he wants wearing apparel he'll hunt up a different tailor, and his companions will be able to profit by his example and not get themselves in shape to don the zebra outfit in the first place," explained the Macon *Times-Democrat*. Agreeing with Folk and Hadley that, in the governor's words, "it should be just as serious an offense to violate the antitrust laws as it is to violate the larceny statutes," the 1907 legislature added prison sentences to the antitrust laws.[29]

By threatening corporate officers with the same fear of public disgrace, punishment, and loss of liberty that criminal law had long used to deter people, Folk and Hadley sought to persuade others to follow their daring path. In 1909 Hadley told United States attorney general George Wickersham that prosecution of Standard Oil's officers for "practically every crime in the calendar, from murder in the first degree to petit larceny . . . in connection with . . . the crushing out of competition . . . would do more to secure fair and lawful trade" than antitrust civil suits. He advised St. Louis circuit attorney Seebert Jones in 1910 that Kansas City's criminal indictment of several commission merchants under the 1907 criminal antitrust law restored competition better than had his own suits, which had not prevented businessmen from forming new corporations.[30]

Folk and Hadley persuaded the 1907 legislature to broaden the Missouri Idea to include other forms of consumer protection. In addition to the freight and passenger rate laws that aided consumers when they rode trains or purchased merchandise, the 1907 legislature enacted fifteen minor railroad laws and seven more protecting life insurance policyholders against corrupt company officers. Legislators also passed a law to protect consumers against adulterated and mislabeled foods and beverages. Heeding an angry chorus of consumers from St. Louis and Kansas City, Folk called a special session in 1907 at which legislators gave cities and their consumers the power to regulate the rates and services of local utilities. The measure, Folk promised, would save consumers millions of dollars. By enacting laws to protect insurance policyholders, beef eaters, and streetcar riders, the 1907 legislature extended the Missouri Idea beyond Hadley's prosecutions.[31]

But Missourians wanted to extend their participation in popular control beyond the passive act of cheering Folk and Hadley. They wanted to empower themselves with the collective capacity to control their own political fates. The 1907 legislature expanded Folk's most creative contribution to the Missouri Idea, the bribery prosecutions, into permanent structural changes that gave voters greater power. In the same spirit in which Hadley had marshaled traditional beliefs about crime to restrain commercial practices, Folk hoped to turn political traditions into reforms that would arm the popular majority to recapture government from the wealthy and powerful. "The nearer government can be brought to the people the better and purer that government will be," Folk told 1907 legislators. The way to bring government closer was to lower barriers that intervened between voters and laws. Proclaiming "the right of the people to have their laws untainted by venal influences," Folk convinced the legislature to enact a tough antilobbying law. The law required paid lobbyists to register and report their employers' names, their business, and their expenditures.[32]

The central mechanism to give "ordinary citizens" power over "professional politicians," Folk believed, was the direct primary for nominating candidates. Removing the nominating caucuses and conventions at which power brokers had used patronage and money to deflect voters, the 1907 legislature gave a popular majority the direct power to nominate candidates for state office. "It is a crystallizing into law of the sentiment that the rights of the people are safest with the people," concluded Cornelius Roach, editor of the *Carthage Democrat*. The legislature even adopted Folk's proposal for a popular vote on candidates for U.S. Senate with the hope that legislatures would select the voters' choice until the time, "not far distant," when he hoped that the federal constitution would permit voters to elect senators directly.[33]

Although it fell short of the "political revolution" Folk had envisaged, the direct primary did assist "ordinary citizens" by bringing more issues into elections, and wider popular participation. Between 10 and 20 percent of Missouri citizens had traditionally attended the caucuses and conventions that nominated candidates, but over the eighteen years after the direct primary an average of 51 percent of Republican voters and 61 percent of Democratic ones attended the new primaries. Wider popular participation encouraged candidates to identify their candidacies with issues. Although ethnic and sectional allegiances continued to guide most voters at general elections, they felt freer to respond to other issues in primary elections.[34]

Folk championed the most radical form of direct democracy when he convinced legislators to enact an initiative and referendum law. Folk made it part of the Missouri Idea because it "puts an effective stop to bribery in legislative halls, for bribery of legislators would be useless where the people are the final arbiter of a measure." But the consumer-oriented 1907 legislature approved the constitutional ammendment for initiative and referendum because urban consumers had come to believe that direct democracy could best mobilize their political strength as a loosely organized majority.[35] Direct majority rule, they hoped, would overcome the traditional barriers that had divided them in general elections.

After approving direct legislation at the 1908 election, Missouri voters defended it even against popular critics. By an 85–15 margin voters in 1912 rejected the Single Tax, but when opponents of the tax proposed on the 1914 ballot to prohibit Single Taxers from ever using initiative and referendum again, Missouri voters protected the initiative system for all Missourians by a 71–29 margin.[36]

Initiative and referendum, in practice, widened the political agenda and encouraged voters to cast off traditional partisanship as they voted on issues. In the 1910s citizens forced prohibition, woman suffrage, and the Single Tax onto the political agenda by collecting enough initiative signatures to require a popular vote. Each issue mobilized voters to participate in spirited campaigns on issues and policies, not candidates and parties. While in the 1910 election, for example, voters felt so constrained by partisanship that only one in a thousand voted for a candidate from a different party for the two top offices on the ballot, they voted more independently on issues. Only 20 percent favored a pay raise for legislators, while 36 percent favored bonds for a new state capitol. In 1914 17 percent favored a state highway fund, while 46 percent favored pensions for the blind.[37]

Missourians knew that before law enforcement and direct democracy could carry them to an unlimited future of popular control they would have to confront the structures and traditions of representative government that had restrained earlier reform movements. They had come to identify the Missouri Idea with two remarkable politicians, and since Missouri law limited officeholders to a single term, they knew that the challenge would come in the 1908 election. Folk, Hadley, and their supporters believed that the election of leaders to higher office was the surest way to advance the movement. They feared, of course, that the election might erode the Missouri Idea, for elections had traditionally divided voters along ethnic, sectional, racial, and partisan lines. While unprecedented thousands of voters had shunned these divisions in 1904 to support Democrat Folk and Republican Hadley, no one knew how voters would weigh the Missouri Idea against traditional appeals in either the state's first statewide primary election or in the general election.

Folk paid the political price in 1908 for allowing ethnic and religious divisions to divert his campaign for law enforcement. He challenged incumbent Democrat William J. Stone in Missouri's first popular primary for the Senate. The colorful Stone was popular with voters and party organizers for his fiercely partisan rhetoric and his talent for party building and patronage. Professional politicians, particularly from the cities, seized Stone's candidacy to punish Folk and to halt further erosion of their power. While Stone boasted of his "party fidelity," Folk proudly acknowledged that "I have offended many professional politicians. . . ." "Folk was never popular with the political leaders of the party," Hadley told journalist Mark Sullivan, and as governor "he did not succeed in binding men to him personally." Knowing that Folk's attacks on party leaders won him more votes than they lost, machine politicians appealed to the many city dwellers who had cheered Folk's campaign against bribery but disliked his war on drinking and gambling. They urged urban Democrats from ethnic backgrounds more tolerant of a drink or a bet to embrace the more tolerant Stone. In this appeal machine politicians echoed criticisms by Folk's initial supporters. The anti-machine *St. Louis Post-Dispatch* had charged that Folk had betrayed reform when it attacked him in 1907 as a "master busybody": "When one considers what magnificent opportunities Gov. Folk enjoyed to concentrate his . . . tremendous energies on vital reforms . . . , it is impossible not to view, with profound regret, the dissipation of his energy and his influence on aims that are not vital. . . ." In the same vein the St. Louis *Censor* had lamented: "In this day . . . when the enormous question [is] whether plutocracy or people should rule, Folk . . . spends his whole time in seeking to drive home the fact that drinking beer on Sunday is a sin. . . ." Many urban Democrats wanted no part of a Missouri Idea that featured Sunday closing. In the end Folk carried rural Missouri but Stone won the primary by carrying the two largest cities by 23,000 votes. Machine politicians had created that urban majority by their familiar fraudulent tactics, charged the *Kansas City Times*.[38] But it is clear that by subordinating his progressivism to traditional ethnic and religious concerns, Folk had undermined his own ambition for higher office.

Herbert Hadley, by contrast, emerged as Missouri's most popular politician when he sought the governorship in 1908. By uniting Missourians as consumers across the cultural barriers that had defeated Folk, Hadley had shown how law could restrain the powerful. No Republican challenged him in the primary. The Democratic primary, on the other hand, was a religious and ethnic battleground on which machine politicians hoped to separate immigrants from the reform movement. Concerned about evangelical attacks on their culture, the German-American Alliance, for example, supported William S. Cowherd, the conservative candidate. Cowherd emerged as the Democratic nominee after a bitter struggle; Folk's choice, David Ball, plausibly blamed urban vote fraud for his defeat. Roasting Cowherd as the candidate of special interests, Hadley promised to carry on the Missouri Idea. Machine Democrats sought to activate the same ethnic, sectional, racial, and partisan appeals they had used against Ball and Folk by charging that Hadley was a hated Kansan who threatened white supremacy. He was a Republican in a state that had not elected a Republican governor in thirty-seven years. But Hadley refused to be diverted.[39]

Hadley won a spectacular victory, garnering more votes than had any political candidate in the state's history. Since "the combination of Special Interests against him was complete," the *Kansas City Times* concluded, "Hadley's victory lacks no detail of a popular triumph." He "won for the people and with the people." He was the only victorious Republican candidate for statewide office. For the second time in four years voters backed the Missouri Idea, turning over the governorship to a prosecutor who had used traditional values and traditional concepts of law to check the rich and powerful. They turned back ethnic and partisan challenges to the Missouri Idea's democratic appeal. Machine politicians may have secured Cowherd's nomination, but Hadley's victory in the general election was a "repudiation of the reactionary policies of the old discredited Democratic machine," concluded the Democratic *Post-Dispatch*.[40]

From the vantage point of 1907 or 1908 there seemed no limit to how far voters, legislators, journalists, and politicians might broaden and deepen the Missouri Idea. From its origins in boodle prosecutions the Missouri Idea had grown until it looked as though major corporations would be fined, expelled, or dissolved and the voters asume politicans' powers to govern. Folk had fairly called the 1907 legislative session "the most fruitful in good laws that the State has ever had."[41] There was no telling how much more the next session might empower citizens at the expense of politicians or corporations.

Missourians recognized that they were part of a national movement that seemed to be picking up speed as it hurtled toward an unlimited democratic future. "The ethical awakening shows signs of becoming universal and lasting, instead of local and transitory," Folk told audiences. "In this era of conscience the people are realizing that the government of city, state and nation belongs to them, and they can take it into their own hands." Since "the era of conscience demands the same standard of morality for corporations as is required of the individuals that compose them," corporate prosecutions increasingly promised popular control. By the summer of 1907 prosecutors proscribed new commercial practices as traditional crimes. During August alone the Cole County grand jury returned twenty-one indictments against the Missouri Pacific Railroad for failing to run scheduled trains and for overworking its telegraphers, and the new dairy and food commissioner came down on many dairies in Carthage, Jefferson City, and Columbia for selling adulterated milk. That same summer a Texas jury levied an unprecedented state fine of $1,623,900 on the Waters-Pierce Oil Company; a Toledo judge sentenced twenty-three lumbermen and bridge contractors to six months in prison for violating Ohio's antitrust law; San Francisco's bribery prosecutors focused on the city's business elite; and a federal judge in Chicago socked Standard Oil with the largest fine in history, over $29 million. Standard Oil alone was the object of suits by ten states and the federal government. President Theodore Roosevelt and his attorney general, Charles J. Bonaparte, predicted that the prosecutions would not stop until E. H. Harriman, John D. Rockefeller, and other "malefactors of great wealth" all landed in prison.[42]

Popular control, at last, seemed near.

2. The Changing Context of Popular Control

The very speed with which resisters seemed to be moving toward a democratic future in which they held real power focused several interrelated developments in ways that transformed the battle for popular control over corporate power. The unprecedented attempt to prosecute commercial activities, for example, posed special challenges to prosecutors, corporations, and judges, as each sought to translate judicial verdicts into changes in actual corporate behavior or structure. Promoters of the new order and the new pressure groups insisted that economic growth was more important than prosecution. Corporations mounted a huge counteroffensive against the prosecutors.

Stunned by popular condemnation and judicial convictions, corporations fought desperately to shift the debate from guilt to growth. Fresh from the legal defeats and unprecedented fines his Standard Oil empire had suffered in Missouri, Texas, Chicago, and Washington, and with President Roosevelt and his attorney general threatening to imprison the individuals who had built the Standard empire, John D. Rockefeller warned in August 1907 that "the policy of the present administration toward great business combinations of all kinds can have only one result. It means disaster to the country, financial depression and financial chaos" because it destroyed investor confidence, "the basis of all prosperity." Roosevelt replied that Rockefeller and other corporate leaders were conspiring "to bring about as much financial stress as they possibly can in order to discredit the policy of the government and thereby to secure a reversal of that policy, so that they may enjoy the fruits of their own evil doings." Fearing the anticorporate thrust, investors began selling. The stock market crashed in October, and the resulting Panic of 1907 broadened into a depression. Conservatives called Roosevelt "our chief panic-maker," while Roosevelt blamed greedy corporate officials who hid "behind the breastworks of corporate organization."[43]

Back in Missouri, St. Louis businessmen formed a Prosperity League that joined with the Kansas City Commercial Club in demanding an end to agitation and prosecution against corporations in order to restore growth and jobs. Too "much muckraking and denunciation of all corporations" had depressed business investment, complained St. Louis hardware merchant Edward C. Simmons. To Reedy's *Mirror* and other supporters of the Missouri Idea the Panic of 1907 was a deliberate effort "to enable the big money interests to run a bluff upon" reformers and "discredit" their antitrust policies.[44]

Progressives faced a desperate choice, for corporate officials proved in 1907–8 that they did indeed possess the power to retaliate against prosecutions by creating recessions and unemployment. Some urged a slowing of the pace of reform in order to restore investor confidence. The *New York World* declared that it was time to "give legitimate business a breathing spell and permit the restoration of confidence and credit."[45]

The courts themselves gave particular shape to the choice between prosecution and growth by handing down decisions that left extremely ambiguous the meaning of prosecutors' legal victories. "The Supreme Court recognizes that the recognition and condemnation of monopoly is a simple matter," observed the St. Louis *Republic*. "The real problem is the practical one of building up what it has destroyed and restoring what has been appropriated." The difficulty of turning legal victories into popular control was greatly aggravated by what Hadley termed the "somewhat cumbersome process" of the law, with its "delays," "technicalities," "harshness," and "ineffectiveness." The Missouri Supreme Court first decided that Standard Oil had violated the state's antitrust law in 1908, but the court did not finally translate that legal victory into a decision on how the company could conduct its business in Missouri until 1913.[46] Many progressives feared that the courts stripped the substance from the progressives' legal victories by permitting corporations, sometimes after paying small fines, to continue to conduct business after making only minor and largely technical changes in their structure and behavior.

Progressives received a major judicial setback from the United States Supreme Court in 1911. The court permitted investors "to breathe a sigh of relief," declared Chairman A. B. Hepburn of the Chase National Bank, by ruling that corporations did not violate the antitrust laws simply because they monopolized trade and that the courts would decide whether monopolistic practices were "reasonable" or "unreasonable." The question now became not whether a corporation had committed a crime, but whether the crime was "reasonable" or not. "No such a thing as reasonable or unreasonable crimes heretofore have been known in law," thundered the St. Louis *Republic*.[47]

By shifting the focus from whether a particular behavior was criminal in the eyes of the community to whether it was reasonable in the eyes of the courts, the judges established a middle ground where both corporations and progressives could claim some control. Corporate officers sought relief from the combination of journalistic exposure and criminal prosecution that seemed to mean that the community was mobilizing to deny their very right to exist. The "fundamental purpose" of any resolution between progressives and corporations "must be to restore public confidence in corporate methods by bringing back the corporation into harmony with the popular sense of fair play—fair play both towards the public as a consumer and the public as a stockholder in the corporation," James T. Young, director of the Wharton School of Finance, told the Missouri Bankers Association in 1908. Corporations were willing, even eager, for public supervision that restored public confidence. Progressives, for their part, grew increasingly weary of what the Kansas City *Star* called "fruitless efforts at dissolution" that only caused investors to lose confidence and thus workers to lose jobs. After more than a decade of warfare between Kansas City's consumers and its street railway monopoly, Mayor Henry L. Jost proposed government regulation in 1912 as a compromise. Acknowledging that among consumers "there has grown up a sentimental hostility to the company, mainly because of its intolerable conduct," Jost offered "to go to the limit to protect the bonds of the company. But I demand in return that the city shall have the power to regulate fares and the service." Both sides welcomed compromise. "'We, the people,' are beginning to supervise our affairs through our agent, the government, more than ever before," summarized the *Kansas City Times* in 1912.[48]

The way to narrow conflicts over the forms of regulation, many corporations agreed with many progressives, was to empower independent experts, whose training led them to resolve conflicts within a framework that assumed the desirability of growth and the undesirability of popular participation. Many businessmen wanted nonpartisan regulators to use impartial data to protect them against greedy competitors and angry consumers alike. Regulators had the impartiality of the courts along with the speed and flexibility that courts lacked.

The evolution of the campaign for popular control over the middlemen who manufactured and sold increasingly diluted, mislabeled, and adulterated foods and beverages was typical. To tradition-minded Missourians the middlemen were liars and "poisoners," in the words of the St. Louis *Censor*, who deserved to be prosecuted as criminals. Following the lead of the trade associations and professional organizations through which other producers had used the state to suppress competitors and escape popular censure, food and beverage processors welcomed government regulation in hopes that it would preserve public confidence in their industries and protect the biggest corporations against small operators whose greed transcended the industry norm. The state food and drug commissioner, whose office was established at the peak of the consumer uprising in 1907, reassured consumers about the safety of the food industry by assuming responsibility for weighing, analyzing, and approving what the public ate and drank. By 1911 groups like the Kansas City Retail Grocers' Association, State Bottlers' Association, Missouri Vall- Canners' Association, and Missouri Ice Cream Manufacturers' Association were expecting regulation by the food and drug commissioner to assist the growth of their industries. The commissioner sought to secure compliance with health regulations by persuasion and education that would not harm the reputation of businessmen: "In no instance has a prosecution been made when it was possible to accomplish results without it."[49]

3. The Decline of the Missouri Idea and the Rise of Regulation

Missourians hoped that the Missouri Idea would extend its reach at the state level when Herbert Hadley became governor in 1909. They could not have known that the very things that had made him a creative trust-buster as attorney general would leave him particularly vulnerable to the larger currents flowing around him, the trend away from prosecution and toward regulation. While Hadley's secularism had immunized him from the appeal of Folk's evangelical crusades, it also diluted the moral dimensions of his commercial outlook so that he was reluctant to do things that corporations claimed might retard growth. As an attorney, Hadley welcomed law enforcement, but he also believed that disputes should be settled by independent tribunals on the basis of unassailable expertise, and this made regulation appealing. And as a Republican, Hadley had shared the Republican antislavery legacy, which drew both on the zeal to unleash individual ambition by promoting competition and growth, on the one hand, and the belief that the community ought to use strong governmental sanctions against malefactors, on the other. His trust-busting had balanced both sides, encouraging competition and restraining corporations. As a progressive Republican governor, he was not hampered by Democratic fears of a strong administrative state. Moreover, he was drawn toward regulation because Theodore Roosevelt made it the policy issue in the ferocious conflict that flared within the Republican party while Hadley was governor, climaxing in the 1912 presidential campaign. The changes around him redirected Hadley's natural instincts, and as governor he sought not expanded prosecutions, but regulation.

Hadley began his journey from prosecutor to regulator toward the end of his term as attorney general, when he responded to the corporate counter-attack that followed the Panic of 1907. "On account of the disturbed business conditions resulting from the recent panic," he announced in 1908, he would not prosecute the beef and lumber monopolies. "It would be better to permit these evils to go uncorrected and unpunished for a while than to undertake the work of their correction under [economic] circumstances which would result in a more serious injury to the public and the business world." When the railroads tried to add political fears to Hadley's commercial sympathies by urging their employees to oppose his election in 1908, Hadley publicly denounced their blackmail—but declared that "a radical change in existing schedules would disorganize and seriously injure the business interests." This fear of offending investors was eroding the Missouri Idea at its moral core, warned the evangelical Joseph Folk. Cried Folk, "The man who says that the depression in the industrial world is caused by punishing crooks argues that there can be no such thing as honest prosperity. . . . If the country had to choose between great prosperity coupled with crookedness, and less prosperity and more honesty, it would undoubtedly take the latter."[50] Hadley did not agree. Parting ways with his fellow builder of the Missouri Idea, Hadley began to search for an alternative form of public control that would not threaten economic growth.

Over the course of his governorship Hadley's concern with growth moved ever closer to the center of his attempts to establish justice. "All other questions are capable of adjustment and solution if production exceeds consumption and supply keeps ahead of demand," declared the new governor. Soon he was emphasizing that government could assist consumers by encouraging economic growth. In his 1909 inaugural Hadley declared that the best way to narrow the gap between producer and consumer was not for the community to discipline powerful middlemen like the railroads, but to cheapen transportation costs by creating competition to the railroads that would encourage growth. He called for massive state highway building and river improvements. The idea that improved transportation would encourage economic growth became the theme of his governorship. And growth would stem the recession. What began as aid to consumers ended up leading him to cooperate with commercial groups and railroads and echo the earliest promoters of the new order. He sparked creation of regional development groups. He urged better roads.[51]

Hadley wanted public control that would simultaneously encourage growth and restrain corporate practices, reassure investors and protect consumers. He proposed a public service commission to regulate railroads and related corporations. The commission would both "give to the owners of such enterprises a reasonable return" on their investments and "regulate the charges and the conduct of business enterprises to which the public must resort." Since regulators would be "trained and experienced by study and investigation" to evaluate commercial practices within the limits of insuring a fair return, they promised investors more stability than did legislatures and courts, declared Hadley. Legislative regulation, as in the 1905 and 1907 rate laws, responded not to commercial realities but to the desire by politicians to win votes and partisan advantage by appealing to voters' anger. Judicial regulation was unresponsive to commercial needs because it was slow, arbitrary, cumbersome, "and seems harsh in its severity and unfortunate in its effect on general business conditions." An appointed commission of experts would not permit popular or partisan pressures to guide its decisions, and consumers would not have to await court decisions before securing relief. In any case, consumers culd hardly expect judicial or legislative regulation during Hadley's governorship, because the rate laws remained tied up in the courts.[52]

The courts forced Hadley to decide what specific changes in corporate structure would translate his legal victory in the Standard Oil case into effective popular control. His decision outraged many old supporters of the Missouri Idea by opening a huge gap between the realities of prosecution and of regulation. The state supreme court set the stage in December 1908 by ruling that Standard Oil broke the state antitrust law. Standard attorney Frank Hagerman knew that public officials would be eager not to threaten the company's new million-dollar refinery, which dominated the Kansas City suburb of Sugar Creek. Hoping to preserve his company's right to continue operating in Missouri, he proposed that the state and Indiana Standard jointly manage the company's property in Missouri. The state and the industry would each name a trustee, the two trustees would run Missouri's oil business, and the supreme court would arbitrate any differences between the trustees. Hagerman termed the proposal an "unparalleled advance in the management of a great property" by which "we have told the State to step in and watch us carefully. If prices don't suit, the State may change them." Hadley thought it an effective way for consumers to control oil prices. He termed it "the beginning of monopoly regulation" in Missouri, because it gave the state greater authority over the oil industry while preserving the refinery and its jobs. To supporters of the Missouri Idea, however, Hagerman's proposal was "diametrically opposed to the principles which underlie" the antimonopoly laws. The *St. Louis Post-Dispatch* protested that Hadley and Standard proposed "putting the State into the business of running monopolies," a step that "would revolutionize the government of Missouri" and destroy the Missouri Idea. By agreeing to the compromise the government was announcing that Standard was too "powerful" and "entrenched in resources and advantages" to pay the penalty for its crime, namely, ouster from Missouri. The government, in short, would ratify the company's crime. In the end, however, the court denied Hadley the chance to run oil as a state monopoly by rejecting the Hagerman plan.[53]

Hadley increasingly ignored critics and promoted regulation. He urged the 1911 legislature to enact his commission proposal, both to protect consumers and reassure investors "that no radical, extreme or retaliatory orders would be adopted or enforced." In 1913 he told legislators that an expert commission was the best way for government to supervise large corporations.[54]

Democratic legislators used traditional partisanship with appeals to Missourians' long-held fears of government to defeat Hadley's proposals for an administrative state in 1909 and 1911. In 1909 the Democratic Senate refused to support any of Hadley's measures that the Republican House had passed. At their 1910 convention Democrats hoped to rekindle fears of big taxes and government by contrasting Hadley's "inexcusable extravagances" with traditional Democratic "thrift." Democrats also declared that the legislature should set railroad rates, arguing that it was a more responsive body than an appointive commission because it was directly accountable to the voters. Hadley, in turn, blamed Missouri's slow rate of growth on "the niggardly policy in the matter of expenditures that was pursued by Democratic Governors" who pandered to a "sort of conservatism on the part of Missourians" that led them "to glory in a system of low taxes."[55]

Prevented by supporters of partisanship and weak government from securing the kind of progressive legislative record that Folk had achieved in 1907, Hadley followed the example of Theodore Roosevelt and informally assumed regulatory powers. As he turned from prosecution to persuasion, Hadley sought informal ways of establishing administrative regulation. He tried to persuade corporations to accept regulations of the type a commission would have adopted by showing them that he understood their needs. In 1909 he painstakingly worked out an agreement by the railroads to install new headlights. He took Missouri Pacific president Benjamin F. Bush on a fishing trip in 1911 to try to persuade him to cut the passenger fare from 3 to 2½ cents a mile, arguing that the road made unnecessary enemies by its intransigence. When health officials became alarmed that public drinking cups on trains spread diseases, Hadley asked the Missouri Pacific on November 25, 1911, whether it would obey a Missouri Board of Health order against such cups. When the railroad said it would, Hadley wrote the state board on November 29 telling it to issue the order. Hadley adopted the informal approach because he doubted whether the board had the authority to issue the order on its own.[56]

Hadley used the same approach in 1911 to defuse the explosive issue of the railroads' political lobby. Arguing that lobbyists heightened popular anger at railroad corruption of politics, leading to stronger antirailroad laws, Hadley persuaded the railroads to withdraw their lobbyists from Jefferson City and simply send specialists to testify on particular bills. They were to trust their industry's political fortunes, in effect, to Hadley. The 1911 legislature enacted seventeen railroad laws. The railroads protested that three were unfair. Hadley vetoed two of those three. Hadley insisted that creation of a regulatory commission would formalize this procedure by sparing the railroads the need for lobbyists.[57]

Hadley listened more and more favorably to reformers who wanted a strong state to assist victims of the new order as well as to promote development and regulation. When unions concluded that growth was the best protector of jobs and wages, they replaced some of their faith in direct democracy and public ownership with appeals for aid from the state. Growing numbers of urban social reformers joined them in turning to the state to fulfill the traditional notion that the strong should care for the weak. Kansas City reformers created the nation's first municipal department of public welfare in 1909. This new role for government drew reformers together across traditional ethnic, religious and partisan barriers. The Kansas City Board of Public Welfare helped established a consensus in favor of economic growth because "through its work the family of small means is able to share in the advantages of the city's progress," observed the Kansas City *Star*. Kansas City residents worked with such St. Louis reformers as Roger Baldwin and with the unions to create an effective statewide lobby in the 1910s.[58]

The more Hadley focused on development and regulation, the more he supported social welfare. He rejected competitive practices that wasted the long-term productivity of forests or workers. He urged the 1913 legislature "to bring about a larger measure of social and industrial justice, and a physical well-being and prosperity which must be the basis of substantial progress towards a better condition of life." He appointed expert commissions on forestry and waterways to recommend solutions to wasted natural resources. He formed commissions on workmen's compensation and tuberculosis to preserve human resources.[59]

As he became more interested in social reform, he discovered another problem in the Missouri Idea's focus on criminal prosecution. Crusades for law enforcement ended sending people to the Missouri State Penitentiary in Jefferson City, which, Hadley discovered on taking office, was the world's largest jail. It also had a reputation for producing hardened criminals. Since prisons ought to create productive members of society who could contribute to development, Hadley set out to transform the state's approach to punishment, using his administrative powers. He abolished flogging, the lock step, and stripes, ordered that showers and better food be provided for prisoners and that job skills be taught, and saw the measure of his success when the number of discipline cases at the prison fell by half. He worked with pardon attorneys to parole several hundred young prisoners, releasing them to citizens who provided them jobs and assumed responsibility for their conduct. Concerned that prejudiced judges and juries had imposed unjust sentences, Hadley won loud applause from the new National Association for the Advancement of Colored People and its magazine, *The Crisis*, for pardoning large numbers of black prisoners.[60]

While Hadley found further reason to support an administrative state when partisan Democratic legislators killed his legislative initiatives, he fought in 1912 to reconcile progressivism with partisanship. Always more popular than his party, Hadley hoped that progressives could capture the Republican party without causing a split that would produce a Democratic victory. He tried to push President William Howard Taft to adopt progressive policies. But Theodore Roosevelt was proposing a program strikingly similar to Hadley's, and he was more popular with Missouri Republicans. Hadley joined seven other Republican governors in calling on Roosevelt to run.[61]

Knowing that progressives would win if the majority of Republican voters, not the Taft-appointed officeholders, could select the national Republican delegates, Hadley tried unsuccessfully to persuade state Republican chairman Charles D. Morris to hold a presidential primary election. Instead, fist fights broke out at many district conventions as the party rank and file defied their officeholders and leaders in a popular movement to nominate Roosevelt and thereby force the party to put popularity and issues at its core. To prevent further violence at the state convention as both sides tested the limits of party, leaders worked out a delicate compromise that gave Roosevelt a majority of Missouri's at-large delegates. But the majority wanted no more political deals. At one in the morning an amateur delegate, R. T. Andrews from Dallas County in the Ozarks, arose to demand that Roosevelt receive votes of all at-large delegates: "We are fighting for the right of the people to rule, and we do not feel bound by any gentlemen's agreement." Roosevelt carried the Missouri convention by 663 to 321½.[62]

The issue was the same at the national convention. Progressives Roosevelt and Robert La Follette carried nine of the ten states where voters had elected delegates by direct primary vote for the first time in 1912. Progressives polled 1,508,440 Republican votes to 761,716 for Taft. But Taft controlled the party machinery, and the party regulars were determined, as Taft supporter Otto F. Stifel had declared at the Missouri convention, "to preserve . . . the party and save it from populism."[63]

When the convention formally opened in Chicago at noon on June 18, Hadley rose and moved to replace seventy-two Taft delegates with Roosevelt delegates. He charged that the party's national committee was a "political oligarchy." Hadley was ruled out of order, but he made a "splendid impression" on the delegates, reported Democrat William Jennings Bryan, and "won the hearts of the convention," according to another observer. The next day delegates spontaneously erupted in a twenty-five minute demonstration for Hadley that frightened both Roosevelt and Taft leaders. Hadley suddenly loomed as a popular compromise. But compromise was impossible at this convention. The conflict between the two candidates was also a conflict over principles: would majority opinion or officeholding shape political parties of the future? When the officeholders won and nominated Taft, many Republicans followed their leader out, shattering party bonds to form the new Progressive party.[64] Party loyalty could not hold their movement.

Hadley recognized that the fracture would doom the Republicans in Missouri, as elsewhere, and he tried to preserve both the party and progressivism. He believed that "the commercial politician," representing "a partnership between big business and politics," had overwhelmed a majority of Republican voters. He wanted to "so shape things that all who are progressive should be able to eventually work together in one organization," he wrote Roosevelt in July. Feeling the ties of partisanship and believing that American government was party government, Hadley stayed within the Republican party. After delaying time and again, after forcing Taft to endorse popular primaries to nominate future presidents as his price, in October he finally gave what he called a "very tepid" endorsement of Taft. With the Republicans split, Woodrow Wilson easily carried Missouri. St. Louis went Democratic for the first time since 1876. Wilson won 47 percent of the Missouri vote, compared to 30 percent for Taft and 18 percent of Roosevelt.[65] Hadley joined Folk in political retirement. Politics existed for officeholders, not democratic movements or issues.

The Missouri Idea of using law and prosecutions to control new commercial practices became increasingly associated with Hadley's attorney general, Elliott W. Major, and the Democratic party. Major carried Hadley's cases against Standard Oil, International Harvester, the meat packers, lumber companies, and railroads through to victory in the United States Supreme Court. The $358,000 fine against the lumber companies for violating the antitrust law cheered taxpayers, who appreciated both the tax savings and prosecution of the powerful. Appealing to popular support for his trust-busting, Major won the Democratic gubernatorial nomination in 1912 against the corporate candidate, William Cowherd. Blasting Republicans for not enforcing the antitrust laws, Missouri Democrats held a special convention in 1912 to attack the process of monopoly itself, because it "oppresses the people, taxes their energies, limits their opportuities, and . . . has raised the price of living to a point where the cost of the very necessities of life is almost beyond the reach of the great industrial classes." Major's antitrust record reinforced Woodrow Wilson's claim that Democrats were the real trust-busters, that Taft's conservatism and Roosevelt's regulation protected monopoly.[66] In any case, the Republican split created a Democratic sweep. By selecting Major for governor, voters for the third time gave that office to a popular prosecutor.

The triumphant Democrats briefly tried to keep trust-busting alive when they regained full control of state government in 1913. The first battleground on which Governor Major sought to defend the Missouri Idea and redeem the Democrats' 1912 trust-busting pledge was the familiar one of Standard Oil and its Sugar Creek refinery. Once again the courts forced the issue. In 1912 the United States Supreme Court upheld the Missouri court's conviction of the Standard subsidiaries for violating the antitrust law. By threatening to dismantle the refinery and rebuild it across the border in Kansas, Standard mobilized the powerful developers in the Kansas City Commercial Club to try to persuade the 1913 legislature to exempt the oil subsidiaries from the antitrust law. Outgoing Governor Hadley supported the exemption bill, arguing that the court had wrongly conferred an oil monopoly on Waters-

Pierce by allowing it to remain while ousting Standard. He reiterated his belief that regulation would permit both growth and public control. The legislature passed the exemption law.[67]

At this point Major and the original supporters of the Missouri Idea tried to defend, however timidly, the state's capacity for trust-busting against the campaign by businessmen, Hadley, and the legislature to exempt Standard Oil. Standard's protectors intended to rewrite criminal law to declare that "we won't punish you or drive you out because we can't get along without you," warned Democratic Representative Charles M. Hay from rural central Missouri. Speaking for urban consumers, the *St. Louis Post-Dispatch* proclaimed that Standard had intimidated political leaders into supporting the legalization of monopoly. And Governor Major seemed to agree. He vetoed the exemption bill, charging that it would "strike down our efficent anti-trust statutes." By this law "the State would be going through the useless performance of thrusting the offending corporation through the window and inviting it to return to the best room in the house through the front door." But Major's vision was shaky. He objected more to the form than the substance of the Standard exemption. Charging that the bill was "a legislative recall of a judicial decision" and thus a Republican Progressive doctrine, Democrat Major wrote in six different places in his veto message that the state supreme court already had the power to grant the exemption that Standard wanted.[68]

Standard's attorneys hoped that the court would sense how tentative Major's defense of the Missouri Idea was. Frank Hagerman threatened "a disastrous blow to this community" of Sugar Creek if the court forced the company to move its refinery to Kansas. A month later the supreme court joined the consensus. By permitting Indiana Standard to resume business in Missouri by operating independently and submitting to judicial regulation, the judges declared that regulation was preferable to trust-busting.[69]

Major and the Democrats chose a second arena in 1913 in which to try to preserve trust-busting against corporate pressures toward regulation. Their 1913 effort to compel large fire insurance companies to submit to Missouri's antitrust laws paralleled the attempt to discipline Standard Oil. The fight began in 1911 when the legislature enacted a regulatory law that permitted the companies to cooperate in setting rates. To the disgust of insurance commissioner Frank Blake and the anger of policyholders, the companies used this law as the excuse to raise their rates over the next two years by 50 to 200 percent. Consumers, led by the *St. Louis Post-Dispatch*, retaliated by dealing the companies a "stinging defeat" in 1913. That year the legislature repealed the 1911 law and enacted a law that made any cooperative rate agreement an automatic antitrust violation. In April 1913 over a hundred companies, copying Standard Oil's example of mobilizing commercial pressure, refused to insure the state's businesses against fire until they were allowed to cooperate in setting rates. On April 30 they stopped writing insurance in Missouri and waited for business to pressure state officials not to enforce the new law.[70]

Major and Attorney General John T. Barker began by trying to resist the insurance companies' blackmail. Major won loud cheers in June from the St. Louis Central Trades and Labor Council and Reedy's *Mirror* when he proposed that the state government fill the void left by the companies by entering the insurance business itself. For three months Major and Barker held out. Finally, as pressures mounted from fire-struck cities—such as Springfield, where investors refused to rebuild burned buildings until they could be insured—the Democratic officials agreed in August to a compromise. The companies agreed to return to Missouri, and Barker promised not to prosecute them under the 1913 law. "The resumption of underwriting by the exiled insurance companies assures the continuation of prosperous industrial and commercial activities," concluded the relieved *Post-Dispatch*, which only a few months earlier had championed trust-busting. Outraged by this "groveling" compromise, Reedy charged that it only proved that "the insurance companies have Missouri by the throat." Governor Major appointed a commission to propose a long-term solution. Seeking a middle ground between policyholders and companies that would protect growth by insuring adequate protection against fire losses, the commission recommended that the 1915 legislature replace trust-busting with regulation and concentrate on reducing fire hazards whose costs hurt both consumers and companies. Converted, Major told legislators that "at the bottom of the whole insurance question lies the reduction of fire waste," an issue on which "the interest of the companies and of the public is one and the same." Legislators enacted regulation into law in 1915. The *Post-Dispatch* summarized the new consensus: "The State and the insurance companies must co-operate under regulations which will enable the companies to do a profitable business and will protect the public from oppression."[71]

The resolutions of the insurance and oil battles highlighted the common ground that Democrats and large corporations had created for the debate over public control of business. It was, after all, the same ground that Hadley had discovered in the aftermath of the Panic of 1907. Economic growth was the basic point of agreement. From the start Major had devoted his greatest energy and imagination to the promotion of state highways. "Good roads are the great Appian way over which true progress must march," he announced. Enlisting in the crusade started by such groups as car dealers' associations and the Kansas City Commerical Club, Major attracted national attention by calling on all Missourians to donate their labor on August 20 and 21, 1913, to improve roads in their communities. "Pull Missouri Out of the Mud," Major implored. Over a quarter of a million Missourians responded, participating on those two days in what the *Kansas City Times* hailed as "the biggest fight ever made for Missouri." Seeing the army of volunteer road builders, the former consumer crusaders on the *St. Louis Post-Dispatch* proclaimed that road repairs, not trust-busting, were the ways to "vitalize the civic spirit."[72] "Civic pride" had come by 1913 to mean economic development.

Economic growth and regulation became for Major and the Democrats intertwined parts of a unified approach to the issue of popular control over the emerging large-scale corporate world. Before they could fully join Hadley and the courts in eroding the Missouri Idea, the Democrats had to abandon the party's 1912 promises and Major his jabs at large corporations early in 1913. Lacking the evangelical passion that had kept Folk deaf to the appeals of the developers, the Democrats who dominated state government after 1913 concluded that growth and regulation were needed to overcome the commercial, judicial, and political uncertainties that the Missouri Idea had unleashed. In his inaugural Major urged fellow Democrats in the legislature to shun policies that might intensify economic insecurities or retard growth:

> You cannot serve the people faithfully and efficiently if you distress the legitimate business interests of the state. Be not radical nor extreme, but rather place your feet upon the middle path, for after all that is the path of safety and will ultimately lead us to the door of success and commercial and civic glory.[73]

These fears left him unwilling to turn his jabs at Standard Oil and the insurance companies into a full-scale campaign to redeem his party's 1912 antitrust promises. Major mobilized traditional Democratic partisanship behind the creation of formal institutions for state regulation. Believing in 1913 that "the people and the public service corporations should be brought closer together," he persuaded Democratic legislators to enact Hadley's old proposal for a public service commission to regulate railroads and utilities. "The creation of such a commission is a progressive step," he explained, because it would bring "a speedy and inexpensive adjustment" to disputes that, with the threat of criminal prosecutions, retarded growth by discouraging investors. Democrats soon enacted the rest of Hadley's program for development and regulation, including a state highway department and authorization for cities to establish commission governments that would shift local controversies from the arena of popular combat to the more stable one of resolution by regulation.[74] Democratic legislators affirmed the vitality of traditional partisanship by refusing to pass any laws defining the structures of development and regulation until a governor of their party was in office to take credit for enacting the legislation.

Over time consumers discovered many subtle ways that the new regulatory bodies eroded their capacity for democratic mobilization and popular control. Regulation in practice did not fulfill its promise of providing speedier and more certain popular control.

After fighting to restore the tradition by which elected legislators heeded popular majorities rather than corporate bribes, consumers believed that legislatures were one place where they could finally control large corporations. After all, the legislature had lowered railroad freight rates in 1905 and passenger rates in 1907. The menace regulation posed to legislation began to appear in 1913, when the United States Supreme Court upheld the 1907 two-cent fare law and the new rates took effect. The railroads protested to the new Public Service Commission that the two-cent fare deprived investors of an adequate return. The commission agreed, and permitted the roads to raise their rates. Supporters of lower rates, including Governor Major, were out-raged. Not only had the new commission betrayed consumers' expectations that regulation would benefit them, but now the power to set rates had been taken from the popularly elected legislature and given to remote experts over whom voters had no influence. Defenders of the legislature's power to set rates sped to the courts to challenge the commission's right to overturn a specific fare enacted by the legislature, but the state supreme court upheld the commission in 1917.[75] Regulation had eroded legislative capacity to discipline corporate power.

The creation of the Public Service Commission undermined a second method of democratic mobilization by which Missourians had traditionally sought to restrain corporate power. In their turn-of-the-century revolts water drinkers, streetcar riders, and users of electricity had mobilized around their local communities to battle for strict controls over or abolition of private utility monoplies. Consumers in the largest cities had won the power from the 1907 legislature to discipline their local utilities in their own communities. Over the years since 1907 local regulatory bodies, particularly in St. Louis, had forced utilities for the first time to provide services demanded by local consumers. Angered that public ownership movements and local regulators had allowed local consumers to turn the tradition of community control into an unprecedented capacity for local majorities to enforce radical remedies, the utilities began a crusade to take regulatory power away from local communities and establish it at the more remote state level, where consumers of particular services in particular communities would have less influence over policy. The establishment of a state commission in 1913 was a political victory for the United Railways of St. Louis because it stripped that city's residents of the power to control their own affairs in their own community, protested local consumers. To the infuriated St. Louis Central Trades and Labor Council the commission was "the finest job ever put over on the people of this state in the past 20 years, and demanded by the public utility compa-nies." By weakening public ownership movements among consumers, state regulation created "the Commission to Head Off Socialism," thundered the St. Louis *Labor.* Over its first few years a majority of urban consumers came to view the commission as the protector of utilities.[76]

Even more dramatic than regulation's erosion of community and legisla-ture as traditional focuses for democratic mobilization was its impact on the democratic competence and confidence of individual citizens. Corporations and regulators sought to persuade consumers that control was an individual, not a collective, issue and that consumers were inadequate to the task. In other words, Missourians should abandon the search for popular controls because they were either too hypocritical or too stupid for the job. At the peak of the Missouri Idea in the summer of 1907 the *Joplin News-Herald* agreed with Lieutenant Governor A. P. Riddle of Kansas that "there needs to be reformation from the ground up before this world will be without com-mercial sin—and that time is a long way off. . . . There will never be real reformation of the trusts until the people" could truthfully say, as individuals, that they returned borrowed books, avoided profane language, tied their horses on the streets, and never sped in their cars or shot game out of season. Fear that they lacked the moral authority to fight corporations sapped the people's democratic confidence. Thus the Kansas City Health Department encouraged consumers to feel inadequate to challenge food processors when it announced, "Don't blame the health department if you or your children become ill," since consumers were "careless or indifferent" to the department's regulations and advise about food preparation.[77] Fears of individual moral or intellectual failure gnawed at consumers' confidence, eroding their vision of collectively building a democratic future.

14

Epilogue

It would be tragic to end a book about democratic aspirations on a note of political defeat. It has become easy, fashionable, to abandon democratic theory and democratic practice because we have no languages other than that of victory and defeat by which to understand them. But the experiences of long-dead Missourians can provide at least a metaphor from which we might build an alternative understanding of democracy.

The central problem of modern democracy is distance. The new order introduced one form of distance when it ripped economic activities from the social and moral fabric into which they had been interwoven in the old order. This separation created the popular sense of injury and outrage that has inspired resisters to fight to draw economic life back toward social and cultural traditions.

The distance between people's economic activities and their social lives and popular traditions has only widened since the days of the Missouri Idea. Driven by the value of growth, the new order has increasingly separated production from consumption and thereby distanced the specialized, secular, economic world of large-scale institutions and bureaucracies ever further from popular traditions and popular control. The managers of giant units of production and power have sought to insulate their institutions from popular pressures in the conviction that distance is the best protection against popular suspicions of and challenges to their very legitimacy. In the years since Standard Oil hired a publicity expert in 1906 to try to deflect Herbert Hadley's prosecution and other popular attempts to control its corporate structure, managers have turned public relations into a dense, almost impenetrable forest protecting their institutions from popular control. The challenge of developing popular controls to restrain the tendency of production and growth to propel large institutions into increasingly remote orbits has come

266

over time to haunt people in all productive systems, socialist as well as capitalist.

When people have fought to reunite their economic activities with their traditions, whether in the Progressive Era or the present, they have come up against obstacles created by a second kind of distance. The democratic challenge of today, as then, is to reach toward a future in which the majority confidently governs itself, from a present whose formal economic, cultural, and political shape has been imposed by others. How can people begin to imagine a democratic future when the circumstances of their present lives are profoundly undemocratic? This distance between a limited present and an unlimited future creates the difficulties of turning the shared commitments and activities of the moment into ultimate power, of reconciling means and ends. The very length and difficulty of this journey led even the passionate democrat Walt Whitman to conclude that democracy was "a great word, whose history, I suppose, remains unwritten, because that history has yet to be enacted." The failure so far to establish a truly democratic society reflects not our inability to act in democratic ways or to dream democratic dreams, but our inability to shorten the distance from present to future.

Democratic movements, now as then, have not reached an unlimited future because they have not overcome huge political and constitutional barriers along the way of their journey. Politics has pivoted on office seeking, not policy. Political parties have been the major mobilizing vehicles, and they have separated voters along ethnic, religious, and sectional lines. Constitutional checks and balances and overlapping jurisdictions limit the extent to which any program can be enacted. Each barrier has diverted resisters from reaching their destination.

The most persistent way that these barriers have transformed and weakened popular movements has been by appealing to resisters' votes while delivering laws that reflect less the original democratic movement than the intervening campaign contributors, major party leaders, and legislative rhythms and traditions. Thousands of Missouri Populists, for example, watched with growing horror during the 1890s as obsession with office seeking led their leaders to divert the movement's original thrust away from programs which promised them a future free from the private credit system and toward the Democratic party's lures of offices and minor reforms. The distance between immediate concerns and ultimate policy has grown steadily wider over the twentieth century. The greatest office-getter of all, Franklin Roosevelt, convinced voters that he favored their hopes for restructuring society, but he diverted their landslide endorsement of 1936 into an unexpected and unpopular war on the Supreme Court. So great had the distance between issues and policy become by 1984 than an unprecedented number of voters cast their ballots for a presidential candidate who disagreed with their views on the major foreign and domestic issues.

From their first encounters with the new order, traditional Missourians concluded that the way to assert popular control was to shorten the distance between the cause of popular anger and its resolution. They first resisted the new railroads and banks by robbing them. Workers first resisted the new machines that threatened their crafts and livelihoods by smashing them. In a single act they bound the resolution to the source.

While the Missourians in this book failed in their political struggles to reintegrate their economic activities with their social traditions and failed to reach a democratic future, they can point us toward two major ways of cutting distance. Their experience is particularly relevant to democracy in our time because both kinds of distance have lengthened in the intervening years. Since the new order's terrifying forms of competition and authority were new to these Missourians, they confronted the new kinds of distance with a freshness and clarity that has escaped our generation. The creativity and resilience of their democratic alternatives underscore for us the crucial importance of shortening distance for democratic movements.

1. The Problem of Cutting Distance: Structure

The problem of structure is the problem of the distance between the present grievances of voters and the policy resolution of those grievances in the future. The democratic test for political and constitutional structures is the ease with which voters can use them to mobilize their concerns into policy.

Missouri's progressives concluded that they required structural changes to shorten the distance between voter and policy in order to mobilize their power as a loosely organized majority of consumers to dislodge corporate political power. Through initiative and referendum elections, they hoped to seize from politicians the capacity to define the political agenda and make policy. As they solicited the signatures and votes of fellow citizens along their way toward making policy directly at the ballot box, progressives shortened the distance to a democratic future by using the new structure to take possession of government. They acquired the confidence that a loosely organized majority could indeed prevail over the producers and politicians who had for so long dominated politics. The great popularity of initiative and referendum pointed toward direct, participatory democracy as the fastest way to shorten the distance between a limited present and an unlimited future.

In the three-quarters of a century since Missouri adopted initiative and referendum in 1908, we have failed to build on the progressives' underlying conclusion that the entire system created by the Constitution was intended precisely to create a very long distance between people and policy. The Founding Fathers, argued progressive historians like J. Allen Smith and Charles Beard, wanted a governmental structure that would make it harder for people to seize power directly as they themselves had during the American Revolution. We have even failed to debate seriously the adoption of initiative and referendum in the federal Constitution, even though a popular majority has favored this change in every recent poll by margins of at least two to one. If voters had possessed the power to declare war, for example, the United States would almost certainly not have entered World War I or sent ground or naval forces to defend its far-flung empire in recent decades. If voters had set federal spending priorities they would have spent their taxes, according to polls, on health and education, not defense and space.

Progressives bequeathed to us the challenge of daring to imagine how we might change our structures of government in order to narrow the political and constitutional distance between grievance and resolution, between voter and policy. The reason that intervening reformers have failed to enact structural changes to narrow this distance is not the failure of the progressives' solutions but a decline in trust in direct majority rule. That failure reflects back to us not an absence of serious alternatives but our own lack of faith in democracy.

Future democratic movements will encounter many of the same problems as did those in the past unless they consider structural changes to shorten distance. The most frequent alternative structure in countries which value popular legitimacy is, of course, the parliamentary system. By this method voters choose among parties that offer dramatic policy alternatives. With tight party discipline directed toward enactment of policies rather than holding of office, parliamentary systems shorten distance by mobilizing voters directly toward policies. We must not let discussion of the democratic possibilities of a parliamentary form be shaped by the vaguely academic and elitist tone of earlier debates on the topic.

While some of the distance that has confronted democratic movements was deliberately placed there by the Constitution's eighteenth-century authors, other structural problems of distance have developed with the new order. The Constitution's geographic basis for representation permitted voters in the localistic old order to be represented in the all-important struggles between Tidewater and Piedmont, North and South, East and West. But the emergence of national markets, corporations, and producer groups has mocked geographic representation, because politicians have frequently paid more attention to these groups' campaign contributions than to their constituents. The distance between the locus of local democratic power, the community, and the locus of national policymaking has usually been too long for voters to span. This distance has continued to pose a central challenge to democratic movements because, as earlier Missourians demonstrated, local communities have retained the participatory vitality to reassert popular restraints long after production came to be shaped by far-flung markets. This country's most widespread experiment with socialism, for example, resulted from campaigns by local consumers and progressives to use their communities for public ownership of local corporations.

There are many structural ways to shorten this distance. One approach to activating the neighborhood traditions and face-to-face exchanges that have strengthened the democratic possibilities in community control is simply to decentralize policymaking and give more power to communities. Another way to bring voters closer to policy is to elect national representatives on the basis of commitments they share with people as feminists, consumers, workers, doves, hawks, or whatever interest or ideology best reflects voters' political consciousness, rather than on the basis of geography. Since representatives would view themselves primarily as spokespersons for particular ideologies or interests, they would be much more under the direct control of those who elected them. For purposes of political representation "community" might be redefined to include people who share commitments rather than residences. The possibilities are limited only by our imaginations, but to fail to explore them is to doom future democratic movements to retrace the same diversions, discouragements, and defeats that their predecessors experienced.

2. The Problem of Cutting Distance: Participation

Collective participation, almost by definition, is the only way to get from a limited present to an unlimited future. It is also, as Missourians discovered in their struggles to free themselves from competition and alien authority, the central means by which people have reunited popular traditions with their daily lives, and turned private losses and injuries into public battlegrounds and then into democratic movements.

Traditional Missourians expected to build their communities of resistance, whether of confrontation or escape, from the richly layered associations of their daily lives. Through lines of allegiance and communication among kinship, friendship, and craft groups they built deep and warm participatory worlds of support around their churches, fraternal lodges, saloons, workplaces, and political parties. Shared traditions predisposed them to analyze changes in similar ways and to participate with others in actions to defend or recover those traditions. Their communities turned questions of power into the basic issue of whom to trust and whom not to trust, and they expected political relief to take the immediate shape of support from and action by family and friends, rather than the more distant form of pressure groups or governmental programs. Loyalty to a threatened tradition inspired more enthusiastic participation than have more recent forms of loyalty—loyalty, say, to an organization which encourages people to think that they need not act themselves because someone else will do the work of protecting the organization.

Remembering how these networks had supported their traditions in their initial encounters with the new order, Missourians recreated that support in their democratic movements in the form of collective participation. Participation, in turn, encouraged them to extend a cherished but threatened tradition into action to recover or gain territory.

From their day to ours, collective participation has been the fuel that has propelled democratic movements across the distance between private injury and public combat and resolution. It has shortened distance by mobilizing supporters into direct assaults on the sources of their injuries. These direct confrontations have generally deprived politicians and others in power of their customary maneuvering room and prevented them from diverting or transforming reformers' demands or escaping the democratic force of their movements.

Participation turned struggles into movements. In the mid-1950s the meetings in traditional religious sanctuaries, the rallies, the songs, the group discipline in the face of hostility all combined to create the sense of participatory community that became the core of the civil rights and antiwar movements. Their intensely participatory experience as parishioners and clergymen in black southern churches provided the encouragement for members to become "activists" in trying to force their white neighbors to practice what their common religious inheritance preached. The most recent feminist movement began with commitments and experiences of women in the deeply participatory New Left student organizations that made them unwilling to accept unequal treatment from male colleagues. In the 1970s the women's movement creatively applied traditional participation to modern resistance by building deep layers of personal networks and sisterhood underneath the dominant male culture. These networks turned personal issues into community ones, private into public, without need for intervening government.

The experience of mutual participation shortened distance in several ways. By cooperating on an equal basis in acts that defied the new leaders, resisters freed their own lives from the new order's pressures for competition, hierarchy, deference, and resignation. The democratic present of their participatory movements gave them the experience, confidence, and vision to reach toward an unlimited democratic future in which they would shape values and institutions. Participants in democratic movements, past and present, have echoed the St. Louis cooper who credited his increasing enthusiasm for more radical and militant action on his "getting well surrounded and fortified" by cheering supporters during the 1877 strike. By the ways they lived and acted, resisters showed that they could govern a world by participatory values inspired by folk memories of moral, family, craft, and community traditions that the new leaders had claimed to have obliterated. By turning private loss into public action, they freed themselves from the republican attitude toward self-government, which encouraged citizens to blame themselves, not their rulers, for their losses. By prefiguring the future in present practice, they brought it much closer than could any program or theory. By using participatory actions, not the quest for office, to set the terms of political struggle, they recruited others who dared hope that the new movement had the potential to avoid the diversions that had slowed earlier democratic movements.

Participatory acts further shortened distance by frightening economic leaders with the specter of defeat in the all-important cultural war for hearts and minds. The new leaders suddenly learned from a sit-down or a sit-in that they had mistaken popular silence for enthusiasm or at least acquiescence. Participatory acts shattered the security and legitimacy of institutions that they thought they fully controlled. The direct action of the civil rights movement, for example, rekindled the same fear that events such as the 1877 strike had kindled—that resisters, not official authorities, had the real power to determine which laws would be obeyed. The new participatory movements forced leaders to surrender strongholds of racial segregation and workplace control to civil rights and labor movements, for example, in ways that the railroads, however much they may have been humiliated by him, never surrendered to Jesse James.

Participatory acts even encouraged resisters to hope for future forms of community discipline based on popular sovereignty to replace the existing imperative of growth. The Missouri Idea turned traditional moral, family, religious, and community values into yardsticks with which to interpret and judge new commercial activities. To redefine new activities as the traditional crimes of murder, treason, robbery, rape, and poisoning was at a stroke to remove most of the distance the new order had created between those activities and traditional values. Consumer movements from the emergence of Missouri Idea to the present have cut distance by creating a modern kind of accountability between buyers and sellers to replace the new oder's focus on cost and growth.

Democratic movements can learn from problems that have vexed collective participation in the past. The very ease with which participatory movements cut distance creates special problems for reformers. In their eagerness for direct action, they sometimes focused on the most accessible target for their anger rather than the institution or the social values that lay behind it, at a train rather than the railroad owners, at an army recruiter rather than the draft or the military, at a segregationist restaurant owner rather than racism. The heady feeling that an unlimited future was near at hand sometimes encouraged an impatient eagerness to speed up the journey. This impatience tempted many resisters to weaken their democratic force by placing their faith in leaders to conclude the journey for them. The new order's hierarchical nature and the traditional focus of politics on officeholding tempted all but the most deeply participatory movements to look for salvation in heroes. Progressives, particularly, came to depend on leaders like Theodore Roosevelt, Joseph Folk, and Herbert Hadley to define the shape of the future and how to reach it. In the years since Folk and Hadley, participatory movements have become entangled in new problems. Television, for example, has created the danger that natural leadership can be trivialized into a kind of stardom and participants reduced to fans in ways that can erode democratic confidence. Television can turn participants into spectators.

Each of these problems, however, only emphasizes anew the central significance of collective participation. From Hadley's day to ours, people have called their crusades "movements" because only through movement can they travel from a limited present to an unlimited future.

3. Winning, Losing, and Democracy

A preoccupation with winning and losing has limited both the practice and the theory of democratic movements. The explicit or implicit criterion for victory is usually a restructuring of institutional relationships in which new groups acquire ownership of farm, factory, guns, or state. This concern with winning and losing assumes a particularly fatalistic flavor at times such as the present, when the objective chances for radical restructuring of power appear slight. The current concern with "hegemony," for example, may deepen our understanding of the dominant culture's power, but it also may encourage resignation, which is a powerful weapon against democratic movements. So long as people conclude that the dominant culture always wins, they will lack the confidence that nourishes resistance.

We need a more democratic standard for evaluating the significance of democratic movements, whether those of the present or of turn-of-the-century Missourians. Missouri's resisters were trying to do something far more serious than win and far broader than rearrange institutional relationships. They were trying to live their lives in ways that allowed them to preserve their own ways of relating to people and nature. With old bonds of mutual obligation shattered by the everyday realities of isolating competition, with society divided into those who gave orders and those who took them, with work separated from life, Missourians sought first and most basically to construct the substance of collective participation for mutual assistance. Active participation by equals challenged the competitive and hierarchical society that the new economic rulers were trying to establish. The employers, teachers, and editors of the new order could fuel the great engine of resignation to deflect democratic movements only if they could succeed in instilling individual feelings of fear, guilt, survival, or greed. By simply participating with others, Missourians learned that only through collective, not individual, action could they control their lives. Their participatory acts, although sometimes neither wise nor just, always nurtured the capacity for democratic resistance.

Collective participation acquired as much political significance in the new order as did institutional arrangements, because nearly all relationships became political in a market economy in which people worked for wages paid by others and in which traditional authorities were replaced by leaders whose claims to legitimacy came from their economic power. Relations between teacher and student, editor and reader, preacher and parishioner, representative and constituent, worker and employer became less bonds of obligation or mutual support and more simple tests of power. Participation turned powerlessness into mutual competence and confidence. In participatory acts people shed feelings of ambivalence and broke through the cultural pressures to blame themselves. Activities that turned the private and individual into the public and collective were political. By turning folk memories into bases for struggle people hoped to fulfill their traditional responsibilities, to restore success and failure as small matters of everyday significance instead of issues on which survival itself might depend, to make trust and fear and judgment and authority once again into relationships among particular people instead of power relationships controlled by ownership and hierarchy.

To measure the vision or practice of democratic movements by a yardstick of success or failure seems particularly inappropriate. For one thing, what does victory look like? Freedom and democracy exist not as theoretical or institutional formulations, but in the cooperative struggle to attain them. Free people are those who are in motion to claim more freedom. People who protest their lack of freedom are likely to be far freer from their would-be rulers, in fact, than people who claim that they are free. For another thing, it is simply not clear that any particular agent—for example, workers—or any particular vehicle—for example, a political party—is the best way to create a democratic society. Why focus on ownership of the means of production, for example, when we have plenty of contemporary examples of undemocratic societies in which the means of production are owned collectively? The Missourians in this book raised a more penetrating issue of power when they used approaches as different as social outlawry and the Missouri Idea to insist that community discipline was the central issue. By encouraging in their practice cooperation over competition, democracy over hierarchy, moral over economic, and, above all, participation over deference or escape, Missourians pointed clearly toward the shape of the future society they wanted to create.

If victory and defeat must remain criteria for studying the hopes and tragedies of participants within social systems, Missouri's resisters won by the values that mattered to them. The new order was strikingly vulnerable because it sought to control hearts and minds as well as behavior. Each time schoolchildren gazed out the window instead of absorbing a teacher's lesson, each time a worker dreamed of escape that came with the quitting bell, each time groups of patrons sang loudly in bars, the new order failed to control hearts and minds. The new leaders urged Missourians to abandon their concerns about family, work, neighbors, community, and the environment. So long as Missourians collectively expressed those concerns, however, they proved that the new order lacked legitimacy. They created their own worlds. So can we.

A Note on Sources

This book is grounded in many kinds of primary sources. The annual reports of state agencies were consistently the most valuable for long-term trends. The reports of the State Board of Agriculture reflected the agricultural developers' fifty-year struggle to persuade and compel the state's farmers to accept the new order. The same campaign is reflected in reports of the State Horticultural Society in the 1860s and 1870s and in particular bulletins of the Agricultural Extension Service of the University of Missouri's College of Agriculture in the twentieth century. The annual reports of the Bureau of Labor Statistics after 1879 not only reported on organized labor's organizing and political activities but also included special reports by commissioners on changes in work. Although they become somewhat less revealing after 1900 as they become more devoted to promoting economic opportunities in Missouri, they still were invaluable. Periodic reports by the State Mine Inspector (particularly in the 1880s and 1890s) and by the State Board of Mediation and Arbitration (particularly for strikes in the twentieth century) were essential. The Superintendent of Insurance, Food and Drug Commissioner, and State Board of Health also wrote helpful and sometimes very revealing reports. But perhaps the most revealing of all state agencies to prepare annual reports was the State Superintendent of Public Schools. The state schoolmen's sense that they were the spearheads of a cultural revolution was echoed in the reports by local school boards and superintendents that are cited in Chapter 6. The *Journals* of the House of Representatives and Senate included popular petitions and governors' messages. The biennial *Official Manuals* reported election results. Federal census reports for population, agriculture, manufacturing, public debt, and religion were crucial to show change over time.

The second major category of sources was newspapers. Some seventy-five different newspapers were consulted for one purpose or another, and the notes indicate which ones were used for what purposes. The *St. Louis Post-Dispatch* was consistently the most helpful for its broad coverage and its interest in democratic movements. The *Kansas City Star* led the state's progressive Republican newspapers. For farm protest movements the Macon *Missouri Granger* was essential for the 1870s, while California's *The Newspaper* and the Memphis *Farmers' Union* were the best Farmers' Alliance and Populist papers. The leading Socialist newspapers were the St. Louis *Labor* for the period after 1900, and the shorter-lived Kennett *Justice* in the 1910s and the Benton *Scott County Kicker* in the 1900s. The Jefferson City *Tribune* gave the best news from the capitol. In a class by itself was William Marion Reedy's St. Louis journal, *The Mirror*, which commented on all social and political matters. The religious press, usually composed of weeklies, provided an important window for many traditional Missourians and was sampled through the Sedalia *Harmony Baptist*, the Methodists' St. Louis *Central Christian Advocate*, the Disciples of Christ's *Western Christian Union* from Boonville and *The Christian* from Sedalia, and the semi-official St. Louis Catholic periodical, *The Review*. These newspapers are located in the Newspaper or Reference rooms of the State Historical Society in Columbia.

Some manuscript collections were essential. Easily the most valuable was the large Herbert Hadley collection, which revealed the gradual evolution of this Republican attorney general (1905-9) and governor (1909-13) from trust-busting to regulation. The political associations of a conservative Democratic loyalist can be followed through the very good papers of Lon Stephens, who served as governor from 1897 to 1901. The papers of Joseph Folk, governor from 1905 to 1909, and of William J. Stone, governor from 1893 to 1897 and senator from 1897 to 1917, are much thinner and less revealing. Two outstanding manuscript collections that trace the daily debates and struggles of craft unions over several decades are the minute books of the St. Louis District Council of the United Brotherhood of Carpenters and Joiners and the St. Louis Typographical Union. The N. D. Houghton Papers, though small, contained valuable reminiscences about the adoption of initiative and referendum in Missouri. All of the above collections are housed at the Joint Manuscript Collections of the University of Missouri and the State Historical Society in Columbia except for the Stephens papers, which are at the State Archives in Jefferson City.

Many of the published proceedings of voluntary associations were essential for Chapter 10, including those of the Missouri Bar Association, the State Medical Association, and the Missouri Press Association. More revealing, however, were the proceedings of the Women's Christian Temperance Union, which sought to balance feminist and pro-labor sympathies with its members' shifting vision of the role of evangelical religion in the new order. The annual proceedings of the Grand Lodge of the Knights of Pythias were crucial for the processes of fraternal discipline because they included, among other things, results of fraternal trials. The most important sources for the values, disciplines, and sometimes membership of labor unions and fraternal lodges were the constitutions, by-laws, and membership directories cited in Chapters 8 and 9. The state proceedings of the Knights and Daughters of Tabor and of the Ancient Free and Accepted Masons were vital for black fraternal orders.

Two trials that played significant parts in struggles over whether law would support growth or community discipline were the cases of the Christian County Bald Knobbers of the 1880s and of the businessmen and city officials Circuit Attorney Joseph Folk prosecuted in St. Louis between 1902 and 1904. The transcripts of the four Bald Knobber cases are in boxes 1143 and 1144 of the Missouri Supreme Court Files, State Archives, Jefferson City. Folk's trials were reprinted in volume 9 of John D. Lawson, ed., *American State Trials* (St. Louis: F. H. Thomas Law Book Co., 1918).

Crucial sources for groups of Missourians who did not otherwise leave records are the pioneering sociological accounts based on surveys and interviews in the early twentieth century. Among the most helpful, if sometimes appalling in their racism, were William Wilson Elwang, *The Negroes of Columbia Missouri* (Columbia: University of Missouri Sociology Department, 1904); William August Crossland, *Industrial Conditions Among Negroes in St. Louis* (St. Louis: Washington University Studies in Social Economics, 1914); Asa E. Martin, *Our Negro Population: A Sociological Study of the Negroes of Kansas City, Missouri* (1913); Stephen Cornish, "Survey of a Rural Negro Community in Pike County Missouri" (M.A. thesis, University of Missouri, 1922); Ruth Crawford, *The Immigrant in St. Louis* (St. Louis: Washington University School of Social Economics, 1914); and W. L. Nelson, "A Rural Survey of Morgan County, Missouri," *Monthly Bulletin of the State Board of Agriculture*, 14 (February 1916).

A few other collections deserve special mention. The State Historical Society's Reference Room has an excellent collection of county histories as well as broadsides from such campaigns as the early twentieth-century struggle for public ownership of utilities in Columbia. It also has a remarkable collection of popular novels and "histories" about the James Gang.

Although the notes indicate the secondary sources that were most helpful for particular topics, there are some general guides to research on Missouri history. For the past several decades monographic research on Missouri history has centered around five major sources: graduate theses and dissertations from St. Louis University, Washington University, and the University of Missouri-Columbia, and articles in the *Missouri Historical Review* (published by the State Historical Society of Missouri, Columbia) and *The Bulletin* and its successor, *Gateway Heritage* (published by the Missouri Historical Society, St. Louis). The most valuable recent bibliographical annotations are in Walter A. Schroeder, *Bibliography of Missouri Geography: A Guide to Written Material on Places and Regions of Missouri* (Columbia: University of Missouri-Columbia Extension Division, 1977); Neal Primm, *Lion of the Valley: St. Louis, Missouri* (Boulder, Colo.: Pruett Pub. Co., 1981); A. Theodore Brown and Lyle W. Dorsett, *K.C.: A History of Kansas*

City, Missouri (Boulder, Colo.: Pruett Pub. Co., 1978); and volumes 1 through 3 of the official *History of Missouri* series edited by William Parrish and published by the University of Missouri Press. There are valuable lists of sources in Selwyn K. Troen, *A Guide to Resources on the History of St. Louis* (St. Louis: Washington University Institute for Urban and Regional Studies, 1971), and Milton D. Rafferty, *The Ozarks: Land and Life* (Norman: University of Oklahoma Press, 1980).

Part I. The Integration of Life in the Old Order

Chapter 1. Traditional Values and the Old Order

1. William Howard Morman, "History of Greer Mill," *Missouri Historical Review* [hereafter cited as *MHR*], 66 (July 1972), 610–21; Priscilla Ann Evans, "Merchant Gristmills and Communities: An Economic Relationship," *MHR*, 68 (April 1974), 321.

2. Philip V. Scarpino, "Development of the Osage River, with Primary Emphasis on the Period 1840 to 1931" (Seminar paper, History 455, University of Missouri-Columbia, 1975), appendix 1.

3. J. A. Dacus and James W. Buel, *A Tour of St. Louis; or, The Inside of a Great City* (St. Louis: Western Publishing Co., 1878), 29. For the persistence of that "local conservatism," see H. B. Wandell, *Wandell's Annual: Louisiana Purchase Exposition in a Nutshell* (St. Louis: Wandell, 1903), 26.

4. *Mining Industries*, 1880 Census, vol. 15, 658–61.

5. *Herald*, July 14, 1870, quoted in Curtis H. Synhorst, *Historical Resources: Chronology of Osage River History*, vol. 1 of *Cultural Resources Survey: Harry S. Truman Dam and Reservoir Project* (Columbia: American Archaeology Division, University of Missouri-Columbia, 1983), 193.

6. *Report of the Manufactures of the United States*, 1880 Census, vol. 2, 143–45.

7. *Statistics of Wealth and Industry*, 1870 Census, vol. 3, 188, 192. Quotation from Leon Parker Ogilvie, "The Development of the Southeast Missouri Lowlands" (Ph.D. diss., University of Missouri, 1967), 139–40.

8. Charles Callison, *Man and Wildlife in Missouri: The History of One State's Treatment of Its Natural Resources* (Harrisburg, Pa.: Stackpole, Co., 1953), 1–7; see "Special Issue: Missouri's Wildlife Trail," *Missouri Conservationist*, 37 (July 1976), 1–17, for nineteenth-century highlights.

9. Quoted in George Denver Jones, "A Study of the Outbreaks of Grasshoppers in Missouri" (M.A. thesis, University of Missouri, 1939), 19.

10. Missouri Bureau of Labor Statistics, *1st Annual Report* (1880), 57–62.

11. The horse-powered hoist is pictured in Arrell M. Gibson, "Lead Mining in Southwest Missouri after 1865," *MHR*, 53 (July 1959), 321.

12. Clarence N. Roberts, "History of the Structural Brick Industry in Missouri," *MHR*, 47 (July 1953), 322–23; Lela Cole, "The Early Tie Industry along the Niangua River," *MHR*, 48 (April 1954), 266–67; Missouri Bureau of Labor Statistics and Inspection, *16th Annual Report* (1894), 34; *Report of the Production of Agriculture*, 1880 Census, vol. 3, 123–25; *Statistics of Wealth and Industry*, 1870 Census, vol. 3, 414, 416, 422–23, 426, 457.

13. James D. Norris, "The Meramec Iron Works, 1826–1876: The History of a Pioneer Iron Works in Missouri" (Ph.D. diss., University of Missouri, 1961), 257. *Mining Industries*, 1880 Census, vol. 15, 896–99.

14. *Report of the Production of Agriculture*, 1880 Census, vol. 3, 123–25; *Agriculture*, 1920 Census, vol. 6, part 1, 578–88.

15. This account follows George Helmuth Kellner, "The German Element on the Urban Frontier: St. Louis, 1830–1860" (Ph.D. diss., University of Missouri-Columbia, 1973) and

Walter Dean Kamphoefner, "Transplanted Westphalians: Persistence and Transformation of Socioeconomic and Cultural Patterns in the Northwest German Migration to Missouri" (Ph.D. diss., University of Missouri-Columbia, 1978). Duden's report has been translated and reissued as *Report on a Journey to the Western States of North America and a Stay of Several Years along the Missouri (During the Years 1824, '25, '26, and 1827)*, English translation by James W. Goodrich, general editor, et. al. (Columbia: State Historical Society of Missouri and University of Missouri Press, 1980).

16. *Statistics of Population*, 1870 Census, vol. 1, 743.

17. Russell Clemens, unpublished compilation from 1870 manuscript census for Macon County, in author's possession.

18. Quoted in Samuel Bannister Harding, *Life of George R. Smith, Founder of Sedalia, Mo.* (Sedalia: privately published, 1904), 31.

19. Suzanna Maria Grenz, "The Black Community in Boone County, Missouri, 1850–1900" (Ph.D. diss., University of Missouri-Columbia, 1979), 74. For apprenticeship origins, see Fern Boan, *A History of Poor Relief Legislation and Administration in Missouri* (Chicago: University of Chicago Press, 1941), 19–21. Seeing the interaction of formal law and the everyday realities of slavery in Missouri requires the varying perspectives of fugitive slave William Wells Brown, *The Narrative of William W. Brown, a Fugitive Slave* (1848), reprinted in Robin W. Winks, ed., *Four Fugitive Slave Narratives* (Reading, Mass: Addison-Wesley, 1969); Harrison Anthony Trexler's proslavery *Slavery in Missouri, 1804–1865* (Baltimore: Johns Hopkins University Press, 1914); Donnie Duglie Bellamy's exploration of political fears of racial equality in "Slavery, Emancipation, and Racism in Missouri, 1850–1865" (Ph.D. diss., University of Missouri-Columbia, 1971); Robert W. Duffner's detailed account of everyday resistance in "Slavery in Missouri River Counties, 1820–1865" (Ph.D. diss., University of Missouri-Columbia, 1974); and Philip V. Scarpino's focus on the economic setting of "Slavery in Callaway County, Missouri, with Primary Emphasis on the Period 1845–1855" (M.A. thesis, University of Missouri-Columbia, 1975).

20. Grenz, "Boone County Black Community," 44.

21. Linda Morice, "The School as an Agent of Industrial Capitalism: A Case Study of German-Americans in the St. Joseph Public Schools, 1871–1887" (seminar paper, History 467, University of Missouri-Columbia, 1972), 10–11.

22. R. S. Douglass, *History of Missouri Baptists* (Kansas City: Western Baptist Publishing Co., 1934), 451; J. C. Maple, ed., *Missouri Baptist Centennial, 1906* (Columbia: E. W. Stephens Publishing Co., 1907), 157, 172; George L. Peters, *The Disciples of Christ in Missouri: Celebrating One Hundred Years of Co-operative Work* (n.p.: Centennial Commission, 1937), 212–21.

23. Walter John Galus, "The History of the Catholic Italians in Saint Louis" (M.A. thesis, St. Louis University, 1936); Margaret Justine Lo Piccolo Sullivan, "Hyphenism in St. Louis, 1900–1921: The View from the Outside" (Ph.D. diss., St. Louis University, 1968), 216–17; Averam B. Bender, "History of the Beth Hamedrosh Hagodol Congregation of St. Louis, 1879–1960," *Bulletin of the Missouri Historical Society*, [hereafter *BMHS*], 27 (Oct. 1970), 69–70; U. S. Census, *Religious Bodies, 1916*, part 1, 280–83.

24. Susan Curtis Mernitz, "Church, Class, and Community in Lexington, Missouri" (M.A. thesis, University of Missouri-Columbia, 1981), 10; Maple, *Missouri Baptist Centennial*, 9–10; *The Doctrines and Disciplines of the Methodist Episcopal Church* (New York: Hunt and Eaton, 1892 ed.), 81.

25. Maple, *Missouri Baptist Centennial*, 56; Wiley Jones Patrick, *The History of the Salt River [Baptist] Association, Missouri* (Columbia: E. W. Stephens Publishing Co., 1909), 385; Mernitz, "Church and Class in Lexington," 12–13.

26. Sedalia *Harmony Baptist*, March 1899; St. Louis *Central Christian Advocate*, Oct. 20, 1886.

27. *Methodist Episcopal Discipline* (1892 ed.), 30; Sedalia *Harmony Baptist*, June 1907; Boonville *Western Christian Union*, Jan. 1899; Sedalia *The Christian*, Jan. 1, 1896.

28. Ann Croft Harrison, "Edward Butler: The Beginnings of a Boss" (M.A. thesis, Washington University, 1969), for his career to 1877; and Harold Zink, *City Bosses in the United States: A Study of Twenty Municipal Bosses* (Durham: Duke University Press, 1930), 302–16.

29. Quotation from William M. Reddig, *Tom's Town: Kansas City and the Pendergast Legend* (Philadelphia: J. B. Lippincott, 1947), 28. See also Lyle W. Dorsett, *The Pendergast Machine* (New York: Oxford University Press, 1968), chs. 1–3, and idem, "Alderman Jim Pendergast," *BMHS*, 21 (Oct. 1964), 3–16.

30. John Samuel Myers, "The Merit System in St. Louis from 1874 to 1937"(Ph.D. diss., Washington University, 1939), 152–53; Herbert S. Hadley to William Howard Taft, Nov. 27, 1909, letterbook 5, 318–19, Hadley Papers, Joint Manuscript Collections, University of Missouri, Western Historical Manuscript Collection and State Historical Society of Missouri-Columbia, [hereafter cited as Joint Manuscript Collections]; Lon Stephens to W. H. Moore, Dec. 29, 1898, box 1, folder 3, p. 35, Stephens Papers, Missouri State Archives, Jefferson City.

31. Frederick Anthony Hodes, "The Urbanization of St. Louis: A Study in Urban Residential Patterns in the Nineteenth Century" (Ph.D. diss., St. Louis University, 1977), 54–56, 130; Jack Muraskin, "St. Louis Municipal Reform in the 1890s: A Study in Failure," *BMHS*, 25 (Oct. 1968), 48.

32. Homer Clevenger, "Agrarian Politics in Missouri, 1880–1896" (Ph.D. diss., University of Missouri, 1940), 148; Missouri *Official Manual, 1891–92*, 353–82; *St. Louis Post-Dispatch*, July 19, 1904.

33. Hodes, "Urbanization of St. Louis," 96–104, 130; *Report of the Statistics of Agriculture*, 1890 Census, vol. 5, 216–17; Missouri *Official Manual, 1891–92*, 10.

34. *Official Directory of Missouri for 1883*, 83; Missouri *Official Manual, 1889–90*, 153; *1891–92*, 7, 9; *1901–1902*, 6–8, 13, 69–76; *1909–10*, 672–73; *1913–14*, 755–56; *1917–18*, 427.

35. Herbert S. Hadley to Theodore Roosevelt, March 9, 1912, folder 811, Hadley Papers; *Tribune* quoted in Kennett *Clipper*, Sept. 29, 1892; Missouri *Official Manual, 1893–94*, 277–87, 419; Ed Star to Lon Stephens, March 24, 1899, box 32, folder 1, Stephens Papers.

Part II. Creation of the New Order

Chapter 2. The Engine of Growth

1. Charles M. Kurtz, *The Saint Louis World's Fair of 1904* (St. Louis: Gottschalk, 1903), 11–23; *Louisiana Purchase Centennial: Dedication Ceremonies* (n.p., n.d.), 13–18; *Official Guide to the Louisiana Purchase Exposition* (St. Louis: Official Guide Co., 1904), 15, 17.

2. Mark Bennitt, ed., *History of the Louisiana Purchase Exposition* (St. Louis: Universal Exposition Publishing Co., 1905), 673; *The Universal Exposition of 1904* (St. Louis: Exposition Co., 1904), 63; Walker, "The World's Fair," *Cosmopolitan*, Sept. 1904, 493.

3. *Report on Manufacturing Industries*, 1890 Census, vol. 6, part I, 68; *Manufactures*, 1920 Census, vol. 8, 18; *Compendium of the Tenth Census*, 1880 Census, 713; *Agriculture*, 1920 Census, vol. 5, 18; *Population*, 1920 Census, vol. 1, 20.

4. *Official Guide*, 7.

5. Missouri State Board of Agriculture, *19th Annual Report . . . 1886–87*, 6, 8; Agriculture Board, *23rd Annual Report . . . 1890–91*, 724, 726; Agriculture Board, *43rd Annual Report . . . 1910*, 43.

6. Philip V. Scarpino, "Development of the Osage River, with Primary Emphasis on the Period 1840 to 1931" (Seminar paper, History 455, University of Missouri-Columbia, Fall 1975), 3–4, 15–18; Curtis H. Synhorst, *Historical Resources: Chronology of Osage River History*, vol. 1 of *Cultural Resources Survey: Harry S. Truman Dam and Reservoir Project* (Columbia: American Archaeology Division, University of Missouri-Columbia, 1983), 187; William E. Parrish, *A History of Missouri: Volume 3, 1860 to 1875* (Columbia: University of Missouri Press, 1973), 207; Missouri Railroad and Warehouse Commissioners, *17th Annual Report . . . 1891*, 6.

7. Fletcher quoted in H. Craig Miner, *The St. Louis–San Francisco Transcontinental Railroad: The Thirty-fifth Parallel Project, 1853–1890* (Lawrence: University Press of Kansas, 1972), 46; Jefferson City *Daily Tribune*, July 11, Oct. 10, 1879; Springfield *Missouri Weekly*

Patriot, May 3, 1866. Quotation from Edwin L. Lopata, *Local Aid to Railroads in Missouri* (New York: Columbia University, 1937), 67.

8. Lopata, *Local Aid to Railroads*, 62, 63; Charles N. Glaab, *Kansas City and the Railroads: Community Policy in the Growth of a Regional Metropolis* (Madison: State Historical Society of Wisconsin, 1962), ch. 2; Leon Parker Ogilvie, "The Development of the Southeast Missouri Lowlands" (Ph.D. diss., University of Missouri-Columbia, 1967), ch. 2.

9. Missouri Railroad and Warehouse Commissioners, *17th Annual Report . . . 1891*, 6; *34th Annual Report . . . 1909*, 49.

10. Miner, *St. Louis–San Francisco Railroad*, 56, 71–72.

11. *Statistics of the Population of the United States*, 1870 Census, vol. 1, 194; *Statistics of the Population of the United States*, 1880 Census, vol. 1, 241, 245; Synhorst, *Osage River*, 156, 213.

12. *Population of the United States*, 1870 Census, vol. 1, 186–95; *Population*, 1900 Census, vol. 1, bulletin no. 32, 18–19.

13. Lopata, *Local Aid to Railroads*, 65.

14. *Mining Industries*, 1880 Census, vol. 15, 658–61, 896; *Report on Mineral Industries*, 1890 Census, vol. 8, 387–89.

15. Leslie G. Hill, "History of the Missouri Lumber and Mining Company, 1890–1909" (Ph.D. diss., University of Missouri, 1949), 25–27, 30–33, 36, 41, 82, 142–43, 210; John A. Galloway, "John Barber White: Lumberman" (Ph.D. diss., University of Missouri, 1961), 22–23, 163.

16. St. Louis Union Merchants' Exchange, *Annual Statement of the Trade and Commerce of St. Louis . . . 1870*, 124, 325; Merchants' Exchange of St. Louis, *Annual Statement . . . 1880*, 120, 194; *Annual Statement . . . 1890*, 229, 246; *Annual Statement . . . 1900*, 244, 254; *Annual Statement . . . 1910*, 260, 268; Missouri Railroad and Warehouse Commissioners, *7th Annual Report . . . 1881*, 87; *29th Annual Report . . . 1904*, 388.

17. Doris R. H. Beuttenmuller, "The Granite City Steel Company: History of an American Enterprise," *BMHS*, 10 (Jan. 1954), 139–42, 199–200.

18. Fernando de Lara Baluyut, "Anheuser-Busch—A Study in Firm Growth" (M.S. thesis, St. Louis University, 1961).

19. G. K. Renner, "The Kansas City Meat Packing Industry Before 1900," *MHR*, 55 (Oct. 1960), 22–29; Merchants' Exchange of St. Louis, *Annual Statement . . . 1875*, 126, 132; *Annual Statement . . . 1890*, 231, 240.

20. Renner, "Kansas City Meat Packing," 24; *Manufactures*, 1880 Census, vol. 2, 144; *Manufacturing Industries*, 1890 Census, vol. 6, part 1, 491.

21. Hugh P. Williamson and Arnold Bedsworth, "Duley's Mill," *BMHS*, 21 (April 1965), 247; Priscilla Ann Evans, "Merchant Gristmills and Communities, 1820–1880. An Economic Relationship," *MHR*, 68 (April 1974), 324–25; Alice Lanterman, "The Development of Kansas City as a Grain and Milling Center," *MHR*, 42 (Oct. 1947), 23–24; Kansas City Board of Trade, *Annual Statistical Report . . . 1907*, 10.

22. Quoted in Kathleen White Miles, ed., *Annals of Henry County* (Clinton: The Printery, 1973), vol. 1, 164.

23. The pamphlets are among the uncatalogued railroad materials of the State Historical Society of Missouri. Missouri State Board of Agriculture, *12th Annual Report . . . 1876*, 59–67; Larry A. McFarlane, "The Missouri Land and Live Stock Company, Limited, of Scotland: Foreign Investment on the Missouri Farming Frontier, 1882–1908" (Ph.D. diss., University of Missouri, 1963), 18, 51–54, 63, 96–130; *Proceedings of the Missouri Horticultural Society . . . 1872*, 41.

24. *Horticultural Society . . . 1876*, 177; *Horticultural Society . . . 1879*, 302; Missouri State Board of Agriculture, *15th Annual Report . . . 1880–81*, 267.

25. Agriculture Board, *18th Annual Report . . . 1885*, 307, 308–9, 311; Swallow quoted in Jonas Viles, *The University of Missouri: A Centennial History* (Columbia: University of Missouri, 1939), 298.

26. Agriculture Board, *11th Annual Report . . . 1875*, 62.

27. Agriculture Board, *12th Annual Report . . . 1876*, 5–9, 37–38.

28. *Horticultural Society . . . 1876*, 183–84; Agriculture Board, *19th Annual Report . . . 1886*, 32; *32nd Annual Report . . . 1900*, 34–35.

29. Henry D. Hooker, "George Husmann," *MHR*, 23 (April 1929), 353–60, and idem, "George Husmann," in *Dictionary of American Biography*, ed., Dumas Malone (New York: Charles Scribner's Sons, 1943), vol. 9, 430, for his life. Quotations from *The Cultivation of the Native Grape, and Manufacture of American Wines* (New York: George and F. W. Woodward, 1866), 192, and Agriculture Board, *12th Annual Report . . . 1876*, 83. Isidor Bush describes the phylloxera story in Agriculture Board, *11th Annual Report . . . 1875*, 259–70. Husmann's books are at the Wine Institute in San Francisco. David Keyes provided copies.

30. Viles, *University of Missouri*, 299–301; Frederick B. Mumford, *History of the Missouri College of Agriculture* (Columbia: Agricultural Experiment Station bulletin no. 482, 1944), 48–57. Riley quoted in Agriculture Board, *12th Annual Report . . . 1876*, 32, but see also pages 86–96 for the conflict.

31. Missouri Agricultural Experiment Station, bulletin no. 1 (1888), 7–8, 12–13; bulletin no. 2 (1888), 1; and, for Texas fever, bulletins 11 (1890), 37 (Jan. 1897), esp. 117–29, and 48 (Oct. 1899); and Agriculture Board, *33rd Annual Report . . . 1901*, 28; *34th Annual Report . . . 1902*, 35; Mumford, *College of Agriculture*, 98; John H. Longwell, *The Centennial Report, 1870–1970, of the College of Agriculture, University of Missouri-Columbia* (Columbia: University of Missouri-Columbia College of Agriculture, 1970), 32–33, 239.

32. Agriculture Board, *22nd Annual Report . . . 1889–90*, 21; *23rd Annual Report . . . 1890–91*, 21; *24th Annual Report . . . 1891*, 17–18; *38th Annual Report . . . 1905*, 5.

33. Agriculture Board, *23rd Annual Report . . . 1890–91*, 19; *24th Annual Report . . . 1891*, 16; *25th Annual Report . . . 1892*, 321.

34. Agriculture Board, *23rd Annual Report . . . 1890–91*, 59; *41st Annual Report . . . 1908*, 257; *44th Annual Report . . . 1912*, 97; *45th Annual Report . . . 1913*, 384.

35. *Past and Present of Nodaway County, Missouri* (Indianapolis: B. F. Bowen, 1910), vol. 1, 237–38; Agriculture Board, *46th Annual Report . . . 1914*, 70–74.

36. Agriculture Board, *19th Annual Report . . . 1886–87*, 278; Dorothy J. Caldwell, "David Rankin: 'Cattle King' of Missouri," *MHR*, 66 (April 1972), 386, 390.

37. Agriculture Board, *33rd Annual Report . . . 1901*, 29; *44th Annual Report . . . 1912*, 180, 302.

38. Agriculture Board, *17th Annual Report . . . 1883*, 10; *18th Annual Report . . . 1885*, 39; *35th Annual Report . . . 1903*, 14–15; *37th Annual Report . . . 1904*, 11; *41st Annual Report . . . 1908*, 21.

39. Agriculture Board, *43rd Annual Report . . . 1911*, 413–23; *44th Annual Report . . . 1912*, 35; Agriculture Board, *Missouri Yearbook of Agriculture . . . 1915*, 39; Mumford, *College of Agriculture*, 106, 119–20, 124.

40. "The Farm Adviser in Missouri," University of Missouri Agricultural Experiment Station, *Circular No. 59* (March 1913), 189–96.

41. Agriculture Board, *45th Annual Report . . . 1913*, 347.

42. Agriculture Board, *44th Annual Report . . . 1912*, 119; *45th Annual Report . . . 1913*, 342–43; Vera Busiek Schuttler, *A History of the Missouri Farm Bureau Federation* (n.p.: Missouri Farm Bureau Federation, 1948), 3.

43. Agriculture Board, *46th Annual Report . . . 1914*, 218.

44. Agriculture Board, *1915 Yearbook*, 92; *1916 Yearbook*, 76; Schuttler, *Missouri Farm Bureau*, 6, 8–14; Mumford, *College of Agriculture*, 121–22, 125; Longwell, *College of Agriculture*, 82–86.

Chapter 3. The New Insecurities

1. Kathleen White Miles, ed., *Annals of Henry County* (Clinton: The Printery, 1974), vol. 2, 148.

2. Agriculture Board, *23rd Annual Report . . . 1890–91*, 724; Clarence N. Roberts, "Developments in the Missouri Pottery Industry, 1800–1950," *MHR*, 58 (July 1965), 468.

3. *Statistics of Agriculture*, 1870 Census, 188, 192; *Agriculture*, 1900 Census, part 1, 285–87, 692–93; Agriculture Board, *24th Annual Report . . . 1891*, 186; Curtis H. Synhorst, *Historical Resources: Chronology of Osage River History*, vol. 1 of *Cultural Resources Survey: Harry S. Truman Dam and Reservoir Project* (Columbia: American Archaeology Division, University of Missouri Columbia, 1983), 220.

4. Agriculture Board, *19th Annual Report . . . 1886–87*, 344; F. B. Mumford, "A Century of Missouri Agriculture," *MHR*, 15 (Jan. 1921), 287.

5. *Statistics of Wealth and Industry*, 1870 Census, vol. 3, 540–41; *Manufactures*, 1920 Census, vol. 9, 800–807. The sample for St. Joseph was based on the first 700 white males in the city directories of 1867–68 and 1908. The Springfield conclusion comes from the first 600 names of males with clear occupations in the 1873–74 and 1911–12 directories.

6. St. Louis *Missouri Republican*, July 26, 1877; *St. Louis Globe-Democrat*, July 23, 1877; Missouri Bureau of Labor Statistics, *16th Annual Report . . . 1894*, 136–37, 142, 146, 147, 163, 186, 197, 199; Labor Bureau, *30th Annual Report . . . 1908*, 782–93.

7. Labor Bureau, *16th Annual Report . . . 1894*, 40–52; Asa E. Martin, *Our Negro Population: A Sociological Study of the Negroes of Kansas City, Missouri* (1913; New York: Negro Universities Press, 1969 ed.), 59; Labor Bureau, *17th Annual Report . . . 1895*, 240–62, 313–27.

8. Labor Bureau, *2nd Annual Report . . . 1880*, 7, 15–42; *11th Annual Report . . . 1889*, 12–13, 14–66; *17th Annual Report . . . 1895*, 9–55; *21st Annual Report . . . 1899*, 304–8; *34th Annual Report . . . 1912*, 3, 194.

9. *St. Louis Globe-Democrat*, July 30, 1877; Labor Bureau, *17th Annual Report . . . 1895*, 95–96; also *15th Annual Report . . . 1893*, 91, and *16th Annual Report . . . 1894*, 224–26; Clarence N. Roberts, "The History of the Brick and Tile Industry in Missouri" (Ph.D. diss., University of Missouri, 1950), 142.

10. Thomas L. Norton, *Trade-Union Policies in the Massachusetts Shoe Industry, 1919–1929* (New York: Columbia University Press, 1932), 23; *Statistics of Wealth and Industry*, 1870 Census, vol. 3, 540; *Manufactures*, 1920 Census, vol. 9, 800–807.

11. Mark Bennitt, ed., *History of the Louisiana Purchase Exposition* (St. Louis: Universal Exposition Pub. Co., 1905), 618, 619. *Amerika*, Aug. 8, 1877, translated and quoted in Walter Kamphoefner, "The St. Louis *Amerika* from 1877 to 1886: The Immigrant Catholic Press and the Labor Question" (Research paper, History 356, University of Missouri-Columbia, 1974), 5. Note 5 in this chapter describes the sampling method from city directories.

12. Howard S. Miller and Quinta Scott, *The Eads Bridge* (Columbia: University of Missouri Press, 1979), 106–7.

13. Labor Bureau, *2nd Annual Report . . . 1880*, 166; *19th Annual Report . . . 1897*, 437–38; Miles, *Henry County*, vol. 1, 130.

14. Labor Bureau, *28th Annual Report . . . 1906*, 88; *36th Annual Report . . . 1914*, 4, 6–9.

15. Labor Bureau, *10th Annual Report . . . 1888*, 8–50, 61; William Barclay Napton, *Past and Present of Saline County, Missouri* (Indianapolis: B. F. Bowen, 1910), 248; Labor Bureau, *36th Annual Report . . . 1914*, 15.

16. Don Crinklaw, "The Battle of the Breweries," *St. Louis Post-Dispatch Pictures*, June 9, 1974; Labor Bureau, *10th Annual Report . . . 1888*, 153; *2nd Annual Report . . . 1880*, 107, 108, 138–39; *32nd Annual Report . . . 1910*, 253; *34th Annual Report . . . 1912*, 10.

17. Labor Bureau, *2nd Annual Report . . . 1880*, 166, 167.

18. Fern Boan, *A History of Poor Relief Legislation and Administration in Missouri* (Chicago: University of Chicago Press, 1941), 19.

19. Labor Bureau, *15th Annual Report . . . 1893*, 42; *17th Annual Report . . . 1895*, 94, 97.

20. Labor Bureau, *6th Annual Report . . . 1884*, 168–78, 186–92, 214–17; *27th Annual Report . . . 1905*, 412–21; *36th Annual Report . . . 1914*, 125; Boan, *Missouri Poor Relief*, 186.

21. Labor Bureau, *1st Annual Report . . . 1879*, 6–7, 27; *2nd Annual Report . . . 1880*, 280; Mary Beth Norton et al., *A People and a Nation* (Boston: Houghton Mifflin, 1982), 456.

22. Labor Bureau, *2nd Annual Report . . . 1880*, 147; *Coopers' International Journal*, 11 (Dec. 1901), 15.

23. St. Louis *Daily Times*, July 25, 1877; *St. Louis Globe-Democrat*, July 25, 1877; Labor Bureau, *6th Annual Report . . . 1884*, 259.

24. *Statistics of Wealth and Industry*, 1870 Census, vol. 3, 538, 394; *Manufactures*, 1920 Census, vol. 9, 800–807, and vol. 8, 296; Labor Bureau, *38th and 39th Annual Report . . . 1916–17*, 59; Martin, *Our Negro Population, 59.*

25. *Statistics of Wealth and Industry*, 1870 Census, vol. 3, 538, 540; *Manufacturing Industries*, 1890 Census, vol. 6, part 1, 486–87; *Manufactures*, 1920 Census, vol. 9, 800–807; Labor Bureau, *2nd Annual Report . . . 1880*, 171.

26. Labor Bureau, *13th Annual Report . . . 1891*, 483, 486; *Occupations*, 1900 Census, ccxxii; *Population: Occupations*, 1920 Census, vol. 4, 743.

27. *Manufacturing Industries*, 1890 Census, vol. 6, part 1, 88–89.

28. Russell Clemens, unpublished compilation from 1870 and 1900 manuscript censuses for Macon County, in author's possession; Christopher C. Gibbs, "The Lead Belt Riot and World War One," *MHR*, 71 (July 1977), 402–3, 410; *Statistics of the Population*, 1870 Census, vol. 1, 743; *Occupations*, 1900 Census, 318–25.

29. Clemens, compilation from 1900 Macon County manuscript census; William August Crossland, *Industrial Conditions among Negroes in St. Louis* (St. Louis: Washington University Studies in Social Economics, 1914), 74–79; Martin, *Our Negro Population*, 51; *Report of the Population*, 1890 Census, vol. 1, part 2, 678–79, 724–25; *Population: Occupations*, 1920 Census, vol. 4, 1125, 1128.

30. Crossland, *Industrial Conditions*, 64; *Report of the Population*, 1890 Census, vol. 1, part 2, 678–79, 724–25; *Population: Occupations*, 1920 Census, vol. 4, 1125, 1128.

31. *Amerika*, translated and quoted in Kamphoefner, "St. Louis *Amerika*," 7; Labor Bureau, *7th Annual Report . . . 1885*, 18; *9th Annual Report . . . 1887*, 7; *10th Annual Report . . . 1888*, 130–31, 136–37; *32nd Annual Report . . . 1910*, 398–99; Herbert Hadley to Jack Briscoe, May 27, 1910, letterbook 11, p. 552, Hadley Papers.

32. Woman's Christian Temperance Union of Missouri, *Report of the 14th Annual Convention* (1896), 41; *Minutes of the 50th Session of the St. Louis Annual Conference of the Methodist Episcopal Church South . . . 1897*, 61, 70.

33. E. T. Behrens, "I Been Workin' on a Railroad,' *Railway Clerk*, Feb. 1940, 64; copy kindly provided by Michael Cassity.

34. Missouri State Board of Mediation and Arbitration, *Biennial Report to the 43rd General Assembly . . . 1905*, 6–7.

35. Hannibal *Daily Clipper*, July 24, 1877.

Part III. Primitive Resistance to the New Order

1. Quoted in Albany [N.Y.] *Cultivator and Country Gentleman*, 44 (Jan. 23, 1879), 52, courtesy of Peter Argersinger.

Chapter 4. The Law, Outlaws, and Railroads

1. *Official Manual of the State of Missouri . . . 1891–92*, 250; Arthur Roy Kirkpatrick, "Missouri on the Eve of the Civil War," *MHR*, 55 (Jan. 1961), 99–106; (April 1961), 235–37; W. Wayne Smith, "An Experiment in Counterinsurgency: The Assessment of Confederate Sympathizers in Missouri," *Journal of Southern History*, 35 (Aug. 1969), 361–80; William Barclay Napton, *Past and Present of Saline County Missouri* (Indianapolis: B. F. Bowen, 1910), 161.

2. St. Louis *Missouri Republican*, June 23, 1866; St. Louis *Tri-Weekly Missouri Democrat*, Nov. 17, 1865; Robert Sidney Douglass, *History of Southeast Missouri* (1912; reprinted Cape Girardeau: Ramfre Press, 1961), 340, 443–44.

3. Minnie M. Brashear, "The Anti-Horse Thief Association of Northeast Missouri," *MHR*, 45 (July 1951), 345; *Goodspeed's History of Southeast Missouri* (1888, reprinted Independence: BNL Library Service, 1978), 392.

4. Fred DeArmond, "Reconstruction in Missouri," *MHR*, 61 (April 1967), 377; Jonathan Fairbanks and Clyde Edwin Tuck, *Past and Present of Greene County, Missouri* (Indianapolis: A. W. Bowen, 1915), 224–26; Margaret L. Dwight, "Black Suffrage in Missouri, 1861–1877" (Ph.D. diss.; University of Missouri-Columbia, 1978), ch. 9; Floyd Calvin Shoemaker, *Missouri and Missourians: Land of Contrasts—People of Achievements* (Chicago: Lewis Pub. Co., 1943), vol. 1, 1015–16; William Young, *Young's History of Lafayette County, Missouri* (Indianapolis: B. F. Bowen, 1910), vol 1, 360–61.

5. Osceola *Voice of the People*, May 12, 19, 26, 1880.

6. John W. Million, *State Aid to Railways in Missouri* (Chicago: University of Chicago Press, 1896), 188; *Boonville Weekly Eagle*, Sept. 11, 1874.

7. Missouri *Journal of the House of Representatives . . . 1885*, 29; Springfield *Missouri Weekly Patriot*, March 3, 1870.

8. William E. Parrish, *A History of Missouri, Volume 3: 1860 to 1875* (Columbia: University of Missouri Press, 1973), 198; Edwin L. Lopata, *Local Aid to Railroads in Missouri* (New York: Columbia University, 1937), 135–45; Homer Clevenger, "Railroads in Missouri Politics, 1875–1887," *MHR*, 43 (April 1949), 224; *Statistics of Wealth and Industry*, 1870 Census, vol. 3, 11, 42–44; *Report on Valuation, Taxation, and Public Indebtedness*, 1880 Census, vol. 7, 674–75.

9. Lopata, *Local Aid to Railroads*, 96, 135–45; *Statistics of the Population of the United States*, 1870 Census, vol. 1, 43–44; *Statistics of the Wealth and Industry*, 1870 Census, vol. 3, 42–44.

10. Curtis Synhorst, "Direct Legislation in Missouri" (Paper for Missouri Conference on History, n.d. [c. 1975]), 5; E. M. Violette, "The Missouri and Mississippi Railroad Debt," *MHR*, 15 (April 1921), 504–6, 513–15; Lopata, *Local Aid to Railroads*, 138, 140, 142–44.

11. *History of Lewis, Clark, Knox and Scotland Counties* (1887, reprinted Marceline: Walsworth Pub. Co., 1981), 722; St. Louis *Missouri Republican*, June 9, 1870; Lopata, *Local Aid to Railroads*, 104; Synhorst, "Direct Legislation," 5.

12. Sedalia *Daily Bazoo*, Oct. 6, 1869; *Sedalia Democrat*, Nov. 4, 1869; Michael J. Cassity, "Defending a Way of Life: The Development of Industrial Market Society and the Transformation of Social Relationships in Sedalia, Missouri, 1850–1890" (Ph.D. diss., University of Missouri-Columbia, 1973), 39–41.

13. *Kansas City Times*, April 25, 26, 28, 30, May 1–3, 1872; George H. Preston, *A History of the Cass County, Missouri, Bond Swindle* (St. Louis: Southwestern Book Co., 1873), esp. 85–89; John F. Philips and F. M. Cockrell to B. Gratz Brown, May 1, 1872, folder 30, box 1, B. Gratz Brown Papers, Office of Governor Collection, State Archives, Jefferson City; Sedalia *Democrat*, April 29, 1872; Sedalia *Daily Bazoo*, April 25, 27, 30, 1872; *History of Cass and Bates Counties* (St. Joseph: National Historical Co., 1883), 204–6, 391–429; *History and Directory of Cass County, Missouri* (Harrisonville: Cass County Leader, 1908), 177–203.

14. Lopata, *Local Aid to Railroads*, 104–5, 107–11.

15. Ibid., 111–12.

16. Violette, "Missouri and Mississippi Railroad Debt," *MHR*, 15 (July 1921), 629–47; 16 (Oct. 1921), 90–118; Virginia Rust Frazer, "Dallas County Railroad Bonds," *MHR*, 61 (July 1967), 444–45.

17. Lopata, *Local Aid to Railroads*, 123–27; *History and Directory of Cass County*, 200; Frazer, "Dallas County Bonds," 454–60.

18. St. Louis *Missouri Republican*, July 26, 1877; Clinton *Henry County Democrat*, Dec. 20, 27, 1877, Jan. 10, 31, 1878; Osceola *Sun*, May 29, 1879; folder 18132, Historical Records Survey, Works Projects Administration, Western Historical Manuscripts Collection; Curtis H. Synhorst, *Historical Resources: Chronology of Osage River History* (Columbia: American Archaeology Division, University of Missouri Columbia, 1983), 196–97, 208, 210–11, 228–30; *The History of Henry and St. Clair Counties* (1883, reprinted Clinton: Henry County Historical Society, 1968), 903–24.

19. W. F. Switzler, "Constitutional Conventions of Missouri, 1865–1875," *MHR*, 1 (Jan. 1907), 109–20; Isidor Loeb, "Constitutions and Constitutional Conventions of Missouri," *MHR*, 16 (Jan. 1922), 207–24; *Statistics of Wealth and Industry*, 1870 Census, vol. 3, 42–44;

Frederick N. Judson, *A Treatise upon the Law and Practice of Taxation in Missouri* (Columbia: E. W. Stephens, 1900), 66–69; Lopata, *Local Aid to Railroads*, 135–45; Frederic Arthur Culmer, *A New History of Missouri* (Mexico, Mo.: McIntyre Pub. Co., 1938), 480–81; Grace Gilmore Avery and Floyd C. Shoemaker, eds., *Messages and Proclamations of the Governors* (Columbia: State Historical Society of Missouri, 1924), vol. 6, 12.

20. Quoted in Frazer, "Dallas County Bonds," 462. See also Agriculture Board, *15th Annual Report . . . 1880–81*, 84.

21. William A. Settle, Jr., *Jesse James Was His Name; or, Fact and Fiction Concerning the Careers of the Notorious James Brothers of Missouri* (Columbia: University of Missouri Press, 1966), 66–67.

22. Sedalia *Daily Democrat*, April 13, 1882; J. A. Dacus, *Illustrated Lives and Adventures of Frank and Jesse James* (St. Louis: N. D. Thompson, 1881), 111–15; Robertus Love, *The Rise and Fall of Jesse James* (New York: G. P. Putnam's Sons, 1926), 297–98; Homer Croy, *Jesse James Was My Neighbor* (New York: Duell, Sloan and Pearce, 1949), 36–38; Richard S. Brownlee, *Gray Ghosts of the Confederacy: Guerrilla Warfare in the West, 1861–1865* (Baton Rouge: Louisiana State University Press, 1958), 63, 241–46; Carl W. Breihan, *Quantrill and His Civil War Guerrillas* (Denver: Sage Books, 1959), 43–44.

23. *Kansas City Times*, Sept. 27, 1872; Croy, *Jesse James Was My Neighbor*, 38; Settle, *Jesse James Was His Name*, 33–46.

24. *St. Louis Republican*, Feb. 1, 1874; St. Louis *Dispatch*, Feb. 2, 1874; Settle, *Jesse James Was His Name*, 47–48, 70–72, 88–89, 92–103, 107–9, 111–12; R. T. Bradley, *The Outlaws of the Border; or, The Lives of Frank and Jesse James* (St. Louis: J. W. Marsh, 1882), 56, 73–79; Dacus, *Illustrated Lives*, 281–88; Croy, *Jesse James Was My Neighbor*, 114–27.

25. William Anderson Settle, Jr., "Frank and Jesse James and Missouri Politics" (M.A. thesis, University of Missouri, 1941), 8–9, 26, 35–36, 44.

26. *Kansas City Times*, Oct. 15, 1872; Lexington *Weekly Caucasian*, Dec. 12, 1874; *Journal*, quoted in *Caucasian*, Sept. 19, 1874; Missouri *Journal of the House of Representatives . . . 1885*, 29; St. Louis *Dispatch*, Feb. 10, 1874.

27. *Train and Bank Robbers of the West* (Chicago: Belfore-Clarke, 1883), 173–74; 176–83; Croy, *Jesse James Was My Neighbor*, 82–86; Jay Donald, *Outlaws of the Border . . . Frank and Jesse James* (Chicago: Coburn and Newman, 1882), 220–24; Settle, *Jesse James Was His Name*, 59–60; St. Louis *Dispatch*, Jan. 27, 1875.

28. St. Louis *Dispatch*, Jan. 27, 1875; John N. Edwards, *Noted Guerrillas; or, The Warfare of the Border* (St. Louis: Bryan, Brand and Co., 1877), 456–57; Croy, *Jesse James Was My Neighbor*, 88–94; Frank Triplett, *The Life, Times and Treacherous Death of Jesse James* (Chicago: J. H. Chambers, 1882), 133–38; Settle, *Jesse James Was His Name*, 76–80; Frank James quoted in D. Weyermann, "Shades of Future Shock: the Social Bandit, 1860–1890" (Research paper, History 356, University of Missouri-Columbia, 1974), 8.

29. Lexington *Weekly Caucasian*, Oct. 17, 1874; Donald, *Outlaws of the Border*, 256–62, 473–74; J. W. Buel, *The Border Bandits* (Chicago: Donohue, Henneberry, 1893), 276–277; *Train and Bank Robbers*, 325; Settle, *Jesse James Was His Name*, 6–8, 69–70.

30. Donald, *Outlaws of the Border*, 377; *St. Louis Globe-Democrat*, April 5, 1882.

31. *Kansas City Times*, Oct. 15, 1872; St. Louis *Republic*, Feb. 2, 1874; *Train and Bank Robbers*, 135.

32. H. H. Crittenden, comp., *The Crittenden Memoirs* (New York: G. P. Putnam's Sons, 1936), 241; Buel, *Border Bandits*, 207–15.

33. *Kansas City Times*, Oct. 15, 1872; St. Louis *Republic*, Feb. 2, 1874; Settle, *Jesse James Was His Name*, 171–72, 227.

34. Sedalia *Daily Democrat*, April 4, 5, 7, 20, 1882; Crittenden, *Memoirs*, 225–29, 255–61; Settle, *Jesse James Was His Name*, 110–11, 116–19, 130–31; Croy, *Jesse James Was My Neighbor*, 202–5, 206–9.

35. *Train and Bank Robbers*, 317–18; *Journal of the Missouri Senate . . . 1883*, 23; *St. Louis Republic*, April 4, 6, 1882.

36. Sedalia *Daily Democrat*, April 7, 13, 15, 1882; *Journal* quoted in *Democrat*, April 19, 1882; Jennie Edwards, ed., *John N. Edwards: Biography, Memoirs, Reminiscences and Recollections* (Kansas City: Jennie Edwards, 1889), 163–65.

37. Settle, *Jesse James Was His Name*, 123, 139–44, 162; Homer Clevenger, "Agrarian Politics in Missouri, 1880–1896" (Ph.D. diss., University of Missouri, 1940), 112–21.

38. Croy, *Jesse James Was My Neighbor*, 241–43, 245; Settle, *Jesse James Was His Name*, 173–74, 180–195, 227, 239, 242–51.

39. *St. Louis Globe-Democrat*, July 27, 1877; David Burbank, "The First International in St. Louis," *BMHS*, 18 (Jan. 1962), 163–71; Robert V. Bruce, *1877: Year of Violence* (1959, reprint Chicago: Quadrangle paperback ed., 1970), 276; Saul K. Padover, comp. and trans., *The Letters of Karl Marx* (Englewood Cliffs: Prentice-Hall, 1979), 318.

40. St. Joseph *Daily Herald*, July 24, 1877.

41. Sedalia *Daily Democrat*, July 24, 26, 1877; *St. Louis Daily Times*, July 23, 28, 1877; Walter Kamphoefner, "The St. Louis *Amerika* from 1877 to 1886: The Immigrant Catholic Press and the Labor Question" (Research paper, History 356, University of Missouri Columbia, 1974), 5; Hannibal *Clipper*, July 24, 1877.

42. Bruce, *1877*, part 2: David Burbank, *Reign of the Rabble: The St. Louis General Strike of 1877* (New York: Augustus M. Kelley, 1966), 15–17; St. Joseph *Daily Herald*, July 24, 1877.

43. Sedalia *Daily Democrat*, July 27, 1877; *St. Louis Globe-Democrat*, July 24, 1877.

44. *St. Louis Globe-Democrat*, July 24–26, 1877; Hannibal *Clipper*, July 25, 1877; Sedalia *Daily Democrat*, July 25, 27, 1877; St. Louis *Missouri Republican*, July 25, 26, 1877; *St. Louis Daily Times*, July 25, 28, 1877.

45. Sedalia *Daily Democrat*, July 26, 27, 1877; St. Louis *Missouri Republican*, July 25, 1877; *St. Louis Globe-Democrat*, July 26, 1877; *St. Louis Daily Times*, July 27, 1877; Burbank, *Reign of Rabble*, 48.

46. Sedalia *Daily Democrat*, July 26, 1877; Hannibal *Clipper*, July 25, 26, 30, 1877; *St. Louis Globe-Democrat*, July 26, 1877.

47. Sedalia *Daily Democrat*, July 31, 1877; Hannibal *Clipper*, July 24, 1877.

48. Burbank, *Reign of Rabble*, 5, 20; Lucius E. Guese, "St. Louis and the Great Whisky Ring," *MHR*, 36 (Jan. 1942), 160–79.

49. *St. Louis Globe-Democrat*, July 24, 1877; Burbank, *Reign of Rabble*, 33–34.

50. *St. Louis Globe-Democrat*, July 25, 26, 1877; *St. Louis Daily Times*, July 25, 1877; Burbank, *Reign of Rabble*, 4, 53–58.

51. *St. Louis Globe-Democrat*, July 26, 29, 1877; St. Louis *Missouri Republican*, July 26, 1877.

52. *St. Louis Globe-Democrat*, July 26, 1877; St. Louis *Missouri Republican*, July 26, 27, 28, 1877; *St. Louis Daily Times*, July 27, 1877.

53. St. Louis *Missouri Republican*, July 26, 28, 1877; St. Louis *Dispatch*, July 25, 1877; *St. Louis Daily Times*, July 24, 1877; St. Joseph *Daily Herald*, July 25, 1877.

54. *St. Louis Globe-Democrat*, July 25, 27, 28, 1877; St. Louis *Missouri Republican*, July 27, Aug. 1, 1877; *St. Louis Daily Times*, July 27, 1877; Burbank, *Reign of Rabble*, 104–6, 129–32, 140–45.

55. *St. Louis Globe-Democrat*, July 27, 1877; St. Louis *Missouri Republican*, July 26, 27, 28, 1877; *St. Louis Daily Times*, July 24, 26, 27, 1877.

56. Hannibal *Clipper*, July 24, 25, 26, 27, 30, 1877.

57. Sedalia *Daily Democrat*, July 26, 27, 29, 31, 1877.

Chapter 5. Communities, Economic Development, and Vigilantes

1. Lucille Morris, *Bald Knobbers* (Caldwell, Idaho: Caxton Printers, 1939), 35–36, 99, 141–42; Thomas Hart Benton, *An Artist in America* (New York: Robert M. McBride, 1937), 85–86, 111–12; Harvey N. Castleman, *The Bald Knobbers* (Girard, Kans.: Haldeman-Julius Pubs., 1944), 6.

2. Fred De Armond, "Guerrillas in the Ozarks," Springfield *Sunday News and Leader*, January 18, 1976, pp. E1–2; Robert L. Harper, *Among the Bald Knobbers: A History of the Desperadoes of the Ozark Mountains* (n.p.: Harper & Taylor, 1888), 13–14; Castleman, *Bald Knobbers*, 5; Morris, *Bald Knobbers*, 25–32.

3. F. McConkey, *The Bald Knobbers or Citizen's Committee of Taney and Christian Counties, Missouri* (Forsyth, Mo.: Groom & McConkey, 1887), 4–5.

4. McConkey, *Bald Knobbers*, 37–38; *Report on Population*, 1890 Census, vol. 1, 2, 4, 213, 214, 219, 222; *Statistics of the Population*, 1870 Census, vol. 1, 43–44.

5. McConkey, *Bald Knobbers*, 7; Castleman, *Bald Knobbers*, 6; Morris, *Bald Knobbers*, 49–52.

6. Morris, *Bald Knobbers*, 37–40, 45, 48, 53–59; McConkey, *Bald Knobbers*, 34–36, 41; Castleman, *Bald Knobbers*, 7; Jefferson City *Daily Tribune*, Nov. 10, 1885.

7. Castleman, *Bald Knobbers*, 10, 11–12, 13; McConkey, *Bald Knobbers*, 7–10; Morris, *Bald Knobbers*, 62–66, 70.

8. Jefferson City *Daily Tribune*, Nov. 10, 1885; Castleman, *Bald Knobbers*, 27; McConkey, *Bald Knobbers*, 15–20.

9. McConkey, *Bald Knobbers*, 20–24, 28–32; Castleman, *Bald Knobbers*, 14–18, 27–28; Morris, *Bald Knobbers*, 74–82, 84–85, 98; Springfield *Daily Herald*, April 17, 1886.

10. Harper, *Among the Bald Knobbers*, 35–38; Castleman, *Bald Knobbers*, 19; A. M. Haswell, "The Story of the Bald Knobbers," *MHR*, 18 (October 1923), 28–29; Morris, *Bald Knobbers*, 34–35, 104–7.

11. Morris, *Bald Knobbers*, 69, 71–73; Harper, *Among the Bald Knobbers*, 87, 105–8, 121–22; Castleman, *Bald Knobbers*, 24; trial transcript, *State of Missouri* v. *Wiley Mathews*, case 8, box 1143, Missouri Supreme Court Files, State Archives, Jefferson City.

12. Harper, *Among the Bald Knobbers*, 39–40; Castleman, *Bald Knobbers*, 19; Haswell, "Bald Knobbers," 30–32; McConkey, *Bald Knobbers*, 44–46; Morris, *Bald Knobbers*, 108.

13. Trial transcripts, *State* v. *Wiley Mathews*, *State* v. *David Walker* (case 4, box 1144), *State* v. *William Walker* (case 1, box 1144), *State* v. *John Mathews* (case 7, box 1144), Missouri Supreme Court Files, State Archives; Morris, *Bald Knobbers*, 114, 122–28, 135, 137; Harper, *Among the Bald Knobbers*, 53–56, 59; Springfield *Daily Herald*, Sept. 3, 1887.

14. Trial transcripts for Wiley Mathews, John Mathews, David Walker, William Walker; Springfield *Daily Herald*, Sept. 7, 8, 1887; Springfield *Leader*, Aug. 25, Sept. 1, 1887; Harper, *Among the Bald Knobbers*, 78–81; Morris, *Bald Knobbers*, 149–57, 174, 189, 193, 197, 204–6.

15. Harper, *Among the Bald Knobbers*, 99; Morris, *Bald Knobbers*, 218, 223, 224–32; Cosmo Joseph Pusateri, "A Businessman in Politics: David R. Francis, Missouri Democrat" (Ph.D. diss., St. Louis University, 1965), 142–52; Springfield *Leader*, May 9, 10, 1889; Springfield *Express*, May 10, 1889; *St. Louis Globe-Democrat*, May 9, 11, 1889; Springfield *Republican*, May 11, 1889.

16. Harper, *Among the Bald Knobbers*, 33.

17. Irvin G. Wyllie, "Race and Class Conflict on Missouri's Cotton Frontier," *Journal of Southern History*, 20 (May 1954), 184; *Statistics of Agriculture*, 1890 Census, vol. 5, 216–17; *Population*, 1890 Census, vol. 1, part 1, 211–21.

18. Leon Parker Ogilvie, "The Development of the Southeast Missouri Lowlands" (Ph.D. diss., University of Missouri-Columbia, 1967), 211, 236, 237; Margaret L. Dwight, "Black Suffrage in Missouri, 1865–1877" (Ph.D. diss., University of Missouri-Columbia, 1978), 219–22, 234–35, 238–39, 241.

19. Ogilvie, "Southeast Missouri Lowlands," 100–103, 104, 388.

20. Ibid., 105–106, 109, 115–24, 129; Wyllie, "Race and Class Conflict," 185; J. Sheppard Smith, "Reclamation of Swamp Lands and the Modern Drainage Bond," *Annals of American Academy of Political and Social Science*, 88 (March 1920), 111.

21. *Irrigation and Drainage*, 1920 Census, vol. 7, 578–82; *Report on Wealth, Debt, and Taxation*, 1890 Census, vol. 15, 265–66.

22. *Population*, 1910 Census, vol. 2, 1075, 1080, 1081, 1082, 1085; *Statistics of Agriculture*, 1890 Census, vol. 5, 216–17; *Agriculture*, 1920 Census, vol. 6, 578–88; Wyllie, "Race and Class Conflict," 184.

23. Ogilvie, "Southeast Missouri Lowlands," 209–12; Seth S. Barnes to Herbert Hadley, Oct. 21, 1911, H. R. Post to Herbert Hadley, Nov. 9, 1911, H. R. Post to Edward Regenhardt, Nov. 23, 1911, Hadley Papers.

24. Otto Kochtitzky, *The Story of a Busy Life* (1931, reprinted Cape Girardeau, Mo.: Ramfre Press, 1957), 113–15; Ogilvie, "Southeast Missouri Lowlands," 111, 240, 243.

25. Ogilvie, "Southeast Missouri Lowlands," 212, 375; Charleston *Weekly Enterprise*, July 8, 1910.

26. Kennett *Justice*, Jan. 9, 16, Feb. 20, 1914.

27. C. G. Post to Herbert Hadley, Dec. 5, 1911, F. M. Rumbold to Hadley, Dec. 6, 1911, Hadley Papers.

28. Ogilvie, "Southeast Missouri Lowlands," 238, 240, 241; New Madrid *Weekly Record*, Sept. 16, 23, 1905.

29. New Madrid *Weekly Record*, June 4, 1910.

30. Charleston Weekly *Enterprise*, July 8, 1910.

31. Herbert Hadley to Henry C. Riley, July 7, 1910, letterbook 12: 216, J. M. Haw to Hadley, July 19, 1910, Hadley Papers; Charleston *Weekly Enterprise*, July 8, 22, 1910, April 7, 14, 1911.

32. Seth S. Barnes to Herbert Hadley, Oct. 12, 21, 1911, J. S. Gossom to Hadley, Oct. 17, 1911, Hadley Papers; New Madrid *Southeast Missourian*, Oct. 12, 1911.

33. Caruthersville *Pemiscot Argus*, Oct. 5, 12, 1911; Caruthersville *Twice-a-Week Democrat*, Oct. 3, 5, 1911.

34. Caruthersville *Pemiscot Argus*, Oct. 12, 1911; Caruthersville *Twice-a-Week Democrat*, Oct. 13, 1911.

35. Seth S. Barnes to Herbert Hadley, Oct. 12, 21, 1911, March 12, 1912, Hadley Papers, New Madrid *Weekly Record*, March 23, 1912.

36. Caruthersville *Pemiscot Argus*, Dec. 14, 1911.

37. J. S. Gossom to Herbert Hadley, Oct. 17, 1911, F. M. Rumbold to Hadley, Dec. 6, 1911, Hadley Papers; Caruthersville *Twice-a-Week Democrat*, Oct. 13, 1911.

38. Kennett *Justice*, March 2, April 24, 1914.

39. Kennett *Justice*, Jan. 9, 16, 23, 30, June 26, Aug. 14, 1914.

40. *Missouri Official Manual, 1905–06*, 442–43; *1909–10*, 734–35; *1913–14*, 757–58; Ogilvie, "Southeast Missouri Lowlands," 364.

41. *Missouri Official Manual, 1917–18*, 429–30.

42. Kennett *Justice*, Jan. 9, 1914; Ogilvie, "Southeast Missouri Lowlands," 218, 221, 252, 360; New Madrid *Weekly Record*, March 27, April 3, Dec. 25, 1915; Benton *Scott County Democrat*, Dec. 2, 9, 16, 1915; *St. Louis Post-Dispatch*, Jan. 22, 1916.

43. Kennett *Justice*, Nov. 6, 1914; Sikeston *Standard*, Dec. 24, 1915; New Madrid *Weekly Record*, Nov. 27, Dec. 11, 25, 1915, Jan. 29, 1916; *St. Louis Post-Dispatch*, Jan. 22, 1916.

44. Benton *Scott County Democrat*, Nov. 25, Dec. 2, 16, 1915, Jan. 27, Feb. 23, 1916; New Madrid *Weekly Record*, Nov. 27, 1915; *St. Louis Post-Dispatch*, Jan. 21, 24, 25, 1916; Ogilvie, "Southeast Missouri Lowlands," 218–20.

Part IV. The Cultural War

1. Thomas Hart Benton, *An Artist in America* (New York: Robert M. McBride, 1937), 3; J. E. Cortner to Herbert S. Hadley, July 3, 1911, Hadley Papers.

2. Benton, *Artist in America*, 85; *Lexington News*, Feb. 11, 1892.

3. Benton, *Artist in America*, 27–28.

Chapter 6. Discipline and Self-Discipline

1. Leslie G. Hill, "History of the Missouri Lumber and Mining Company, 1890–1909" (Ph.D. diss., University of Missouri, 1949), 156; Missouri Bureau of Labor Statistics, *13th Annual Report . . . 1891*, 13–14.

2. Mary Jane Quinn, "Local Union No. 6, Brewing, Malting and General Labor Departments, St. Louis, Missouri" (M.A. thesis, University of Missouri, 1947), 71.

3. Katherine Teasdale Condie, "The Temperance Movement in Missouri, 1869–1887" (Ph.D. diss., Washington University, 1937), 15, 79; Hill, "Missouri Lumber and Mining Co.,"

145–47, 173–74, 237–38, 240–42; John A. Galloway, "John Barber White: Lumberman" (Ph.D. diss., University of Missouri, 1961), 226–27, 231–32; 237–38, 248; G. K. Renner, "Prohibition Comes to Missouri, 1910–1919," *MHR*, 62 (July 1968), 384–85.

4. Susan Curtis Mernitz, "Church, Class, and Community in Lexington, Missouri" (M.A. thesis, University of Missouri-Columbia, 1981), traces this process in one community.

5. Grace Gilmore Avery and Floyd C. Shoemaker, eds., *Messages and Proclamations of the Governors* (Columbia: State Historical Society of Missouri, 1924), vol. 6, 45–47, 430.

6. Ibid., 45–47, 351–52, 430–31; Sarah Guitar and Floyd C. Shoemaker, eds., *Messages and Proclamations of the Governors* (Columbia: State Historical Society of Missouri, 1926), vol. 7, 28–29, 168–69, 251; vol. 8, 84–85, 315, 399; Missouri National Guard, *History of the Missouri National Guard* (n. p., 1934), 26–28; William H. Riker, *Soldiers of the States: The Role of the National Guard in American Democracy* (Washington: Public Affairs Press, 1957), 53; Lon Stephens to Jerome Boarman, June 11, 1900, box 2, folder 2, p. 157, Stephens Papers, Missouri State Archives, Jefferson City.

7. *Annual Report of the Board of Police Commissioners of the City of St. Louis . . . 1869*, 18.

8. Marshall S. Snow, *The City Government of Saint Louis* (Baltimore: Johns Hopkins University Studies, 1887), 31–32; St. Louis Police Commissioners, *10th Annual Report . . . 1871*, 40; *38th Annual Report . . . 1899*, 806–17, 827–29; *56th Annual Report . . . 1917*, 15.

9. Mernitz, "Church and Class in Lexington," 43–44; Kathleen White Miles, ed., *Annals of Henry County* (Clinton: The Printery, 1974), vol. 2, 147.

10. *Population*, 1870 Census, vol. 1, 194; St. Louis Police Commissioners, *10th Annual Report . . . 1871*, 41; Asa E. Martin, *Our Negro Population, A Sociological Study of the Negroes of Kansas City, Missouri* (1913; reprinted New York: Negro Universities Press, 1969), 131; Mernitz, "Church and Class in Lexington," 67.

11. Herbert S. Hadley to Thomas R. Marks, July 1, 1910 (letterbook 12, 174–75), to Solon T. Gilmore, July 19, 1910 (letterbook 12, 333), Aug. 8, 1910 (12, 465–66), Sept. 7, 1910, (13, 99–100), Sept. 10, 1910 (13, 135), Sept. 21, 1910 (13, 244); Harry C. Smith to Solon T. Gilmore, Sept. 3, 1910, enclosed in Gilmore to Hadley, Sept. 5, 1910, Hadley Papers; Kansas City *Star*, Aug. 18, 1910.

12. *St. Louis Daily Times*, July 24, 1877.

13. *54th Report of the Public Schools of the State of Missouri . . . 1903*, 102, 112, 113, e.g.; Alice Hayden Turley, "A History of the School District of the City of Hannibal, Missouri, 1866–1931" (M.A. thesis, University of Missouri, 1953), 8, 9; Glenn Freeman Leslie, "The Development of Financial Support for Public Schools in Missouri" (Ed.D. thesis, University of Missouri, 1945), 102–5, 151, 157–58, 272; W. T. Carrington, *History of Education in Missouri: Autobiographical* (n.p., 1931), xv.

14. Selwyn K. Troen, *The Public and the Schools: Shaping the St. Louis System, 1838–1920* (Columbia: University of Missouri Press, 1975), 159–60; Merle Curti, *The Social Ideas of American Educators; with New Chapter on the Last Twenty-Five Years* (Totwa, N. J.: Littlefield, Adams, 1959), 310–12.

15. Missouri *7th Annual Report of the Superintendent of Public Schools . . . 1872*, 77; Board of Directors of the St. Louis Public Schools, *17th Annual Report . . . 1871*, 166; Curti, *Social Ideas*, 323, 330, 332.

16. State School Superintendent, *7th Report . . . 1872*, 78; St. Louis Schools, *21st Annual Report . . . 1875*, 20–21; Troen, *Public and Schools*, 47, 48.

17. State School Superintendent, *7th Report . . . 1872*, 78–79.

18. St. Louis Schools, *20th Annual Report . . . 1874*, 137.

19. State School Superintendent, *5th Report . . . 1870*, xv–xvi.

20. State School Superintendent, *7th Report . . . 1872*, 14.

21. State School Superintendent, *4th Report . . . 1869*, 16, 17.

22. William E. Parrish, *A History of Missouri, Volume 3: 1860 to 1875* (Columbia: University of Missouri Press, 1973), 170–75; Mernitz, "Church and Class in Lexington," 41–43; Carrington, *History of Education in Missouri*, xv, xvi; Leslie, "Financial Support for Missouri Schools," 168–71; State School Superintendent, *26th Report . . . 1875*, 17.

23. State School Superintendent, *7th Report . . . 1872*, 10, 46–47; *4th Report . . . 1869*, 64–65, 142; Avery and Shoemaker, *Governors Messages*, vol. 6, 278; *6th Annual Report of the Kansas City Public Schools . . . 1876–77*, 46; Agriculture Board, *33rd Annual Report . . . 1900*, 354.

24. St. Louis Schools, *30th Annual Report . . . 1884*, 277; J. M. Rice, "The Public Schools of St. Louis and Indianapolis," *Forum*, 14 (Dec. 1892), 432, 433; *Annual Report, Course of Study and Rules and Regulations of the Board of Education of the Columbia Public Schools . . . 1894*, 39; *1st Annual Report of the Public Schools of Lebanon, Missouri . . . 1885–86*, 13; Board of St. Joseph Public Schools, *Annual Report of Superintendent . . . 1865*, 9; *Lexington School Manual . . . 1889–90*, 15; *Annual Report of the Superintendent of Schools of the City of Richmond . . . 1882–83*, 20.

25. St. Joseph Public Schools, *Annual Report . . . 1879–80*, 59, also *1869–70*, 31; *1871–72*, 7–8; *1873–74*, 33–34; *Course of Study and Rules and Regulations for the Public Schools of Kirksville Missouri . . . 1895*, 5; Kansas City Public Schools, *5th Annual Report . . . 1875–76*, 18; St. Louis Schools, *17th Annual Report . . . 1871*, 84–89; State School Superintendent, *4th Report . . . 1869*, 95.

26. State School Superintendent, *4th Report . . . 1869*, 6; Kansas City Public Schools, *Annual Report . . . 1874–75*, 16; St. Joseph Public Schools, *Annual Report . . . 1866*, 21.

27. Wiley Jones Patrick, *The History of the Salt River Association, Missouri* (Columbia: E. W. Stephens, 1909), 284; W. H. Lewis, *History of Methodism in Missouri for a Decade of Years from 1860 to 1870* (Nashville: Methodist Episcopal Church, South, 1890), 444, 445; J. W. Haines, *The History of the Polk County Baptist Association* (Bolivar: Bolivar Herald, 1897), 38; St. Louis *Review*, Aug. 3, 1899, Jan. 4, 1900, Jan. 24, 1901, Sept. 19, 1901.

28. Patrick, *Salt River Association*, 242–44; T. L. Largen, *Shoal Creek Association, with History of Her Churches and Biography of Ministers* (Kansas City: Word and Way Pub. Co., 1908), 13; J. C. Maple, *Missouri Baptist Centennial, 1906* (Columbia: E. W. Stephens, 1907), 211–13; George L. Peters, *The Disciples of Christ in Missouri: Celebrating One Hundred Years of Co-operative Work* (n. p.: Centennial Commission, 1937), 227–28; Troen, *Public and Schools*, 34; Carrington, *History of Education in Missouri*, 9.

29. State School Superintendent, *5th Report . . . 1870*, xv.

30. State School Superintendent, *4th Report . . . 1869*, 139–259, esp. 164, 202.

31. St. Joseph Public Schools, *22nd Annual Report . . . 1886*, 11; State School Superintendent, *7th Annual Report . . . 1872*, 326–29; *35th Report . . . 1884*, 32–35; *43rd Report . . . 1892*, 68–70, 77–79.

32. State School Superintendent, *7th Annual Report . . . 1872*, 323–29; *35th Report . . . 1884*, 32–39; *43rd Report . . . 1892*, 68–70, 77–79; *54th Report . . . 1903*, 50–52, 59–61; *64th Report . . . 1913*, 258–60. For compulsory attendance, see *57th Report . . . 1906*, 22–30.

33. State School Superintendent, *43rd Report . . . 1892*, 111–16; Kansas City Schools, *6th Annual Report . . . 1876–77*, 50.

34. St. Joseph Schools, *Annual Report . . . 1887*, 9; *Annual Report . . . 1866*, 21; *Annual Report . . . 1885*, 50; *Report of the Board of Education of the City of Carthage, Mo., May 1876*, 20; Kansas City Schools, *6th Annual Report . . . 1876–77*, 42.;

Chapter 7. The Democratic Culture of Escape and Ragtime

1. Missouri Bureau of Labor Statistics, *Eleventh Annual Report . . . 1889*, 348–49; Kathleen White Miles, ed., *Annals of Henry County* (Clinton: The Printery, 1973), vol. 1, 160; Thomas Hart Benton, *Artist in America* (New York: Robert M. McBride, 1937), 86; F. M. Rumbold to Herbert S. Hadley, Dec. 6, 1911, Hadley Papers, Joint Manuscript Collections; Kennett *Justice*, March 19, 1914; T. L. Largen, *Shoal Creek Association with History of Her Churches and Biography of Ministers* (Kansas City: Word and Way Pub. Co., 1908), 46–48; Frank C. Tuker, *The Methodist Church in Missouri, 1789–1939: A Brief History* (n.p.: Joint Committee of the Historical Societies of the Missouri East and Missouri West Annual Conferences, 1966), 237–42; Wiley Jones Patrick, *The History of the Salt River Associaion,*

Missouri (Columbia: E. W. Stephens, 1909), 385; New Madrid *Southeast Missourian*, June 23, 1910.

2. Sedalia *Weekly Bazoo*, Feb. 6, 1877.

3. Asa E. Martin, *Our Negro Population: A Sociological Study of the Negroes of Kansas City, Missouri* (1913, reprinted New York: Negro Universities Press, 1969), 160; Benton, *Artist in America*, 28.

4. Benton, *Artist in America*, 17–19, 22, 23; Herbert Hadley to Thomas R. Marks, May 18, 1910, letterbook 11, p. 498, Hadley Papers.

5. John Cleophus Cotter, "The Negro in Music in Saint Louis" (M.A. thesis, Washington University, 1959), 290, 295, 297–98; Rudi Blesh and Harriet Janis, *They All Played Ragtime* (1950, reprinted New York: Oak Publications Paperback, 1971), 14–17, 39–41; interview with Rudi Blesh, Sedalia, July 26, 1975; Sedalia *Democrat-Capital*, Dec. 26, 1976, James Haskins with Kathleen Benson, *Scott Joplin* (Garden City: Doubleday, 1978), 77, 88, 95–98; Terry Waldo, *This Is Ragtime* (New York: Hawthorn Books, 1976), 35–36; Sedalia *Democrat-Capital*, eds., *Scott Joplin Ragtime Festival Souvenir Edition* (n.p., n.d., 1975?), 10; S. Brun Campbell, "The Ragtime Kid (An Autobiography)," *Jazz Report*, 6 (Nov. 1, 1967), 5, courtesy of Michael Cassity.

6. William J. Schafer and Johannes Riedel, *The Art of Ragtime: Form and Meaning of an Original Black American Art* (Baton Rouge: Louisiana State University Press, 1973), 5–37, 111–16; Edward A. Berlin, *Ragtime: A Musical and Cultural History* (Berkeley: University of California Press, 1980), 99–111; Waldo, *This Is Ragtime*, 7–36; David A. Jasen and Trebor Jay Tichenor, *Rags and Ragtime: A Musical History* (New York: Seabury, 1978), 11–20; Alain Locke, *The Negro and His Music: Negro Art, Past and Present*, (New York: Arno Press, 1969), 53–60; Thornton Haggert, "Instrumental Dance Music, 1780s–1920s," 3, notes to accompany Federal Music Society record, *Come and Trip It* (New World Records NW 293), courtesy of John Hasse; Eileen Southern, *The Music of Black America: A History* (New York: W. W. Norton, 1983 ed.), 311–16; Haskins, *Scott Joplin*, 67–75; Peter Gammond, *Scott Joplin and the Ragtime Era* (London: Angus & Robertson, 1975), 20–22.

7. Jasen and Tichenor, *Rags and Ragtime*, 28–33; Blesh and Janis, *They All Played Ragtime*, 54–62, 110–12.

8. Haskins, *Scott Joplin*, 32, 41, 46–62, 75–94; Addison W. Reed, "The Life and Works of Scott Joplin" (Ph.D. diss., University of North Carolina, 1973), 1–25; Theodore Albrecht, "Julius Weiss: Scott Joplin's First Piano Teacher," *College Music Symposium*, 19 (Fall 1979), 89–105; *Scott Joplin Ragtime Festival Souvenir Edition*, 15; Vera Brodsky Lawrence, ed., *The Collected Works of Scott Joplin* (New York: New York Public Library, 1971), vol. 1, 3.

9. Blesh and Janis, *They All Played Ragtime*, 45–52, 58; Gammond, *Joplin and Ragtime Era*, 63–65.

10. Blesh and Janis, *They All Played Ragtime*, 112–18, 235–37, 280–84; Jasen and Tichenor, *Rags and Ragtime*, 83–84, 111–33; Schafer and Riedel, *Art of Ragtime*, 75–88; Waldo, *This Is Ragtime*, 66–75; Rudi Blesh, "Scott Joplin: Black-American Classicist," in Lawrence, *Collected Works of Scott Joplin*, vol. 1, xxx–xxxi.

11. Blesh, "Joplin: Black-American Classicist," xxix, xxxvi; Schafer and Riedel, *Art of Ragtime*, 12–15, 51–52, 95–97; Haskins, *Scott Joplin*, 143; Campbell, "Ragtime Kid," 5; Trebor Jay Tichenor, "Missouri's Role in the Ragtime Revolution," *BMHS*, 17 (April 1961), 239–44; Jasen and Tichenor, *Rags and Ragtime*, 21–27; Trebor Jay Tichenor, ed., *Ragtime Rarities: Complete Original Music for 63 Piano Rags* (New York: Dover, 1975), 39–42; Melissa Fuell, *Blind Boone: His Early Life and His Achievement* (Kansas City: Burton, 1915), 124–25, 207–8, 209–10; William Parrish, "Blind Boone's Ragtime," *Missouri Life*, 7 (Nov.–Dec. 1979), 18–23.

12. *St. Louis Globe-Democrat*, June 7, 1903; Blesh, "Joplin: Black-American Classicist," xxii–xxvii; Haskins, *Scott Joplin*, 104–6, 112–15, 126–27, 131–32, 137–38; Gammond, *Joplin and Ragtime Era*, 129–30; Reed, "Life and Works of Joplin," 37–38; Schafer and Riedel, *Art of Ragtime*, 42, 50, 217–18.

13. Lawrence, *Collected Works of Joplin*, vol. 1, 126, 284; Blesh, "Joplin: Black-American Classicist," xxxvii, xxxiv; Blesh and Janis, *They All Played Ragtime*, 65–66, 141; Reed, "Life

and Works of Joplin," 42–43; Haskins, *Scott Joplin*, 125–26, 163–66, 170; Stark quoted in Berlin, *Ragtime*, 186.

14. Haskins, *Scott Joplin*, 160–62, 171–72, 177–80; Reed, "Life and Works of Joplin," 45–50; Blesh and Janis, *They All Played Ragtime*, 242–44, 248–49; Vera Brodsky Lawrence, "Scott Joplin and *Treemonisha*," 10–12, booklet to accompany Houston Grand Opera recording, *Scott Joplin's Treemonisa* (Deutsche Gramophon 2702-083, 1976).

15. This interpretation is based primarily on the Houston Grand Opera production, Houston, May 1981, for *Treemonisha* must be seen for Joplin's vision to come to life. The Houston text closely follows Joplin's, as reprinted in Lawrence, *Collected Works of Joplin*, vol. 2. The most penetrating musicological analysis is Schafer and Riedel, *Art of Ragtime*, 205–25.

16. *Crisis*, 5 (April 1913), 276–77; poem quoted in Whitcomb, *After the Ball: Pop Music from Rag to Rock* (1972, reprinted Baltimore: Penguin Books, 1974), 16.

17. Lawrence, *Collected Works of Joplin*, vol. 1, 182–84; New Franklin *Howard County News*, March 10, 1904.

18. Berlin, *Ragtime*, 41–44; Isaac Goldberg, *Tin Pan Alley: A Chronicle of the American Popular Music Racket* (New York: John Day, 1930), 145; *Musical America*, 18 (July 5, 1913), 28.

19. Al Rose, *Eubie Blake* (New York: Schirmer Books, 1979), 11–12.

20. Quoted in *Crisis*, 5 (April 1913), 276–77.

Part V. Mutual Aid

Chapter 8. *The Protections of Church, Race, and Language*

1. Clement Simon Mihanovich, "Americanization of the Croats in Saint Louis, Missouri, during the Past Thirty Years" (M.A. thesis, St. Louis University, 1936), 8–9, 16–17.

2. Margaret Justine Lo Piccolo Sullivan, "Hyphenism in St. Louis, 1900–1921: The View from the Outside" (Ph.D. diss., St. Louis University, 1968), 34–39, 96–98, 225–30; John Rothensteiner, *History of the Archdiocese of St. Louis* (St. Louis: Blackwell Wielandy, 1928), vol. 2, 454–59; William Barnaby Faherty, *Dream by the River: Two Centuries of Saint Louis Catholicism, 1766–1967* (St. Louis: Piraeus, 1973), 96; Missouri Conference of Charities and Correction, *8th Annual Report . . . 1907*, 75.

3. Howard F. Sachs, "Development of the Jewish Community of Kansas City, 1864–1908," *MHR*, 60 (April 1966), 353, 356–58; Sullivan, "Hyphenism in St. Louis," 151–65, 174–81; Averam B. Bender, "History of the Beth Hamedrosh Hagodol Congregation of St. Louis, 1879–1960," *BMHS*, 27 (Oct. 1970), 60, 67; Ruth Crawford, *The Immigrant in St. Louis* (St. Louis: Washington University Studies in Social Economics, 1916), 86–88; *St. Louis Globe-Democrat*, May 16, 1911.

4. *Amerika* in Walter Kamphoefner, "The St. Louis *Amerika* from 1877 to 1886: The Immigrant Catholic Press and the Labor Question" (Term paper, History 356, University of Missouri-Columbia, 1974), 11; St. Louis *Review*, May 18, 1899, May 29, 1902.

5. Sister Audrey Olson, "The Nature of an Immigrant Community: St. Louis Germans, 1850–1920," *MHR*, 66 (April 1972), 351–52; Barbara Sanders, "The Germans of Ste. Genevieve, 1830 to 1890" (Seminar paper, History 455, University of Missouri-Columbia, 1980), 14–15; Crawford, *Immigrant in St. Louis*, 89; St. Louis *Review*, June 15, Nov. 2, 9, 1899, March 8, 1900.

6. *History of the Washington Turner Society* (Washington: Historical Committee of the Washington Turner Society, 1900; translated by William Bek, n.d.), 8–11, 15–23.

7. Gary Ross Mormino, "Over Here: St. Louis Italo-Americans and the First World War," *BMHS*, 30 (Oct. 1973), 46; Selwyn K. Troen, *The Public and the Schools: Shaping the*

St. Louis System, 1838–1920 (Columbia: University of Missouri Press, 1975), 55–78; U.S. Census, *Religious Bodies: 1906*, part 1, 43, 122.

8. Giovanni Schiavo, *The Italians in Missouri* (Chicago: Italian American Pub. Co., 1929), 68; Walter John Galus, "The History of the Catholic Italians in Saint Louis" (M.A. thesis, St. Louis University, 1936); St. Louis *Republic*, May 8, 1906; Sullivan, "Hyphenism in St. Louis," 88.

9. St. Louis *Western Watchman*, January 25, 1906; Margaret Sullivan, "Constitutionalism, Revolution and Culture: Irish-American Nationalism in St. Louis, 1902–1914," *BMHS*, 28 (April 1972), 234–45.

10. *Jewish Progress in Saint Louis* (St. Louis: A. Rosenthal, 1904), 36; Sullivan, "'Hyphenism in St. Louis," 169–70, 188–96; Sachs, "Jewish Community of Kansas City," 357.

11. *St. Louis Times*, Oct. 26, 28, Nov. 1, 1915; *St. Louis Globe-Democrat*, Nov. 1, 1915, March 17, 1918; St. Louis *Mirror*, Feb. 12, 1915; St. Louis *Republic*, Nov. 29, 1917.

12. W. Sherman Savage, "The Legal Provisions for Negro Schools in Missouri from 1865 to 1890," *Journal of Negro History*, 16 (July 1931), 313, 319–20; Roger N. Baldwin, "Report of the Committee on the Problems of Negroes," Missouri Conference of Charities and Correction, *15th Annual Meeting . . . 1914*, 24–26; *The Crisis*, 6 (May 1913), 41, (Aug. 1913), 168; 7 (March 1914), 220; Priscilla Alden Stith, "The Negro Migrant in St. Louis" (M.A. thesis, University of Missouri, 1918), 36–38, 39–40, 43; Asa E. Martin, *Our Negro Population: A Sociological Study of the Negroes of Kansas City, Missouri* (1913, reprinted New York: Negro Universities Press, 1969), 92–95, 96; *Eye* quoted in Kathleen White Miles, ed., *Annals of Henry County*, (Clinton: The Printery, 1974), vol. 2, 18.

13. Alberta D. and David O. Shipley, *The History of Black Baptists in Missouri* (n.p.: privately published, 1976), 137–38; *The Crisis*, 1 (March 1911), 6; 3 (Nov. 1911), 19; 5 (Jan. 1913), 122–23; 6 (May 1913), 15; Daniel T. Kelleher, "St. Louis' 1916 Residential Segregation Ordinance," *BMHS*, 26 (April 1970), 239–48; *St. Louis Post-Dispatch*, Feb. 14, 1907.

14. *26th Report of the Public Schools of the State of Missouri . . . 1876*, 17; Public Schools, *53rd Report . . . 1902*, 29–30; Baldwin, "Report on Negroes," 23.

15. *The Crisis*, 6 (May 1913), 24; Henry Sullivan Williams, "The Development of the Negro Public School System in Missouri," *Journal of Negro History*, 5 (April 1920), 165.

16. Martin, *Our Negro Population*, 171; Stephen Cornish, "Survey of a Rural Negro Community in Pike County Missouri" (M.A. thesis, University of Missouri, 1922), 52; Suzanna Maria Grenz, "The Black Community in Boone County, Missouri, 1850–1900" (Ph.D. diss., University of Missouri-Columbia, 1979), 133.

17. Public Schools, *42nd Report . . . 1891*, 56–63; *53rd Report . . . 1902*, 101–9; Martin, *Our Negro Population*, 170; Robert Irving Brigham, "The Education of the Negro in Missouri" (Ph.D. diss., University of Missouri, 1946), 107.

18. Grenz, "Boone County Blacks," 160, 161–62.

19. Public Schools, *26th Report . . . 1876*, 12; *27th Report . . . 1877*, 16; *42nd Report . . . 1891*, 56–63; Troen, *Public and Schools*, 88–92.

20. William August Crossland, *Industrial Conditions among Negroes in St. Louis* (St. Louis: Washington University Studies in Social Economics, 1914), 34; Brigham, "Education of Negro in Missouri," 115, 117; Williams, "Negro Public Schools in Missouri," 162–63; *The Crisis*, 3 (Jan. 1912), 103; Martin, *Our Negro Population*, 174; Thomas C. Cadwallader and Christopher Joyce, "Charles Henry Turner (1867–1923): America's First Black Comparative Psychologist and Animal Behaviorist" (Paper presented to Cheiron, 1978), courtesy of Thomas Cadwallader.

21. W. Sherman Savage, *The History of Lincoln University* (Jefferson City: Lincoln University, 1939), 36, 44, 283; J. W. Evans, "A Brief Sketch of the Development of Education in St. Louis, Missouri," *Journal of Negro Education*, 7 (Oct. 1938), 548–52; Brigham, "Education of Negro," 240–41.

22. *Advance* quoted in *The Crisis*, 4 (July 1912), 124; 3 (Dec. 1911), 51; 4 (Oct. 1912), 274; Crossland, *St. Louis Negroes*, 37–38; Mrs. L. V. DeFrantz, "Social Progress of the Colored People of Kansas City," Missouri Conference of Charities and Correction, *15th Annual Meeting . . . 1914*, 29.

23. Shipley, *Black Baptists*, 166–70, 174, 180, 185; Gaston Hugh Wamble, "Negroes and Missouri Protestant Churches Before and After the Civil War," *MHR*, 61 (April 1967), 321–45; Wilbur D. East, "A Descriptive Survey of the Negro Churches in Columbia" (M.A. thesis, University of Missouri, 1938), 13–14; Cornish, "Pike County Negroes," 61, 63; U.S. Census, *Religious Bodies: 1906*, vol. 1, 552–53.

24. Crossland, *St. Louis Negroes*, 36; William Wilson Elwang, *The Negroes of Columbia, Missouri* (Columbia: University of Missouri Department of Sociology, 1904), 35; Martin, *Our Negro Population*, 180–82.

25. U.S. Census, *Religious Bodies: 1906*, vol. 1, 553; Cornish, "Pike County Negroes," 88; Grenz, "Boone County Blacks," 74–75.

26 Martin, *Our Negro Population*, 96, 185–86; Carter G. Woodson, *The History of the Negro Church* (Washington: Associated Publishers, 1921), 277–78; De Frantz, "Kansas City Colored People," 28; *The Crisis*, 2 (Oct. 1911), 231; 3 (Jan. 1912), 97; 6 (Nov. 1913), 319; 7 (Dec. 1913), 60; Julia Childs Curtis, "A Girls' Clubhouse," *The Crisis*, 6 (Oct. 1913), 294–96.

27. Martin, *Kansas City Negroes*, 38, 40, 43, 53; Shipley, *Black Baptists*, 82–84; W. E. Burghardt Du Bois, ed., *The Negro Church* (Atlanta: Atlanta University Press, 1903), 130, 135; George Everett Slavens, "The Missouri Negro Press, 1875–1920," *MHR*, 64 (July 1970), 413–31; *The Crisis*, 6 (June 1913), 63; Crossland, *St. Louis Negroes*, 39–57.

28. Du Bois, *Negro Church*, 207–8; William E. B. Du Bois, *The Souls of Black Folk* (1903), reprinted in *Three Negro Classics* (New York: Avon Books, 1965), 340–45; Woodson, *Negro Church*, 253–54, 267–68, 273–74, 280, 302–3; Troen, *Public and Schools*, 94–95. See also E. Franklin Frazier, *The Negro Church in America* (1963, reprinted New York: Schocken Books, 1974).

29. U.S. Census, *Religious Bodies: 1906*, vol. 1, 220–25, 552; Cindy Landis, "The Temperance Movement in Jefferson City and New York City, 1890–1895" (Research paper, History 356, University of Missouri-Columbia, 1974), 5–8; Richmond *Conservator*, Aug. 11, 1887; W. E. Burghardt Du Bois, ed., *Some Efforts of American Negroes for Their Own Social Betterment* (Atlanta: Atlanta University Press, 1898), 41.

30. *The Crisis*, 5 (April 1913), 291; also 1 (Nov. 1910), 6; (Dec. 1910), 9; 4 (June 1912), 64; 4 (Oct. 1912), 272; "Dynamite in Kansas City," *The Crisis*, 3 (Feb. 1912), 160–62.

31. *Statistics of Churches*, 1890 Census, vol. 9, 38–43; U.S. Census, *Religious Bodies: 1916*, vol. 1, 190–93; *Population of the United States*, 1890 Census, vol. 1, xcviii; *Population*, 1920 Census, vol. 3, 551.

32. *Statistics of Churches*, 1890 Census, vol. 9, 163–64, 174–75, 182, 186, 195, 197, 198, 203, 349–50, 513, 547–48, 561, 569, 578, 586–87, 601, 606, 615, 639, 661–62, 674, 678, 686, 700; U.S. Census, *Religious Bodies: 1916*, vol. 1, 280–83; *The Statistics of the Population of the United States*, 1870 Census, vol. 1, 361–63; *Population of the United States*, 1890 Census, vol. 1, 211–22; *Population*, 1920 Census, vol. 3, 551–61; *Statistics of Agriculture*, 1890 Census, vol. 5, 216–17; *Agriculture*, 1910 Census, vol. 5, 762–64; *Agriculture*, 1920 Census, vol. 6, 589–610; *Report of the State Auditor . . . 1902*, 273–330.

33. Frederick D. Power, *Bible Doctrine for Young Disciples* (St. Louis: Christian Pub. Co., 1899), 131; *The Doctrines and Discipline of the Methodist Episcopal Church* (Cincinnati: Cranston & Curts, 1892), 39; Sedalia *The Christian*, April 1, 1899; Sedalia *Harmony Baptist*, July 1898.

34. Susan Curtis Mernitz, "Church, Class, and Community in Lexington, Missouri" (M.A. thesis, University of Missouri-Columbia, 1981), 15; Frank C. Tucker, *The Methodist Church in Missouri, 1798–1939: A Brief History* (n.p.: Joint Historical Societies of the Missouri East and Missouri West Annual Conferences, 1966), 296, 301, 302–4; R. S. Douglass, *History of Missouri Baptists* (Kansas City: Western Baptist Pub. Co., 1934), 458, 463.

35. Tucker, *Missouri Methodists*, 277–30; T. L. Largen, *Shoal Creek Association with History of Her Churches and Biography of Ministers* (Kansas City: Word and Way Pub. Co., 1908) 54–56; George L. Peters, *The Disciples of Christ in Missouri: Celebrating One Hundred Years of Co-operative Work* (n.p.: Centennial Commission, 1937), 212–21.

36. Wiley Jones Patrick, *The History of the Salt River Association, Missouri* (Columbia: E. W. Stephens, 1909), 301–2; Largen, *Shoal Creek Association*, 92, 105.

37. St. Louis *Central Christian Advocate*, March 5, 1890, also Sept. 8, 15, 1886, Feb. 12, 1890; Charles Edwin Jones, "Disinherited or Rural? A Historical Case Study in Urban Holiness Religion," *MHR*, 66 (April 1972), 395–412; Tucker, *Missouri Methodists*, 191.

38. *Macon Messenger of Peace*, Dec. 15, 1882; Sedalia *Harmony Baptist*, Jan. 1897, Nov. 1898; St. Louis *Central Christian Advocate*, Sept. 1, 1886; Marceline *Messenger of Peace*, Jan. 1, 1896.

39. Missouri Baptist General Association, *Missouri Baptist Centennial, 1906* (Columbia: E. W. Stephens, 1907), 88, 194; Sedalia *Harmony Baptist*, May 1898.

40. Methodist quoted in St. Louis *Review*, Dec. 7, 1899; Patrick, *Salt River Association*, 379; St. Louis *Central Christian Advocate*, Oct. 20, 1886.

41. Sedalia *Harmony Baptist*, March, Sept. 1899; St. Louis *Central Christian Advocate*, July 28, 1886, Jan. 8, 1890.

42. Quoted in Walter R. Houf, "The Protestant Church in the Rural Midwestern Community, 1820–1870" (Ph.D. diss. University of Missouri-Columbia, 1967), 120.

43. Mernitz, "Church and Class in Lexington," 31–35, 71–78; Wamble, "Negroes and Protestant Churches," 337–39, 341, 343–45; Pomeroy in Michael J. Cassity, "Defending a Way of Life: The Development of Industrial Market Society and the Transformation of Social Relationships in Sedalia, Missouri, 1850–1880" (Ph.D. diss., University of Missouri-Columbia, 1973), 64.

44. St. Louis *Central Christian Advocate*, Aug. 25, 1886; Boonville *Western Christian Union*, Feb. 1899.

45. Cassity, "Way of Life," 53–54; Katherine Teasdale Condie, "The Temperance Movement in Missouri, 1869–1887" (Ph.D. diss., Washington University, 1937), 16–17, 29, 49–50.

46. Cassity, "Way of Life," 128–33; Condie, "Temperance Movement," 16, 21–25; Largen, *Shoal Creek Association*, 51–52; Douglass, *Missouri Baptists*, 295.

47. St. Louis *Central Christian Advocate*, Feb. 19, 26, March 5, 1890.

48. Condie, "Temperance Movement," 16, 20–21, 50–55, 94–99, 123–58.

49. Woman's Christian Temperance Union of Missouri, *Report of the 8th Annual Convention . . . 1890*, 114, 115; *11th Annual Convention . . . 1893*, 27; *14th Annual Convention . . . 1896*, 19; Christopher C. Gibbs, "The Lead Belt Riot and World War One," *MHR*, 71 (July 1977), 409–10; Condie, "Temperance Movement," 52–55, 61–62; Clare Lucile Bradley, "The Prohibition Movement and Dramshop Law Enforcement in Missouri, 1887–1910" (M.A. thesis, Washington University, 1941), 28, 117, 137.

50. Tucker, *Missouri Methodists*, 167–71; Patrick, *Salt River Association*, 259–62; R. S. Duncan, *A History of the Baptists in Missouri* (St. Louis: Scammell, 1882), 916–29; William E. Parrish, *Missouri under Radical Rule, 1865–1870* (Columbia; University of Missouri Press, 1965), 63, 68; Condie, "Temperance Movement," 17–18, 48–49; St. Louis *Central Christian Advocate*, Sept. 22, 1886; St. Louis *Review*, May 11, 1899.

51. Tucker, *Missouri Methodists*, 242, 243.

52. *Register* in G. K. Renner, "Prohibition Comes to Missouri, 1910–1919," *MHR*, 62 (July 1968), 375; U.S. Census, *Religious Bodies: 1916*, vol. 1, 280–83; *Official Manual of the State of Missouri . . . 1917–1918*, 484–85.

Chapter 9. The Fraternal and Cooperative Ethic of Mutual Aid

1. Ray V. Denslow, *Civil War and Masonry in Missouri* (n.p.: Missouri Grand Lodge, Ancient Free & Accepted Masons, 1930), 176; William E. Parrish, *A History of Missouri, Volume 3: 1860 to 1875* (Columbia: University of Missouri Press, 1973), 194–95; Missouri Bureau of Labor Statistics, *36th Annual Report . . . 1914*, 43–47; Knights of Pythias of Missouri, Grand Lodge, *25th Annual Convention . . . 1895*, 55; William Wilson Elwang, *The Negroes of Columbia Missouri* (Columbia: University of Missouri Department of Sociology, 1904), 11, 29; Stephen Cornish, "Survey of a Rural Negro Community in Pike County Missouri" (M.A. thesis, University of Missouri, 1922), 64; Asa E. Martin, *Our Negro Population: A Sociological Study of the Negroes of Kansas City Missouri* (1913, reprinted New York:

Negro Universities Press, 1969), 79; Missouri State Insurance Department, *45th Annual Report . . . 1913*, 15–17.

2. *Hoye's St. Joseph City Directory, 1887–8*, 529–30; *Constitution and By-Laws of M.B. and B.U. of the State of Mo.* (Hannibal, 1886), 3, 6, 11; Missouri Insurance Department, *30th Annual Report . . . 1898*, xxv–xxvii; *35th Annual Report . . . 1903*, xxix–xxxi; *By-Laws of the Bard Temple of Honor and Temperance, No. 5* (Hannibal, n.d.); Katherine Teasdale Condie, "The Temperance Movement in Missouri, 1869–1887" (Ph.D. diss., Washington University, 1937), 17–18, 48, 92–93.

3. *Swick's St. Joseph City Directory, 1867–8*, 169–72; *R. L. Polk Co.'s St. Joseph City Directory, 1908*, 32–40; *Gould's St. Louis Directory, 1895*, 2020–2035; *History of Southeast Missouri* (Chicago: Goodspeed Pub. Co., 1888), 442–43, 453–54.

4. Solon Justus Buck, *The Granger Movement: A Study of Agricultural Organization and Its Political, Economic, and Social Manifestations, 1870–1880* (1913, reprinted Lincoln: University of Nebraska Bison Books, 1963), 58 ff.; D. Sven Nordin, *Rich Harvest: A History of the Grange, 1867–1900* (Jackson: University Press of Mississippi, 1974), 29; O. H. Kelley, *Origin and Progress of the Order of the Patrons of Husbandry . . . 1866 to 1873* (1875, reprinted Westport, Conn.: Hyperion, 1975), 18, 19, 22, 30, 38–39, 68–69; *Constitution, By-Laws, and Rules of Order of the Cigar-Makers' Union, No. 76, of Hannibal, Missouri . . . 1890*, 4.

5. *Columbia Evening Missourian*, May 12, 1921; *By-Laws of Hannibal Post No. 43, G.A.R. . . . 1883*, 2, 13.

6. Bureau of Labor Statistics, *36th Report . . . 1914*, 43.

7. *Proceedings of the Grand Lodge, Knights of Pythias of Missouri, N.A.S.A.E.A.A.&A. . . . 1915*, 19; Missouri Horticultural Society, *16th Annual Meeting . . . 1875*, 127; *Macon Missouri Granger*, March 10, Sept. 15, 1874; *Hannibal Cigar-Makers, Local 76*, 4; *By-Laws, Coeur De Leon Lodge No. 11, Knights of Pythias, of Hannibal, Missouri* (1893), 3–4.

8. Noel P. Gist, *Secret Societies: A Cultural Study of Fraternalism in the United States* (Columbia: University of Missouri Studies, 1940), 123–24; Knights and Daughters of Tabor for Missouri, *15th Annual Grand Session . . . 1902*, 77.

9. *Hannibal Knights of Pythias No. 11*, 4; Knights and Daughters of Tabor, *1894 Proceedings*, 26; Gist, *Secret Societies*, 144.

10. *By-Laws of Hannibal Lodge No. 161, A.O.U.W. of Hannibal, Missouri* (1885), 2; *Constitution and By-Laws of Sedalia Lodge, No. 27, Knights of Pythias . . . 1880*, 39; Charles W. Ferguson, *Fifty Million Brothers: A Panorama of American Lodges and Clubs* (New York: Farrar and Rinehart, 1937), 191–92.

11. *Sedalia Knights of Pythias No. 27*, 33; *Hannibal Knights of Pythias No. 11*, 7.

12. Robert J. Richardson, "Missouri," in H. Morton Bodfish, ed., *History of Building and Loan in the United States* (Chicago: United States Building and Loan League, 1931), 460–67; Bureau of Labor Statistics, *15th Annual Report . . . 1893*, 109–274; S. G. Mead, comp., *Mutual Insurance Manual: A Hand Book* (McPherson, Kans.: National Association of Mutual Co-operative Fire Insurance Companies, 1906), 491–95; Missouri State Board of Agriculture, *30th Annual Report . . . 1893*, 333–57.

13. Amos G. Warner, *Three Phases of Cooperation in the West* (Baltimore: Johns Hopkins University Studies in Historical and Political Science, 1888), 398–400; H. Roger Grant, "Missouri's Utopian Communities," *MHR*, 66 (Oct. 1971), 49–53; St. Louis *Review*, June 21, 1900.

14. *Macon Missouri Granger*, March 3, May 12, 1874; Missouri Bureau of Labor Statistics, *2nd Report . . . 1880*, 213–17; *Constitution and By-Laws of the Workingmen's Co-operative Co., of Hannibal Missouri . . . 1886*, 3, 4; Parrish, *Missouri, Vol. 3*, 286.

15. Phil Chew, *History of the Farmers' Alliance, the Agricultural Wheel, the Farmers' and Laborers' Union, the Farmers' Mutual Benefit Association, the Patrons of Industry, and Other Farmers' Organizations* (St. Louis: Journal of Agriculture, 1890), 84, 369, 373; Leon Parker Ogilvie, "The Development of the Southeast Missouri Lowlands" (Ph.D. diss., University of Missouri-Columbia, 1967), 344.

16. *Cooperation*, 5 (August 1913), 315; *Hannibal Workingmen's Cooperative*, 12.

17. Bureau of Labor Statistics, *20th Report . . . 1898*, 206–12; Michael J. Cassity, "Defending a Way of Life: The Development of Industrial Market Society and the Transformation of Social Relationships in Sedalia, Missouri, 1850–1880" (Ph.D. diss., University of Missouri-Columbia, 1973), 167–75; Martha S. Kayser, "Woman's Exchange," in William Hyde and Howard L. Conrad, *Encyclopedia of the History of St. Louis* (New York: Southern History Co., 1899), vol. 6, 2526–27; *Hoye's City Directory of Kansas City, Missouri . . . 1889*, 719.

18. Herbert Myrick, *How to Cooperate . . . A Manual for Cooperators* (1891, reprinted New York: Orange Judd, 1910), 133–34, 137; Warner, *Cooperation in West*, 413–16; Bureau of Labor Statistics, *7th Report . . . 1885*, 18, 40; *10th Report . . . 1888*, 131; *32nd Report . . . 1910*, 407.

19. Earl A. Collins, "The Multitude Incorporated," *MHR*, 27 (July 1933), 303–6; George McA. Miller, "The School in the Promotion of Progress," *Arena*, 28 (Sept. 1902), 231–37; Ross E. Paulson, *Radicalism and Reform: The Vrooman Family and American Social Thought, 1837–1937* (Lexington: University of Kentucky Press, 1968), 172–85; Grant, "Missouri Utopias," 45–48.

20. *St. Joseph Directory, 1887–8*, 530; *St. Joseph Directory, 1908*, 34–35; *By-Laws of Russell Camp No. 2065, Modern Woodmen of America* (Sedalia, 1901), 16–20; *M. H. McCoy's Sedalia, Mo., City Directory for 1898–1899*; *Hoye's Sedalia City Directory for 1903*; names and occupations for Odd Fellows' Itaska Encampment for Lexington courtesy of Susan Curtis Mernitz.

21. *Masonic Directory, Sedalia, Mo., 1896*, (3–5, 7–9); *Masonic Directory, St. Joseph, Mo., 1901*, 7–19; A Loyd Collins, "A History of a Century of Freemasonry in Clinton, Missouri, 1844–1944" (typescript by Clinton Lodge 548, 1944), 50–51; *Masonic Directory of Kansas City, Missouri, 1912*; *By-Laws of Hannibal Lodge, No. 41, I.O.O.F. . . . 1897*, 14; *By-Laws of Hannibal Lodge, No. 26, I.O.O.F. . . . 1900*, 17–18; *Sedalia Pythias No. 27*, 40–41; *Hannibal Pythias No. 11*, 12–16; *Journal of Proceedings of the Grand Lodge, Knights of Pythias of Missouri . . . 1892*, 217–20; *1893*, 187–90; *1894*, 192–96; *1895*, 135–40; *Hannibal A.O.U.W. No. 161*, 13–14; *Revised By-Laws . . . Bluff City Lodge No. 23, A.O.U.W. of Hannibal, Missouri* (1895), 15; *By-Laws and Roster of Crescent Tent, No. 4 Knights of the Maccabees . . . Sedalia . . . 1898*, 10–19; *Sedalia Modern Woodmen No. 2065*, 16–20; city directories for occupations. Names of fraternal members and their occupations for Lexington are courtesy of Susan Curtis Mernitz.

22. *St. Louis Review*, Jan. 5, 1903, Nov. 2, 1899, Aug. 22, 1901; *Goodspeed's Southeast Missouri*, biographical appendix; Henry J. Browne, *The Catholic Church and the Knights of Labor* (Washington: Catholic University of America Press, 1949), 158–59, 215–16, 279–81; William Barnaby Faherty, *Dream by the River: Two Centuries of Saint Louis Catholicism, 1766–1967* (St. Louis: Piraeus, 1973), 112–14.

23. Names taken from biographical appendix of *Goodspeed's Southeast Missouri*.

24. Arthur Preuss, *Dictionary of Secret and Other Societies* (1924, reprinted Detroit: Gale Research Co., 1966), 336.

25. *Hannibal I.O.O.F. No. 26*, 11; *Hannibal A.O.U.W. No. 161*, 5; *Constitution and By-Laws of Hannibal Typographical Union No. 86* (1884), 10; *By-Laws, Order of Business and Rules of Order of the Iron Molder's Union No. 142 of Hannibal, Mo. . . . , 1896*, 14.

26. *Most Worthy Grand Lodge of Free and Accepted Masons for . . . Missouri . . . 1880*, 25; *Hannibal Typographical No. 88*, 10; Chew, *History of Farmers' Alliance*, 226; *Sedalia Pythias No. 27*, 14; Knights of Pythias, *Missouri State Lodge . . . 1895*, 18; *By-Laws of Hannibal Division No. 39, Order of Railway Conductors . . . 1887*, 6; *By-Laws, Rules and Regulations of Charity Lodge No. 331 A.F.&A.M. . . . St. Joseph . . . 1895*, 16.

27. Gist, *Secret Societies*, 95.

28. Missouri Horticultural Society, *16th Annual Meeting . . . 1875*, 126; *Hannibal Cigar-Makers No. 88*, 12; *Hannibal I.O.O.F. No. 26*, 11; Preuss, *Secret Societies*, 376. Georg Simmel, "The Sociology of Secrecy and of Secret Societies," *American Journal of Sociology*, 11 (Jan. 1906), 441–98, is an interpretive base.

29. Kathleen White Miles, ed., *Annals of Henry County* (Clinton: The Printery, 1973), vol. 1, 53.

30. Black Masons, *1880 State Proceedings*, 25, 28–29; Gist, *Secret Societies*, 70–73, 75–76, 78.

31. Gist, *Secret Societies*, 67, 68; *Hannibal I.O.O. F. No. 26*, 13.

32. Julie Watkins, "Freemasonry in Missouri" (Research paper, History 356, University of Missouri-Columbia, 1981), 3; Macon *Missouri Granger*, March 3, 1874; Chew, *History of Farmers' Alliance*, 226.

33. *Sedalia Pythias No. 27*, 23; *Hannibal Iron Molders No. 142*, 10; *By-Laws of the Gillespie Military Lodge No. 140, A.F.&A.M.* (Hannibal, 1897), 7–8.

34. Black Masons, *1883 State Proceedings*, 26; *1888*, 17; *Hannibal A.O.U.W. No. 23*, 5; *By-Laws and Rules of Order of Eureka Assembly, Knights of Labor No. 3734 of Hannibal Mo . . . 1885*, 5; *Sedalia Pythias No. 27*, 37; *Sedalia Modern Woodmen No. 2065*, 9.

35. *Sedalia Pythias No. 27*, 21; *Sedalia Modern Woodmen No. 2065*, 8; Knights of Pythias, *Missouri State Lodge . . . 1885*, 231; *1891*, 143–44; *1894*, 182–85.

36. *Hannibal A.O.U.W. No. 23*, 7–8; *Sedalia Pythias No. 27*, 19; *Hannibal Iron Molders No. 142*, 9; *Hannibal I.O.O.F. No. 41*, 6–7; *Sedalia Modern Woodmen No. 2065*, 5–6; *Sedalia Maccabees No. 4*, 5–6; *By-Laws of No. 38, St. Vincent De Paul Council, Knights of Father Mathew, Sedalia, Mo. . . . 1892*, 11–12.

37. *Hannibal I.O.O.F. No. 26*, 8; Black Masons, *1880 State Proceedings*, 25–26, 60; Knights of Pythias, *State Lodge . . . 1895*, 134; Knights and Daughters of Tabor, *1894 Proceedings*, 40, 91; anthem in Miles, *Henry County*, vol. 1, 364.

38. St. Louis *Review*, May 31, 1900.

39. Harugari, *Constitution, Statuten der Sterbe-Kasse und Neben-Gesetz der Glasgow Lodge D.O.H., 1885*, 1; Lexington names are courtesy of Susan Curtis Mernitz.

40. Knights of Pythias, *State Lodge . . . 1885*, 254; *1893*, 170; *1894*, 126, 223, 234; *1895*, 98.

41. Knights of Pythias, *State Lodge . . . 1885*, 233.

42. Knights of Pythias, *State Lodge . . . 1887*, 87–88, 97; *1898*, 100–01; *1900*, 105, 137–39; *1906*, 105.

43. *Masonic Directory, Sedalia, Mo., 1905*, 7.

Part VI. The Search for Security in the New Workplaces

Chapter 10. The Economic Organization of the New Order

1. William H. Wilson, ed., "The Diary of a Kansas City Merchant, 1874–1880," *BMHS*, 19 (April 1963), 257.

2. Michael J. Cassity, "Defending a Way of Life: The Development of Industrial Market Society and the Transformation of Social Relationships in Sedalia, Missouri, 1850–1880" (Ph.D. diss., University of Missouri-Columbia, 1973), 104; Ernest D. Kargau, *Mercantile, Industrial and Professional Saint Louis* (St. Louis: Nixon-Jones, 1902), 132–34; Kathleen White Miles, ed., *Annals of Henry County* (Clinton: The Printery, 1973), vol. 1, 47.

3. George H. Morgan, "Merchants' Exchange of St. Louis," *Annals of the American Academy of Political and Social Science*, 38 (Sept. 1911), 222–26; T. J. Tanner, "The Board of Trade of Kansas City," ibid., 237–41; S. S. Huebner, "The Functions of Produce Exchanges," ibid., 1–35; Kargau, *Mercantile St. Louis*, 92–96; Alice Lanterman, "The Development of Kansas City as a Grain and Milling Center," *MHR*, 42 (Oct. 1947), 30–32.

4. Rudolf Alexander Clemen, *The American Livestock and Meat Industry* (New York: Ronald Press, 1923), 204–6.

5. R. E. Riegel, "The Missouri Pacific Railroad to 1879," *MHR*, 18 (Oct. 1923), 22–26; idem, "The Missouri Pacific, 1879–1900," ibid., 18 (Jan. 1924), 178–82, 187–88; idem, "The Southwestern Pool," ibid., 19 (Oct. 1924), 12–24.

6. John A. Galloway, "John Barber White: Lumberman" (Ph.D. diss., University of Missouri, 1961), 71–109; Leslie G. Hill, "History of the Missouri Lumber and Mining Com-

pany, 1890–1909" (Ph.D. diss., University of Missouri, 1949), ch. 3; Southwestern Lumbermen's Association, *50th Anniversary, 1889*–1938, (10, 24); James W. Martin and Jerry J. Presley, *Ozark Land and Lumber Company Organization and Operations, 1887 to 1923* (Columbia: University of Missouri School of Forestry, 1958, dittoed), (73).

7. Clemen, *American Livestock Industry*, 750–51; H. Roger Grant, *Insurance Reform: Consumer Action in the Progressive Era* (Ames: Iowa State University Press, 1979), 76–84; Herbert S. Hadley, 1908 statement on antitrust prosecutions, 10–11, folder 160, Hadley Papers. Joint Manuscript Collections.

8. Riegel, "Missouri Pacific, 1879–1900," 3–26; Cassity, "Way of Life," 100–01; Don Crinklaw, "The Battle of the Breweries," *St. Louis Post-Dispatch Pictures*, June 9, 1974; Hadley 1908 antitrust statement, 12–13; Sherman Morse, "The Taming of Rogers," *American Magazine*, 62 (July 1906), 227–29.

9. James Lee Murphy, "The Consolidation of the Street Railways in the City of St. Louis, Missouri" (M.A. thesis, St. Louis University, 1964); Ted Planje, Jr., "St. Joseph, Missouri, Utilities Before 1900: Franchise, Competitive Franchise, Then Absentee Ownership" (Term paper, History 356, University of Missouri-Columbia, 1971); Union Electric information courtesy of Philip V. Scarpino.

10. G. K. Renner, "The Kansas City Meat Packing Industry Before 1900," *MHR*, 55 (Oct. 1960), 23; Frederick Lewis Deming, "The Boatmen's National Bank, 1847–1941" (Ph.D. diss., Washington University, 1942), 133, 147–51.

11. Susan Curtis Mernitz, "Church, Class, and Community in Lexington, Missouri" (M.A. thesis, University of Missouri-Columbia, 1981), 32.

12. Missouri Bureau of Labor Statistics, *40–41st Annual Report . . . 1918–20*, 622–23.

13. Mernitz, "Church and Class in Lexington," 31–33.

14. "The First Veiled Prophet Carnival, October 8, 1878," *BMHS*, 9 (Oct. 1952), 7–35; *His Mysterious Majesty, The Veiled Prophet's Golden Jubilee, 1878–1928* (n.p.), (12–13); *Veiled Prophet's Sixth Annual Festival* (1883), (4); Ernest Kirschten, *Catfish and Crystal* (Garden City: Doubleday, 1965), 31–33.

15. Max A. Goldstein, ed., *One Hundred Years of Medicine and Surgery in Missouri* (St. Louis: St. Louis Star, 1900), 92, 97; State School Superintendent, *64th Annual Report . . . 1913*, 49; Missouri Press Association, *42nd Annual Meeting . . . 1908*, 106; E. W. Moore to Lon Stephens, June 22, 1899, box 34, folder 4, Stephens Papers, Missouri State Archives, Jefferson City.

16. State School Superintendent, *47th Annual Report . . . 1896*, 67; *55th Annual Report . . . 1904*, 13; Missouri Bar Association, *Proceedings of the 33rd Annual Meeting . . . 1915*, 153; *13th Annual Meeting . . . 1893*, 148; Missouri Press Association, *42nd Annual Meeting . . . 1908*, 110; A. J. D. Stewart, ed., *The History of the Bench and Bar of Missouri* (St. Louis: Legal Pub. Co., 1898), 73; *Journal of the Missouri State Medical Association*, 1 (July 1904), 9.

17. E. J. Goodwin, *A History of Medicine in Missouri* (St. Louis: W. L. Smith, 1905), 123–24, 125–26; *Constitution, By-Laws, and Fee-Bill of the Saint Joseph Medical Society . . . 1889*, 3–4; *Charter, Constitution and By-Laws of the Bar Association of Saint Louis . . . 1885*, 5–6.

18. Missouri State Teachers Association, *A Brief History of the Missouri State Teachers' Association* (n.p., n.d.), 43–44.

19. Stewart, *Bench and Bar*, 42–43, 407–8; Goodwin, *Missouri Medicine*, 129–32, 137–40, 143–44; Jonas Viles, *The University of Missouri: A Centennial History* (Columbia: University of Missouri, 1939), 360–61, 381–83, 455, 463–71; Frank F. Stephens, *A History of the University of Missouri* (Columbia: University of Missouri Press, 1962), 216–17, 218–20, 232–35, 238, 283–84, 382–83, 387; William F. Fratcher, *The Law Barn: A Brief History of the School of Law, University of Missouri-Columbia* (Columbia: University of Missouri-Columbia School of Law, 1978), 1–4; State School Superintendent, *30th Annual Report . . . 1879*, 111–12; Missouri Press Association, *42nd Annual Meeting . . . 1908*, 106–7.

20. Manley O. Hudson, *The Bar and Legal Education in Missouri* (Missouri Bar Association, 1913), 3; Harold Walter Eickoff, "The Organization and Regulation of Medicine in

Missouri, 1883–1901" (Ph.D. diss., University of Missouri-Columbia, 1964), 23–25, 31–41, 114–55; *Journal of the Missouri State Medical Association*, 1 (Sept. 1904), 139.

21. State School Superintendent, *64th Report . . . 1913*, 7; Husdon, *Bar and Legal Education*, 2.

22. Eickoff, "Medical Regulation," ch. 9.

23. Ray G. Hurlburt, "A. T. Still, Founder of Osteopathy," *MHR*, 19 (Oct. 1924), 25–33.

24. Eickoff, "Medical Regulation," chs. 7, 8, 10, 11, 12.

25. Missouri Bar Association, *22nd Annual Meeting . . . 1904*, 17–19; *23rd Annual Meeting . . . 1905*, 12, 15, 62–64; *26th Annual Meeting . . . 1908*, 95.

26. State School Superintendent, *57th Report . . . 1906*, 71; *64th Report . . . 1913*, 31–32, 41–44, 123–24; Dorothy J. Caldwell, "A Look at the Missouri State Teachers Association," *MHR*, 51 (Oct. 1956), 31–41; Claude A. Phillips, *A History of Education in Missouri* (Jefferson City: Hugh Stephens, 1911), 129, 133, 266; Marvin Shamberger, "The Legislative Policies and Activities of the Missouri State Teachers Association" (Ed.D. diss., University of Missouri, 1945), 69–84, 96–102.

27. State School Superintendent, *26th Report . . . 1875*, 189; *28th Report . . . 1877*, 287; *30th Report . . . 1879*, 101; *55th Report . . . 1904*, 15; *59th Report . . . 1908*, 219, 221, 228; *64th Report . . . 1913*, 14; Phillips, *History of Education*, 105.

28. Mernitz, "Church and Class in Lexington," 32–33; Miles, *Henry County*, vol. 2, 93; *St. Joseph Medical Society . . . 1889*, 13–16; *Bulletin of the Bar Association of St. Louis . . . 1915*, 48–49.

29. California *The Newspaper*, Aug. 25, 1892; Shamberger, "Missouri State Teachers' Association," 31–32; Missouri Bar Association, *22nd Report . . . 1904*, 12, 20, 24.

30. Missouri Bureau of Labor Statistics, *6th Report . . . 1884*, 168–78.

31. Labor Bureau, *2nd Report . . . 1880*, 201–4; *23rd Report . . . 1901*, 315–25; *26th Report . . . 1904*, 298; Minutes, St. Louis Typographical Union, Jan. 3, 1869, Joint Manuscript Collections.

32. *By-Laws, Order of Business, and Rules of Order of the Iron Molders Union No. 142, of Hannibal, Mo.* (1896), 19; *Constitution, By-Laws and Scale of Prices, Hannibal Typographical Union, No. 88* (1893), 15–16; Minutes, St. Louis Typographical Union, passim; *By-Laws of Local Union No. 333 of the Amalgamated Sheet Metal Workers' Industrial Alliance* (Sedalia, 1904), 5; *By-Laws of Sedalia Union No. 1792 of United Brotherhood of Carpenters and Joiners of America* (n.d.), 1; *Constitution and By-Laws of Bricklayers' and Masons' Union Number 14 of Sedalia, Missouri* (n.d.), 7; St. Louis Carpenters' District Council Minutes, Aug. 8, 1899, April 3, 1900, April 23, 1907, March 21, 1911, Joint Manuscript Collections.

33. *Hannibal Iron Molders Local 142*, 19; *Sedalia Carpenters Local 1792*, 1–2; Minutes, St. Louis Carpenters' District Council, July 7, 21, 1896; Aug. 29, 1899, March 21, 1911; Minutes, Kansas City Carpenters' District Council, summary courtesy of Russell Clemens; Minutes, St. Louis Machine Woodworkers Local 2, April 4, 1902, Joint Manuscript Collections.

34. Minutes, St. Louis Typographical Union, Dec. 14, 26, 1864, May 7, 1865, Aug. 1, Dec. 1, 1866, April 5, 1872, April 29, 1877, Dec. 16, 1884, Jan. 31, 1886, June 26, 1887, Feb. 5, Nov. 5, 1893.

35. Labor Bureau, *9th Report . . . 1887*, 266, 270; *13th Report . . . 1891*, 1–12; Minutes, St. Louis Typographical Union, Sept. 26, 1880, Nov. 25, 1887, Jan. 7, 1891; Minutes, St. Louis Carpenters' District Council, April 10, 1900, April 11, 1911.

36. Labor Bureau, *16th Report . . . 1894*, 526–27; *21st Report . . . 1899*, 273; *Sedalia Bricklayers Local 14*, 9; Minutes, St. Louis Typographical Union, Nov. 6, 1864, Feb. 2, 1873; minutes, St. Louis Carpenters' District Council, August 1901, Aug. 16, 23, 30, 1910.

37. Minutes, St. Louis Carpenters' District Council, Dec. 26, 1899, Dec. 26, 1904, Feb. 5, 1908, Jan. 10, 1911, Nov. 18, 25, 1913.

38. Mary Jane Quinn, "Local Union No. 6, Brewing, Malting and General Labor Departments, St. Louis, Missouri" (M.A. thesis, University of Missouri, 1947), 8, 12–14, 16, 53;

Labor Bureau, *2nd Report . . . 1880*, 203–4; *14th Report . . . 1892*, 51, 55, 69; Minutes, St. Louis Typographical Union, April 6, 1873, March 25, 1883, April 2, 1893; Edwin James Forsythe, "The St. Louis Central Trades and Labor Union, 1887–1945" (Ph.D. diss., University of Missouri, 1956), 16–17.

39. *Moberly Daily Enterprise Monitor*, May 16, 1877.

40. *National Labor Tribune*, Feb. 25, 1888, courtesy of Mark Hirsch.

41. Quoted in Joseph Patrick Blough, "Southwestern Railroad Strike of 1886" (M.A. thesis, St. Louis University, 1949), 36, 38.

42. Minutes, St. Louis Typographical Union, Oct. 11, 1871, Nov. 27, 1881, July 29, 1883; Forsythe, "St. Louis Central Trades," 18; Fred Richard Graham, "A History of the Missouri State Federation of Labor" (M.A. thesis, University of Missouri, 1934), 13; Minutes, St. Louis Carpenters' District Council, July 1, 1913.

43. Minutes, St. Louis Typographical Union, Nov. 6, 1864, Sept. 26, 1880, Jan. 30, April 24, 1881.

44. Michael J. Cassity, "Modernization and Social Crisis: The Knights of Labor and a Midwest Community, 1885–1886," *Journal of American History*, 66 (June 1979), 49; Quinn, "Local 6," 41–46; Graham, "Missouri Federation of Labor," 2; Minutes, St. Louis Carpenters' District Council, Feb. 11, April 3, 1902; Steven L. Piott, "Modernization and the Anti-Monopoly Issue: The St. Louis Transit Strike of 1900," *BMHS*, 35 (Oct. 1978), 3–16.

45. Minutes, St. Louis Typographical Union, July 22, 1888, July 28, 1889; minutes, St. Louis Carpenters' District Council, Nov. 18, 1913.

46. St. Louis *Republic*, Aug. 16, 1890; Minutes, St. Louis Machine Woodworkers, Local 2, Aug. 8, 1902, April 23, Aug. 25, 1903, Aug. 1, 1905; Minutes, Local 1100, United Brotherhood of Carpenters and Joiners, Aug. 6, 1903, Joint Manuscript Collections.

47. Sedalia *Daily Bazoo*, July 26, 1877.

48. Labor Bureau, *13th Report . . . 1891*, 11–12; *15th Report . . . 1893*, 37; Report of Arbitration Committee, June 16, 1910, Hadley Papers, Joint Manuscript Collections.

49. Minutes, St. Louis Typographical Union, Dec. 11, 1864, June 7, 1874, Jan. 4, Oct. 3, 26, 1875, July 28, Oct. 1, 1876, July 1, 25, 1877, Aug. 17, 1879, Jan. 30, Nov. 14, 1887.

50. Labor Bureau, *32nd Report . . . 1910*, 293; *38–39th Report . . . 1916–17*, 161–62.

51. Cassity, "Modernization and Social Crisis," 41–61.

52. Minutes, St. Louis Typographical Union, Aug. 24, 1879; Minutes, Machine Woodworkers Local 6, Dec. 20, 1904.

53. Jefferson City *Tribune*, quoted in Lyle E. Harris, "The Great Southwest Strike of 1886" (Research paper, History 356, University of Missouri-Columbia, 1974), 6.

54. Minutes, St. Louis Carpenters' District Council, July 25, Aug. 15, 1899, Dec. 15, 1908, July 21, 1914, Aug. 17, 24, 1915, Sept. 11, 18, Oct. 16, 1917; minutes, Carpenters Local 1100, Nov. 5, 1908.

55. Labor Bureau, *21st Report . . . 1899*, 273–74; *32nd Report . . . 1910*, 278; *33rd Report . . . 1911*, 42–43, 45, 47–48, 63–64, 66–67, 69–70, 76–77, 95, 96, 98, 99.

Part VII. Political Resistance in the New Order

1. Lon Stephens to R. W. Mitchell, May 29, 1900, Letterbooks, Box 2, Folder 2, p. 32, Stephens Papers, Missouri State Archives, Jefferson City.

2. Frederick N. Judson, *A Treatise Upon the Law and Practice of Taxation in Missouri* (Columbia: E. W. Stephens, 1900), 40–41; Sarah Guitar and Floyd C. Shoemaker, eds., *The Messages and Proclamations of the Governors of the State of Missouri* (Columbia: State Historical Society of Missouri, 1926), vol. 9, 28; Missouri Bureau of Labor Statistics, *40–41st Report . . . 1918–20*, 559–60; Eugene Fair, *Public Administration in Missouri* (Kirksville: Bulletin of the State Teachers College, 1923), 55–58.

3. Guitar and Shoemaker, eds., *Governors' Messages*, vol. 9, 356–57; vol. 11, 82; Missouri State Board of Agriculture, *44th Report . . . 1912*, 110; Herbert S. Hadley to C. L. Hobart, Feb. 19, 1910, letterbook 10, pp. 350, Hadley Papers, Joint Manuscript Collections.

Chapter 11. *Traditional Resistance, Populism, and the Limits of Politics*

1. Alma Beatrice Wilkinson, "The Granger Movement in Missouri" (M.A. thesis, University of Missouri, 1926), 47, 106–7; Phil Chew, *History of the Farmers' Alliance, the Agricultural Wheel, the Farmers' and Laborers' Union, the Farmers' Mutual Benefit Association, the Patrons of Industry, and Other Farmers' Organizations* (St. Louis: Journal of Agriculture, 1890), 212, 226; W. Scott Morgan, *History of the Wheel and Alliance* (St. Louis: C. B. Woodward, 1891), 258; Sedalia *Harmony Baptist*, Nov. 1898; St. Louis *Labor*, Jan. 24, March 28, 1903.

2. Chew, *History of Farmers' Alliance*, 16, 210; Wiley Jones Patrick, *The History of the Salt River Association* (Columbia: E. W. Stephens, 1909), 281; Minutes, St. Louis Typographical Union, Oct. 19, 26, Nov. 30, 1890, Joint Manuscript Collections.

3. Missouri Bureau of Labor Statistics, *2nd Report . . . 1880*, 15–18, 24–28; *11th Report . . . 1889*, 14–66; Joseph Patrick Blough, "Southwestern Railroad Strike of 1886" (M.A. thesis, St. Louis University, 1949), 36, 38; Chew, *History of Farmers' Alliance*, 114, 115, 362; Gary M. Fink, *Labor's Search for Political Order: The Political Behavior of the Missouri Labor Movement, 1890–1940* (Columbia: University of Missouri Press, 1973), 13.

4. Chew, *History of Farmers' Alliance*, 216–18; Fink, *Labor's Search*, 13.

5. Herbert S. Hadley to Theodore Roosevelt, March 9, 1912, folder 811, Hadley Papers; *Memphis Farmers' Union*, Feb. 5, 1891; St. Louis *Central Christian Advocate*, Oct. 6, 1886; Fink. *Labor's Search*, 32.

6. *St. Louis Globe-Democrat*, July 26, 1877.

7. Wilkinson, "Grange in Missouri," 135–36; Missouri, *Journal of the House of Representatives of the Thirty-first General Assembly . . . 1881*, xxix–xxxii; *Journal of . . . 1883*, xxx–xxxix; *Journal of . . . 1887*, 21–27, 48–50, 59–60, 73–74, 82–83, 96–98, 109–11, 118–20, 151–52, 154–56, 171–73, 188–94, 202–7, 223–29, 242–48, 259–63, 281–84, 307–9, 315–16, 331–33, 348–50, 361, 380, 389, 398, 436–37, 460, 492–93.

8. Minutes, St. Louis Typographical Union, July 30, 1882; Edwin James Forsythe, "The St. Louis Central Trades and Labor Union, 1887–1945" (Ph.D. diss., University of Missouri, 1956), 22; St. Louis *Labor*, Jan. 24, 1903; Fink, *Labor's Search*, 23.

9. Missouri *Official Manual . . . 1909–10*, 466–70; *1913–14*, 767–97; Kennett *Justice*, March 19, 1914; St. Louis *Review*, March 20, 1902.

10. Minutes, St. Louis Typographical Union, Jan. 18, 1885; California *The Newspaper*, Aug. 11, 1892; Fink, *Labor's Search*, ch. 3; Fred Richard Graham, "A History of the Missouri State Federation of Labor" (M.A. thesis, University of Missouri, 1934), 9–12, 58–68, 78–97.

11. Clare Lucile Bradley, "The Prohibition Movement and Dramshop Law Enforcement, 1887–1910" (M.A. thesis, Washington University, 1941), 68, 70–88.

12. Missouri *Official Manual . . . 1909–10*, 24–68.

13. Forsythe, "St. Louis Central Trades," 26–27, 44, 55–56; Graham, "Missouri Federation of Labor," 31–32; St. Louis *Mirror*, Feb. 28, 1901.

14. Homer Clevenger, "Agrarian Politics in Missouri, 1880–1896" (Ph.D. diss., University of Missouri, 1940), 17–18, 88–89, 91; Sedalia *Morning Gazette*, Aug. 15, 1890.

15. Steven Lawrence Piott, "From Dissolution to Regulation: The Popular Movement against Trusts and Monopoly in the Midwest, 1877–1913" (Ph.D. dissertation, University of Missouri-Columbia, 1978), 44–54; Clevenger, "Agrarian Politics," 101, 205, 226–27, 228–29; Kennett *Clipper*, July 10, 1890.

16. Leon Parker Ogilvie, "Populism and Socialism in the Southeast Missouri Lowlands," *MHR*, 65 (Jan. 1971), 159–64.

17. St. Louis *Republic*, Aug. 17, 1890, also Sedalia *Morning Gazette*, Aug. 17, 1890; California *The Newspaper*, Aug. 21, 1890; Homer Clevenger, "The Farmers' Alliance in Missouri," *MHR*, 39 (Oct. 1944), 36–39.

18. Clevenger, "Agrarian Politics," 198–99.

19. St. Louis *National Reformer*, Feb. 2, 1891; California *The Newspaper*, Sept. 10, Oct. 15, 1891.

20. St. Louis *National Reformer*, March 1, 1982; Morgan, *History of Wheel*, 265, 266; California *The Newspaper*, June 23, 1892.

21. Morgan, *History of Wheel*, 248, 250, 251, 253; Lamar *Union*, in *Memphis Farmers' Union*, July 7, 1892.

22. St. Louis *National Reformer*, March 1, 1892; *Memphis Farmers' Union*, Aug. 20, Oct. 1, 1891, July 7, Aug. 4, 1892; Morgan, *History of Wheel*, 261; California *The Newspaper*, March 24, 1891.

23. Missouri *Official Manual . . . 1893–94*, 19–40, 239.

24. Butler *Free Press*, Feb. 11, 1897, June 12, 1896; California *The Newspaper*, July 2, 1891.

25. William Vincent Byars, ed., *"An American Commoner": The Life and Times of Richard Parks Bland* (Columbia: E. W. Stephens, 1900), 194–203, 223–24, 230–39.

26. St. Louis *Republic*, July 26, 1896; Clevenger, "Agrarian Politics," 310–12; Lon Stephens to A. Rozelle, Feb. 4, 1899, letterbooks, box 1, folder 3, 355, Stephens Papers.

27. Agriculture Board, *30th Report . . . 1898*, 89; Delphine Roberta Meyer, "Joseph Wingate Folk, Governor of Missouri" (M.A. thesis, Washington University, 1932), 23; John Samuel Myers, "The Merit System in St. Louis from 1874 to 1937" (Ph.D. diss., Washington University, 1939), 55–56; *Post-Dispatch* in Nicholas Clare Burckel, "Progressive Governors in the Border States: Reform Governors of Missouri, Kentucky, West Virginia and Maryland, 1900–1918" (Ph.D. diss., University of Wisconsin-Madison, 1971), 151; Herbert Hadley to George Williams, Sept. 13, 1910, letterbooks 13, 163–64, Hadley Papers.

Chapter 12. The Consumer Revolt and the Grass-Roots Origins of the Missouri Idea

1. *St. Louis Post-Dispatch*, Dec. 9, 1897, Jan. 20, 1898; *Gould's St. Louis Directory of 1898*, 423, 1206, 1602.

2. Kansas City *Star*, Dec. 4, 1912; Agriculture Board, *33rd Annual Report . . . 1901*, 81–83.

3. For an elaboration of the following argument, see David Thelen, "Patterns of Consumer Consciousness in the Progressive Movement: Robert M. La Follette, the Antitrust Persuasion, and Labor Legislation," in Ralph M. Aderman, ed., *The Quest for Social Justice: The Morris Fromkin Memorial Lectures* (Madison: University of Wisconsin Press, 1983), 19–47.

4. Kansas City *Star*, June 29, 1901.

5. Columbia Municipal Ownership League flier, *Scenes along the Source of Columbia's Water Supply* (1903); *Boonville Advance*, Oct. 1, 1903; St. Charles *Cosmos*, March 29, April 12, 1899, April 11, 1900; *St. Louis Post-Dispatch*, Jan. 15, 1895; David Paul Nord, *Newspapers and New Politics: Midwestern Municipal Reform, 1890–1900* (Ann Arbor: UMI Research Press, 1981), 73.

6. Nord, *Newspapers and New Politics*, 72, 141; Columbia Municipal Ownership League, *Municipal Ownership vs. Private Ownership* (1903), 3.

7. *St. Louis Post-Dispatch*, May 18, 19, 20, July 27, 29, 1899; Lon Stephens to L. C. Nelson, June 22, 1899, letterbook, box 2, folder 1, pp. 14–15; Stephens to W. T. Dameron, June 24, 1899, box 2, folder 1, p. 49; Stephens to H. S. Priest, July 6, 1899, box 2, folder 1, p. 147; Scott Miller to Lon Stephens, June 9, 1899, box 33, folder 4; Theodore Fisher to Stephens, June 26, 1899, box 33, folder 5; J. T. Bradshaw to Stephens, June 30, 1899, box 33, folder 4, Stephens Papers. Stephens's dependence on corporate attorneys is obvious if his

message (June 19, 1899, box 33, folder 5) is compared to letters from W. M. Williams (June 3, 1899) and Henry S. Priest (June 5, 1899). The consolidation is traced in James Lee Murphy, "The Consolidation of the Street Railways in the City of St. Louis, Missouri" (M.A. thesis, St. Louis University, 1964).

8. Lincoln Steffens, *The Shame of the Cities* (1904, reprint New York: American Century paperback, 1957), 27–37; St. Louis *Mirror*, March 10, April 19, 1900; *Commonwealth* in Jean Loraine Seeger, "The Rhetoric of the Muckraking Movement in Saint Louis: The Inception Phase" (M.A. thesis, Washington University, 1955), 85.

9. St. Louis *Mirror*, May 17, 1900; *St. Louis Post-Dispatch*, May 9, 10, 20, June 1, 4, 7, 11, July 1, 3, 4, 1900; Claude Wetmore, *The Battle against Bribery: Being the Only Complete Narrative of Joseph W. Folk's Warfare on Boodlers* (St. Louis: Pan American, 1904), 22–23; Frank Tyrell, *Political Thuggery; or, Missouri's Battle with the Boodlers* (St. Louis: Puritan Pub. Co., 1904), 34; Lon Stephens to Frederick N. Judson, June 5, 1900, letterbooks, box 2, folder 2, p. 194; Stephens to William A. Hudson, June 18, 1900, box 2, folder 2, p. 241, Stephens Papers; Steven L. Piott, "Modernization and the Anti-Monopoly Issue: The St. Louis Transit Strike of 1900," *BMHS*, 35 (Oct. 1978), 3–16.

10. St. Louis *Mirror*, March 7, 1901; *St. Louis Post-Dispatch*, March 26, 29, 30, April 4, 1897; *St. Louis Globe-Democrat*, March 8, 14, 19, 26, 1897; Missouri Bureau of Labor Statistics, *18th Annual Report . . . 1896*, 1–82; Jack Muraskin, "St. Louis Municipal Reform in the 1890's: A Study in Failure," *BMHS*, 25 (Oct. 1968), 46–49.

11. St. Louis *Mirror*, March 15, 1900; *St. Louis Post-Dispatch*, March 28, 1901; Seeger, "Muckraking in St. Louis," 43–45, 85.

12. St. Louis *Mirror*, Feb. 28, March 21, 1901; *St. Louis Star*, March 25, April 1, 1901; *St. Louis Post-Dispatch*, April 1, 1901; Lee Meriwether, *My Yesterdays: An Autobiography* (Webster Groves, Mo.; International Mark Twain Society, 1942), 160–68.

13. Missouri *Official Manual . . . 1901–2*, 62–68, 113–16; Lee Meriwether, *My First 100 Years, 1862–1962* (St. Louis: privately published, n.d.), 92–93; Louis G. Geiger, *Joseph W. Folk of Missouri* (Columbia: University of Missouri Studies, vol. 25, 1953), 25.

14. Columbia Municipal Ownership League fliers, *Municipal Ownership vs. Private Ownership*; *Scenes along the Source of Columbia's Water Supply*; *Contaminated Water and Typhoid Fever; Pure Water and Public Health* (all 1903); *Columbia Missouri Statesman*, Feb. 26, 1904.

15. *Boonville Advance*, Aug. 27, Sept. 3, 17, 24, Oct. 1, 8, 1903; *St. Charles Banner News*, July 25, 1901; St. Charles *Cosmos*, March 28, 1900, April 3, 1901; Missouri Bureau of Labor Statistics, *29th Annual Report . . . 1907*, 774, 778, 780–81, 788.

16. John Robert Moore to Herbert S. Hadley, April 6, 1912, folder 266, Hadley Papers.

17. Agriculture Board, *37th Annual Report . . . 1905*, 186.

18. *St. Louis Post-Dispatch*, Jan. 22, 1893.

19. *St. Louis Post-Dispatch*, Nov. 17, 1897; St. Louis *Mirror*, May 23, 1901; Robert Dale Grinder, "The Anti-Smoke Crusades: Early Attempts to Reform the Urban Environment, 1893–1918" (Ph.D. diss., University of Missouri-Columbia, 1973), 52–60; Richard E. Oglesby, "Smoke Gets in Your Eyes," *BMHS*, 26 (April 1970), 184–85, 187.

20. *St. Louis Globe-Democrat*, May 13, July 12, 1911; *St. Louis Times*, May 15, 1911; *St. Louis Post-Dispatch*, May 15, 1911; Civic League of St. Louis, *1911 Year Book*, 33–34; Civic League of St. Louis, *Civic Bulletin*, vol. 1 (Jan. 23, Feb. 8, March 6, Dec. 1, 1911); Mrs. Ernest R. Kroeger, "Smoke Abatement in St. Louis," *American City*, 6 (June 1912), 907; Grinder, "Anti-Smoke Crusades," 99–101; Oglesby, "Smoke Gets in Your Eyes," 188.

21. Kennett *Clipper*, Sept. 29, 1892; Agriculture Board, *30th Annual Report . . . 1898*, 33; *32nd Annual Report . . . 1900*, 107, 108–25; *33rd Annual Report . . . 1901*, 73–81; Eugene Fair, *Public Administration in Missouri* (Kirksville: Bulletin of the State Teachers College, vol. 8, 1923), 231–33; St. Louis *Review*, Dec. 7, 1899; Missouri Food and Drug Commissioner, *Annual Report . . . 1909*, 9–10; *Annual Report . . . 1914*, 5, 11–17.

22. Stephen J. Raiche, "The World's Fair and the New St. Louis, 1896–1904," *MHR* 67 (Oct. 1972), 112–14; Hadley quoted in unidentified *St. Louis Globe-Democrat* clipping, Hadley Papers.

23. Sedalia *Weekly Gazette*, Sept. 11, 1894; *Kansas City Times*, July 23, 25, 28, Aug. 1, 1897; H. Roger Grant, *Insurance Reform: Consumer Action in the Progressive Era* (Ames: Iowa State University Press, 1979), 76–83; Steven L. Piott, "From Dissolution to Regulation: The Popular Movement against Trusts and Monopoly in the Midwest, 1887–1913" (Ph.D. diss., University of Missouri-Columbia, 1978), 54–57, 60–62, 67, 69–76.

24. *St. Louis Post-Dispatch*, July 28, 1899, June 1, 1900, April 13, 1904.

25. *St. Louis Labor Compendium*, May 4, 1902; *News* in Jefferson City *Republican*, April 18, 1902; *Kansas City Journal*, April 19, 1902; St. Louis *Mirror*, April 24, May 15, 1902; *St. Louis Post-Dispatch*, April 24, 1902; Steven L. Piott, "Missouri and the Beef Trust: Consumer Action and Investigation, 1902," *MHR*, 76 (Oct. 1981), 42–49.

26. Kansas City *Star*, June 27, 28, July 3, 4, 6, 7, 13, 1901; *Kansas City Times*, Aug. 4, 29, 1901. See also Christian J. Eck III, "The Kansas City Ice Trust of 1901" (Research paper, History 356, University of Missouri-Columbia, 1976).

27. *St. Louis Post-Dispatch*, March 11, 1904.

28. Missouri *Official Manual . . . 1895–96*, 256, 269; *1901–2*, 317, 322, 325; *1905–6*, 274; William P. Hill to N. D. Houghton, Oct. 23, 1922, Houghton Papers, Joint Manuscript Collections; Gary M. Fink, *Labor's Search for Political Order: The Political Behavior of the Missouri Labor Movement, 1890–1940* (Columbia: University of Missouri Press, 1973), 13, 34–37; Nealie Doyle Houghton, "The Initiative and Referendum in Missouri" (M.A. thesis, University of Missouri, 1923), 11–13, 18.

29. Houghton, "Initiative and Referendum," 9, 14, 18; H. D. Sarman to N. D. Houghton, March 8, 1923, Houghton Papers; Missouri *Official Manual . . . 1901–2*, 334; Norman L. Crockett, "The 1912 Single Tax Campaign in Missouri," *MHR*, 56 (Oct. 1961), 42.

30. Missouri *Official Manual . . . 1905–6*, 541–42; *1909–10*, 808–10; William Preston Hill, *National Decay Caused by Political Corruption and the Remedy* (St. Louis: Missouri Referendum League, n.d. [1908?]), 23.

31. Kathleen White Miles, ed., *Annals of Henry County* (Clinton: The Printery, 1974), vol. 2, 63–64; Lloyd Edson Worner, "The Public Career of Herbert Spencer Hadley" (Ph.D. diss., University of Missouri, 1946), 45–46; Nicholas Clare Burckel, "Progressive Governors in the Border States: Reform Governors of Missouri, Kentucky, West Virginia and Maryland, 1900–1918" (Ph.D. diss., University of Wisconsin-Madison, 1971), 111; "The Great American Lobby: The Typical Example of Missouri," *Frank Leslie's Popular Monthly*, 56 (Aug. 1903), 382.

32. Nord, *Newspapers and New Politics*, 34, 49–50; Seeger, "Muckraking in St. Louis," 47–59; Frances Patton Landen, "The Joseph W. Folk Campaign for Governor in 1904 as Reflected in the Rural Press of Missouri" (M.A. thesis, University of Missouri, 1938), 26; Wetmore, *Battle against Bribery*, 3.

33. W. R. Draper, "The St. Louis Bribery Disclosures," *Independent*, 54 (Oct. 9, 1902), 2402–6; *Outlook*, 70 (Feb. 8, 1902), 353–54; John D. Lawson, *American State Trials: A Collection of the Important and Interesting Criminal Trials Which Have Taken Place in the United States* (St. Louis: F. H. Thomas Law Book Co., 1918), vol 9, 584; Geiger, *Folk*, ch. 3; Landen, "Folk Campaign," ch. 3; Steffens, *Shame of the Cities*, 40; Delphine Roberta Meyer, "Joseph Wingate Folk, Governor of Missouri" (M.A. thesis, Washington University, 1932), 13; Seeger, "Muckraking in St. Louis," 62.

34. William Allen White, "Folk," *McClure's*, 25 (Dec. 1905), 120; Geiger, *Folk*, 51–54; Wetmore, *Battle against Bribery*, 155–79; "Great American Lobby," 382–93.

35. Lawson, *American State Trials*, vol. 9, 445–46, 559–69, 549, 592.

36. Seeger, "Muckraking in St. Louis," 31–39; Geiger, *Folk*, 31.

37. St. Louis *Mirror*, Nov. 2, 1899; Lawson, *American State Trials*, vol. 9, 533; Jack David Muraskin, "Missouri Politics during the Progressive Era, 1896–1916" (Ph.D. diss., University of California-Berkeley, 1969), 161.

38. White, "Folk," 117; J. W. Folk, "Municipal Corruption," *Independent*, 55 (Nov. 26, 1903), 2804; unidentified magazine article in Joseph W. Folk Papers, Joint Manuscript Collections; *St. Louis Post-Disptach*, Jan. 3, 1904; Reedy in Seeger, "Muckraking in St. Louis," 83.

39. Lawson, *American State Trials*, vol. 9, 411–12, 415.

40. Ibid., 487, 488, 490.

41. Ibid., xix; Geiger, *Folk*, 50.

42. Geiger, *Folk*, 50; *Republican* in *Boonville Advance*, Aug. 6, 1903; Steffens, *Shame of the Cities*, 100.

43 White, "Folk," 126; *Paris Mercury*, May 29, 1903; Geiger, *Folk*, 60, 63; Burckel, "Progressive Governors in Border States," 57, 59; Landen, "Folk Campaign," ch. 5.

44. *Columbia Missouri Herald*, Sept. 18, 1903; Landen, "Folk Campaign," 68–70, 89–90.

45. *Democrat* quoted in Meyer, "Folk," 25; *St. Louis Post-Dispatch*, Jan. 3, March 16, 22, 1904; *Columbia Missouri Herald*, Sept. 11, 18, 1903; Geiger, *Folk*, 68.

46. *Gallatin Democrat*, Feb. 11, 1904.

47. Meyer, "Folk," 23; *St. Louis Post-Dispatch*, March 12–18, 20, 25, April 1, 2, 4, 12, 13, 1904; Sturgeon *Missouri Leader*, July 2, 1903.

48. *St. Louis Post-Dispatch*, Jan. 3, 1904; St. Louis *Mirror*, Jan. 7, 1904; Pineville *Democrat*, Aug. 21, 1903, Tyrell, *Political Thuggery*, 17.

49. Missouri *Official Manual . . . 1905–6*, 254–55; *Gallatin Democrat*, July 28, 1904; Landen, "Folk Campaign," 134.

50. *St. Louis Post-Dispatch*, July 18–21, 1904; *Literary Digest*, 29 (July 30, 1904), 129; Geiger, *Folk*, ch. 6.

51. Missouri *Official Manual . . . 1905–6*, 446–502, esp. 468.

Chapter 13. The Missouri Idea and State Politics

1. St. Louis *Mirror*, March 29, 1906.

2. Sarah Guitar and Floyd C. Shoemaker, eds., *The Messages and Proclamations of the Governors of the State of Missouri* (Columbia: State Historical Society of Missouri, 1926), vol. 9, 285–88, 296–97.

3. Guitar and Shoemaker, *Governors' Messages*, vol. 9, 286–88; Charles M. Harvey, "Reform in Missouri," *World To-Day*, 8 (June 1905), 599; St. Louis *Republic*, Feb. 7, 10, 11, Oct. 1, 1905; *St. Louis Post-Dispatch*, Jan. 18, 24, 25, 1905, May 19, 1906; W. D. Vandiver, "What Governor Folk Has Done," *Independent*, 60 (Feb. 1, 1906), 258–59; Delphine Roberta Meyer, "Joseph Wingate Folk, Governor of Missouri" (M.A. thesis, Washington University, 1932), 98; Louis G. Geiger, *Joseph W. Folk of Missouri* (Columbia: University of Missouri Studies, 1953), 93, 100–102; Benton *Scott County Kicker*, Oct. 7, 21, 1905.

4. Vandiver, "What Folk Has Done," 259–60; Joseph W. Folk, "The Enforcement of Law," *Independent*, 59 (July 6, 1905), 9–10; Guitar and Shoemaker, *Governors' Messages*, vol. 9, 294; St. Louis *Republic*, Jan. 29, 30, Feb. 19, March 10, 1905, Feb. 27, 1906; St. Louis *Mirror*, Feb. 16, 1905; *St. Louis Post-Dispatch*, Jan. 23, 24, 1905; *Literary Digest*, 31 (July 22, 1905), 110; *Proceedings of the 23rd Annual Convention of the Woman's Christian Temperance Union of Missouri . . . 1905*, 32; Geiger, *Folk*, 102–4.

5. St. Louis *Censor*, February 16, 23, 1905; St. Louis *Mirror*, Jan. 26, Feb. 9, 1905.

6. St. Louis *Republic*, Oct. 5, 8, 1905; *New York Times*, Jan. 4, 5, 1906; H. Roger Grant, "W. D. Vandiver and the 1905 Life Insurance Scandals," *BMHS*, 29 (Oct. 1972), 7; H. Roger Grant, *Insurance Reform: Consumer Action in the Progressive Era* (Ames: Iowa State University Press, 1979), 152.

7. Grant, "Vandiver," 10–11, 18; Grant, *Insurance Reform*, 152; St. Louis *Censor*, Oct. 25, 1906.

8. State Board of Agriculture, *39th Annual Meeting . . . 1906*, 292, 294, 295.

9. *St. Louis Post-Dispatch*, Oct. 19, 1905; *New York Times*, Jan. 11, March 28, 1906; Sherman Morse, "The Taming of Rogers," *American Magazine*, 62 (July 1906), 228–29, 232–35; Hazel Tutt Long, "Attorney General Herbert S. Hadley *versus* The Standard Oil Trust," *MHR*, 35 (Jan. 1941), 179, 180; Scrapbook 27, Hadley papers.

10. Morse, "Rogers," 227–29, 235.

11. Ibid., 233–34, 235–37; *New York Times*, Jan. 6, 9, 1906; *New York World*, Jan. 10, 1906; *Literary Digest*, 32 (Jan. 20, 1906), 75.

12. *New York Times*, March 25, 1906; *Literary Digest*, 32 (March 24, 1906), 429–30; Morse, "Rogers," 237; *Kansas City World*, March 20, 1906.

13. *New York Times*, March 25, 1906; Morse, "Rogers," 230, 237–38.

14. Morse, "Rogers," 230; *World To-Day*, 10 (March 1906), 229, 315–16; St. Louis *Mirror*, March 29, 1906; St. Louis *Censor*, Jan. 18, March 29, 1906.

15. Jefferson City *Tribune*, March 10, 1909; Long, "Attorney General Hadley," 185–86; Ida M. Tarbell to Herbert S. Hadley, Nov. 25, 1907, folder 51, Hadley Papers.

16. Hadley, "My Work in the Office of Attorney General" (folder 60, 1908 manuscript), 6–10, Hadley Papers; *Joplin News Herald*, Dec. 17, 1905, Dec. 24, 1908; Jefferson City *Tribune*, Jan. 1, 1909; *St. Louis Globe-Democrat*, Sept. 20, 1908.

17. *St. Louis Post-Dispatch*, Nov. 12, 1907, Nov. 14, 1911; Jefferson City *Tribune*, Nov. 13, 1907; Steven Lawrence Piott, "From Dissolution to Regulation: The Popular Movement against Trusts and Monopoly in the Midwest, 1877–1913" (Ph.D. diss., University of Missouri-Columbia, 1978), 197–205.

18. Hadley, "My Work," 13–14; Lloyd Edson Worner, "The Public Career of Herbert Spencer Hadley" (Ph.D., diss., University of Missouri, 1946), 125–26.

19. Hadley, "My Work," 10–11; *St. Louis Globe-Democrat*, Sept. 20, 1908.

20. Hadley, "My Work," 14–15.

21. Hadley, "Argument on Behalf of the Defendant" (n.d., Folder 59); Herbert S. Hadley to B. F. Yoakum, Oct. 26, 1911, letterbook 18, 768, Hadley Papers.

22. Warrensburg *Weekly Standard-Herald*, June 19, July 17, 24, 31, 1903; *Republican* in *Boonville Advance*, Aug. 6, 1903.

23. Herbert S. Hadley to A. P. Murphy, April 13, 1909, letterbook 6, 353–56, Hadley Papers; Guitar and Shoemaker, *Governors' Messages*, vol. 10, 341.

24. Hadley to Murphy, April 13, 1909; Hadley, "My Work," 17–18; Guitar and Shoemaker, *Governors' Messages*, vol. 9, 375–76.

25. Hadley, "My Work," 19–20; Hadley to Murphy, April 13, 1909; H. J. Haskell, "The People His Clients," *Outlook*, 88 (March 28, 1908), 717–18.

26. Hadley, "My Work," 19–20; Hadley to Murphy, April 13, 1909; Hadley to St. Louis *Republic*, April 13, 1909, letterbook 5, 78–80, Hadley Papers; Jefferson City *Tribune*, March 9, 1909; Worner, "Hadley," 133.

27. Kansas City *World*, March 30, 1906.

28. Guitar and Shoemaker, *Governors' Messages*, vol. 9, 318; "Governor Folk on Public Servants and the Law-Defying Criminal Rich," *The Arena*, 39 (June 1908), 747.

29. *St. Louis Post-Dispatch*, Aug. 3, 1907; *Times-Democrat* in Jefferson City *Daily Tribune*, Aug. 3, 1907; *Joplin News Herald*, Aug. 6, 1907; Joseph W. Folk, "The Era of Conscience" (manuscript for lecture, [1909?]), 4, Joseph W. Folk Papers, Joint Manuscript Collections; Guitar and Shoemaker, *Governors' Messages*, vol. 9, 317, 513.

30. Herbert S. Hadley to George W. Wickersham, Nov. 29, 1909, letterbook 9, 220–22; Hadley to Seebert Jones, Jan. 21, 1910, Letterbook 10, 126, Hadley Papers.

31. *St. Louis Post-Dispatch*, Feb. 14, May 8, Aug. 1, 1907; Jefferson City *Tribune*, Aug. 6, 1907; Guitar and Shoemaker, *Governors' Messages*, vol. 9, 343–45, 513; Meyer, "Folk," 24–25; Geiger, *Folk*, 115–21.

32. Guitar and Shoemaker, *Governors' Messages*, vol. 9, 307–10, 372–73.

33. Ibid., 309–10, 374–75; Missouri Press Association, *42nd Annual Meeting . . . 1908*, 66; Thomas S. Barclay, "A Period of Political Uncertainty, 1900–1912," in Walter Williams and Floyd Calvin Shoemaker, *Missouri: Mother of the West* (Chicago: American Historical Society, 1930), vol. 2, 454–56.

34. Myron August Spohrer, "Some Aspects of the Operation of the Direct Primary in Missouri" (M.A. thesis, University of Missouri, 1926), 24–26, 52.

35. "The Biennial Message of Governor Joseph W. Folk," *The Arena*, 37 (March 1907), 293–94; Guitar and Shoemaker, *Governors' Messages*, vol. 9, 336; St. Louis *Mirror*, Dec. 12, 1907; Nealie Doyle Houghton, "The Initiative and Referendum in Missouri" (M.A. thesis, University of Missouri, 1923), 29–43.

36. State of Missouri, *Official Manual . . . 1909–10*, 808–10; *Official Manual . . . 1915–16*, 575; Kansas City *Star*, March 10, 1913; *Kansas City Times*, Nov. 2, 1908; Norman L. Crockett, "The 1912 Single Tax Campaign in Missouri," *MHR*, 56 (Oct. 1961), 51–52.

37. Official Manual . . . *1911–12*, 780–89; *1913–14*, 107–9; *1915–16*, 570–76; *1917–18*, 484–85; Crockett, "1912 Single Tax Campaign," 40–50.

38. Herbert S. Hadley to Mark Sullivan, Oct. 30, 1911, Hadley Papers; Geiger, *Folk*, 124–29; Jack David Muraskin, "Missouri Politics during the Progressive Era, 1896–1915" (Ph.D. diss., University of California at Berkeley, 1969), 197–203, 207–8; St. Louis *Censor*, Nov. 22, 1906; *St. Louis Post-Dispatch*, Feb. 14, 1907; *Kansas City Times*, Nov. 9, 10, 1908.

39. *Joplin News Herald*, Nov. 5, 6, 1908; Jefferson City *Tribune*, July 21, 1908; St. Louis *Mirror*, Nov. 7, Dec. 12, 1907; *St. Louis Globe-Democrat*, Sept. 11, 20, 1908; Muraskin, "Missouri Progressive Politics," 204–7.

40. *Kansas City Times*, Nov. 5, 7, 1908; *St. Louis Post-Dispatch*, Oct. 21, Nov. 4, 1908.

41. Guitar and Shoemaker, *Governors' Messages*, vol. 9, 512.

42. Folk, "Era of Conscience," 4, 6; Jefferson City *Tribune*, June 2, Aug. 4, 9, 13, 21, 1907; *Joplin News Herald*, Aug. 6, 22, 1907; *St. Louis Post-Dispatch*, July 21, Aug. 3, 1907.

43. Jefferson City *Tribune*, Aug. 14, 21, 1907; *Literary Digest*, 35 (Aug. 31, 1907), 279–80; (Nov. 2, 1907), 631–33; (Nov. 9, 1907), 671–76; *The Nation*, 85 (Aug. 15, 1907), 151–52.

44. St. Louis *Mirror*, Dec. 12, 1907; Muraskin, "Missouri Progressive Politics," 242–43, 245–46; *St. Louis Post-Dispatch*, Oct. 9, 1910.

45. *World* in *Literary Digest*, 35 (Aug. 31, 1907), 279.

46. St. Louis *Republic*, May 30, 1911; Guitar and Shoemaker, *Governors' Messages*, vol. 10, 31.

47. St. Louis *Republic*, May 17, 18, 22, 1911.

48. Missouri Bankers Association, *Proceedings of the 18th Annual Convention . . . 1908*, 101; Kansas City *Star*, March 31, 1913; *Kansas City Times*, Dec. 4, 1912.

49. St. Louis *Censor*, Sept. 27, 1906; Missouri Food and Drug Commissioner, *Annual Report . . . 1910*, 5, 17; *Report . . . 1911*, 5, 10, 12, 113; *Report . . . 1915*, 13. See also Kansas City *Star*, Aug. 17, 1910.

50. Hadley, "My Work," 14–15, 20; Nicholas Clare Burckel, "Progressive Governors in the Border States: Reform Governors of Missouri, Kentucky, West Virginia and Maryland, 1900–1918" (Ph.D. diss., University of Wisconsin-Madison, 1971), 130–31; Folk, "Era of Conscience," 7.

51. Hadley, unidentified speech, folder 297, Hadley Papers; Guitar and Shoemaker, *Governors' Messages*, vol. 10, 34, 40–41, 65–68, 92–95, 292–97; Kansas City *Star*, Aug. 17, 1910; Hadley to C. L. Hobart, Feb. 19, 1910, letterbook 10, 350; Hadley to Ben Deering, May 10, 1910, letterbook 11, 367; Hadley to Columbus Bradford, May 14, 1910, letterbook 11, 438; Hadley to G. M. Sebree, May 4, 1911, letterbook 16, 607–8, Hadley Papers.

52. Guitar and Shoemaker, *Governors' Messages*, vol. 10, 26, 27, 30; *St. Louis Globe-Democrat*, April 1, 1909.

53. Jefferson City *Tribune*, Jan. 1, 3, 1909; *St. Louis Post-Dispatch*, Feb. 2, 7, 10, 1909; *St. Louis Globe-Democrat*, Feb. 3, 4, 1909; Paul H. Giddens, *Standard Oil Company (Indiana): Oil Pioneer of the Middle West* (New York: Appleton-Century-Crofts, 1955), 94–97.

54. Guitar and Shoemaker, *Governors' Messages*, vol. 10, 59, 99.

55. Jefferson City *Tribune*, Feb. 5, 1909; *St. Louis Globe-Democrat*, April 5, 1909; Herbert S. Hadley to M. E. Rhodes, June 1, 1909, letterbook 5, 127, Hadley Papers; Missouri *Official Manual . . . 1911–12*, 367; Agriculture Board, *44th Annual Report . . . 1911*, 108, 110.

56. Herbert S. Hadley to A. H. Hamel, July 28, 1909, letterbook 11, 96–97; Hadley to Frank W. Wightman, July 17, 1909, letterbook 11, 7–9; Hadley to C. S. Clarke, Sept. 14, 1909, letterbook 11, 242–45; Hadley to Benjamin F. Bush, June 5, 1911, letterbook 17, 179–81; Hadley to Bush, Nov. 25, 1911, letterbook 22, 52; Hadley to W. F. Evans, Nov. 29, 1911, letterbook 22, 116; Hadley to E. L. Scarritt, Nov. 29, 1911, letterbook 22, 120; Hadley to F. B. Hiller, Nov. 29, 1911, letterbook 22, 122, Hadley Papers.

57. Guitar and Shoemaker, *Governors' Messages*, vol. 10, 112–13.

58. Muraskin, "Missouri Progressive Politics," 100–104, 253–75; Kansas City *Star*, April 19, 1913; Missouri State Conference of Charities and Corrections, *13th Annual Meeting . . . 1912*, 34–40, 103–5; *14th Annual Meeting . . . 1913*, 35–38.

59. Guitar and Shoemaker, *Governors' Messages*, vol. 10, 67, 83–84, 85–86, 113.

60. Ibid., 10, 368–69, 456–61; *Crisis*, 3 (April 1912), 233; *St. Louis Post-Dispatch*, Feb. 1, 1909; Herbert S. Hadley to John S. Phillips, June 16, 1910, letterbook 12, 47–48, Hadley Papers.

61. *American Review of Reviews*, 45 (March 1912), 267; Muraskin, "Missouri Progressive Politics," 286–89, 295–98; Worner, "Hadley," 187–91, 198.

62. Worner, "Hadley," 207–8; *St. Louis Post-Dispatch*, April 26, 1912.

63. George E. Mowry, *Theodore Roosevelt and the Progressive Movement* (1946, reprinted New York: Hill and Wang, 1960), 236; Worner, "Hadley," 210.

64. Charles Moreau Hargen, "The Two National Conventions," *Independent*, 73 (July 4, 1912), 7; William Jennings Bryan, *A Tale of Two Conventions* (New York: Funk and Wagnalls, 1912), 41; *Official Report of the Proceedings of the 15th Republican National Convention . . . 1912*, 33, 35, 106–11; *Kansas City Times*, June 20, 1912; Worner, "Hadley," 234–38.

65. Herbert S. Hadley to Selden P. Spencer, Sept. 25, 1912, letterbook 25, 288; Hadley to Theodore Roosevelt, July 29, 1912, letterbook 24, 736–37; Hadley to Walter A. Evans, Oct. 5, 1912, letterbook 25, 356–60; Missouri *Official Manual . . . 1913–14*, 755–56.

66. Guitar and Shoemaker, *Governors' Messages*, vol. 11, 3–4, 34–35; Missouri *Official Manual . . . 1913–14*, 360, 367.

67. "'Trust Busting' vs. Regulation," *Outlook*, 104 (Aug. 2, 1913), 731–32; Kansas City *Star*, March 21, 23, 1913.

68. Piott, "Dissolution to Regulation," 210; *St. Louis Post-Dispatch*, April 9, 1913; Kansas City *Star*, April 9, 1913; Guitar and Shoemaker, *Governors' Messages*, vol. 11, 112–17.

69. *St. Louis Post-Dispatch*, May 10, 1913; St. Louis *Republic*, April 10, May 11, 1913.

70. Grant, *Insurance Reform*, 113–23; *St. Louis Post-Dispatch*, March 22, 26, May 1, 3, 1913; Kansas City *Star*, April 10, 14, 17, 1913.

71. St. Louis *Labor*, June 14, 1913; St. Louis *Mirror*, June 6, Aug. 8, 1913; *St. Louis Post-Dispatch*, May 9, Aug. 6, 7, 8, 1912; Guitar and Shoemaker, *Governors' Messages*, vol. 11, 47–49.

72. Guitar and Shoemaker, *Governors' Messages*, vol. 11, 13–14; *Kansas City Times*, Aug. 4, 15, 19, 21, 1913; *St. Louis Post-Dispatch*, Aug. 21, 1913; Kansas City *Star*, Aug. 5, 1913.

73. Guitar and Shoemaker, *Governors' Messages*, vol. 11, 10.

74. Ibid., 18–20, 30.

75. St. Louis *Republic*, June 10, 1913; Edwin J. Bean, "Service with the Public Service Commission," *BMHS*, 17 (Jan. 1961), 155–56.

76. St. Louis *Labor*, March 29, April 26, May 3, 1913; Eugene Fair, *Public Administration in Missouri* (Kirksville: Bulletin of the State Teachers College, 1923), 191.

77. *Joplin News Herald*, Aug. 25, 1907; Kansas City *Star*, Aug. 17, 1910.

Index

Adair County, 152
Agricultural Wheel, 205, 206
agriculture, 28, 45–46; and political reform, 205, 206, 207, 208, 211–16; promoted as a business, 35–43, 51; traditional, 14–17
air pollution, 226–27
Allen, Albert, 237
Allen, John M., 212
Allen, T. R., 158, 167
Altgeld, John Peter, 223
Amalgamated Association of Iron and Steel Workers, 191, 196
Amalgamated Association of Street Railway Employees, 195, 222
Amalgamated Sheet Metal Workers, 190
American Federation of Labor, 194, 199
American Medical Association, 184
American Pork Packers' Association, 179
American Pressed Brick Company, 48
American Sabbath Union, 150
American School of Osteopathy, 186
Ancient Order of Hibernians, 135, 157, 159
Ancient Order of United Workmen, 157, 159, 160, 164, 165, 166, 169, 197
Andrews, R. T., 259
Anheuser-Busch brewery, 33
Anti-Horse Thief Association, 61
Anti-Liquor League, 154
Anti-Saloon League, 154, 210
antitrust, 211–12, 227–29, 247, 251–54, 256–57; Hadley prosecutions, 241–46; Major and, 260–63

apprenticeship, 19; erosion of, 50–51
Armour, P. D., 34
Army Corps of Engineers, 29
artisans, 14–18, 47–48
Atchison County, 23
Atlantic and Pacific Railroad, 29, 31

Bacote, S. W., 144
Bald Knobbers, 87–92, 158
Baldwin, Roger, 258
Ball, David, 250
Bank, Clement W., 24
banking, 180
Baptists, 19–20, 21, 113, 147–55. *See also* Salt River Baptist Association
Barker, John T., 261–62
Barnes, Seth, 94, 96, 97
Barry County, 114
Bates County, 32, 63–64, 66
Beard, Charles A., 268
Behrens, E. H., 211
Behrens, E. T., 56
Benton, Thomas Hart, 87, 101, 102, 117, 118, 119
Blackmore, Henry, 210
blacks, 5, 19, 23, 139–46; bootheel farm tenants, 92–93, 95, 96, 99; employment of, 46, 53, 54; family, 19, 52, 145–46; fraternal organizations, 158, 166, 167; music, 120–21; and penal system, 107, 258; religion, 119, 143–45; schools, 140–43; work traditions, 117. *See also* Joplin, Scott; segregation
Blake, Eubie, 129
Blake, Frank, 261
Bland, Richard, 215

311